Study Guide & Working Papers

for

College Accounting
CHAPTERS 1-30

Thirteenth Edition

John Ellis Price, Ph.D., CPA
President and Professor of Accounting
University of North Texas at Dallas
Dallas, Texas

M. David Haddock, Jr., Ed.D., CPA
Professor of Accounting Emeritus
Chattanooga State Community College
Director of Training
Lattimore Black Morgan & Cain, PC
Brentwood, Tennessee

Michael J. Farina, MBA, CPA
Professor of Accounting
Cerritos College
Norwalk, California

McGraw-Hill
Irwin

Study Guide & Working Papers for
COLLEGE ACCOUNTING, Thirteenth Edition
Chapters 1-30
John Ellis Price, M. David Haddock, Jr., and Michael J. Farina

Published by McGraw-Hill/Irwin, an imprint of The McGraw-Hill Companies, Inc., 1221 Avenue of the
Americas, New York, NY 10020. Copyright © 2012, 2009, 2007, 2003, 1999, 1996, 1994, 1990, 1986, 1981, 1974, 1969, 1966
by The McGraw-Hill Companies, Inc. All rights reserved. Printed in the United States of America.

1 2 3 4 5 6 7 8 9 0 QDB/QDB 1 0 9 8 7 6 5 4 3 2 1

ISBN: 978-0-07-743058-0
MHID: 0-07-743058-1

www.mhhe.com

Table of Contents

CHAPTER 1

Accounting: The Language of Business

STUDY GUIDE

Understanding the Chapter

Objectives	**1.** Define accounting. **2.** Identify and discuss career opportunities in accounting. **3.** Identify the users of financial information. **4.** Compare and contrast the three types of business entities. **5.** Describe the process used to develop generally accepted accounting principles. **6.** Define the accounting terms new to this chapter.
Reading Assignment	Read Chapter 1 in the textbook. Complete the textbook Section Self Review as you finish reading each section of the chapter, and the Comprehensive Self Review at the end of the chapter. Refer to the Chapter 1 Glossary or to the Glossary at the end of the book to find definitions for terms that are not familiar to you.

Activities

❑ **Thinking Critically**	Answer the *Thinking Critically* questions for Google and Managerial Implications.
❑ **Discussion Questions**	Answer each assigned discussion question in Chapter 1.
❑ **Critical Thinking Problem**	Complete the critical thinking problem as assigned.
❑ **Business Connections**	Complete the Business Connections activities as assigned to gain a deeper understanding of Chapter 1 concepts.

Practice Tests

Complete the Practice Tests, which cover the main points in your reading assignment. Compare your answers with those in the Practice Test Answer Key for Chapter 1 at the end of this chapter. If you have answered any questions incorrectly, review the related section of the text.

Part A True-False *For each of the following statements, circle T in the answer column if the answer is true or F if the answer is false.*

T   F   **1.** Passing a test called the Uniform CPA Examination is required for one to become a certified public accountant.

T   F   **2.** The Securities and Exchange Commission has a great deal of power to dictate accounting methods used by companies whose stock is traded on the stock exchanges.

T   F   **3** The Securities and Exchange Commission often relies on pronouncements of the Financial Accounting Standards Board.

T   F   **4.** The Financial Accounting Standards Board issues income tax rules.

T   F   **5.** Because of the separate entity assumption, the personal financial activities of the owner of a sole proprietorship are combined with the financial affairs of his or her business in the accounting records of the business.

T   F   **6.** All accounting principles are established by law.

T   F   **7.** Because of the difference in the structures of the three types of business entities, certain aspects of their financial affairs are accounted for in different ways.

T   F   **8.** A sole proprietorship is a form of business entity owned by two or more people.

T   F   **9.** There is little difference between a corporation and other forms of business entities.

T   F   **10.** Shares of stock represent ownership in a corporation.

T   F   **11.** Employees should have no particular interest in the financial information about the business for which they work.

T   F   **12.** The American Institute of Certified Public Accountants is a governmental agency.

T   F   **13.** In a large company, the auditing process is completed by bookkeepers.

Part B Completion *In the answer column, supply the missing word or words needed to complete each of the following statements.*

_____ 1. The _____ and other tax authorities are interested in financial information about a firm.

_____ 2. Corporate owners are called _____.

_____ 3. Ownership in a corporation is evidenced by _____.

_____ 4. The three major types of business entities are sole proprietorships, corporations, and _____.

_____ 5. An economic entity is an organization whose major purpose is to produce a profit, whereas a(n) _____ is a nonprofit organization.

_____ 6. The accounting process involves _____, _____, summarizing, interpreting, and communicating financial information about an economic or social entity.

_____ 7. Periodic reports prepared from accounting records are called _____.

_____ 8. Many people call accounting the _____ _____ _____.

_____ 9. _____ is the study of accounting principles used by different countries.

_____ 10. The IRS and the _____ have large numbers of accountants on their staff and use them to uncover possible violations of the law.

_____ 11. Major areas of accounting are public accounting, managerial accounting, and _____.

_____ 12. The _____ is an organization of accounting educators.

_____ 13. The _____ is a national association of professional accountants.

_____ 14. _____ are developed by the Financial Accounting Standards Board.

_____ 15. The _____ was created to review and oversee the accounting methods of publicly owned corporations.

_____

_____

_____

_____

_____

_____

_____

_____

_____

_____

_____

_____

_____

_____

_____

_____

_____

_____

_____

_____

_____

_____

_____

Chapter 1 Practice Test Answer Key

Part A True-False	Part B Completion
1. T	1. IRS
2. T	2. stockholders or shareholders
3. T	3. shares of stock
4. F	4. partnerships
5. F	5. social entity
6. F	6. recording, classifying
7. T	7. financial statements
8. F	8. language of business
9. F	9. International accounting
10. T	10. FBI
11. F	11. governmental accounting
12. F	12. AAA
13. F	13. AICPA
	14. Generally accepted accounting principles
	15. SEC

CHAPTER 2

Analyzing Business Transactions

STUDY GUIDE

Understanding the Chapter

Objectives

1. Record in equation form the financial effects of a business transaction. **2.** Define, identify, and understand the relationship between asset, liability, and owner's equity accounts. **3.** Analyze the effects of business transactions on a firm's assets, liabilities, and owner's equity and record these effects in accounting equation form. **4.** Prepare an income statement. **5.** Prepare a statement of owner's equity and a balance sheet **6.** Define the accounting terms new to this chapter.

Reading Assignment

Read Chapter 2 in the textbook. Complete the textbook Section Self Review as you finish reading each section of the chapter, and the Comprehensive Self Review at the end of the chapter. Refer to the Chapter 2 Glossary or to the Glossary at the end of the book to find definitions for terms that are not familiar to you.

Activities

❑ **Thinking Critically**

Answer the *Thinking Critically* questions for Southwest Airlines and Managerial Implications.

❑ **Discussion Questions**

Answer each assigned discussion question in Chapter 2.

❑ **Exercises**

Complete each assigned exercise in Chapter 2. Use the forms provided in this SGWP. The objectives covered by an exercise are given after the exercise number. If you need help with an exercise, review the portion of the chapter related to the objective(s) covered.

❑ **Problems A/B**

Complete each assigned problem in Chapter 2. Use the forms provided in this SGWP. The objectives covered by a problem are given after the problem number. If you need help with a problem, review the portion of the chapter related to the objective(s) covered.

❑ **Critical Thinking Problems 2.1 and 2.2**

Complete Critical Thinking Problems 2.1 and 2.2 as assigned. Use the forms provided in this SGWP.

❑ **Business Connections**

Complete the Business Connections activities as assigned to gain a deeper understanding of Chapter 2 concepts.

Practice Tests

Complete the Practice Tests, which cover the main points in your reading assignment. Compare your answers with those in the Practice Test Answer Key for Chapter 2 at the end of this chapter. If you have answered any questions incorrectly, review the related section of the text.

Part A True-False   *For each of the following statements, circle T in the answer column if the answer is true or F if the answer is false.*

T   F   **1.** When equipment is purchased for cash, there is no change in the total value of the firm's property.

T   F   **2.** The balance sheet is prepared at the end of the accounting period to show the results of operations.

T   F   **3.** A net loss results if total expenses exceed total revenue.

T   F   **4** Profit and loss statement is another name for the income statement.

T   F   **5.** The balance sheet shows the financial position of a business on a specific date.

T   F   **6.** The net income or net loss for the period is shown in the Assets section of the balance sheet.

T   F   **7.** The net income or net loss for the period is shown on both the income statement and the statement of owner's equity.

T   F   **8.** The collection of cash from accounts receivable increases owner's equity.

T   F   **9.** Expenses decrease owner's equity.

T   F   **10.** Revenue decreases owner's equity.

Part B Matching   *For each numbered item, choose the matching term from the box and write the identifying letter in the answer column.*

_____   **1.** Amounts owed by charge account customers.

_____   **2.** Amount remaining when total revenue is more than total expenses.

_____   **3.** Those to whom money is owed.

_____   **4.** Owner's financial interest in the business.

_____   **5.** Property owned by a business.

_____   **6.** A business obligation or debt.

_____   **7.** An expression of the relationship in which assets equal liabilities plus owner's equity.

_____   **8.** Inflows of money or other assets resulting from sales of goods or service.

a. Accounts Receivable
b. Assets
c. Creditors
d. Revenue
e. Owner's equity
f. Liability
g. Net income
h. Fundamental accounting equation

Part C Completion *In the answer column, supply the missing word or words needed to complete each of the following statements.*

_____ 1. Accountants must _____ each business transaction before they can intelligently record, report, and interpret it.

_____ 2. The purchase of new equipment on account creates a debt that is called a(n) _____.

_____ 3. When property values and financial interest increase or decrease, the sum of the items on both sides of the equation always remains _____.

_____ 4. The basic reason for starting a business is the possibility of making a _____.

_____ 5. Accounts receivable result when goods are sold or services are performed on _____.

_____ 6. When expenses are paid, the owner's equity is _____.

_____ 7. Regardless of the number and variety of transactions, liabilities plus owner's equity always equal _____.

_____ 8. When supplies are first purchased for use in operations, they are considered a type of _____.

Demonstration Problem

The account balances for Thomas Neal, CPA, for the month of January 2013 are shown below in random order.

Rent Expense	$ 8,000	Advertising Expense	$ 5,000
Fees Earned	138,240	Office Equipment	51,120
Accounts Payable	29,824	T. Neal, Drawing	15,156
Salaries Expense	23,780	Accounts Receivable	29,800
Cash	182,276	T. Neal, Capital 1/1	?

Instructions

1. Determine the balance for **Thomas Neal, Capital,** on January 1, 2013.
2. Prepare an income statement, a statement of owner's equity, and a balance sheet as of January 31, 2013.
3. List the expenses on the income statement in alphabetical order.

SOLUTION

Determine the balance for Thomas Neal Capital, on January 1, 2013.
Let Thomas Neal, Capital = X. Solving for X:

		Assets			=	Liabilities +		Owner's Equity				
		Accts.		Office		Accounts		T. Neal,				
Cash	+	Rec.	+	Equip.	=	Payable	+	Capital	− Drawing	+ Revenue	− Expenses
182,276	+	29,800	+	51,120	=	29,824	+	X	− 15,156	+ 138,240	− 36,780
				263,196	=	116,128	+	X			
		263,196	−	116,128	=	116,128	−	116,128 +	X		
				116,128	=	X					

Thomas Neal, Capital, January 1, 2013 = **$147,068**

Total Expenses:

Rent Expense	$ 8,000
Salaries Expense	23,780
Advertising Expense	5,000
	$36,780

Thomas Neal, CPA
Income Statement
Month Ended January 31, 2013

Revenue		
Fees Earned		138 2 4 0 00
Expenses		
Rent Expense	8 0 0 0 00	
Salaries Expense	23 7 8 0 00	
Advertising Expense	5 0 0 0 00	
Total Expenses		36 7 8 0 00
Net Income		101 4 6 0 00

Thomas Neal, CPA
Statement of Owner's Equity
Month Ended January 31, 2013

Thomas Neal, Capital, January 1, 2013		147 0 6 8 00
Net Income	101 4 6 0 00	
Less Withdrawals	15 1 5 6 00	
Increase in Capital		86 3 0 4 00
Thomas Neal, Capital, January 31, 2013		233 3 7 2 00

SOLUTION (continued)

Thomas Neal, CPA

Balance Sheet

January 31, 2013

Assets					Liabilities				
Cash	182	2 7 6	00		Accounts Payable	29	8 2 4	00	
Accounts Receivable	29	8 0 0	00		Owner's Equity				
Office Equipment	51	1 2 0	00		Thomas Neal, Capital	233	3 7 2	00	
Total Assets	263	1 9 6	00		Total Liabilities and Owner's Equity	263	1 9 6	00	

WORKING PAPERS

Name _____

EXERCISE 2.1

Assets _____

Liabilities _____

Owner's Equity _____

EXERCISE 2.2

1. _____

2. _____

3. _____

4. _____

5. _____

EXERCISE 2.3

	Assets	=	Liabilities	+	Owner's Equity
1.	_____	=	_____	+	_____
2.	_____	=	_____	+	_____
3.	_____	=	_____	+	_____
4.	_____	=	_____	+	_____
5.	_____	=	_____	+	_____

EXERCISE 2.4

Transaction	Assets	=	Liabilities	+	Owner's Equity
1.	+	=	_____	+	+
2.	_____	=	_____	+	_____
3.	_____	=	_____	+	_____
4.	_____	=	_____	+	_____
5.	_____	=	_____	+	_____

EXERCISE 2.5

	Cash	+	Accounts Receivable	+	Equipment	=	Accounts Payable	+	Amos Roberts Capital	+	Revenue	–	Expenses
			Assets			=	Liabilities	+			Owner's Equity		
1.													
2.													
3.													
4.													
5.													
6.													
7.													
8.													
Totals		+		+		=		+		+		–	

EXERCISE 2.6

Revenue

Expenses

EXERCISE 2.7

1. _____
2. _____
3. _____
4. _____
5. _____
6. _____
7. _____

EXERCISE 2.8

EXERCISE 2.9

Revenue

Expenses

EXERCISE 2.10

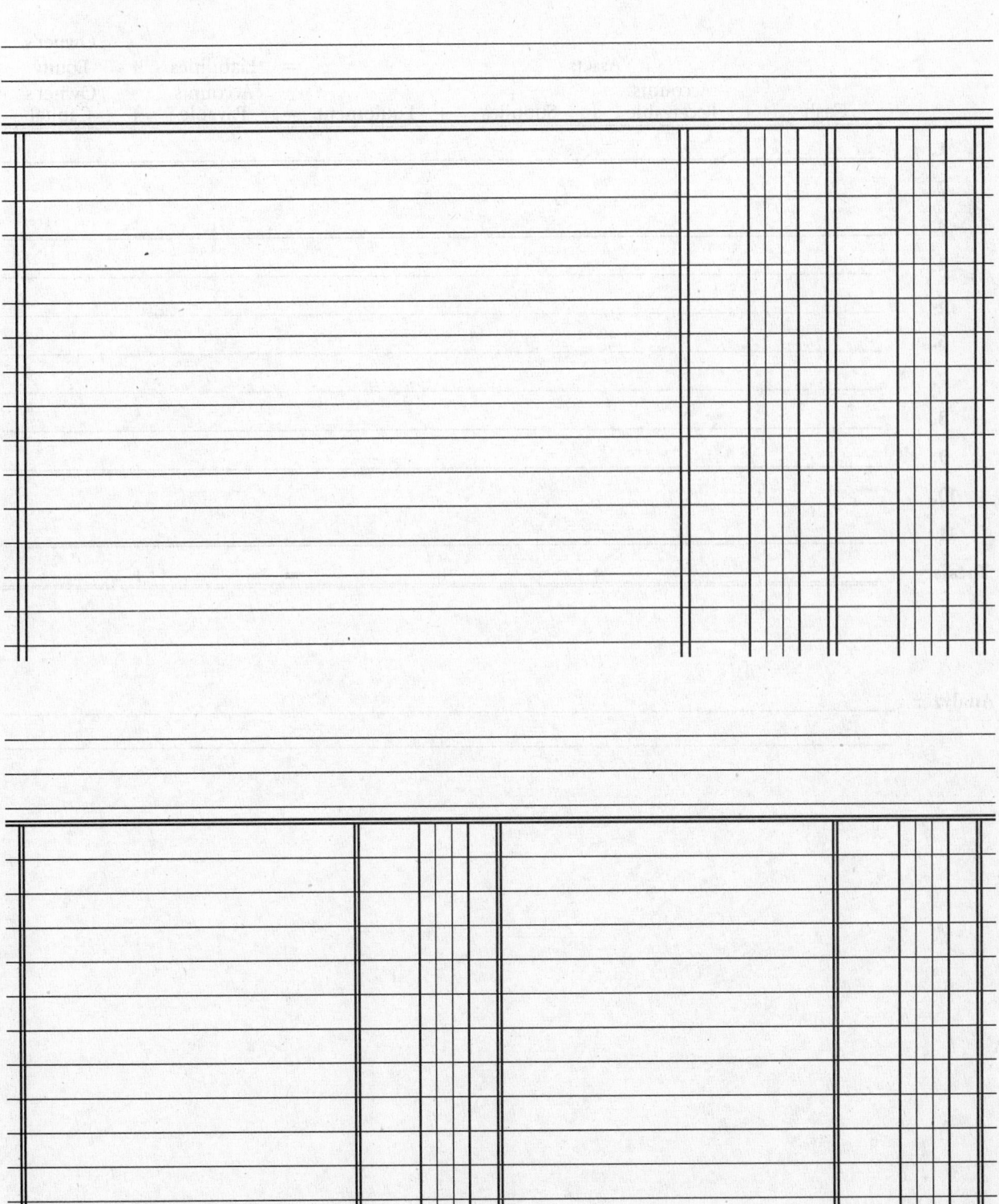

PROBLEM 2.1A or 2.1B

	Cash	+	Accounts Receivable	+	Supplies	+	Equipment	=	Accounts Payable	+	Owner's Capital
					Assets			=	Liabilities	+	Owner's Equity
1.											
2.											
3.											
4.											
5.											
6.											
7.											
8.											
9.											
10.											
11.											
Totals		+		+		+		=		+	

Analyze: _____
_____

PROBLEM 2.2A or 2.2B

	Assets			=	Liabilities +		Owner's Equity	
	Cash	+ Accounts Receivable +	+ _____ +	=	Accounts Payable +	Capital +	Revenue −	Expenses
Beginning Balances	_____	+_____	+_____ +_____	=	+_____	+_____	+_____	−_____
1.	_____	_____	_____					
New Balances	_____	+_____	+_____ +_____	=	+_____	+_____	+_____	−_____
2.	_____	_____	_____					
New Balances	_____	+_____	+_____ +_____	=	+_____	+_____	+_____	−_____
3.	_____	_____	_____					
New Balances	_____	+_____	+_____ +_____	=	+_____	+_____	+_____	−_____
4.	_____	_____	_____					
New Balances	_____	+_____	+_____ +_____	=	+_____	+_____	+_____	−_____
5.	_____	_____	_____					
New Balances	_____	+_____	+_____ +_____	=	+_____	+_____	+_____	−_____
6.	_____	_____	_____					
New Balances	_____	+_____	+_____ +_____	=	+_____	+_____	+_____	−_____
7.	_____	_____	_____					
New Balances	_____	+_____	+_____ +_____	=	+_____	+_____	+_____	−_____
8.	_____	_____	_____					
New Balances	_____	+_____	+_____ +_____	=	+_____	+_____	+_____	−_____
9.	_____	_____	_____					
New Balances	_____	+_____	+_____ +_____	=	+_____	+_____	+_____	−_____
10.	_____	_____	_____					
New Balances	_____	+_____	+_____ +_____	=	+_____	+_____	+_____	−_____

Analyze: _____

_____

PROBLEM 2.3A or 2.3B

Analyze: _____

PROBLEM 2.4A or 2.4B

PROBLEM 2.4A or 2.4B (continued)

Analyze:

CRITICAL THINKING PROBLEM 2.1

CRITICAL THINKING PROBLEM 2.2

Determine the balance for **Dolly Garcia**, April 30, 2013.

	Assets			= Liabilities +		Owner's Equity		
		Accounts		Accounts	D. Garcia	D. Garcia		
Cash	+ Receivable	+ Machinery	= Payable	+ Capital	− Drawing	+ Revenue	− Expenses	
$26,000	+ $10,800	+ $19,000	= $12,800	+ ?	− $5,200	+ $23,800	− $17,150	

Let Dolly Garcia, Capital = X.

Solving for X:

Dolly Garcia, Capital, April 1, 2013, = _____

Advertising Expense	$ 3,750
Maintenance Expense	4,400
Salaries Expense	9,000
Total Expenses	=======

CRITICAL THINKING PROBLEM 2.2 (continued)

Chapter 2 Practice Test Answer Key

Part A True-False		Part B Matching		Part C Completion	
1. T	**6.** F	**1.** a	**5.** b	**1.** analyze	**5.** credit or on account
2. F	**7.** T	**2.** g	**6.** f	**2.** accounts payable or liability	**6.** reduced or decreased
3. T	**8.** F	**3.** c	**7.** h	**3.** equal	**7.** assets
4. T	**9.** T	**4.** e	**8.** d	**4.** profit	**8.** asset or property
5. T	**10.** F				

Analyze: _____

CHAPTER 3

Analyzing Business Transactions Using T Accounts

STUDY GUIDE

Understanding the Chapter

Objectives

1. Set up T accounts for assets, liabilities, and owner's equity. 2. Analyze business transactions and enter them in the accounts. 3. Determine the balance of an account. 4. Set up T accounts for revenue and expenses. 5. Prepare a trial balance from T accounts. 6. Prepare an income statement, a statement of owner's equity, and a balance sheet. 7. Develop a chart of accounts. 8. Define the accounting terms new to this chapter.

Reading Assignment

Read Chapter 3 in the textbook. Complete the textbook Section Self Review as you finish reading each section of the chapter, and the Comprehensive Self Review at the end of the chapter. Refer to the Chapter 3 Glossary or to the Glossary at the end of the book to find definitions for terms that are not familiar to you.

Activities

☐ **Thinking Critically**   Answer the *Thinking Critically* questions for AT&T and Managerial Implications.

☐ **Discussion Questions**   Answer each assigned discussion question in Chapter 3.

☐ **Exercises**   Complete each assigned exercise in Chapter 3. Use the forms provided in this SGWP. The objectives covered by an exercise are given after the exercise number. If you need help with an exercise, review the portion of the chapter related to the objective(s) covered.

☐ **Problems A/B**   Complete each assigned problem in Chapter 3. Use the forms provided in this SGWP. The objectives covered by a problem are given after the problem number. If you need help with a problem, review the portion of the chapter related to the objective(s) covered.

☐ **Critical Thinking Problems**   Complete the critical thinking problems as assigned. Use the forms provided in this SGWP.

☐ **Business Connections**   Complete the Business Connections activities as assigned to gain a deeper understanding of Chapter 3 concepts.

Practice Tests

Complete the Practice Tests, which cover the main points in your reading assignment. Compare your answers with those in the Practice Test Answer Key for Chapter 3 at the end of this chapter. If you have answered any questions incorrectly, review the related section of the text.

Part A True-False

For each of the following statements, circle T in the answer column if the answer is true or F if the answer is false.

T   F   **1.** The **Accounts Payable** account is decreased by a debit entry.

T   F   **2.** Increases in expense accounts are recorded by credit entries.

T   F   **3.** Accountants keep a separate record for each asset, liability, and owner's equity item.

T   F   **4.** The T account allows increases and decreases to be separated and recorded on different sides.

T   F   **5.** Increases in assets are recorded on the debit side of an account.

T   F   **6.** Decreases in assets are recorded on the left side of an account.

T   F   **7.** The owner's beginning investment is entered as a debit in the owner's capital account.

T   F   **8.** Increases in liabilities are recorded on the debit side of an account.

T   F   **9.** A cash payment by a business is recorded as a debit entry in the **Cash** account.

T   F   **10.** Decreases in liabilities are credited to the liability account.

T   F   **11.** An increase in the owner's investment is recorded by crediting the owner's capital account.

T   F   **12.** Revenue accounts are increased by credits.

T   F   **13.** An entry on the left side of any account is called a debit.

T   F   **14.** A reduction in the equity of the owners is recorded by making a debit entry in the **Owner's Drawing** account.

T   F   **15.** The receipt of cash is recorded by a debit entry to the **Cash** account.

Part B Matching
For each numbered item, choose the matching item from the box and write the identifying letter in the answer column.

_____	1. An operating cost that decreases owner's equity.
_____	2. The system of accounting that requires equality of the entries on each side of the equation.
_____	3. Accounts whose balances are carried forward to start a new period.
_____	4. An entry on the left side of an account.
_____	5. An entry on the right side of an account.
_____	6. A system for arranging accounts in logical order.
_____	7. Accounts whose balances are transferred to a summary account at the end of the accounting period.
_____	8. A subdivision of owner's equity that is used to record various types of income of a business.
_____	9. A separate written record that is kept for each asset, liability, and owner's equity item.

a. Account
b. Double-entry system
c. Credit
d. Permanent accounts
e. Temporary accounts
f. Expense
g. Revenue
h. Chart of accounts
i. Debit

Part C Completion
In the answer column, supply the missing word or words needed to complete each of the following statements.

_____	1. The _____ of an account is where increases in the account are recorded and where the balance is recorded.
_____	2. The _____ is a statement prepared to test the accuracy of the figures recorded in the accounts.
_____	3. A(n) _____ is an error where the digits of a number are switched.
_____	4. A(n) _____ is an error where the decimal point is misplaced.
_____	5. A(n) _____ is the total of several entries on either side of an account that is entered in small pencil.

Demonstration Problem

Nina Turner is an investment broker who operates her own business, Turner Investment Counseling.

Instructions

1. Analyze the transactions for the month of January 2013, and record each in the appropriate T accounts. Use plus and minus signs to show increases and decreases. Identify each entry in the T accounts by writing the number of the transaction next to the entry.

2. Determine the balance for each T account. Prepare a trial balance.

Transactions

1. Nina Turner invested $50,000 in cash to start the business.

2. Turner Investment Counseling purchased office furniture for $9,000 on account.

3. Paid $3,000 for one month's rent.

4. Sold an investment portfolio to the Dotson Family and received fees of $50,000.

5. Purchased a computer for $4,000, paying $2,000 in cash and putting the balance on account for 60 days.

6. Paid $8,400 for employee salaries.

7. Purchased office equipment for $7,500 with credit terms of 60 days.

8. Sold an investment portfolio to the Carter Family and will receive commission fees of $21,000 in 30 days.

9. Issued a check for $3,750 for partial payment of the amount for office equipment.

10. Nina Turner withdrew $5,000 in cash for personal use.

11. Issued a check for $1,040 to pay the utility bill.

SOLUTION

Cash

(1)	+ 50,000	(3)	− 3,000
(4)	+ 50,000	(5)	− 2,000
		(6)	− 8,400
		(9)	− 3,750
	100,000	(10)	− 5,000
		(11)	− 1,040
Bal.	76,810		23,190

Accounts Receivable

(8)	+ 21,000

Office Furniture

(2)	+ 9,000

Office Equipment

(5)	+ 4,000
(7)	+ 7,500
Bal.	11,500

Accounts Payable

(9)	− 3,750	(2)	+ 9,000
		(5)	+ 2,000
		(7)	+ 7,500
		Bal.	14,750

Nina Turner, Capital

(1)	+ 50,000

Nina Turner, Drawing

(10)	+ 5,000

Fees Income

(4)	+ 50,000
(8)	+ 21,000
Bal.	71,000

Rent Expense

(3)	+ 3,000

Salaries Expense

(6)	+ 8,400

Utilities Expense

(11)	+ 1040

SOLUTION (continued)

Turner Investment Counseling

Trial Balance

January 31, 2013

ACCOUNT NAME	DEBIT	CREDIT
Cash	76 8 1 0 00	
Accounts Receivable	2 1 0 0 00	
Office Furniture	9 0 0 0 00	
Office Equipment	11 5 0 0 00	
Accounts Payable		14 7 5 0 00
Nina Turner, Capital		50 0 0 0 00
Nina Turner, Drawing	5 0 0 0 00	
Fees Income		71 0 0 0 00
Rent Expense	3 0 0 0 00	
Salaries Expense	8 4 0 0 00	
Utilities Expense	1 0 4 0 00	
Totals	135 7 5 0 00	135 7 5 0 00

WORKING PAPERS

Name _____

EXERCISE 3.1

EXERCISE 3.2

EXERCISE 3.3

1. _____
2. _____
3. _____
4. _____

5. _____
6. _____
7. _____
8. _____

EXERCISE 3.4

1. _____
2. _____
3. _____
4. _____
5. _____

EXERCISE 3.5

_____   _____
_____   _____
_____   _____
_____   _____
_____   _____

EXERCISE 3.6

_____
_____

ACCOUNT NAME	DEBIT	CREDIT

EXERCISE 3.6 (continued)

EXERCISE 3.7

EXERCISE 3.7 (continued)

EXERCISE 3.8

PROBLEM 3.1A or 3.1B

1.

2.

3.

4.

5.

6.

7.

8.

Analyze:

PROBLEM 3.2A or 3.2B

1.

2.

3.

4.

5.

6.

7.

8.

Analyze:

PROBLEM 3.3A or 3.3B

1. _____|_____   _____|_____

2. _____|_____   _____|_____

3. _____|_____   _____|_____

4. _____|_____   _____|_____

5. _____|_____   _____|_____

6. _____|_____   _____|_____

7. _____|_____   _____|_____

8. _____|_____   _____|_____

9. _____|_____   _____|_____

10. _____|_____   _____|_____

11. _____|_____   _____|_____

12. _____|_____   _____|_____

PROBLEM 3.4A or 3.4B

Analyze: _____

_____

PROBLEM 3.5A or 3.5B

ACCOUNT NAME	DEBIT	CREDIT

PROBLEM 3.5A or 3.5B (continued)

Analyze: _____

CRITICAL THINKING PROBLEM 3.1

CRITICAL THINKING PROBLEM 3.1 (continued)

CRITICAL THINKING PROBLEM 3.1 (continued)

CRITICAL THINKING PROBLEM 3.1 (continued)

_____
_____
_____
_____
_____
_____
_____
_____
_____
_____
_____
_____
_____
_____
_____
_____
_____
_____
_____
_____
_____
_____
_____
_____
_____
_____
_____
_____
_____
_____
_____
_____
_____
_____
_____
_____

CRITICAL THINKING PROBLEM 3.2

CRITICAL THINKING PROBLEM 3.2 (continued)

_____

_____

ACCOUNT NAME	DEBIT	CREDIT

CRITICAL THINKING PROBLEM 3.2 (continued)

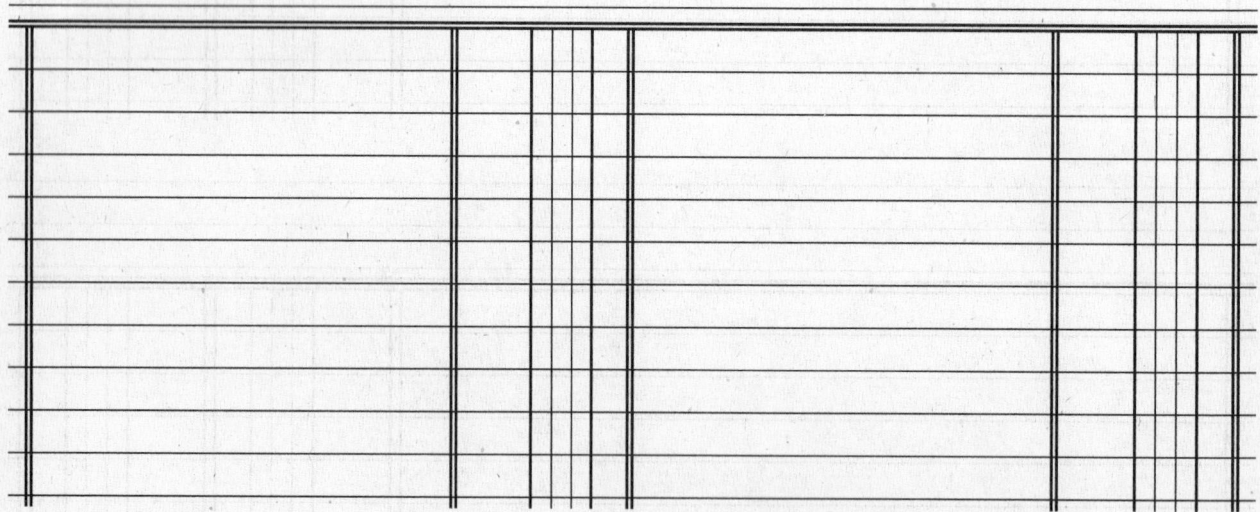

Analyze: _____

Chapter 3 Practice Test Answer Key

Part A True-False

1. T	6. F	11. T
2. F	7. F	12. T
3. T	8. F	13. T
4. T	9. F	14. T
5. T	10. F	15. T

Part B Matching

1. f	6. h
2. b	7. e
3. d	8. g
4. i	9. a
5. c	

Part C Completion

1. normal balance
2. trial balance
3. transposition
4. slide
5. footing

CHAPTER 4

The General Journal and the General Ledger

STUDY GUIDE

Understanding the Chapter

Objectives

1. Record transactions in the general journal. 2. Prepare compound journal entries. 3. Post journal entries to general ledger accounts. 4. Correct errors made in the journal or ledger. 5. Define the accounting terms new to this chapter.

Reading Assignment

Read Chapter 4 in the textbook. Complete the textbook Section Self Review as you finish reading each section of the chapter, and the Comprehensive Self Review at the end of the chapter. Refer to the Chapter 4 Glossary or to the Glossary at the end of the book to find definitions for terms that are not familiar to you.

Activities

❏ **Thinking Critically**

Answer the *Thinking Critically* questions for Willamette Valley Vineyards and Managerial Implications.

❏ **Discussion Questions**

Answer each assigned discussion question in Chapter 4.

❏ **Exercises**

Complete each assigned exercise in Chapter 4. Use the forms provided in this SGWP. The objectives covered by an exercise are given after the exercise number. If you need help with an exercise, review the portion of the chapter related to the objective(s) covered.

❏ **Problems A/B**

Complete each assigned problem in Chapter 4. Use the forms provided in this SGWP. The objectives covered by a problem are given after the problem number. If you need help with a problem, review the portion of the chapter related to the objective(s) covered.

❏ **Critical Thinking Problems**

Complete the critical thinking problems as assigned. Use the forms provided in this SGWP.

❏ **Business Connections**

Complete the Business Connections activities as assigned to gain a deeper understanding of Chapter 4 concepts.

Practice Tests

Complete the Practice Tests, which cover the main points in your reading assignment. Compare your answers with those in the Practice Test Answer Key for Chapter 4 at the end of this chapter. If you have answered any questions incorrectly, review the related section of the text.

Part A Matching *For each numbered item, choose the matching term from the box and write the identifying letter in the answer column.*

_____	1. A ledger account form that always shows the current balance of an account.
_____	2. A journal entry that consists of more than one debit or more than one credit.
_____	3. A permanent, classified record of all accounts used by a business.
_____	4. Used to analyze transactions but not used to maintain financial records.
_____	5. The process of transferring information from the journal to the ledger.
_____	6. An entry that is made when there is an error in data that has been journalized and posted.
_____	7. Record of original entry.
_____	8. The process of recording transactions in the journal.
_____	9. Invoices and other business forms that contain the original data about transactions.
_____	10. A chain of references that makes it possible to trace information about transactions through an accounting system.

a. journal

b. source documents

c. posting

d. general ledger

e. T accounts

f. journalizing

g. correcting entry

h. compound entry

i. balance ledger form

j. audit trail

Part B Completion *In the answer column, supply the missing word or words needed to complete each of the following statements.*

_____ 1. The accountant always records the _____ items first in the Description column of the journal.

_____ 2. The _____ is always entered at the top of the Date column.

_____ 3. The accountant enters transactions in the general journal in _____ order.

_____ 4. The pages in the ledger are usually organized so that the _____ come first.

_____ 5. If an error is discovered in a journal before the entry is _____, the error can be neatly crossed out and the correct data written above it.

_____ 6. All the accounts together constitute a(n) _____, or a record of final entry.

_____ 7. Notations that allow the data in journals and ledgers to be easily traced are called _____.

_____ 8. Descriptions in the general journal should be complete but _____.

_____ 9. On the balance ledger form the second money column is used to record _____ amounts.

_____ 10. On the balance ledger form the first money column is used to record _____ amounts.

Demonstration Problem

On January 1, 2013, John Wilson opened his consulting office and began business as Wilson Consulting Services. Selected transactions for the first month of operations follow.

Instructions

1. Journalize the transactions on page 1 of a general journal. Write the year at the top of the Date column; include an explanation for each entry.

2. Post to the general ledger accounts.

3. Prepare a trial balance.

DATE	TRANSACTIONS
January 1	John Wilson invested $90,000 cash in the business.
2	Issued Check 101 for $5,000 to pay the January rent.
5	Purchased office equipment for $30,000 from Davis Office Supply, Invoice 7045; issued Check 102 for $10,000 down payment with the balance due in 30 days.
12	Wrote a lease contract for Ned Lee for $6,000 cash.
15	Performed consulting services for a client, Jones Supply Company, for $20,000 to be received in 30 days.
28	Issued Check 103 for $10,000 for payment to Davis Office Supply.
29	Issued Check 104 for $10,000 to John Wilson for personal use.
31	Received $9,000 from Jones Supply Company for partial payment of their account.

SOLUTION

PAGE ___1___

	DATE		DESCRIPTION	POST. REF.	DEBIT	CREDIT	
1	2013						1
2	Jan.	1	Cash	101	90 0 0 0 00		2
3			John Wilson, Capital	301		90 0 0 0 00	3
4			Investment to start business				4
5							5
6		2	Rent Expense	514	5 0 0 0 00		6
7			Cash	101		5 0 0 0 00	7
8			Issued Check 101 for January rent				8
9							9
10		5	Office Equipment	131	30 0 0 0 00		10
11			Cash	101		10 0 0 0 00	11
12			Accounts Payable	202		20 0 0 0 00	12
13			Issued Check 102 for office equipment,				13
14			balance due in 30 days.				14
15							15
16		12	Cash	101	6 0 0 0 00		16
17			Fees Income	401		6 0 0 0 00	17
18			Performed services for cash.				18
19							19
20		15	Accounts Receivable	111	20 0 0 0 00		20
21			Fees Income	401		20 0 0 0 00	21
22			Performed services on account.				22
23							23
24		28	Accounts Payable	202	10 0 0 0 00		24
25			Cash	101		10 0 0 0 00	25
26			Paid Invoice 7045, Check 103				26
27							27
28		29	John Wilson, Drawing	302	10 0 0 0 00		28
29			Cash	101		10 0 0 0 00	29
30			Issued Check 104 to owner for personal use.				30
31							31
32		31	Cash	101	9 0 0 0 00		32
33			Accounts Receivable	111		9 0 0 0 00	33
34			Received partial payment				34
35			from Jones Supply Company				35
36							36
37							37
38							38
39							39

44 ◼ Chapter 4

SOLUTION (continued)

GENERAL LEDGER

ACCOUNT _Cash_ **ACCOUNT NO.** ___101___

DATE		DESCRIPTION	POST. REF.	DEBIT	CREDIT	BALANCE DEBIT	BALANCE CREDIT
2013							
Jan.	1		J1	90 0 0 0 00		90 0 0 0 00	
	2		J1		5 0 0 0 00	85 0 0 0 00	
	5		J1		10 0 0 0 00	75 0 0 0 00	
	12		J1	6 0 0 0 00		81 0 0 0 00	
	28		J1		10 0 0 0 00	71 0 0 0 00	
	29		J1		10 0 0 0 00	61 0 0 0 00	
	31		J1	9 0 0 0 00		70 0 0 0 00	

ACCOUNT _Accounts Receivable_ **ACCOUNT NO.** ___111___

DATE		DESCRIPTION	POST. REF.	DEBIT	CREDIT	BALANCE DEBIT	BALANCE CREDIT
2013							
Jan.	15		J1	20 0 0 0 00		20 0 0 0 00	
	31		J1		9 0 0 0 00	11 0 0 0 00	

ACCOUNT _Office Equipment_ **ACCOUNT NO.** ___131___

DATE		DESCRIPTION	POST. REF.	DEBIT	CREDIT	BALANCE DEBIT	BALANCE CREDIT
2013							
Jan.	5		J1	30 0 0 0 00		30 0 0 0 00	

ACCOUNT _Accounts Payable_ **ACCOUNT NO.** ___202___

DATE		DESCRIPTION	POST. REF.	DEBIT	CREDIT	BALANCE DEBIT	BALANCE CREDIT
2013							
Jan.	5		J1		20 0 0 0 00		20 0 0 0 00
	28		J1	10 0 0 0 00			10 0 0 0 00

ACCOUNT _John Wilson, Capital_ **ACCOUNT NO.** ___301___

DATE		DESCRIPTION	POST. REF.	DEBIT	CREDIT	BALANCE DEBIT	BALANCE CREDIT
2013							
Jan.	1		J1		90 0 0 0 00		90 0 0 0 00

SOLUTION (continued)

ACCOUNT   __John Wilson, Drawing__   ACCOUNT NO. ____302____

DATE		DESCRIPTION	POST. REF.	DEBIT	CREDIT	BALANCE DEBIT	BALANCE CREDIT
2013							
Jan.	29		J1	10 0 0 0 00		10 0 0 0 00	

ACCOUNT   __Fees Income__   ACCOUNT NO. ____401____

DATE		DESCRIPTION	POST. REF.	DEBIT	CREDIT	BALANCE DEBIT	BALANCE CREDIT
2013							
Jan.	12		J1		6 0 0 0 00		6 0 0 0 00
	15		J1		20 0 0 0 00		26 0 0 0 00

ACCOUNT   __Rent Expense__   ACCOUNT NO. ____514____

DATE		DESCRIPTION	POST. REF.	DEBIT	CREDIT	BALANCE DEBIT	BALANCE CREDIT
2013							
Jan.	2		J1	5 0 0 0 00		5 0 0 0 00	

Wilson Consulting Services
Trial Balance
January 31, 2013

ACCOUNT NAME	DEBIT	CREDIT
Cash	70 0 0 0 00	
Accounts Receivable	11 0 0 0 00	
Office Equipment	30 0 0 0 00	
Accounts Payable		10 0 0 0 00
John Wilson, Capital		90 0 0 0 00
John Wilson, Drawing	10 0 0 0 00	
Fees Income		26 0 0 0 00
Rent Expense	5 0 0 0 00	
Totals	126 0 0 0 00	126 0 0 0 00

WORKING PAPERS

Name _____

EXERCISE 4.1

	Debit	Credit			Debit	Credit			Debit	Credit
1.			5.				8.			
2.			6.				9.			
3.			7.				10.			
4.										

EXERCISE 4.2

GENERAL JOURNAL

PAGE _____

	DATE		DESCRIPTION	POST. REF.	DEBIT	CREDIT	
1							1
2							2
3							3
4							4
5							5
6							6
7							7
8							8
9							9
10							10
11							11
12							12
13							13
14							14
15							15
16							16
17							17
18							18
19							19
20							20
21							21
22							22
23							23
24							24
25							25
26							26
27							27
28							28
29							29

EXERCISE 4.2 (continued)

GENERAL JOURNAL

PAGE _____

	DATE	DESCRIPTION	POST. REF.	DEBIT	CREDIT	
1						1
2						2
3						3
4						4
5						5
6						6
7						7
8						8
9						9
10						10
11						11
12						12
13						13
14						14
15						15
16						16

EXERCISE 4.3

GENERAL LEDGER

ACCOUNT _____ ACCOUNT NO. _____

DATE	DESCRIPTION	POST. REF.	DEBIT	CREDIT	BALANCE	
					DEBIT	CREDIT

EXERCISE 4.3 (continued)

GENERAL LEDGER

ACCOUNT _____ ACCOUNT NO. _____

DATE	DESCRIPTION	POST. REF.	DEBIT	CREDIT	BALANCE	
					DEBIT	CREDIT

ACCOUNT _____ ACCOUNT NO. _____

DATE	DESCRIPTION	POST. REF.	DEBIT	CREDIT	BALANCE	
					DEBIT	CREDIT

ACCOUNT _____ ACCOUNT NO. _____

DATE	DESCRIPTION	POST. REF.	DEBIT	CREDIT	BALANCE	
					DEBIT	CREDIT

ACCOUNT _____ ACCOUNT NO. _____

DATE	DESCRIPTION	POST. REF.	DEBIT	CREDIT	BALANCE	
					DEBIT	CREDIT

ACCOUNT _____ ACCOUNT NO. _____

DATE	DESCRIPTION	POST. REF.	DEBIT	CREDIT	BALANCE	
					DEBIT	CREDIT

EXERCISE 4.3 (continued)

GENERAL LEDGER

ACCOUNT _____ ACCOUNT NO. _____

DATE	DESCRIPTION	POST. REF.	DEBIT	CREDIT	BALANCE	
					DEBIT	CREDIT

ACCOUNT _____ ACCOUNT NO. _____

DATE	DESCRIPTION	POST. REF.	DEBIT	CREDIT	BALANCE	
					DEBIT	CREDIT

ACCOUNT _____ ACCOUNT NO. _____

DATE	DESCRIPTION	POST. REF.	DEBIT	CREDIT	BALANCE	
					DEBIT	CREDIT

ACCOUNT _____ ACCOUNT NO. _____

DATE	DESCRIPTION	POST. REF.	DEBIT	CREDIT	BALANCE	
					DEBIT	CREDIT

ACCOUNT _____ ACCOUNT NO. _____

DATE	DESCRIPTION	POST. REF.	DEBIT	CREDIT	BALANCE	
					DEBIT	CREDIT

ACCOUNT _____ ACCOUNT NO. _____

DATE	DESCRIPTION	POST. REF.	DEBIT	CREDIT	BALANCE	
					DEBIT	CREDIT

EXERCISE 4.4

GENERAL JOURNAL   PAGE _____

	DATE		DESCRIPTION	POST. REF.	DEBIT	CREDIT	
1							1
2							2
3							3
4							4
5							5
6							6
7							7
8							8
9							9
10							10
11							11
12							12
13							13
14							14
15							15
16							16
17							17
18							18
19							19
20							20
21							21
22							22
23							23
24							24
25							25
26							26
27							27
28							28
29							29
30							30
31							31
32							32
33							33
34							34
35							35
36							36
37							37

EXERCISE 4.5

GENERAL JOURNAL   PAGE _____

	DATE	DESCRIPTION	POST. REF.	DEBIT	CREDIT	
1						1
2						2
3						3
4						4
5						5
6						6

EXERCISE 4.6

GENERAL JOURNAL   PAGE _____

	DATE	DESCRIPTION	POST. REF.	DEBIT	CREDIT	
1						1
2						2
3						3
4						4
5						5
6						6

EXTRA FORM

GENERAL JOURNAL   PAGE _____

	DATE	DESCRIPTION	POST. REF.	DEBIT	CREDIT	
1						1
2						2
3						3
4						4
5						5
6						6
7						7
8						8
9						9
10						10
11						11
12						12
13						13

PROBLEM 4.1A or 4.1B

GENERAL JOURNAL

PAGE _____

	DATE	DESCRIPTION	POST. REF.	DEBIT	CREDIT	
1						1
2						2
3						3
4						4
5						5
6						6
7						7
8						8
9						9
10						10
11						11
12						12
13						13
14						14
15						15
16						16
17						17
18						18
19						19
20						20
21						21
22						22
23						23
24						24
25						25
26						26
27						27
28						28
29						29
30						30
31						31
32						32
33						33
34						34
35						35
36						36
37						37
38						38

PROBLEM 4.1A or 4.1B (continued)

GENERAL JOURNAL   PAGE _____

	DATE		DESCRIPTION	POST. REF.	DEBIT	CREDIT	
1							1
2							2
3							3
4							4
5							5
6							6
7							7
8							8
9							9
10							10
11							11
12							12
13							13
14							14
15							15
16							16
17							17
18							18
19							19
20							20
21							21
22							22
23							23
24							24
25							25
26							26
27							27
28							28
29							29
30							30
31							31
32							32
33							33
34							34
35							35
36							36
37							37

Analyze: _____

PROBLEM 4.2A or 4.2B

GENERAL JOURNAL   PAGE _____

	DATE	DESCRIPTION	POST. REF.	DEBIT	CREDIT	
1						1
2						2
3						3
4						4
5						5
6						6
7						7
8						8
9						9
10						10
11						11
12						12
13						13
14						14
15						15
16						16
17						17
18						18
19						19
20						20
21						21
22						22
23						23
24						24
25						25
26						26
27						27
28						28
29						29
30						30
31						31
32						32
33						33
34						34
35						35
36						36
37						37

PROBLEM 4.2A or 4.2B (continued)

GENERAL JOURNAL   PAGE _____

	DATE	DESCRIPTION	POST. REF.	DEBIT	CREDIT	
1						1
2						2
3						3
4						4
5						5
6						6
7						7
8						8
9						9
10						10
11						11
12						12
13						13
14						14
15						15
16						16
17						17
18						18
19						19
20						20
21						21
22						22
23						23
24						24
25						25
26						26
27						27
28						28
29						29
30						30
31						31
32						32
33						33
34						34
35						35
36						36
37						37

PROBLEM 4.2A or 4.2B (continued)

GENERAL LEDGER

ACCOUNT _____ ACCOUNT NO. _____

DATE		DESCRIPTION	POST. REF.	DEBIT	CREDIT	BALANCE	
						DEBIT	CREDIT

ACCOUNT _____ ACCOUNT NO. _____

DATE		DESCRIPTION	POST. REF.	DEBIT	CREDIT	BALANCE	
						DEBIT	CREDIT

ACCOUNT _____ ACCOUNT NO. _____

DATE		DESCRIPTION	POST. REF.	DEBIT	CREDIT	BALANCE	
						DEBIT	CREDIT

ACCOUNT _____ ACCOUNT NO. _____

DATE		DESCRIPTION	POST. REF.	DEBIT	CREDIT	BALANCE	
						DEBIT	CREDIT

Name _____

PROBLEM 4.2A or 4.2B (continued)

GENERAL LEDGER

ACCOUNT _____ ACCOUNT NO. _____

DATE	DESCRIPTION	POST. REF.	DEBIT	CREDIT	BALANCE DEBIT	CREDIT

ACCOUNT _____ ACCOUNT NO. _____

DATE	DESCRIPTION	POST. REF.	DEBIT	CREDIT	BALANCE DEBIT	CREDIT

ACCOUNT _____ ACCOUNT NO. _____

DATE	DESCRIPTION	POST. REF.	DEBIT	CREDIT	BALANCE DEBIT	CREDIT

ACCOUNT _____ ACCOUNT NO. _____

DATE	DESCRIPTION	POST. REF.	DEBIT	CREDIT	BALANCE DEBIT	CREDIT

ACCOUNT _____ ACCOUNT NO. _____

DATE	DESCRIPTION	POST. REF.	DEBIT	CREDIT	BALANCE DEBIT	CREDIT

PROBLEM 4.2A or 4.2B (continued)

GENERAL LEDGER

ACCOUNT _____ ACCOUNT NO. _____

DATE	DESCRIPTION	POST. REF.	DEBIT	CREDIT	BALANCE	
					DEBIT	CREDIT

ACCOUNT _____ ACCOUNT NO. _____

DATE	DESCRIPTION	POST. REF.	DEBIT	CREDIT	BALANCE	
					DEBIT	CREDIT

ACCOUNT _____ ACCOUNT NO. _____

DATE	DESCRIPTION	POST. REF.	DEBIT	CREDIT	BALANCE	
					DEBIT	CREDIT

ACCOUNT _____ ACCOUNT NO. _____

DATE	DESCRIPTION	POST. REF.	DEBIT	CREDIT	BALANCE	
					DEBIT	CREDIT

ACCOUNT _____ ACCOUNT NO. _____

DATE	DESCRIPTION	POST. REF.	DEBIT	CREDIT	BALANCE	
					DEBIT	CREDIT

Analyze: _____

_____

PROBLEM 4.3A or 4.3B

_____

_____

_____

_____

_____

_____

Analyze: _____

_____

PROBLEM 4.4A or 4.4B

GENERAL JOURNAL

PAGE _____

	DATE	DESCRIPTION	POST. REF.	DEBIT	CREDIT	
1						1
2						2
3						3
4						4
5						5
6						6
7						7
8						8
9						9
10						10
11						11
12						12
13						13
14						14
15						15
16						16
17						17
18						18
19						19
20						20
21						21
22						22
23						23
24						24
25						25
26						26

PROBLEM 4.4A or 4.4B (continued)

GENERAL LEDGER

ACCOUNT _____ ACCOUNT NO. _____

DATE	DESCRIPTION	POST. REF.	DEBIT	CREDIT	BALANCE	
					DEBIT	CREDIT

ACCOUNT _____ ACCOUNT NO. _____

DATE	DESCRIPTION	POST. REF.	DEBIT	CREDIT	BALANCE	
					DEBIT	CREDIT

ACCOUNT _____ ACCOUNT NO. _____

DATE	DESCRIPTION	POST. REF.	DEBIT	CREDIT	BALANCE	
					DEBIT	CREDIT

ACCOUNT _____ ACCOUNT NO. _____

DATE	DESCRIPTION	POST. REF.	DEBIT	CREDIT	BALANCE	
					DEBIT	CREDIT

ACCOUNT _____ ACCOUNT NO. _____

DATE	DESCRIPTION	POST. REF.	DEBIT	CREDIT	BALANCE	
					DEBIT	CREDIT

PROBLEM 4.4A or 4.4B (continued)

GENERAL LEDGER

ACCOUNT _____ ACCOUNT NO. _____

DATE	DESCRIPTION	POST. REF.	DEBIT	CREDIT	BALANCE	
					DEBIT	CREDIT

ACCOUNT _____ ACCOUNT NO. _____

DATE	DESCRIPTION	POST. REF.	DEBIT	CREDIT	BALANCE	
					DEBIT	CREDIT

ACCOUNT _____ ACCOUNT NO. _____

DATE	DESCRIPTION	POST. REF.	DEBIT	CREDIT	BALANCE	
					DEBIT	CREDIT

ACCOUNT _____ ACCOUNT NO. _____

DATE	DESCRIPTION	POST. REF.	DEBIT	CREDIT	BALANCE	
					DEBIT	CREDIT

Analyze: _____

_____

EXTRA FORM

GENERAL LEDGER

ACCOUNT _____ ACCOUNT NO. _____

DATE	DESCRIPTION	POST. REF.	DEBIT	CREDIT	BALANCE	
					DEBIT	CREDIT

CRITICAL THINKING PROBLEM 4.1

_____
_____
_____
_____
_____
_____
_____
_____
_____
_____
_____
_____
_____
_____
_____
_____
_____
_____
_____
_____
_____
_____

CRITICAL THINKING PROBLEM 4.1 (continued)

CRITICAL THINKING PROBLEM 4.2

GENERAL JOURNAL   PAGE _____

	DATE		DESCRIPTION	POST. REF.	DEBIT	CREDIT	
1							1
2							2
3							3
4							4
5							5
6							6
7							7
8							8
9							9
10							10
11							11
12							12
13							13
14							14
15							15
16							16
17							17
18							18
19							19
20							20
21							21
22							22
23							23
24							24
25							25
26							26
27							27
28							28
29							29
30							30
31							31
32							32
33							33
34							34
35							35
36							36
37							37
38							38

CRITICAL THINKING PROBLEM 4.2 (continued)

GENERAL JOURNAL

PAGE _____

	DATE	DESCRIPTION	POST. REF.	DEBIT	CREDIT	
1						1
2						2
3						3
4						4
5						5
6						6
7						7
8						8
9						9
10						10
11						11
12						12
13						13
14						14
15						15
16						16
17						17
18						18
19						19
20						20
21						21
22						22
23						23
24						24
25						25
26						26
27						27
28						28
29						29
30						30
31						31
32						32
33						33
34						34
35						35
36						36
37						37

CRITICAL THINKING PROBLEM 4.2 (continued)

GENERAL JOURNAL

PAGE _____

	DATE	DESCRIPTION	POST. REF.	DEBIT	CREDIT	
1						1
2						2
3						3
4						4
5						5
6						6
7						7
8						8
9						9
10						10
11						11
12						12
13						13
14						14

GENERAL LEDGER

ACCOUNT _____ ACCOUNT NO. _____

DATE	DESCRIPTION	POST. REF.	DEBIT	CREDIT	BALANCE	
					DEBIT	CREDIT

CRITICAL THINKING PROBLEM 4.2 (continued)

GENERAL LEDGER

ACCOUNT _____ ACCOUNT NO. _____

DATE	DESCRIPTION	POST. REF.	DEBIT	CREDIT	BALANCE DEBIT	CREDIT

ACCOUNT _____ ACCOUNT NO. _____

DATE	DESCRIPTION	POST. REF.	DEBIT	CREDIT	BALANCE DEBIT	CREDIT

ACCOUNT _____ ACCOUNT NO. _____

DATE	DESCRIPTION	POST. REF.	DEBIT	CREDIT	BALANCE DEBIT	CREDIT

ACCOUNT _____ ACCOUNT NO. _____

DATE	DESCRIPTION	POST. REF.	DEBIT	CREDIT	BALANCE DEBIT	CREDIT

ACCOUNT _____ ACCOUNT NO. _____

DATE	DESCRIPTION	POST. REF.	DEBIT	CREDIT	BALANCE DEBIT	CREDIT

CRITICAL THINKING PROBLEM 4.2 (continued)

GENERAL LEDGER

ACCOUNT _____   ACCOUNT NO. _____

DATE	DESCRIPTION	POST. REF.	DEBIT	CREDIT	BALANCE	
					DEBIT	CREDIT

ACCOUNT _____   ACCOUNT NO. _____

DATE	DESCRIPTION	POST. REF.	DEBIT	CREDIT	BALANCE	
					DEBIT	CREDIT

ACCOUNT _____   ACCOUNT NO. _____

DATE	DESCRIPTION	POST. REF.	DEBIT	CREDIT	BALANCE	
					DEBIT	CREDIT

ACCOUNT _____   ACCOUNT NO. _____

DATE	DESCRIPTION	POST. REF.	DEBIT	CREDIT	BALANCE	
					DEBIT	CREDIT

ACCOUNT _____   ACCOUNT NO. _____

DATE	DESCRIPTION	POST. REF.	DEBIT	CREDIT	BALANCE	
					DEBIT	CREDIT

CRITICAL THINKING PROBLEM 4.2 (continued)

GENERAL LEDGER

ACCOUNT _____ ACCOUNT NO. _____

DATE	DESCRIPTION	POST. REF.	DEBIT	CREDIT	BALANCE	
					DEBIT	CREDIT

ACCOUNT _____ ACCOUNT NO. _____

DATE	DESCRIPTION	POST. REF.	DEBIT	CREDIT	BALANCE	
					DEBIT	CREDIT

ACCOUNT _____ ACCOUNT NO. _____

DATE	DESCRIPTION	POST. REF.	DEBIT	CREDIT	BALANCE	
					DEBIT	CREDIT

EXTRA FORMS

GENERAL LEDGER

ACCOUNT _____ ACCOUNT NO. _____

DATE	DESCRIPTION	POST. REF.	DEBIT	CREDIT	BALANCE	
					DEBIT	CREDIT

ACCOUNT _____ ACCOUNT NO. _____

DATE	DESCRIPTION	POST. REF.	DEBIT	CREDIT	BALANCE	
					DEBIT	CREDIT

CRITICAL THINKING PROBLEM 4.2 (continued)

ACCOUNT NAME	DEBIT	CREDIT

ACCOUNT NAME	DEBIT	CREDIT

CRITICAL THINKING PROBLEM 4.2 (continued)

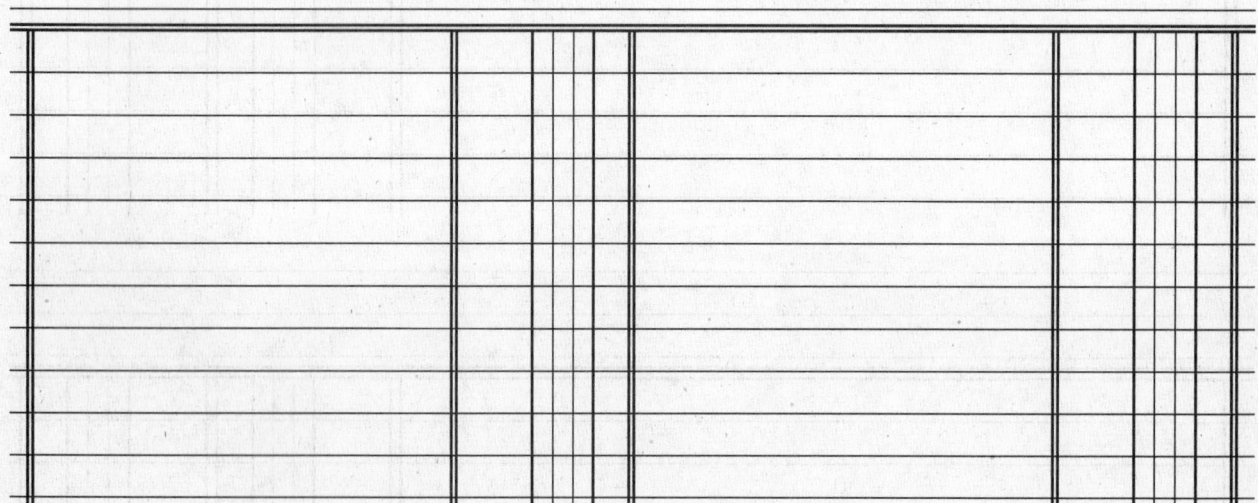

Analyze: _____

Chapter 4 Practice Test Answer Key

Part A Matching

1. i	**6.** g	
2. h	**7.** a	
3. d	**8.** f	
4. e	**9.** b	
5. c	**10.** j	

Part B Completion

1. debit   **6.** ledger

2. year   **7.** posting references

3. chronological or date   **8.** brief or concise

4. assets or balance sheet accounts   **9.** credit

5. posted   **10.** debit

CHAPTER 5   Adjustments and the Worksheet

STUDY GUIDE

Understanding the Chapter

Objectives

1. Complete a trial balance on a worksheet. 2. Prepare adjustments for unrecorded business transactions. 3. Complete the worksheet. 4. Prepare an income statement, statement of owner's equity, and balance sheet from the completed worksheet. 5. Journalize and post the adjusting entries. 6. Define the accounting terms new to this chapter.

Reading Assignment

Read Chapter 5 in the textbook. Complete the textbook Section Self Review as you finish reading each section of the chapter, and the Comprehensive Self Review at the end of the chapter. Refer to the Chapter 5 Glossary or to the Glossary at the end of the book to find definitions for terms that are not familiar to you.

Activities

❑ **Thinking Critically**
Answer the *Thinking Critically* questions for Boeing and Managerial Implications.

❑ **Discussion Questions**
Answer each assigned discussion question in Chapter 5.

❑ **Exercises**
Complete each assigned exercise in Chapter 5. Use the forms provided in this SGWP. The objectives covered by an exercise are given after the exercise number. If you need help with an exercise, review the portion of the chapter related to the objective(s) covered.

❑ **Problems A/B**
Complete each assigned problem in Chapter 5. Use the forms provided in this SGWP. The objectives covered by a problem are given after the problem number. If you need help with a problem, review the portion of the chapter related to the objective(s) covered.

❑ **Critical Thinking Problems**
Complete the critical thinking problems as assigned. Use the forms provided in this SGWP.

❑ **Business Connections**
Complete the Business Connections activities as assigned to gain a deeper understanding of Chapter 5 concepts.

Practice Tests

Complete the Practice Tests, which cover the main points in your reading assignment. Compare your answers with those in the Practice Test Answer Key for Chapter 5 at the end of this chapter. If you have answered any questions incorrectly, review the related section of the text.

Part A True-False

For each of the following statements, circle T in the answer column if the statement is true or F if the statement is false.

T   F   **1.** The balances of the expense accounts are normally transferred to the Income Statement Debit column of the worksheet.

T   F   **2.** When the Balance Sheet columns of the worksheet are first added, the total of the Debit column should equal the total of the Credit column.

T   F   **3.** After the net income (or net loss) is computed in the Income Statement section of the worksheet, this amount is transferred to the Balance Sheet section of the worksheet.

T   F   **4.** On a worksheet, the difference between the Debit and Credit Column totals in the Income Statement section must equal the difference between the Debit and Credit column totals in the Balance Sheet section.

T   F   **5.** The Income Statement columns and Balance Sheet columns provide the figures for preparing the financial statements.

T   F   **6.** The ledger must be in balance before financial statements are prepared.

T   F   **7.** Accountants use a worksheet as a means of organizing their figures quickly.

T   F   **8.** The first two money columns of the worksheet contain a trial balance of the general ledger accounts.

T   F   **9.** Asset account balances from the trial balance are normally transferred to the Income Statement Debit column of the worksheet.

T   F   **10.** Liability account balances from the trial balance are normally transferred to the Balance Sheet credit column of the worksheet.

Part B Matching

For each numbered item, choose the matching term from the box and write the identifying letter in the answer column.

_____ 1. A form used to organize the amounts needed to prepare the financial statements.

_____ 2. The term used when referring to an account in which there is an excess of credits over debits.

_____ 3. The term used when the total of the debit amounts in the general ledger and the total of the credit amounts are equal.

_____ 4. The term used for an account with an excess of debits over credits.

_____ 5. A way to test the accuracy of the figures recorded in the general ledger.

_____ 6. Assets = Liabilities + Owner's Equity.

> **a.** Worksheet
> **b.** Trial balance
> **c.** Debit balance
> **d.** Fundamental accounting equation
> **e.** Credit balance
> **f.** In balance

Demonstration Problem

The general ledger accounts listed on the worksheet for the Amos Graphics Design Company on January 31, 2013, show the results of the first month of operation.

Instructions

1. Record the following adjustments in the Adjustments section of the worksheet using the information below.

   a. Supplies used during the month, $8,850.

   b. The amount in the **Prepaid Rent** account represents a payment made on January 1 for the rent for 12 months.

   c. The equipment, purchased in January, has an estimated useful life of 10 years with no salvage value. The firm uses the straight-line method of depreciation.

2. Complete the worksheet.

3. Journalize and post the adjusting entries. Use journal page number 2.

SOLUTION

Amos Graphics Design Company
Worksheet
Month Ended January 31, 2013

ACCOUNT NAME	TRIAL BALANCE DEBIT	TRIAL BALANCE CREDIT	ADJUSTMENTS DEBIT	ADJUSTMENTS CREDIT	ADJUSTED TRIAL BALANCE DEBIT	ADJUSTED TRIAL BALANCE CREDIT	INCOME STATEMENT DEBIT	INCOME STATEMENT CREDIT	BALANCE SHEET DEBIT	BALANCE SHEET CREDIT
Cash	74,700.00				74,700.00				74,700.00	
Accounts Receivable	101,400.00				101,400.00				101,400.00	
Supplies	17,400.00			(a) 8,850.00	8,550.00				8,550.00	
Prepaid Rent	252,000.00			(b) 21,000.00	231,000.00				231,000.00	
Equipment	252,000.00				252,000.00				252,000.00	
Accum. Depr.—Equipment				(c) 2,100.00		2,100.00				2,100.00
Accounts Payable		160,800.00				160,800.00				160,800.00
John Amos, Capital		295,200.00				295,200.00				295,200.00
John Amos, Drawing	18,000.00				18,000.00				18,000.00	
Fees Income		453,030.00				453,030.00		453,030.00		
Advertising Expense	22,800.00				22,800.00		22,800.00			
Insurance Expense	24,000.00				24,000.00		24,000.00			
Salaries Expense	135,000.00				135,000.00		135,000.00			
Supplies Expense			(a) 8,850.00		8,850.00		8,850.00			
Rent Expense			(b) 21,000.00		21,000.00		21,000.00			
Telephone Expense	5,250.00				5,250.00		5,250.00			
Utilities Expense	6,480.00				6,480.00		6,480.00			
Depr. Expense—Equipment			(c) 2,100.00		2,100.00		2,100.00			
Totals	909,030.00	909,030.00	31,950.00	31,950.00	911,130.00	911,130.00	225,480.00	453,030.00	685,650.00	458,100.00
Net Income							227,550.00			227,550.00
							453,030.00	453,030.00	685,650.00	685,650.00

SOLUTION (continued)

GENERAL JOURNAL

PAGE 2

	DATE		DESCRIPTION	POST. REF.	DEBIT	CREDIT	
1			**Adjusting Entries**				1
2	2013						2
3	Jan.	31	Supplies Expense	518	8 8 5 0 00		3
4			Supplies	121		8 8 5 0 00	4
5							5
6		31	Rent Expense	519	2 1 0 0 00		6
7			Prepaid Rent	131		2 1 0 0 00	7
8							8
9		31	Depreciation Expense—Equipment	524	2 1 0 00		9
10			Accumulated Depreciation—Equipment	142		2 1 0 00	10
11							11

GENERAL LEDGER (PARTIAL)

ACCOUNT Supplies   ACCOUNT NO. 121

DATE		DESCRIPTION	POST. REF.	DEBIT	CREDIT	BALANCE DEBIT	BALANCE CREDIT
2013							
Jan.	3		J1	1 7 4 0 0 00		1 7 4 0 0 00	
	31	Adjusting	J2		8 8 5 0 00	8 5 5 0 00	

ACCOUNT Prepaid Rent   ACCOUNT NO. 131

DATE		DESCRIPTION	POST. REF.	DEBIT	CREDIT	BALANCE DEBIT	BALANCE CREDIT
2013							
Jan.	2		J1	252 0 0 0 00		252 0 0 0 00	
	31	Adjusting	J2		2 1 0 0 00	231 0 0 0 00	

ACCOUNT Accumulated Depreciation—Equipment   ACCOUNT NO. 142

DATE		DESCRIPTION	POST. REF.	DEBIT	CREDIT	BALANCE DEBIT	BALANCE CREDIT
2013							
Jan.	31	Adjusting	J2		2 1 0 00		2 1 0 00

SOLUTION (continued)

GENERAL LEDGER (PARTIAL)

ACCOUNT **Supplies Expense**   ACCOUNT NO. **518**

DATE		DESCRIPTION	POST. REF.	DEBIT	CREDIT	BALANCE DEBIT	BALANCE CREDIT
2013							
Jan.	31	Adjusting	J2	8 8 5 0 00		8 8 5 0 00	

ACCOUNT **Rent Expense**   ACCOUNT NO. **519**

DATE		DESCRIPTION	POST. REF.	DEBIT	CREDIT	BALANCE DEBIT	BALANCE CREDIT
2013							
Jan.	31	Adjusting	J2	21 0 0 0 00		21 0 0 0 00	

ACCOUNT **Depreciation Expense—Equipment**   ACCOUNT NO. **524**

DATE		DESCRIPTION	POST. REF.	DEBIT	CREDIT	BALANCE DEBIT	BALANCE CREDIT
2013							
Jan.	31	Adjusting	J2	2 1 0 0 00		2 1 0 0 00	

STUDY GUIDE

WORKING PAPERS

Name _____

EXERCISE 5.1

1. _____
_____
_____
_____

2. _____
_____
_____
_____

3. _____
_____
_____
_____

EXERCISE 5.2

1. _____
_____
_____
_____

2. _____
_____
_____
_____

EXERCISE 5.3

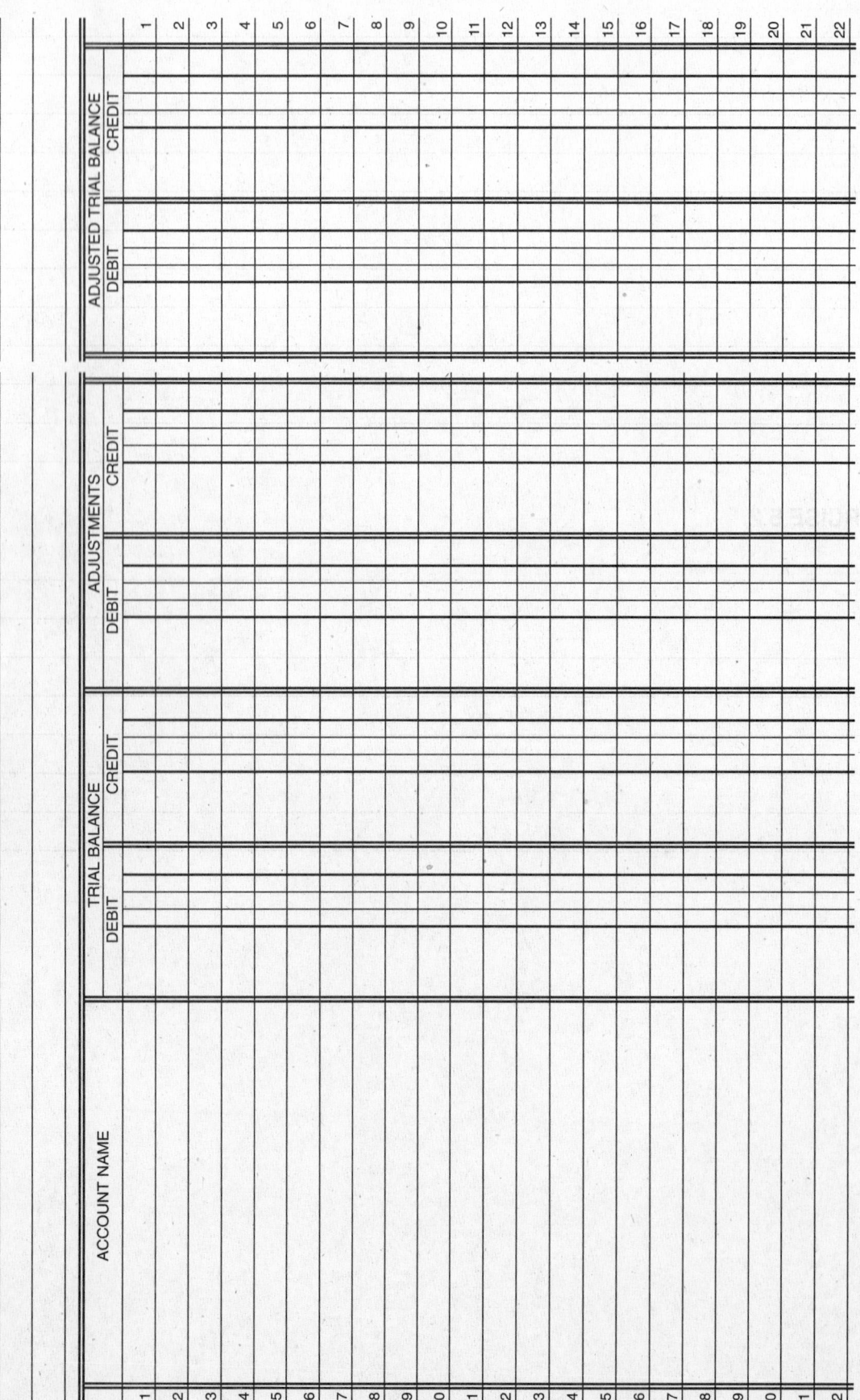

EXERCISE 5.4

_____
_____
_____
_____
_____
_____
_____
_____
_____
_____
_____
_____
_____
_____
_____
_____

EXERCISE 5.5

GENERAL JOURNAL   PAGE _____

	DATE	DESCRIPTION	POST. REF.	DEBIT	CREDIT	
1						1
2						2
3						3
4						4
5						5
6						6
7						7
8						8
9						9
10						10
11						11

GENERAL LEDGER

ACCOUNT __Supplies__   ACCOUNT NO. ___121___

DATE	DESCRIPTION	POST. REF.	DEBIT	CREDIT	BALANCE DEBIT	BALANCE CREDIT

ACCOUNT __Prepaid Insurance__   ACCOUNT NO. ___131___

DATE	DESCRIPTION	POST. REF.	DEBIT	CREDIT	BALANCE DEBIT	BALANCE CREDIT

ACCOUNT __Accumulated Depreciation—Equipment__   ACCOUNT NO. ___142___

DATE	DESCRIPTION	POST. REF.	DEBIT	CREDIT	BALANCE DEBIT	BALANCE CREDIT

EXERCISE 5.5 (continued)

GENERAL LEDGER

ACCOUNT __Depreciation Expense—Equipment__   ACCOUNT NO. ____517____

DATE	DESCRIPTION	POST. REF.	DEBIT	CREDIT	BALANCE DEBIT	BALANCE CREDIT

ACCOUNT __Insurance Expense__   ACCOUNT NO. ____521____

DATE	DESCRIPTION	POST. REF.	DEBIT	CREDIT	BALANCE DEBIT	BALANCE CREDIT

ACCOUNT __Supplies Expense__   ACCOUNT NO. ____523____

DATE	DESCRIPTION	POST. REF.	DEBIT	CREDIT	BALANCE DEBIT	BALANCE CREDIT

EXTRA FORMS

ACCOUNT _____   ACCOUNT NO. _____

DATE	DESCRIPTION	POST. REF.	DEBIT	CREDIT	BALANCE DEBIT	BALANCE CREDIT

ACCOUNT _____   ACCOUNT NO. _____

DATE	DESCRIPTION	POST. REF.	DEBIT	CREDIT	BALANCE DEBIT	BALANCE CREDIT

PROBLEM 5.1A or 5.1B

	ACCOUNT NAME	TRIAL BALANCE		ADJUSTMENTS	
		DEBIT	CREDIT	DEBIT	CREDIT
1					
2					
3					
4					
5					
6					
7					
8					
9					
10					
11					
12					
13					
14					
15					
16					
17					
18					
19					
20					
21					
22					
23					
24					
25					
26					
27					
28					
29					
30					
31					
32					

PROBLEM 5.1A or 5.1B (continued)

_____

_____

	ADJUSTED TRIAL BALANCE		INCOME STATEMENT		BALANCE SHEET		
	DEBIT	CREDIT	DEBIT	CREDIT	DEBIT	CREDIT	
							1
							2
							3
							4
							5
							6
							7
							8
							9
							10
							11
							12
							13
							14
							15
							16
							17
							18
							19
							20
							21
							22
							23
							24
							25
							26
							27
							28
							29
							30
							31
							32

Analyze: _____

_____

PROBLEM 5.2A or 5.2B

	ACCOUNT NAME	TRIAL BALANCE		ADJUSTMENTS	
		DEBIT	CREDIT	DEBIT	CREDIT
1					
2					
3					
4					
5					
6					
7					
8					
9					
10					
11					
12					
13					
14					
15					
16					
17					
18					
19					
20					
21					
22					
23					
24					
25					
26					
27					
28					
29					
30					
31					
32					

86 ■ Chapter 5   Copyright © 2012 The McGraw-Hill Companies, Inc. All rights reserved.

PROBLEM 5.2A or 5.2B (continued)

_____

ADJUSTED TRIAL BALANCE		INCOME STATEMENT		BALANCE SHEET		
DEBIT	CREDIT	DEBIT	CREDIT	DEBIT	CREDIT	
						1
						2
						3
						4
						5
						6
						7
						8
						9
						10
						11
						12
						13
						14
						15
						16
						17
						18
						19
						20
						21
						22
						23
						24
						25
						26
						27
						28
						29
						30
						31
						32

Analyze: _____

_____

PROBLEM 5.3A or 5.3B

PROBLEM 5.3A or 5.3B (continued)

Analyze: _____

PROBLEM 5.4A or 5.4B

	ACCOUNT NAME	TRIAL BALANCE		ADJUSTMENTS	
		DEBIT	CREDIT	DEBIT	CREDIT
1					
2					
3					
4					
5					
6					
7					
8					
9					
10					
11					
12					
13					
14					
15					
16					
17					
18					
19					
20					
21					
22					
23					
24					
25					
26					
27					
28					
29					
30					
31					
32					

PROBLEM 5.4A or 5.4B (continued)

_____
_____

ADJUSTED TRIAL BALANCE		INCOME STATEMENT		BALANCE SHEET		
DEBIT	CREDIT	DEBIT	CREDIT	DEBIT	CREDIT	
						1
						2
						3
						4
						5
						6
						7
						8
						9
						10
						11
						12
						13
						14
						15
						16
						17
						18
						19
						20
						21
						22
						23
						24
						25
						26
						27
						28
						29
						30
						31
						32

PROBLEM 5.4A or 5.4B (continued)

PROBLEM 5.4A or 5.4B (continued)

PROBLEM 5.4A or 5.4B (continued)

GENERAL JOURNAL   PAGE _____

	DATE	DESCRIPTION	POST. REF.	DEBIT	CREDIT	
1						1
2						2
3						3
4						4
5						5
6						6
7						7
8						8
9						9
10						10
11						11
12						12
13						13
14						14

GENERAL LEDGER

ACCOUNT _____ ACCOUNT NO. _____

DATE	DESCRIPTION	POST. REF.	DEBIT	CREDIT	BALANCE DEBIT	BALANCE CREDIT

ACCOUNT _____ ACCOUNT NO. _____

DATE	DESCRIPTION	POST. REF.	DEBIT	CREDIT	BALANCE DEBIT	BALANCE CREDIT

ACCOUNT _____ ACCOUNT NO. _____

DATE	DESCRIPTION	POST. REF.	DEBIT	CREDIT	BALANCE DEBIT	BALANCE CREDIT

PROBLEM 5.4A or 5.4B (continued)

GENERAL LEDGER

ACCOUNT _____ ACCOUNT NO. _____

DATE	DESCRIPTION	POST. REF.	DEBIT	CREDIT	BALANCE	
					DEBIT	CREDIT

ACCOUNT _____ ACCOUNT NO. _____

DATE	DESCRIPTION	POST. REF.	DEBIT	CREDIT	BALANCE	
					DEBIT	CREDIT

ACCOUNT _____ ACCOUNT NO. _____

DATE	DESCRIPTION	POST. REF.	DEBIT	CREDIT	BALANCE	
					DEBIT	CREDIT

ACCOUNT _____ ACCOUNT NO. _____

DATE	DESCRIPTION	POST. REF.	DEBIT	CREDIT	BALANCE	
					DEBIT	CREDIT

ACCOUNT _____ ACCOUNT NO. _____

DATE	DESCRIPTION	POST. REF.	DEBIT	CREDIT	BALANCE	
					DEBIT	CREDIT

Analyze: _____

_____

CRITICAL THINKING PROBLEM 5.1

	ACCOUNT NAME	TRIAL BALANCE		ADJUSTMENTS	
		DEBIT	CREDIT	DEBIT	CREDIT
1					
2					
3					
4					
5					
6					
7					
8					
9					
10					
11					
12					
13					
14					
15					
16					
17					
18					
19					
20					
21					
22					
23					
24					
25					
26					
27					
28					
29					
30					
31					

CRITICAL THINKING PROBLEM 5.1 (continued)

_____

	ADJUSTED TRIAL BALANCE		INCOME STATEMENT		BALANCE SHEET		
	DEBIT	CREDIT	DEBIT	CREDIT	DEBIT	CREDIT	
							1
							2
							3
							4
							5
							6
							7
							8
							9
							10
							11
							12
							13
							14
							15
							16
							17
							18
							19
							20
							21
							22
							23
							24
							25
							26
							27
							28
							29
							30
							31
							32

CRITICAL THINKING PROBLEM 5.1 (continued)

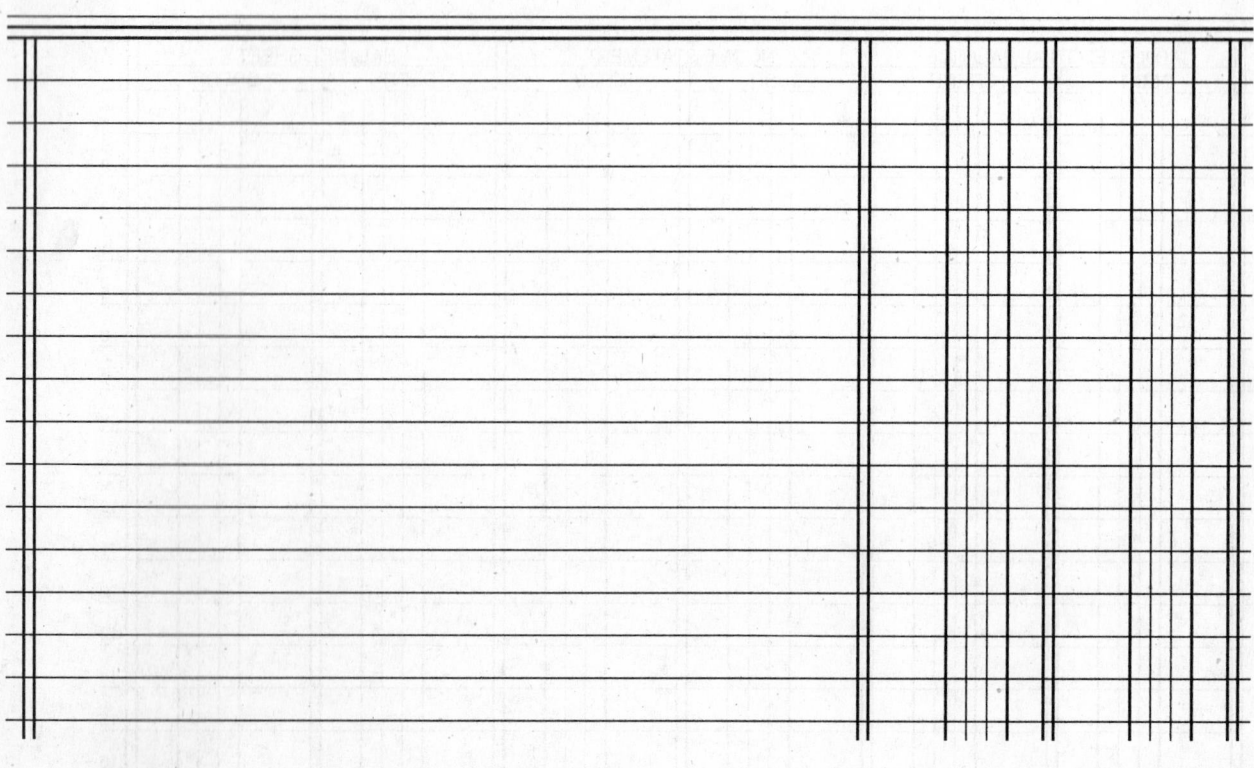

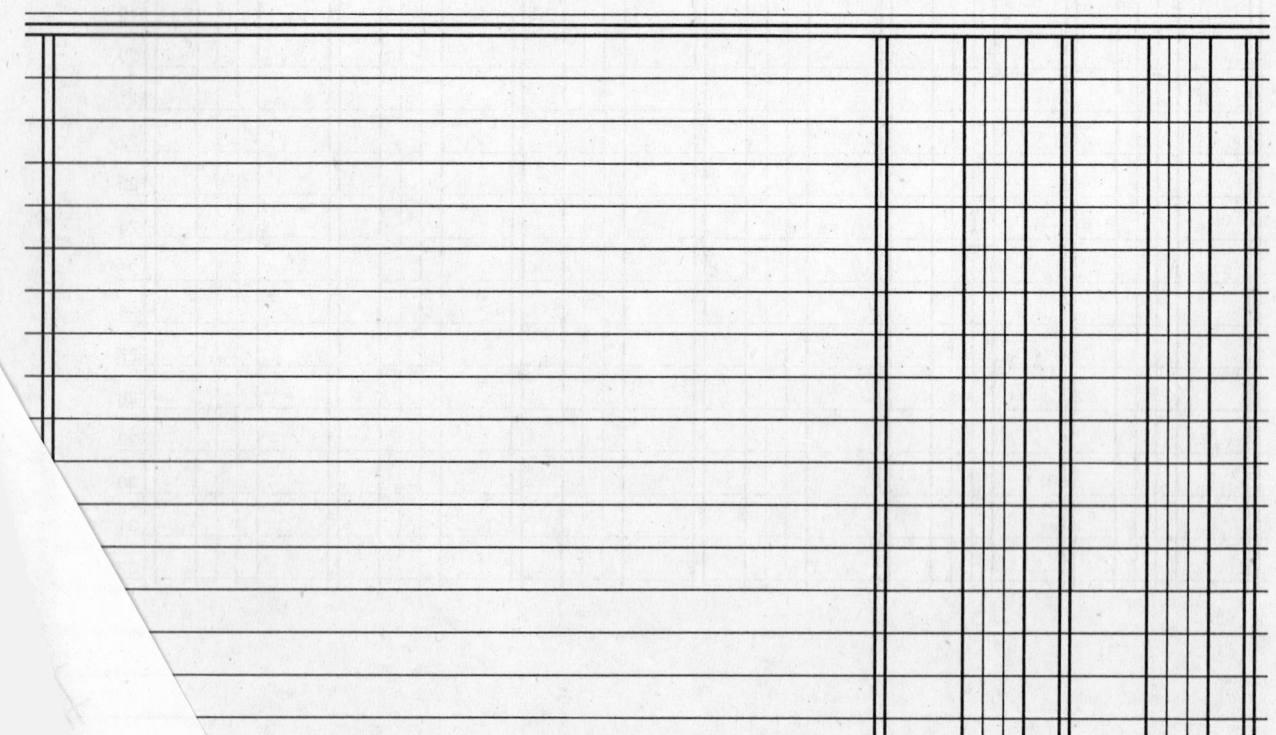

CRITICAL THINKING PROBLEM 5.1 (continued)

CRITICAL THINKING PROBLEM 5.1 (continued)

GENERAL JOURNAL

PAGE _____

	DATE	DESCRIPTION	POST. REF.	DEBIT	CREDIT	
1						1
2						2
3						3
4						4
5						5
6						6
7						7
8						8
9						9
10						10
11						11

GENERAL LEDGER

ACCOUNT _____ ACCOUNT NO. _____

DATE	DESCRIPTION	POST. REF.	DEBIT	CREDIT	BALANCE DEBIT	BALANCE CREDIT

ACCOUNT _____ ACCOUNT NO. _____

DATE	DESCRIPTION	POST. REF.	DEBIT	CREDIT	BALANCE DEBIT	BALANCE CREDIT

ACCOUNT _____ ACCOUNT NO. _____

DATE	DESCRIPTION	POST. REF.	DEBIT	CREDIT	BALANCE DEBIT	BALANCE CREDIT

CRITICAL THINKING PROBLEM 5.1 (continued)

GENERAL LEDGER

ACCOUNT _____ ACCOUNT NO. _____

DATE	DESCRIPTION	POST. REF.	DEBIT	CREDIT	BALANCE	
					DEBIT	CREDIT

ACCOUNT _____ ACCOUNT NO. _____

DATE	DESCRIPTION	POST. REF.	DEBIT	CREDIT	BALANCE	
					DEBIT	CREDIT

ACCOUNT _____ ACCOUNT NO. _____

DATE	DESCRIPTION	POST. REF.	DEBIT	CREDIT	BALANCE	
					DEBIT	CREDIT

Analyze: _____

_____

EXTRA FORMS

ACCOUNT _____ ACCOUNT NO. _____

DATE	DESCRIPTION	POST. REF.	DEBIT	CREDIT	BALANCE	
					DEBIT	CREDIT

ACCOUNT _____ ACCOUNT NO. _____

DATE	DESCRIPTION	POST. REF.	DEBIT	CREDIT	BALANCE	
					DEBIT	CREDIT

CRITICAL THINKING PROBLEM 5.2

TO: _____

FROM: _____

DATE: _____

SUBJECT: _____

_____

_____

_____

_____

_____

_____

_____

_____

_____

_____

_____

_____

_____

_____

_____

_____

_____

_____

_____

_____

_____

_____

_____

Chapter 5 Practice Test Answer Key

Part A True-False		Part B Matching	
1. T	6. T	1. a	4. c
2. F	7. T	2. e	5. b
3. T	8. T	3. f	6. d
4. T	9. F		
5. T	10. T		

Closing Entries and the Postclosing Trial Balance

STUDY GUIDE

Understanding the Chapter

Objectives	**1.** Journalize and post closing entries. **2.** Prepare a postclosing trial balance. **3.** Interpret financial statements. **4.** Review the steps in the accounting cycle. **5.** Define the accounting terms new to this chapter.
Reading Assignment	Read Chapter 6 in the textbook. Complete the textbook Section Self Review as you finish reading each section of the chapter, and the Comprehensive Self Review at the end of the chapter. Refer to the Chapter 6 Glossary or to the Glossary at the end of the book to find definitions for terms that are not familiar to you.

Activities

❏ **Thinking Critically**	Answer the *Thinking Critically* questions for Carnival Corporation and Managerial Implications.
❏ **Discussion Questions**	Answer each assigned discussion question in Chapter 6.
❏ **Exercises**	Complete each assigned exercise in Chapter 6. Use the forms provided in this SGWP. The objectives covered by an exercise are given after the exercise number. If you need help with an exercise, review the portion of the chapter related to the objective(s) covered.
❏ **Problems A/B**	Complete each assigned problem in Chapter 6. Use the forms provided in this SGWP. The objectives covered by a problem are given after the problem number. If you need help with a problem, review the portion of the chapter related to the objective(s) covered.
❏ **Critical Thinking Problems**	Complete the critical thinking problems as assigned. Use the forms provided in this SGWP.
❏ **Business Connections**	Complete the Business Connections activities as assigned to gain a deeper understanding of Chapter 6 concepts.

Practice Tests

Complete the Practice Tests, which cover the main points in your reading assignment. Compare your answers with those in the Practice Test Answer Key for Chapter 6 at the end of this chapter. If you have answered any questions incorrectly, review the related section of the text.

Part A True-False   *For each of the following statements, circle T in the answer column if the statement is true or F if the statement is false.*

T   F   **1.** The general ledger is a continuing record.

T   F   **2.** The postclosing trial balance will show figures for asset, liability, owner's equity, revenue, and expense accounts.

T   F   **3.** The total of all expenses appears on the credit side of the **Income Summary** account.

T   F   **4.** To close a revenue account, the accountant debits that account and credits the **Income Summary** account.

T   F   **5.** All asset accounts are closed into the **Income Summary** account.

T   F   **6.** The balance of the **Income Summary** account—net income or net loss—is transferred to the owner's capital account.

T   F   **7.** The Income Summary is a financial statement prepared at the end of each accounting period.

T   F   **8.** Adjusting entries create a permanent record of any changes in account balances that are shown on the worksheet.

T   F   **9.** If an adjustment is not made for supplies used, the net income for the period will be understated.

T   F   **10.** Closing entries reduce the balance of revenue and asset accounts to zero so that they are ready to receive data for the next period.

Part B Matching   *For each numbered item, choose the matching term from the box and write the identifying letter in the answer column.*

_____   **1.** The procedure of journalizing and posting the results of operations at the end of an accounting period.

_____   **2.** Journal entries used to transfer the balances of the revenue and expense accounts to the summary accounts as part of the end-of-period procedures.

_____   **3.** Term used when referring to an account after its balance has been transferred out.

_____   **4.** Special account in the general ledger used for combining data about revenue and expenses.

_____   **5.** The last step in the end-of-period procedure, which shows the accountant that it is safe to proceed with entries for the new period.

a. Closing the accounting records
b. Closing entries
c. Closed account
d. Postclosing trial balance
e. Income Summary

Demonstration Problem

The Income Statement and Balance Sheet sections of the worksheet for James Wilson for the period ended December 31, 2013 are shown below.

Instructions

1. Journalize the closing entries on page 24 of a general journal.
2. Determine the new balance for Capital once the closing entries have been posted.

James Wilson
Worksheet
Month Ended December 31, 2013

	ACCOUNT NAME	INCOME STATEMENT DEBIT	INCOME STATEMENT CREDIT	BALANCE SHEET DEBIT	BALANCE SHEET CREDIT
1	Cash			96 0 0 0 00	
2	Accounts Receivable			6 0 0 0 00	
3	Supplies			12 0 0 0 00	
4	Prepaid Rent			9 0 0 0 00	
5	Equipment			60 0 0 0 00	
6	Accumulated Depreciation—Equipment				1 4 4 0 00
7	Accounts Payable				15 0 0 0 00
8	James Wilson, Capital				109 5 0 0 00
9	James Wilson, Drawing			6 0 0 0 00	
10	Fees Income		90 0 0 0 00		
11	Salaries Expense	14 4 0 0 00			
12	Utilities Expense	2 1 0 0 00			
13	Supplies Expense	4 8 0 0 00			
14	Advertising Expense	4 2 0 0 00			
15	Depreciation Expense—Equipment	1 4 4 0 00			
16	Totals	26 9 4 0 00	90 0 0 0 00	189 0 0 0 00	125 9 4 0 00
17	Net Income	63 0 6 0 00			63 0 6 0 00
18		90 0 0 0 00	90 0 0 0 00	189 0 0 0 00	189 0 0 0 00
19					

SOLUTION

GENERAL JOURNAL   PAGE ___24___

	DATE		DESCRIPTION	POST. REF.	DEBIT	CREDIT	
1			**Closing Entries**				1
2	2013						2
3	Dec.	31	Fees Income	401	90 0 0 0 00		3
4			Income Summary	399		90 0 0 0 00	4
5							5
6		31	Income Summary	399	26 9 4 0 00		6
7			Salaries Expense	511		14 4 0 0 00	7
8			Utilities Expense	514		2 1 0 0 00	8
9			Supplies Expense	517		4 8 0 0 00	9
10			Advertising Expense	522		4 2 0 0 00	10
11			Depreciation Expense—Equipment	523		1 4 4 0 00	11
12							12
13		31	Income Summary	399	63 0 6 0 00		13
14			James Wilson, Capital	301		63 0 6 0 00	14
15							15
16		31	James Wilson, Capital	301	6 0 0 0 00		16
17			James Wilson, Drawing	302		6 0 0 0 00	17
18							18

New Capital Balance:

James Wilson, Capital, December 1, 2013		$109,500.00
Add: Net Income	63,060.00	
Less Withdrawals for December	6,000.00	
Increase in Capital		57,060.00
James Wilson, Capital, December 31, 2013		$166,560.00

WORKING PAPERS

Name _____

EXERCISE 6.1

GENERAL JOURNAL
PAGE _____

	DATE	DESCRIPTION	POST. REF.	DEBIT	CREDIT	
1						1
2						2
3						3
4						4
5						5
6						6
7						7
8						8
9						9
10						10
11						11
12						12
13						13
14						14
15						15
16						16
17						17
18						18
19						19
20						20
21						21

EXERCISE 6.2

1. _____
2. _____
3. _____
4. _____
5. _____
6. _____
7. _____
8. _____
9. _____

EXERCISE 6.3

1. _____   5. _____

2. _____   6. _____

3. _____   7. _____

4. _____

EXERCISE 6.4

1. _____   6. _____   11. _____

2. _____   7. _____   12. _____

3. _____   8. _____   13. _____

4. _____   9. _____   14. _____

5. _____   10. _____   15. _____

EXERCISE 6.5

1. Total revenue for the period is _____ .

2. Total expenses for the period are _____ .

3. Net income for the period is _____ .

4. Owner's withdrawals for the period are _____ .

EXERCISE 6.6

GENERAL JOURNAL

PAGE _____

	DATE		DESCRIPTION	POST. REF.	DEBIT	CREDIT	
1							1
2							2
3							3
4							4
5							5
6							6
7							7
8							8
9							9
10							10
11							11
12							12
13							13
14							14
15							15
16							16
17							17
18							18
19							19
20							20
21							21
22							22
23							23
24							24
25							25
26							26
27							27
28							28
29							29
30							30
31							31
32							32
33							33
34							34
35							35
36							36
37							37

EXERCISE 6.6 (continued)

GENERAL LEDGER

ACCOUNT __Gloria Bahamon, Capital__   ACCOUNT NO. ____301____

DATE		DESCRIPTION	POST. REF.	DEBIT	CREDIT	BALANCE DEBIT	BALANCE CREDIT
2013							
Mar.	31	Balance	✔				120 0 0 0 00

ACCOUNT __Gloria Bahamon, Drawing__   ACCOUNT NO. ____302____

DATE		DESCRIPTION	POST. REF.	DEBIT	CREDIT	BALANCE DEBIT	BALANCE CREDIT
2013							
Mar.	31	Balance	✔			12 0 0 0 00	

ACCOUNT __Income Summary__   ACCOUNT NO. ____399____

DATE		DESCRIPTION	POST. REF.	DEBIT	CREDIT	BALANCE DEBIT	BALANCE CREDIT

ACCOUNT __Fees Income__   ACCOUNT NO. ____401____

DATE		DESCRIPTION	POST. REF.	DEBIT	CREDIT	BALANCE DEBIT	BALANCE CREDIT
2013							
Mar.	31	Balance	✔				325 0 0 0 00

ACCOUNT __Depreciation Expense—Equipment__   ACCOUNT NO. ____510____

DATE		DESCRIPTION	POST. REF.	DEBIT	CREDIT	BALANCE DEBIT	BALANCE CREDIT
2013							
Mar.	31	Balance	✔			20 1 6 0 00	

EXERCISE 6.6 (continued)

GENERAL LEDGER

ACCOUNT __Insurance Expense__   ACCOUNT NO. ___511___

DATE		DESCRIPTION	POST. REF.	DEBIT	CREDIT	BALANCE	
						DEBIT	CREDIT
2013							
Mar.	31	Balance	✔			10 4 0 0 00	

ACCOUNT __Rent Expense__   ACCOUNT NO. ___514___

DATE		DESCRIPTION	POST. REF.	DEBIT	CREDIT	BALANCE	
						DEBIT	CREDIT
2013							
Mar.	31	Balance	✔			32 0 0 0 00	

ACCOUNT __Salaries Expense__   ACCOUNT NO. ___517___

DATE		DESCRIPTION	POST. REF.	DEBIT	CREDIT	BALANCE	
						DEBIT	CREDIT
2013							
Mar.	31	Balance	✔			156 0 0 0 00	

ACCOUNT __Supplies Expense__   ACCOUNT NO. ___518___

DATE		DESCRIPTION	POST. REF.	DEBIT	CREDIT	BALANCE	
						DEBIT	CREDIT
2013							
Mar.	31	Balance	✔			4 6 0 0 00	

ACCOUNT __Telephone Expense__   ACCOUNT NO. ___519___

DATE		DESCRIPTION	POST. REF.	DEBIT	CREDIT	BALANCE	
						DEBIT	CREDIT
2013							
Mar.	31	Balance	✔			5 8 0 0 00	

Chapter 6 ■ 111

EXERCISE 6.6 (continued)

GENERAL LEDGER

ACCOUNT __Utilities Expense__   ACCOUNT NO. ___523___

DATE		DESCRIPTION	POST. REF.	DEBIT	CREDIT	BALANCE DEBIT	BALANCE CREDIT
2013							
Mar.	31	Balance	✔			8 4 0 0 00	

EXTRA FORMS

ACCOUNT _____   ACCOUNT NO. _____

DATE	DESCRIPTION	POST. REF.	DEBIT	CREDIT	BALANCE DEBIT	BALANCE CREDIT

ACCOUNT _____   ACCOUNT NO. _____

DATE	DESCRIPTION	POST. REF.	DEBIT	CREDIT	BALANCE DEBIT	BALANCE CREDIT

ACCOUNT _____   ACCOUNT NO. _____

DATE	DESCRIPTION	POST. REF.	DEBIT	CREDIT	BALANCE DEBIT	BALANCE CREDIT

EXERCISE 6.7

GENERAL JOURNAL   PAGE _____

	DATE		DESCRIPTION	POST. REF.	DEBIT	CREDIT	
1							1
2							2
3							3
4							4
5							5
6							6
7							7
8							8

EXERCISE 6.8

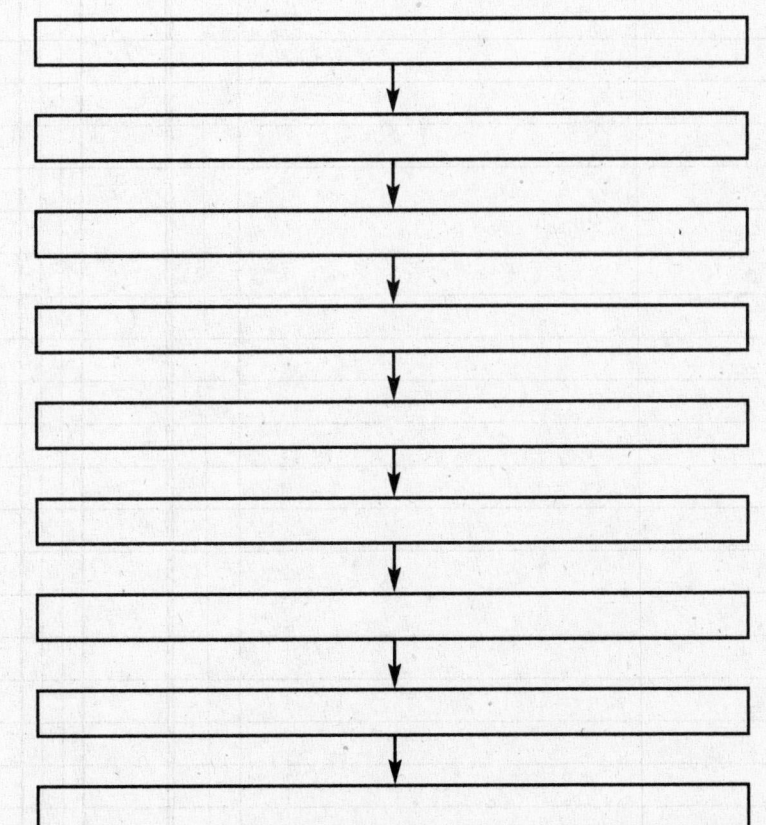

PROBLEM 6.1A or 6.1B

GENERAL JOURNAL

PAGE _____

	DATE	DESCRIPTION	POST. REF.	DEBIT	CREDIT	
1						1
2						2
3						3
4						4
5						5
6						6
7						7
8						8
9						9
10						10
11						11

GENERAL JOURNAL

PAGE _____

	DATE	DESCRIPTION	POST. REF.	DEBIT	CREDIT	
1						1
2						2
3						3
4						4
5						5
6						6
7						7
8						8
9						9
10						10
11						11
12						12
13						13
14						14
15						15
16						16
17						17
18						18
19						19
20						20

Analyze: _____

_____

PROBLEM 6.2A or 6.2B

GENERAL JOURNAL
PAGE _____

	DATE	DESCRIPTION	POST. REF.	DEBIT	CREDIT	
1						1
2						2
3						3
4						4
5						5
6						6
7						7
8						8
9						9
10						10
11						11

GENERAL JOURNAL
PAGE _____

	DATE	DESCRIPTION	POST. REF.	DEBIT	CREDIT	
1						1
2						2
3						3
4						4
5						5
6						6
7						7
8						8
9						9
10						10
11						11
12						12
13						13
14						14
15						15
16						16
17						17
18						18

PROBLEM 6.2A or 6.2B (continued)

GENERAL LEDGER

ACCOUNT __Supplies__   ACCOUNT NO. ___121___

	DATE	DESCRIPTION	POST. REF.	DEBIT	CREDIT	BALANCE DEBIT	BALANCE CREDIT

ACCOUNT __Prepaid Advertising__   ACCOUNT NO. ___131___

	DATE	DESCRIPTION	POST. REF.	DEBIT	CREDIT	BALANCE DEBIT	BALANCE CREDIT

ACCOUNT __Accumulated Depreciation—Equipment__   ACCOUNT NO. ___142___

	DATE	DESCRIPTION	POST. REF.	DEBIT	CREDIT	BALANCE DEBIT	BALANCE CREDIT

ACCOUNT __Capital__   ACCOUNT NO. ___301___

	DATE	DESCRIPTION	POST. REF.	DEBIT	CREDIT	BALANCE DEBIT	BALANCE CREDIT

ACCOUNT __Drawing__   ACCOUNT NO. ___302___

	DATE	DESCRIPTION	POST. REF.	DEBIT	CREDIT	BALANCE DEBIT	BALANCE CREDIT

PROBLEM 6.2A or 6.2B (continued)

GENERAL LEDGER

ACCOUNT __Income Summary__ ACCOUNT NO. ____399____

DATE	DESCRIPTION	POST. REF.	DEBIT	CREDIT	BALANCE	
					DEBIT	CREDIT

ACCOUNT __Fees Income__ ACCOUNT NO. ____401____

DATE	DESCRIPTION	POST. REF.	DEBIT	CREDIT	BALANCE	
					DEBIT	CREDIT

GENERAL LEDGER

ACCOUNT __Salaries Expense__ ACCOUNT NO. ____511____

DATE	DESCRIPTION	POST. REF.	DEBIT	CREDIT	BALANCE	
					DEBIT	CREDIT

ACCOUNT __Utilities Expense__ ACCOUNT NO. ____514____

DATE	DESCRIPTION	POST. REF.	DEBIT	CREDIT	BALANCE	
					DEBIT	CREDIT

ACCOUNT __Supplies Expense__ ACCOUNT NO. ____517____

DATE	DESCRIPTION	POST. REF.	DEBIT	CREDIT	BALANCE	
					DEBIT	CREDIT

PROBLEM 6.2A or 6.2B (continued)

ACCOUNT __Depreciation Expense—Equipment__   ACCOUNT NO. ____523____

DATE	DESCRIPTION	POST. REF.	DEBIT	CREDIT	BALANCE DEBIT	BALANCE CREDIT

ACCOUNT __Advertising Expense__   ACCOUNT NO. ____526____

DATE	DESCRIPTION	POST. REF.	DEBIT	CREDIT	BALANCE DEBIT	BALANCE CREDIT

ACCOUNT NAME	DEBIT	CREDIT

Analyze: _____

PROBLEM 6.3A or 6.3B

GENERAL JOURNAL   PAGE _____

	DATE		DESCRIPTION	POST. REF.	DEBIT	CREDIT	
1							1
2							2
3							3
4							4
5							5
6							6
7							7
8							8
9							9
10							10
11							11
12							12
13							13
14							14
15							15
16							16
17							17
18							18
19							19
20							20
21							21
22							22
23							23
24							24
25							25
26							26
27							27
28							28
29							29
30							30
31							31
32							32
33							33
34							34
35							35
36							36
37							37

PROBLEM 6.3A or 6.3B (continued)

GENERAL LEDGER

ACCOUNT _____ **Capital** _____ ACCOUNT NO. _____ **301**

DATE	DESCRIPTION	POST. REF.	DEBIT	CREDIT	BALANCE	
					DEBIT	CREDIT

ACCOUNT _____ **Drawing** _____ ACCOUNT NO. _____ **302**

DATE	DESCRIPTION	POST. REF.	DEBIT	CREDIT	BALANCE	
					DEBIT	CREDIT

ACCOUNT __**Income Summary**_____ ACCOUNT NO. _____ **399**

DATE	DESCRIPTION	POST. REF.	DEBIT	CREDIT	BALANCE	
					DEBIT	CREDIT

ACCOUNT __**Fees Income**_____ ACCOUNT NO. _____ **401**

DATE	DESCRIPTION	POST. REF.	DEBIT	CREDIT	BALANCE	
					DEBIT	CREDIT

PROBLEM 6.3A or 6.3B (continued)

GENERAL LEDGER

ACCOUNT __Advertising Expense__   ACCOUNT NO. ___511___

DATE	DESCRIPTION	POST. REF.	DEBIT	CREDIT	BALANCE	
					DEBIT	CREDIT

ACCOUNT __Depreciation Expense—Equipment__   ACCOUNT NO. ___514___

DATE	DESCRIPTION	POST. REF.	DEBIT	CREDIT	BALANCE	
					DEBIT	CREDIT

ACCOUNT __Rent Expense__   ACCOUNT NO. ___517___

DATE	DESCRIPTION	POST. REF.	DEBIT	CREDIT	BALANCE	
					DEBIT	CREDIT

ACCOUNT __Salaries Expense__   ACCOUNT NO. ___519___

DATE	DESCRIPTION	POST. REF.	DEBIT	CREDIT	BALANCE	
					DEBIT	CREDIT

ACCOUNT __Utilities Expense__   ACCOUNT NO. ___523___

DATE	DESCRIPTION	POST. REF.	DEBIT	CREDIT	BALANCE	
					DEBIT	CREDIT

Analyze: _____

_____

PROBLEM 6.3A or 6.3B (continued)

GENERAL LEDGER

ACCOUNT _____ ACCOUNT NO. _____

DATE	DESCRIPTION	POST. REF.	DEBIT	CREDIT	BALANCE	
					DEBIT	CREDIT

ACCOUNT _____ ACCOUNT NO. _____

DATE	DESCRIPTION	POST. REF.	DEBIT	CREDIT	BALANCE	
					DEBIT	CREDIT

ACCOUNT _____ ACCOUNT NO. _____

DATE	DESCRIPTION	POST. REF.	DEBIT	CREDIT	BALANCE	
					DEBIT	CREDIT

ACCOUNT _____ ACCOUNT NO. _____

DATE	DESCRIPTION	POST. REF.	DEBIT	CREDIT	BALANCE	
					DEBIT	CREDIT

ACCOUNT _____ ACCOUNT NO. _____

DATE	DESCRIPTION	POST. REF.	DEBIT	CREDIT	BALANCE	
					DEBIT	CREDIT

PROBLEM 6.3A or 6.3B (continued)

GENERAL LEDGER

ACCOUNT _____ ACCOUNT NO. _____

	DATE	DESCRIPTION	POST. REF.	DEBIT	CREDIT	BALANCE	
						DEBIT	CREDIT

ACCOUNT _____ ACCOUNT NO. _____

	DATE	DESCRIPTION	POST. REF.	DEBIT	CREDIT	BALANCE	
						DEBIT	CREDIT

ACCOUNT _____ ACCOUNT NO. _____

	DATE	DESCRIPTION	POST. REF.	DEBIT	CREDIT	BALANCE	
						DEBIT	CREDIT

ACCOUNT _____ ACCOUNT NO. _____

	DATE	DESCRIPTION	POST. REF.	DEBIT	CREDIT	BALANCE	
						DEBIT	CREDIT

ACCOUNT _____ ACCOUNT NO. _____

	DATE	DESCRIPTION	POST. REF.	DEBIT	CREDIT	BALANCE	
						DEBIT	CREDIT

PROBLEM 6.4A or 6.4B

	ACCOUNT NAME	TRIAL BALANCE		ADJUSTMENTS	
		DEBIT	CREDIT	DEBIT	CREDIT
1					
2					
3					
4					
5					
6					
7					
8					
9					
10					
11					
12					
13					
14					
15					
16					
17					
18					
19					
20					
21					
22					
23					
24					
25					
26					
27					
28					
29					
30					
31					
32					

PROBLEM 6.4A or 6.4B (continued)

_____

ADJUSTED TRIAL BALANCE		INCOME STATEMENT		BALANCE SHEET		
DEBIT	CREDIT	DEBIT	CREDIT	DEBIT	CREDIT	
						1
						2
						3
						4
						5
						6
						7
						8
						9
						10
						11
						12
						13
						14
						15
						16
						17
						18
						19
						20
						21
						22
						23
						24
						25
						26
						27
						28
						29
						30
						31
						32

PROBLEM 6.4A or 6.4B (continued)

GENERAL JOURNAL

PAGE _____

	DATE	DESCRIPTION	POST. REF.	DEBIT	CREDIT	
1						1
2						2
3						3
4						4
5						5
6						6
7						7
8						8
9						9
10						10
11						11
12						12
13						13

GENERAL JOURNAL

PAGE _____

	DATE	DESCRIPTION	POST. REF.	DEBIT	CREDIT	
1						1
2						2
3						3
4						4
5						5
6						6
7						7
8						8
9						9
10						10
11						11
12						12
13						13
14						14
15						15
16						16
17						17
18						18

PROBLEM 6.4A or 6.4B (continued)

GENERAL LEDGER

ACCOUNT __Supplies__   ACCOUNT NO. ___121___

DATE	DESCRIPTION	POST. REF.	DEBIT	CREDIT	BALANCE	
					DEBIT	CREDIT

ACCOUNT __Prepaid Advertising__   ACCOUNT NO. ___131___

DATE	DESCRIPTION	POST. REF.	DEBIT	CREDIT	BALANCE	
					DEBIT	CREDIT

ACCOUNT __Accumulated Depreciation—__   ACCOUNT NO. ___142___

DATE	DESCRIPTION	POST. REF.	DEBIT	CREDIT	BALANCE	
					DEBIT	CREDIT

ACCOUNT __Capital__   ACCOUNT NO. ___301___

DATE	DESCRIPTION	POST. REF.	DEBIT	CREDIT	BALANCE	
					DEBIT	CREDIT

ACCOUNT __Drawing__   ACCOUNT NO. ___302___

DATE	DESCRIPTION	POST. REF.	DEBIT	CREDIT	BALANCE	
					DEBIT	CREDIT

PROBLEM 6.4A or 6.4B (continued)

GENERAL LEDGER

ACCOUNT __Income Summary__   ACCOUNT NO. ____399____

DATE	DESCRIPTION	POST. REF.	DEBIT	CREDIT	BALANCE DEBIT	BALANCE CREDIT

ACCOUNT __Fees Income__   ACCOUNT NO. ____401____

DATE	DESCRIPTION	POST. REF.	DEBIT	CREDIT	BALANCE DEBIT	BALANCE CREDIT

GENERAL LEDGER

ACCOUNT __Salaries Expense__   ACCOUNT NO. ____511____

DATE	DESCRIPTION	POST. REF.	DEBIT	CREDIT	BALANCE DEBIT	BALANCE CREDIT

ACCOUNT __Utilities Expense__   ACCOUNT NO. ____514____

DATE	DESCRIPTION	POST. REF.	DEBIT	CREDIT	BALANCE DEBIT	BALANCE CREDIT

ACCOUNT __Supplies Expense__   ACCOUNT NO. ____517____

DATE	DESCRIPTION	POST. REF.	DEBIT	CREDIT	BALANCE DEBIT	BALANCE CREDIT

PROBLEM 6.4A or 6.4B (continued)

ACCOUNT __Depreciation Expense—_____ ACCOUNT NO. ___523___

DATE	DESCRIPTION	POST. REF.	DEBIT	CREDIT	BALANCE	
					DEBIT	CREDIT

ACCOUNT __Advertising Expense_____ ACCOUNT NO. ___526___

DATE	DESCRIPTION	POST. REF.	DEBIT	CREDIT	BALANCE	
					DEBIT	CREDIT

ACCOUNT NAME	DEBIT	CREDIT

Analyze: _____
_____

CRITICAL THINKING PROBLEM 6.1

Contemporary Fashions

Worksheet

Month Ended December 31, 2013

	ACCOUNT NAME	TRIAL BALANCE DEBIT	TRIAL BALANCE CREDIT	ADJUSTMENTS DEBIT	ADJUSTMENTS CREDIT
1	Cash	163 2 0 0 00			
2	Accounts Receivable	36 0 0 0 00			
3	Supplies	28 8 0 0 00			(a) 14 4 0 0 00
4	Prepaid Insurance	43 2 0 0 00			(b) 9 6 0 0 00
5	Machinery	336 0 0 0 00			
6	Accumulated Depreciation—Machinery				(c) 4 8 0 0 00
7	Accounts Payable		54 0 0 0 00		
8	Jada McBride, Capital		298 3 2 0 00		
9	Jada McBride, Drawing	24 0 0 0 00			
10	Fees Income		330 0 0 0 00		
11	Supplies Expense			(a) 14 4 0 0 00	
12	Insurance Expense			(b) 9 6 0 0 00	
13	Salaries Expense	44 4 0 0 00			
14	Depreciation Expense—Machinery			(c) 4 8 0 0 00	
15	Utilities Expense	6 7 2 0 00			
16	Totals	682 3 2 0 00	682 3 2 0 00	28 8 0 0 00	28 8 0 0 00
17	Net Income				
18					
19					
20					
21					
22					
23					
24					
25					
26					
27					
28					
29					
30					
31					
32					

CRITICAL THINKING PROBLEM 6.1 (continued)

_____

_____

ADJUSTED TRIAL BALANCE		INCOME STATEMENT		BALANCE SHEET		
DEBIT	CREDIT	DEBIT	CREDIT	DEBIT	CREDIT	
						1
						2
						3
						4
						5
						6
						7
						8
						9
						10
						11
						12
						13
						14
						15
						16
						17
						18
						19
						20
						21
						22
						23
						24
						25
						26
						27
						28
						29
						30
						31
						32

CRITICAL THINKING PROBLEM 6.1 (continued)

Name _____

CRITICAL THINKING PROBLEM 6.1 (continued)

_____

GENERAL JOURNAL   PAGE _____

	DATE	DESCRIPTION	POST. REF.	DEBIT	CREDIT	
1						1
2						2
3						3
4						4
5						5
6						6
7						7
8						8
9						9
10						10
11						11
12						12
13						13
14						14
15						15
16						16

CRITICAL THINKING PROBLEM 6.1 (continued)

GENERAL JOURNAL

PAGE _____

	DATE		DESCRIPTION	POST. REF.	DEBIT	CREDIT	
1							1
2							2
3							3
4							4
5							5
6							6
7							7
8							8
9							9
10							10
11							11
12							12
13							13
14							14
15							15
16							16
17							17
18							18

ACCOUNT NAME	DEBIT	CREDIT

Analyze: _____

_____

CRITICAL THINKING PROBLEM 6.2

1. _____

_____

_____

_____

_____

_____

_____

_____

_____

_____

2.

GENERAL JOURNAL   PAGE _____

	DATE	DESCRIPTION	POST. REF.	DEBIT	CREDIT	
1						1
2						2
3						3
4						4
5						5
6						6

3. _____

_____

_____

_____

_____

_____

_____

_____

_____

_____

_____

_____

_____

_____

_____

CRITICAL THINKING PROBLEM 6.2 (continued)

_____

_____

_____

_____

_____

_____

_____

_____

_____

_____

_____

_____

_____

_____

_____

_____

_____

_____

_____

_____

_____

_____

Chapter 6 Practice Test Answer Key

Part A True-False	Part B Matching
1. T	1. a
2. F	2. b
3. F	3. c
4. T	4. e
5. F	5. d
6. T	
7. F	
8. T	
9. F	
10. F	

MINI-PRACTICE SET 1

Service Business Accounting Cycle

GENERAL JOURNAL

PAGE _____

	DATE	DESCRIPTION	POST. REF.	DEBIT	CREDIT	
1						1
2						2
3						3
4						4
5						5
6						6
7						7
8						8
9						9
10						10
11						11
12						12
13						13
14						14
15						15
16						16
17						17
18						18
19						19
20						20
21						21
22						22
23						23
24						24
25						25
26						26
27						27
28						28
29						29
30						30
31						31
32						32
33						33
34						34

GENERAL JOURNAL   PAGE _____

	DATE	DESCRIPTION	POST. REF.	DEBIT	CREDIT	
1						1
2						2
3						3
4						4
5						5
6						6
7						7
8						8
9						9
10						10
11						11
12						12
13						13
14						14
15						15
16						16
17						17
18						18
19						19
20						20
21						21
22						22
23						23
24						24
25						25
26						26
27						27
28						28
29						29
30						30
31						31
32						32
33						33
34						34
35						35
36						36
37						37
38						38
39						39

GENERAL JOURNAL   PAGE _____

	DATE		DESCRIPTION	POST. REF.	DEBIT	CREDIT	
1							1
2							2
3							3
4							4
5							5
6							6
7							7
8							8
9							9
10							10
11							11
12							12
13							13
14							14
15							15
16							16
17							17
18							18
19							19
20							20
21							21
22							22
23							23
24							24
25							25
26							26
27							27
28							28
29							29
30							30
31							31
32							32
33							33
34							34
35							35
36							36
37							37
38							38
39							39

GENERAL JOURNAL   PAGE _____

	DATE		DESCRIPTION	POST. REF.	DEBIT	CREDIT	
1							1
2							2
3							3
4							4
5							5
6							6
7							7
8							8
9							9
10							10
11							11
12							12
13							13
14							14
15							15
16							16
17							17
18							18
19							19
20							20
21							21
22							22
23							23
24							24
25							25
26							26
27							27
28							28
29							29
30							30
31							31
32							32
33							33
34							34
35							35
36							36
37							37
38							38
39							39

Name _____

GENERAL LEDGER

ACCOUNT _____ ACCOUNT NO. _____

DATE	DESCRIPTION	POST. REF.	DEBIT	CREDIT	BALANCE	
					DEBIT	CREDIT

ACCOUNT _____ ACCOUNT NO. _____

DATE	DESCRIPTION	POST. REF.	DEBIT	CREDIT	BALANCE	
					DEBIT	CREDIT

GENERAL LEDGER

ACCOUNT _____ ACCOUNT NO. _____

DATE	DESCRIPTION	POST. REF.	DEBIT	CREDIT	BALANCE	
					DEBIT	CREDIT

ACCOUNT _____ ACCOUNT NO. _____

DATE	DESCRIPTION	POST. REF.	DEBIT	CREDIT	BALANCE	
					DEBIT	CREDIT

ACCOUNT _____ ACCOUNT NO. _____

DATE	DESCRIPTION	POST. REF.	DEBIT	CREDIT	BALANCE	
					DEBIT	CREDIT

ACCOUNT _____ ACCOUNT NO. _____

DATE	DESCRIPTION	POST. REF.	DEBIT	CREDIT	BALANCE	
					DEBIT	CREDIT

ACCOUNT _____ ACCOUNT NO. _____

DATE	DESCRIPTION	POST. REF.	DEBIT	CREDIT	BALANCE	
					DEBIT	CREDIT

Name _____

GENERAL LEDGER

ACCOUNT _____ ACCOUNT NO. _____

DATE	DESCRIPTION	POST. REF.	DEBIT	CREDIT	BALANCE	
					DEBIT	CREDIT

ACCOUNT _____ ACCOUNT NO. _____

DATE	DESCRIPTION	POST. REF.	DEBIT	CREDIT	BALANCE	
					DEBIT	CREDIT

ACCOUNT _____ ACCOUNT NO. _____

DATE	DESCRIPTION	POST. REF.	DEBIT	CREDIT	BALANCE	
					DEBIT	CREDIT

ACCOUNT _____ ACCOUNT NO. _____

DATE	DESCRIPTION	POST. REF.	DEBIT	CREDIT	BALANCE	
					DEBIT	CREDIT

Name _____

GENERAL LEDGER

ACCOUNT _____ ACCOUNT NO. _____

DATE		DESCRIPTION	POST. REF.	DEBIT	CREDIT	BALANCE	
						DEBIT	CREDIT

ACCOUNT _____ ACCOUNT NO. _____

DATE		DESCRIPTION	POST. REF.	DEBIT	CREDIT	BALANCE	
						DEBIT	CREDIT

ACCOUNT _____ ACCOUNT NO. _____

DATE		DESCRIPTION	POST. REF.	DEBIT	CREDIT	BALANCE	
						DEBIT	CREDIT

ACCOUNT _____ ACCOUNT NO. _____

DATE		DESCRIPTION	POST. REF.	DEBIT	CREDIT	BALANCE	
						DEBIT	CREDIT

ACCOUNT _____ ACCOUNT NO. _____

DATE		DESCRIPTION	POST. REF.	DEBIT	CREDIT	BALANCE	
						DEBIT	CREDIT

GENERAL LEDGER

ACCOUNT _____   ACCOUNT NO. _____

DATE	DESCRIPTION	POST. REF.	DEBIT	CREDIT	BALANCE DEBIT	BALANCE CREDIT

ACCOUNT _____   ACCOUNT NO. _____

DATE	DESCRIPTION	POST. REF.	DEBIT	CREDIT	BALANCE DEBIT	BALANCE CREDIT

ACCOUNT _____   ACCOUNT NO. _____

DATE	DESCRIPTION	POST. REF.	DEBIT	CREDIT	BALANCE DEBIT	BALANCE CREDIT

ACCOUNT _____   ACCOUNT NO. _____

DATE	DESCRIPTION	POST. REF.	DEBIT	CREDIT	BALANCE DEBIT	BALANCE CREDIT

ACCOUNT _____   ACCOUNT NO. _____

DATE	DESCRIPTION	POST. REF.	DEBIT	CREDIT	BALANCE DEBIT	BALANCE CREDIT

	ACCOUNT NAME	TRIAL BALANCE		ADJUSTMENTS	
		DEBIT	CREDIT	DEBIT	CREDIT
1					
2					
3					
4					
5					
6					
7					
8					
9					
10					
11					
12					
13					
14					
15					
16					
17					
18					
19					
20					
21					
22					
23					
24					
25					
26					
27					
28					
29					
30					
31					
32					
33					
34					
35					
36					
37					

ADJUSTED TRIAL BALANCE		INCOME STATEMENT		BALANCE SHEET		
DEBIT	CREDIT	DEBIT	CREDIT	DEBIT	CREDIT	
						1
						2
						3
						4
						5
						6
						7
						8
						9
						10
						11
						12
						13
						14
						15
						16
						17
						18
						19
						20
						21
						22
						23
						24
						25
						26
						27
						28
						29
						30
						31
						32
						33
						34
						35
						36
						37

MINI-PRACTICE SET 1 (continued)

ACCOUNT NAME	DEBIT	CREDIT

Analyze: _____

_____

_____

_____

_____

_____

_____

_____

_____

_____

_____

_____

_____

_____

_____

_____

_____

_____

_____

_____

_____

_____

_____

_____

_____

_____

_____

_____

_____

_____

_____

CHAPTER 7

Accounting for Sales and Accounts Receivable

STUDY GUIDE

Understanding the Chapter

Objectives	**1.** Record credit sales in a sales journal. **2.** Post from the sales journal to the general ledger accounts. **3.** Post from the sales journal to the customers' accounts in the accounts receivable subsidiary ledger. **4.** Record sales returns and allowances in the general journal. **5.** Post sales returns and allowances. **6.** Prepare a schedule of accounts receivable. **7.** Compute trade discounts. **8.** Record credit card sales in appropriate journals. **9.** Prepare the state sales tax return. **10.** Define the accounting terms new to this chapter.
Reading Assignment	Read Chapter 7 in the textbook. Complete the textbook Section Self Review as you finish reading each section of the chapter, and the Comprehensive Self Review at the end of the chapter. Refer to the Chapter 7 Glossary or to the Glossary at the end of the book to find definitions for terms that are not familiar to you.

Activities

❏ **Thinking Critically**	Answer the *Thinking Critically* questions for indi and Managerial Implications.
❏ **Discussion Questions**	Answer each assigned discussion question in Chapter 7.
❏ **Exercises**	Complete each assigned exercise in Chapter 7. Use the forms provided in this SGWP. The objectives covered by an exercise are given after the exercise number. If you need help with an exercise, review the portion of the chapter related to the objective(s) covered.
❏ **Problems A/B**	Complete each assigned problem in Chapter 7. Use the forms provided in this SGWP. The objectives covered by a problem are given after the problem number. If you need help with a problem, review the portion of the chapter related to the objective(s) covered.
❏ **Critical Thinking Problems**	Complete the critical thinking problems 7.1 and 7.2 as assigned. Use the forms provided in this SGWP.
❏ **Business Connections**	Complete the Business Connections activities as assigned to gain a deeper understanding of Chapter 7 concepts.

Practice Tests	Complete the Practice Tests, which cover the main points in your reading assignment. Compare your answers with those in the Practice Test Answer Key for Chapter 7 at the end of this chapter. If you have answered any questions incorrectly, review the related section of the text.

Part A True-False *For each of the following statements, circle T in the answer column if the statement is true and F if the statement is false.*

T   F   **1.** The accountant must keep an individual record of dealings with each customer to answer questions received from managers and salespeople of the company, from the customers themselves, and from banks and credit bureaus.

T   F   **2.** A credit sale made on a credit card issued by a credit card company is accounted for in the same manner as a credit sale made on a bank credit card.

T   F   **3.** The **Accounts Receivable** account in the general ledger is known as a control account because it contains a summary of all activities involving accounts receivable.

T   F   **4.** As proof of accuracy, the total of all customers' accounts in the accounts receivable ledger is compared with the balance of the **Accounts Receivable** account in the general ledger.

T   F   **5.** The basic procedure for posting totals from the sales journal to the general ledger is not affected by the use of an accounts receivable ledger.

T   F   **6.** When the balance-form ledger sheet is used in the accounts receivable ledger, the accountant figures the running balance of each account after each posting during the month.

T   F   **7.** The accounts receivable ledger is called a subsidiary ledger because it is only a part of the general ledger.

T   F   **8.** The amount of each credit sale is posted daily to the customer's account in the accounts receivable ledger.

T   F   **9.** When a customer returns goods on which sales tax was charged, the firm gives credit for the price of goods but not the sales tax.

T   F   **10.** The **Accounts Receivable** account in the general ledger must be individually debited for each credit sale as it is made.

T   F   **11.** The larger the volume of credit sales, the more desirable it is to use a special sales journal.

T   F   **12.** The amount of a sales allowance is debited to the Sales account because the revenue from sales has been reduced.

T   F   **13.** The Sales Slip Number column in the sales journal shows where to look when more information is needed.

T   F   **14.** The use of a special sales journal enables more than one person to work on the journals of a business at the same time.

T   F   **15.** Special journals are needed when the transactions of a business include groups of repetitive entries.

T   F   **16.** Sales on credit require debits to **Accounts Payable.**

T   F   **17.** The Sales account may be credited for a sale made for cash but not on account.

T   F   **18.** The special sales journal is used for recording both cash sales and sales on credit.

T   F   **19.** The columns and headings in the sales journal eliminate the need for a description of each entity.

T   F   **20.** The use of a special sales journal makes posting individual sales transactions to accounts in the general ledger unnecessary.

Part B Matching

For each numbered item, choose the matching term from the box and write the identifying letter in the answer column.

_____ 1. A reduction in the amount charged to a customer who has received defective goods or services.

_____ 2. A liability account for recording a tax levied by some states on certain retail sales.

_____ 3. A special journal for recording only the credit sales of a company.

_____ 4. Identification cards used by some banks to individuals for use in making credit card purchases at participating businesses.

_____ 5. Identification cards given by some businesses to their customers who have established credit.

_____ 6. The type of credit usually given by a business on the basis of the personal knowledge of the customer.

_____ 7. A reduction in price, based on volume purchased, given by wholesalers to retailers who buy goods for resale.

> **a.** Trade discount
>
> **b.** Sales return or allowance
>
> **c.** Business credit card
>
> **d.** Sales tax payable
>
> **e.** Open-account credit
>
> **f.** Sales journal
>
> **g.** Bank credit cards

Part C Exercise

Answer each question about the accounts receivable subsidiary ledger account shown below.

ACCOUNTS RECEIVABLE SUBSIDIARY LEDGER

NAME **Charles Kronos**   TERMS _____

ADDRESS **1891 Windsor Drive, Dallas, TX 75623-6998**

DATE		DESCRIPTION	POST. REF.	DEBIT	CREDIT	BALANCE DEBIT	BALANCE CREDIT
2013							
Jan.	1	Balance	✔			4 0 0 00	
	4	Sales Slip 101	S1	6 0 00		4 6 0 00	
	7	Sales Slip 167	S1	9 0 00		5 5 0 00	
	18		J1		8 0 00	4 7 0 00	

1. Where did the $400 entry come from?

_____

2. How could you find a complete description of the $60 charge on January 4?

_____

_____

3. What was the probable reason for the $80.00 entry? How can you find out for sure?

_____

_____

Demonstration Problem

Coastal Auto Supply sells tires and auto supplies to retail stores. The firm offers a trade discount of 40 percent on tires and 20 percent on auto supplies. Transactions involving credit sales and sales returns and allowances for the month of April 2013 follow, along with the general ledger accounts used to record these transactions. Account balances shown are for the beginning of April 2013.

Instructions

1. Open the general ledger accounts; enter the balance for **Accounts Receivable.**
   - 111 Accounts Receivable $61,020
   - 401 Sales
   - 451 Sales Returns and Allowances

2. Set up the accounts receivable subsidiary ledger. Open an account for each credit customer and enter the balances as of April 1, 2013. All customers have terms of n/45.

Auto Warehouse	$ —
Dave's Auto Mart	$14,790
Jazzy Wheels and Window Tint Center	$42,000
Mike's Car Care Center	$4,230
Paso Auto Express	$ —

3. Record the transactions on page 6 of a sales journal and on page 16 of the general journal. (Be sure to enter each sale at its net price.)

4. Post individual entries from the sales journal and the general journal to the appropriate ledger accounts.

5. Total and rule the sales journal as of April 30, 2013.

6. Post from the sales journal to the appropriate general ledger accounts.

7. Prepare a schedule of accounts receivable for April 30, 2013.

8. Compare the total of the schedule of accounts receivable to the balance of the **Accounts Receivable** account. The two should be equal.

DATE	TRANSACTIONS
April 1	Sold tires to Auto Warehouse; issued sales slip 6701 with a list price of $50,000.
5	Sold auto supplies to Mike's Car Care Center; issued sales slip 6702 with a list price of $50,200.
9	Sold auto supplies to Jazzy Wheels and Window Tint Center; issued sales slip 6703 with a list price of $19,800.
14	Sold tires to Dave's Auto Mart, issued sales slip 6704 with a list price of $49,200.
18	Accepted a return of all auto supplies damaged in shipment to Jazzy Wheels and Window Tint Center; issued Credit Memorandum 251. The original sale was made on sales slip 6703 on April 9.
22	Sold auto supplies to Auto Warehouse; issued sales slip 6705 with a list price of $83,480.
29	Sold tires to Mike's Car Care Center; issued sales slip 6706 with a list price of $87,230.
30	Sold tires to Paso Auto Express; issued sales slip 6707 with a list price of $43,230.

SOLUTION

SALES JOURNAL

PAGE ___6___

	DATE		INVOICE NO.	CUSTOMER'S NAME	POST. REF.	ACCOUNTS RECEIVABLE/ DR. SALES CR.	
1	2013						1
2	April	1	6701	Auto Warehouse	✔	30 0 0 0 00	2
3		5	6702	Mike's Car Care Center	✔	40 1 6 0 00	3
4		9	6703	Jazzy Wheels and Window Tint Center	✔	15 8 4 0 00	4
5		14	6704	Dave's Auto Mart	✔	29 5 2 0 00	5
6		22	6705	Auto Warehouse	✔	66 7 8 4 00	6
7		29	6706	Mike's Car Care Center	✔	52 3 3 8 00	7
8		30	6707	Paso Auto Express	✔	25 9 3 8 00	8
9				Totals		260 5 8 0 00	9
10						(1 1 1 /4 01)	10
11							11

GENERAL JOURNAL

PAGE ___16___

	DATE		DESCRIPTION	POST. REF.	DEBIT	CREDIT	
1	2013						1
2	April	18	Sales Returns and Allowances	451	15 8 4 0 00		2
3			Accounts Rec./Jazzy Wheels	111 ✔		15 8 4 0 00	3
4			and Window Tint Center				4
5			Accepted return of damaged supplies,				5
6			Credit Memo 251; original sale				6
7			made on Invoice 6703 of April 9				7
8							8

GENERAL LEDGER

ACCOUNT ___Accounts Receivable___   ACCOUNT NO. ___111___

DATE		DESCRIPTION	POST. REF.	DEBIT	CREDIT	BALANCE DEBIT	BALANCE CREDIT
2013							
April	1	Balance	✔			61 0 2 0 00	
	18		J16		15 8 4 0 00	45 1 8 0 00	
	30		S6	260 5 8 0 00		305 7 6 0 00	

SOLUTION (continued)

GENERAL LEDGER

ACCOUNT __Sales__ ACCOUNT NO. __401__

DATE		DESCRIPTION	POST. REF.	DEBIT	CREDIT	BALANCE DEBIT	BALANCE CREDIT
2013							
April	30		S6		260 5 8 0 00		260 5 8 0 00

ACCOUNT __Sales Returns and Allowances__ ACCOUNT NO. __451__

DATE		DESCRIPTION	POST. REF.	DEBIT	CREDIT	BALANCE DEBIT	BALANCE CREDIT
2013							
April	18		J16	15 8 4 0 00		15 8 4 0 00	

ACCOUNTS RECEIVABLE SUBSIDIARY LEDGER

NAME __Auto Warehouse__ TERMS __n/45__

DATE		DESCRIPTION	POST. REF.	DEBIT	CREDIT	BALANCE DEBIT	BALANCE CREDIT
2013							
April	1	Sales Slip 6701	S6	30 0 0 0 00		30 0 0 0 00	
	22	Sales Slip 6705	S6	66 7 8 4 00		96 7 8 4 00	

NAME __Dave's Auto Mart__ TERMS __n/45__

DATE		DESCRIPTION	POST. REF.	DEBIT	CREDIT	BALANCE DEBIT	BALANCE CREDIT
2013							
April	1	Balance	✔			14 7 9 0 00	
	14	Sales Slip 6704	S6	29 5 2 0 00		44 3 1 0 00	

SOLUTION (continued)

ACCOUNTS RECEIVABLE SUBSIDIARY LEDGER

NAME __Jazzy Wheels and Window Tint Center__   TERMS ____n/45____

DATE		DESCRIPTION	POST. REF.	DEBIT	CREDIT	BALANCE DEBIT	BALANCE CREDIT
2013							
April	1	Balance	✔			42 0 0 0 00	
	9	Sales Slip 6703	S6	15 8 4 0 00		57 8 4 0 00	
	18	CM 251	J16		15 8 4 0 00	42 0 0 0 00	

NAME __Mike's Car Care Center__   TERMS ____n/45____

DATE		DESCRIPTION	POST. REF.	DEBIT	CREDIT	BALANCE DEBIT	BALANCE CREDIT
2013							
April	1	Balance	✔			4 2 3 0 00	
	5	Sales Slip 6702	S6	40 1 6 0 00		44 3 9 0 00	
	29	Sales Slip 6706	S6	52 3 3 8 00		96 7 2 8 00	

NAME __Paso Auto Express__   TERMS ____n/45____

DATE		DESCRIPTION	POST. REF.	DEBIT	CREDIT	BALANCE DEBIT	BALANCE CREDIT
2013							
April	30	Sales Slip 6707	S6	25 9 3 8 00		25 9 3 8 00	

Coastal Auto Supply

Schedule of Accounts Receivable

April 30, 2013

Auto Warehouse	96 7 8 4 00
Dave's Auto Mart	44 3 1 0 00
Jazzy Wheels and Window Tint Center	42 0 0 0 00
Mike's Car Care Center	96 7 2 8 00
Paso Auto Express	25 9 3 8 00
Total	305 7 6 0 00

WORKING PAPERS

Name _____

EXERCISE 7.1

1. _____   5. _____
2. _____   6. _____
3. _____   7. _____
4. _____   8. _____

EXERCISE 7.2

Dr.	Cr.		Dr.	Cr.
1. _____	_____	4.	_____	_____
2. _____	_____	5.	_____	_____
3. _____	_____	6.	_____	_____

EXERCISE 7.3

SALES JOURNAL

PAGE _____

	DATE	SALES SLIP NO.	CUSTOMER'S NAME	POST. REF.	ACCOUNTS RECEIVABLE DEBIT	SALES TAX PAYABLE CREDIT	SALES CREDIT	
1								1
2								2
3								3
4								4
5								5

EXERCISE 7.4

	DATE		DESCRIPTION	POST. REF.	DEBIT	CREDIT	
1							1
2							2
3							3
4							4
5							5
6							6
7							7
8							8
9							9
10							10
11							11
12							12
13							13
14							14
15							15

GENERAL JOURNAL PAGE _____

EXERCISE 7.5

1. _____
   _____
   _____

2. _____
   _____
   _____

3. _____
   _____
   _____

4. _____
   _____
   _____

EXERCISE 7.6

1. _____
2. _____
3. _____

EXERCISE 7.7

1. _____
2. _____
3. _____

EXERCISE 7.8

GENERAL JOURNAL

PAGE _____

	DATE	DESCRIPTION	POST. REF.	DEBIT	CREDIT	
1						1
2						2
3						3
4						4
5						5

EXERCISE 7.9

_____
_____

Balance of Accounts Receivable: _____

EXERCISE 7.10

GENERAL LEDGER

ACCOUNT _____ ACCOUNT NO. _____

	DATE	DESCRIPTION	POST. REF.	DEBIT	CREDIT	BALANCE	
						DEBIT	CREDIT

ACCOUNT _____ ACCOUNT NO. _____

	DATE	DESCRIPTION	POST. REF.	DEBIT	CREDIT	BALANCE	
						DEBIT	CREDIT

ACCOUNT _____ ACCOUNT NO. _____

	DATE	DESCRIPTION	POST. REF.	DEBIT	CREDIT	BALANCE	
						DEBIT	CREDIT

ACCOUNTS RECEIVABLE SUBSIDIARY LEDGER

NAME _____ TERMS _____

	DATE	DESCRIPTION	POST. REF.	DEBIT	CREDIT	BALANCE

NAME _____ TERMS _____

	DATE	DESCRIPTION	POST. REF.	DEBIT	CREDIT	BALANCE

PROBLEM 7.1A or 7.1B

SALES JOURNAL   PAGE _____

	DATE	SALES SLIP NO.	CUSTOMER'S NAME	POST. REF.	ACCOUNTS RECEIVABLE DEBIT	SALES TAX PAYABLE CREDIT	SALES CREDIT	
1								1
2								2
3								3
4								4
5								5
6								6
7								7
8								8
9								9
10								10
11								11
12								12

GENERAL LEDGER

ACCOUNT _____   ACCOUNT NO. _____

DATE	DESCRIPTION	POST. REF.	DEBIT	CREDIT	BALANCE DEBIT	BALANCE CREDIT

ACCOUNT _____   ACCOUNT NO. _____

DATE	DESCRIPTION	POST. REF.	DEBIT	CREDIT	BALANCE DEBIT	BALANCE CREDIT

ACCOUNT _____   ACCOUNT NO. _____

DATE	DESCRIPTION	POST. REF.	DEBIT	CREDIT	BALANCE DEBIT	BALANCE CREDIT

Analyze: _____

_____

PROBLEM 7.2A or 7.2B

SALES JOURNAL

PAGE _____

	DATE	SALES SLIP NO.	CUSTOMER'S NAME	POST. REF.	ACCOUNTS RECEIVABLE DEBIT	SALES TAX PAYABLE CREDIT	SALES CREDIT	
1								1
2								2
3								3
4								4
5								5
6								6
7								7
8								8
9								9
10								10
11								11
12								12

GENERAL JOURNAL

PAGE _____

	DATE	DESCRIPTION	POST. REF.	DEBIT	CREDIT	
1						1
2						2
3						3
4						4
5						5
6						6
7						7
8						8
9						9
10						10
11						11
12						12
13						13
14						14
15						15
16						16
17						17
18						18
19						19
20						20
21						21

PROBLEM 7.2A or 7.2B (continued)

GENERAL LEDGER

ACCOUNT _____ ACCOUNT NO. _____

	DATE	DESCRIPTION	POST. REF.	DEBIT	CREDIT	BALANCE	
						DEBIT	CREDIT

ACCOUNT _____ ACCOUNT NO. _____

	DATE	DESCRIPTION	POST. REF.	DEBIT	CREDIT	BALANCE	
						DEBIT	CREDIT

ACCOUNT _____ ACCOUNT NO. _____

	DATE	DESCRIPTION	POST. REF.	DEBIT	CREDIT	BALANCE	
						DEBIT	CREDIT

ACCOUNT _____ ACCOUNT NO. _____

	DATE	DESCRIPTION	POST. REF.	DEBIT	CREDIT	BALANCE	
						DEBIT	CREDIT

PROBLEM 7.2A or 7.2B (continued)

Analyze: _____

PROBLEM 7.3A or 7.3B

							SALES JOURNAL							PAGE _____		

	DATE	SALES SLIP NO.	CUSTOMER'S NAME	POST. REF.	ACCOUNTS RECEIVABLE DEBIT	SALES TAX PAYABLE CREDIT	SALES CREDIT	
1								1
2								2
3								3
4								4
5								5
6								6
7								7
8								8
9								9
10								10
11								11
12								12

PROBLEM 7.3A or 7.3B (continued)

GENERAL JOURNAL

PAGE _____

	DATE		DESCRIPTION	POST. REF.	DEBIT	CREDIT	
1							1
2							2
3							3
4							4
5							5
6							6
7							7
8							8
9							9
10							10
11							11
12							12
13							13
14							14
15							15

GENERAL LEDGER

ACCOUNT _____   ACCOUNT NO. _____

DATE	DESCRIPTION	POST. REF.	DEBIT	CREDIT	BALANCE DEBIT	BALANCE CREDIT

ACCOUNT _____   ACCOUNT NO. _____

DATE	DESCRIPTION	POST. REF.	DEBIT	CREDIT	BALANCE DEBIT	BALANCE CREDIT

PROBLEM 7.3A or 7.3B (continued)

GENERAL LEDGER

ACCOUNT _____ ACCOUNT NO. _____

DATE	DESCRIPTION	POST. REF.	DEBIT	CREDIT	BALANCE	
					DEBIT	CREDIT

ACCOUNT _____ ACCOUNT NO. _____

DATE	DESCRIPTION	POST. REF.	DEBIT	CREDIT	BALANCE	
					DEBIT	CREDIT

ACCOUNTS RECEIVABLE SUBSIDIARY LEDGER

NAME _____ TERMS _____

DATE	DESCRIPTION	POST. REF.	DEBIT	CREDIT	BALANCE

NAME _____ TERMS _____

DATE	DESCRIPTION	POST. REF.	DEBIT	CREDIT	BALANCE

NAME _____ TERMS _____

DATE	DESCRIPTION	POST. REF.	DEBIT	CREDIT	BALANCE

PROBLEM 7.3A or 7.3B (continued)

ACCOUNTS RECEIVABLE SUBSIDIARY LEDGER

NAME _____ TERMS _____

	DATE	DESCRIPTION	POST. REF.	DEBIT	CREDIT	BALANCE

NAME _____ TERMS _____

	DATE	DESCRIPTION	POST. REF.	DEBIT	CREDIT	BALANCE

NAME _____ TERMS _____

	DATE	DESCRIPTION	POST. REF.	DEBIT	CREDIT	BALANCE

NAME _____ TERMS _____

	DATE	DESCRIPTION	POST. REF.	DEBIT	CREDIT	BALANCE

NAME _____ TERMS _____

	DATE	DESCRIPTION	POST. REF.	DEBIT	CREDIT	BALANCE

NAME _____ TERMS _____

	DATE	DESCRIPTION	POST. REF.	DEBIT	CREDIT	BALANCE

PROBLEM 7.3A or 7.3B (continued)

Balance of Accounts Receivable account: _____

Analyze: _____

_____

PROBLEM 7.4A or 7.4B

SALES JOURNAL   PAGE _____

	DATE	SALES SLIP NO.	CUSTOMER'S NAME	POST. REF.	ACCOUNTS RECEIVABLE DR./ SALES CR.	
1						1
2						2
3						3
4						4
5						5
6						6
7						7
8						8
9						9
10						10
11						11
12						12

PROBLEM 7.4A or 7.4B (continued)

GENERAL JOURNAL

PAGE _____

	DATE		DESCRIPTION	POST. REF.	DEBIT	CREDIT	
1							1
2							2
3							3
4							4
5							5
6							6
7							7
8							8
9							9
10							10
11							11
12							12
13							13

GENERAL LEDGER

ACCOUNT _____ ACCOUNT NO. _____

DATE	DESCRIPTION	POST. REF.	DEBIT	CREDIT	BALANCE	
					DEBIT	CREDIT

ACCOUNT _____ ACCOUNT NO. _____

DATE	DESCRIPTION	POST. REF.	DEBIT	CREDIT	BALANCE	
					DEBIT	CREDIT

ACCOUNT _____ ACCOUNT NO. _____

DATE	DESCRIPTION	POST. REF.	DEBIT	CREDIT	BALANCE	
					DEBIT	CREDIT

PROBLEM 7.4A or 7.4B (continued)

ACCOUNTS RECEIVABLE SUBSIDIARY LEDGER

NAME _____ TERMS _____

DATE	DESCRIPTION	POST. REF.	DEBIT	CREDIT	BALANCE

NAME _____ TERMS _____

DATE	DESCRIPTION	POST. REF.	DEBIT	CREDIT	BALANCE

NAME _____ TERMS _____

DATE	DESCRIPTION	POST. REF.	DEBIT	CREDIT	BALANCE

NAME _____ TERMS _____

DATE	DESCRIPTION	POST. REF.	DEBIT	CREDIT	BALANCE

NAME _____ TERMS _____

DATE	DESCRIPTION	POST. REF.	DEBIT	CREDIT	BALANCE

PROBLEM 7.4A or 7.4B (continued)

ACCOUNTS RECEIVABLE SUBSIDIARY LEDGER

NAME _____ TERMS _____

DATE	DESCRIPTION	POST. REF.	DEBIT	CREDIT	BALANCE

Balance of Accounts Receivable account: _____

Analyze: _____

_____

CRITICAL THINKING PROBLEM 7.1

SALES JOURNAL

PAGE _____

	DATE	SALES SLIP NO.	CUSTOMER'S NAME	POST. REF.	ACCOUNTS RECEIVABLE DR./ SALES CR.	
1						1
2						2
3						3
4						4
5						5
6						6
7						7
8						8
9						9
10						10
11						11

CRITICAL THINKING PROBLEM 7.1 (continued)

GENERAL JOURNAL

PAGE _____

	DATE		DESCRIPTION	POST. REF.	DEBIT	CREDIT	
1							1
2							2
3							3
4							4
5							5
6							6
7							7

GENERAL LEDGER

ACCOUNT _____   ACCOUNT NO. _____

DATE	DESCRIPTION	POST. REF.	DEBIT	CREDIT	BALANCE DEBIT	BALANCE CREDIT

ACCOUNT _____   ACCOUNT NO. _____

DATE	DESCRIPTION	POST. REF.	DEBIT	CREDIT	BALANCE DEBIT	BALANCE CREDIT

ACCOUNT _____   ACCOUNT NO. _____

DATE	DESCRIPTION	POST. REF.	DEBIT	CREDIT	BALANCE DEBIT	BALANCE CREDIT

CRITICAL THINKING PROBLEM 7.1 (continued)

ACCOUNTS RECEIVABLE LEDGER

NAME _____ TERMS _____

DATE	DESCRIPTION	POST. REF.	DEBIT	CREDIT	BALANCE

NAME _____ TERMS _____

DATE	DESCRIPTION	POST. REF.	DEBIT	CREDIT	BALANCE

NAME _____ TERMS _____

DATE	DESCRIPTION	POST. REF.	DEBIT	CREDIT	BALANCE

NAME _____ TERMS _____

DATE	DESCRIPTION	POST. REF.	DEBIT	CREDIT	BALANCE

NAME _____ TERMS _____

DATE	DESCRIPTION	POST. REF.	DEBIT	CREDIT	BALANCE

CRITICAL THINKING PROBLEM 7.1 (continued)

ACCOUNTS RECEIVABLE SUBSIDIARY LEDGER

NAME _____ TERMS _____

	DATE		DESCRIPTION	POST. REF.	DEBIT	CREDIT	BALANCE

Balance of Accounts Receivable account: _____

Analyze: _____

_____

CRITICAL THINKING PROBLEM 7.2

1. _____
   _____
   _____

2. _____
   _____
   _____
   _____
   _____

3. _____
   _____
   _____
   _____
   _____
   _____
   _____

4. _____
   _____
   _____
   _____
   _____
   _____
   _____

Chapter 7 Practice Test Answer Key

Part A True-False		Part B Matching	Part C Exercises
1. T	11. T	1. b	
2. F	12. F	2. d	
3. T	13. T	3. f	
4. T	14. T	4. g	
5. T	15. T	5. c	
6. T	16. F	6. e	
7. F	17. F	7. a	
8. T	18. F		
9. F	19. T		
10. F	20. T		

Part C Exercises

1. The balance was carried over from December 2012.

2. By referring to a copy of Sales Slip 101.

3. It was most likely a sales return or allowance. Refer to the January 18 entry on page 1 of the general journal.

Accounting for Purchases and Accounts Payable

STUDY GUIDE

Understanding the Chapter

Objectives

1. Record purchases of merchandise on credit in a three-column purchases journal. **2.** Post from the three-column purchases journal to the general ledger accounts. **3.** Post credit purchases from the purchases journal to the accounts payable subsidiary ledger. **4.** Record purchases returns and allowances in the general journal and post them to the accounts payable subsidiary ledger. **5.** Prepare a schedule of accounts payable. **6.** Compute the net delivered cost of purchases. **7.** Demonstrate a knowledge of the procedures for effective internal control of purchases. **8.** Define the accounting terms new to this chapter.

Reading Assignment

Read Chapter 8 in the textbook. Complete the textbook Section Self Review as you finish reading each section of the chapter, and the Comprehensive Self Review at the end of the chapter. Refer to the Chapter 8 Glossary or to the Glossary at the end of the book to find definitions for terms that are not familiar to you.

Activities

❏ **Thinking Critically**

Answer the *Thinking Critically* questions for Williams Sonoma and Managerial Implications.

❏ **Discussion Questions**

Answer each assigned discussion question in Chapter 8.

❏ **Exercises**

Complete each assigned exercise in Chapter 8. Use the forms provided in this SGWP. The objectives covered by an exercise are given after the exercise number. If you need help with an exercise, review the portion of the chapter related to the objective(s) covered.

❏ **Problems A/B**

Complete each assigned problem in Chapter 8. Use the forms provided in this SGWP. The objectives covered by a problem are given after the problem number. If you need help with a problem, review the portion of the chapter related to the objective(s) covered.

❏ **Critical Thinking Problems**

Complete the critical thinking problems as assigned. Use the forms provided in this SGWP.

❏ **Business Connections**

Complete the Business Connections activities as assigned to gain a deeper understanding of Chapter 8 concepts.

Practice Tests

Complete the Practice Tests, which cover the main points in your reading assignment. Compare your answers with those in the Practice Test Answer Key for Chapter 8 at the end of this chapter. If you have answered any questions incorrectly, review the related section of the text.

Part A True-False

For each of the following statements, circle T in the answer column if the statement is true or F if the statement is false.

T F **1.** The special purchases journal is used to record all transactions in which merchandise or equipment is purchased on credit.

T F **2.** A receiving report is prepared to show the quantity of goods received and their condition.

T F **3.** Freight In becomes part of the cost of purchases shown in the Cost of Goods Sold section of the income statement.

T F **4.** The procedure for posting totals from the purchases journal remains the same, whether or not an accounts payable ledger is used.

T F **5.** A payment is first recorded in the cash payments journal and then debited immediately to the supplier's account in the accounts payable ledger.

T F **6.** As soon as it is recorded in the **Purchases** journal, the amount of a purchase is posted as a credit to the supplier's account in the accounts payable ledger.

T F **7.** After all postings for a period are completed, the total of the individual balances in the accounts payable ledger should be equal to the balance of the **Accounts Receivable** control account in the general ledger.

T F **8.** Within the accounts payable ledger, the accounts for creditors are arranged alphabetically or by account number.

T F **9.** The use of the balance ledger form makes each creditor's balance readily available.

T F **10.** At the end of the month, the total of the payments made to creditors is debited to the **Accounts Payable** account.

T F **11.** Returns of merchandise to suppliers are recorded in the general journal.

T F **12.** Purchases Returns and Allowances is a contra-revenue account.

T F **13.** Payments made to creditors are recorded in the cash payments journal.

T F **14.** At the end of the month, the total of the Accounts Payable column in the purchases journal is debited to the **Accounts Payable** control account.

T F **15.** The balance of each creditor's account in the accounts payable ledger is not computed until the end of the accounting period.

T F **16.** Each purchase of merchandise on credit should be recorded in the purchases journal as it occurs during the month.

T F **17.** One of the basic advantages of the purchases journal is that the posting to **Accounts Payable** is simplified.

T F **18.** An account called **Purchases** is charged with the cost of the merchandise as it is sold.

T F **19.** The provision in the purchases journal of special columns for the invoice number, the invoice date, and the credit terms is intended to ensure payment of the bill when it is due.

T F **20.** When properly designed, a purchases journal makes posting to the general ledger unnecessary.

Part B Exercise   *Answer each of the following in the space provided. Make your answers complete but as brief as possible.*

A firm uses a multicolumn purchases journal with the following money columns: Accounts Payable Credit, Purchases Debit, and Freight In Debit

1. How is the **Purchases** account classified?

   _____

   _____

   _____

2. How is the accuracy of the totals verified at the end of the month?

   _____

   _____

   _____

3. Which columns are totaled and summary posted to the general ledger?

   _____

   _____

   _____

4. If the buyer pays freight charges directly to the carrier on a purchase of merchandise, where is the freight transaction recorded?

   _____

   _____

   _____

5. The figures of which column are used to update the accounts payable ledger?

   _____

   _____

6. Where would you record the purchase of office equipment on open account credit terms?

   _____

   _____

7. Where is the **Freight In** account shown on the income statement?

   _____

   _____

   _____

Demonstration Problem

Santa Rosa Office Supply is a retail business that sells office equipment, furniture, and office supplies. Its credit purchases and purchases returns and allowances for the month of October 2013 follow. The general ledger accounts used to record these transactions are given below.

Instructions

1. Open the general ledger accounts and enter the balance of Accounts Payable for October 1, 2013.

2. Using the list of creditors that follows, open the accounts in the accounts payable subsidiary ledger and enter the account balances for October 1, 2013.

3. Record the transactions in a purchases journal, page 12, and a general journal, page 30.

4. Post individual entries from the purchases journal to the accounts payable subsidiary ledger, then post from the general journal to the general ledger and accounts payable subsidiary ledger.

5. Total, prove, and rule the purchases journal as of October 31, 2013.

6. Post the column totals from the purchases journal to the appropriate general ledger accounts.

7. Compute the net delivered cost of the firm's purchases for the month.

8. Prepare a schedule of accounts payable for October 31, 2013.

9. Check the total of the schedule of accounts payable against the balance of the **Accounts Payable** account in the general ledger. The two amounts should be equal.

GENERAL LEDGER ACCOUNTS

205 Accounts Payable	$18,900 Cr.
501 Purchases	
502 Freight In	
503 Purchases Returns and Allowances	

CREDITORS

Name	Terms	Balance
Bolanos Office Supplies	n/30	
Dallas Office Supply	n/60	$2,320
Davis Office Products	n/30	
Golden West Office Center	2/10, n/30	5,670
Trinh Copy and Paper	1/10, n/30	10,910

DATE	TRANSACTIONS
October 4	Purchased desks for $9,160 plus a freight charge of $280 from Davis Office Products, Invoice 3124 dated September 30, terms payable in 30 days.
9	Purchased computers for $7,450 from Bolanos Office Supplies, Invoice 7129 dated October 4, net due and payable in 30 days.
11	Received Credit Memo 165 for $600 from Davis Office Products as an allowance for slightly damaged but usable desks purchased on Invoice 3124 of September 30.
16	Purchased file cabinets for $2,720 plus a freight charge of $124 from Dallas Office Supply, Invoice 9088 dated October 11, terms of 60 days.
21	Purchased electronic calculators for $2,200 from Bolanos Office Supplies, Invoice 7765 dated October 16, net due and payable in 30 days.
24	Purchased laser printer paper for $3,350 plus a freight charge of $320 from Trinh Copy and Paper on Invoice 4891 dated October 19, terms of 1/10, n/30.
29	Received Credit Memo 629 for $540 from Bolanos Office Supplies for defective calculators that were returned. The calculators were originally purchased on Invoice 2765 of October 16.
31	Purchased office chairs for $4,300 plus a freight charge of $156 from Golden West Office Center, Invoice 966 dated October 26, terms of 2/10, n/30.

SOLUTION

PURCHASES JOURNAL

PAGE ___12___

DATE		CUSTOMER'S NAME	INVOICE NUMBER	INVOICE DATE	TERMS	POST. REF.	ACCOUNTS PAYABLE CREDIT	PURCHASES DEBIT	FREIGHT IN DEBIT
2013									
Oct.	4	Davis Office Products	3124	9/30	n/30		9 4 4 0 00	9 1 6 0 00	2 8 0 00
	9	Bolanos Office Supplies	7129	10/4	n/30		7 4 5 0 00	7 4 5 0 00	
	16	Dallas Office Supply	9088	10/11	n/60		2 8 4 4 00	2 7 2 0 00	1 2 4 00
	21	Bolanos Office Supplies	7765	10/16	n/30		2 2 0 0 00	2 2 0 0 00	
	24	Trinh Copy & Paper	4891	10/19	1/10, n/30		3 6 7 0 00	3 3 5 0 00	3 2 0 00
	31	Golden West Office Center	966	10/26	2/10, n/30		4 4 5 6 00	4 3 0 0 00	1 5 6 00
	31						30 0 6 0 00	29 1 8 0 00	8 8 0 00

GENERAL JOURNAL

PAGE ___30___

	DATE		DESCRIPTION	POST. REF.	DEBIT	CREDIT	
1	2013						1
2	Oct.	11	Accounts Payable/Davis Office Products	205 ✔	6 0 0 00		2
3			Purchases Returns and Allowances	503		6 0 0 00	3
4			Received Credit Memo 165 for				4
5			damaged merchandise; original				5
6			purchase was made on Invoice 3124,				6
7			September 30, 2013				7
8							8
9		29	Accounts Payable/Bolanos Office Supplies	205 ✔	5 4 0 00		9
10			Purchases Returns & Allowances	503		5 4 0 00	10
11			Received Credit Memo 629 for damaged				11
12			merchandise that was returned;				12
13			original purchase was made on				13
14			Invoice 2765, October 16, 2013				14
15							15

SOLUTION (continued)

GENERAL LEDGER

ACCOUNT   **Accounts Payable**   ACCOUNT NO. ____205____

DATE		DESCRIPTION	POST. REF.	DEBIT	CREDIT	BALANCE DEBIT	BALANCE CREDIT
2013							
Oct.	1	Balance	✔				18 9 0 0 00
	11		J30	6 0 0 00			18 3 0 0 00
	29		J30	5 4 0 00			17 7 6 0 00
	31		P12		30 0 6 0 00		47 8 2 0 00

ACCOUNT   **Purchases**   ACCOUNT NO. ____501____

DATE		DESCRIPTION	POST. REF.	DEBIT	CREDIT	BALANCE DEBIT	BALANCE CREDIT
2013							
Oct.	31		P12	29 1 8 0 00		29 1 8 0 00	

ACCOUNT   **Freight In**   ACCOUNT NO. ____502____

DATE		DESCRIPTION	POST. REF.	DEBIT	CREDIT	BALANCE DEBIT	BALANCE CREDIT
2013							
Oct.	31		P12	8 8 0 00		8 8 0 00	

ACCOUNT   **Purchases Returns and Allowances**   ACCOUNT NO. ____503____

DATE		DESCRIPTION	POST. REF.	DEBIT	CREDIT	BALANCE DEBIT	BALANCE CREDIT
2013							
Oct.	11		J30		6 0 0 00		6 0 0 00
	29		J30		5 4 0 00		1 1 4 0 00

Purchases	$29,180
Freight In	880
Delivered Cost of Purchases	$30,060
Less Purchases Returns and Allowances	1,140
Net Delivered Cost of Purchases	$28,920

SOLUTION (continued)

ACCOUNTS PAYABLE SUBSIDIARY LEDGER

NAME __Bolanos Office Supplies__   TERMS ___n/30___

DATE		DESCRIPTION	POST. REF.	DEBIT	CREDIT	BALANCE
2013						
Oct.	9	Invoice 7129, 10/4/13	P12		7 4 5 0 00	7 4 5 0 00
	21	Invoice 7765, 10/16/13	P12		2 2 0 0 00	9 6 5 0 00
	29	CM 629	J30	5 4 0 00		9 1 1 0 00

NAME __Dallas Office Supply__   TERMS ___n/60___

DATE		DESCRIPTION	POST. REF.	DEBIT	CREDIT	BALANCE
2013						
Oct.	1	Balance	✔			2 3 2 0 00
	16	Invoice 9088, 10/11/13	P12		2 8 4 4 00	5 1 6 4 00

NAME __Davis Office Products__   TERMS ___n/30___

DATE		DESCRIPTION	POST. REF.	DEBIT	CREDIT	BALANCE
2013						
Oct.	4	Invoice 3124, 9/30/13	P12		9 4 4 0 00	9 4 4 0 00
	11	CM 165	J30	6 0 0 00		8 8 4 0 00

NAME __Golden West Office Center__   TERMS ___2/10, n/30___

DATE		DESCRIPTION	POST. REF.	DEBIT	CREDIT	BALANCE
2013						
Oct.	1	Balance	✔			5 6 7 0 00
	31	Invoice 966, 10/26/13	P12		4 4 5 6 00	10 1 2 6 00

NAME __Trinh Copy and Paper__   TERMS ___1/10, n/30___

DATE		DESCRIPTION	POST. REF.	DEBIT	CREDIT	BALANCE
2013						
Oct.	1	Balance	✔			10 9 1 0 00
	24	Invoice 4891, 10/19/13	P12		3 6 7 0 00	14 5 8 0 00

SOLUTION (continued)

Santa Rosa Office Supply

Schedule of Accounts Payable

October 31, 2013

Bolanos Office Supplies		9	1	1	0	00
Dallas Office Supply		5	1	6	4	00
Davis Office Products		8	8	4	0	00
Golden West Office Center	10	1	2	6	00
Trinh Copy and Paper	14	5	8	0	00
Total	47	8	2	0	00

WORKING PAPERS

Name _____

EXERCISE 8.1

1. _____   4. _____
2. _____   5. _____
3. _____   6. _____

EXERCISE 8.2

	Dr.	Cr.		Dr.	Cr.
1.	_____	_____	4.	_____	_____
2.	_____	_____	5.	_____	_____
3.	_____	_____	6.	_____	_____

EXERCISE 8.3

PURCHASES JOURNAL   PAGE _____

DATE	PURCHASED FROM	INVOICE NUMBER	INVOICE DATE	TERMS	POST. REF.	ACCOUNTS PAYABLE CREDIT	PURCHASES DEBIT	FREIGHT IN DEBIT

EXERCISE 8.4

GENERAL JOURNAL   PAGE _____

	DATE	DESCRIPTION	POST. REF.	DEBIT	CREDIT	
1						1
2						2
3						3
4						4
5						5
6						6
7						7
8						8
9						9
10						10

EXERCISE 8.5

GENERAL JOURNAL

PAGE _____

	DATE		DESCRIPTION	POST. REF.	DEBIT	CREDIT	
1							1
2							2
3							3
4							4
5							5
6							6
7							7

EXERCISE 8.6

_____

_____

_____

_____

_____

EXERCISE 8.7

a. _____

_____

b. _____

c. _____

d. _____

_____

EXERCISE 8.8

a. _____

b. _____

c. _____

d. _____

PROBLEM 8.1A or 8.1B

PURCHASES JOURNAL

PAGE _____

DATE	PURCHASED FROM	INVOICE NUMBER	INVOICE DATE	TERMS	POST. REF.	ACCOUNTS PAYABLE CREDIT	PURCHASES DEBIT	FREIGHT IN DEBIT

GENERAL JOURNAL

PAGE _____

	DATE	DESCRIPTION	POST. REF.	DEBIT	CREDIT	
1						1
2						2
3						3
4						4
5						5
6						6
7						7
8						8
9						9
10						10
11						11
12						12
13						13
14						14
15						15
16						16
17						17
18						18
19						19

PROBLEM 8.1A or 8.1B (continued)

GENERAL LEDGER

ACCOUNT _____   ACCOUNT NO. _____

	DATE	DESCRIPTION	POST. REF.	DEBIT	CREDIT	BALANCE DEBIT	CREDIT

ACCOUNT _____   ACCOUNT NO. _____

	DATE	DESCRIPTION	POST. REF.	DEBIT	CREDIT	BALANCE DEBIT	CREDIT

ACCOUNT _____   ACCOUNT NO. _____

	DATE	DESCRIPTION	POST. REF.	DEBIT	CREDIT	BALANCE DEBIT	CREDIT

ACCOUNT _____   ACCOUNT NO. _____

	DATE	DESCRIPTION	POST. REF.	DEBIT	CREDIT	BALANCE DEBIT	CREDIT

Analyze: _____

PROBLEM 8.2A or 8.2B

ACCOUNTS PAYABLE SUBSIDIARY LEDGER

NAME _____ TERMS _____

	DATE	DESCRIPTION	POST. REF.	DEBIT	CREDIT	BALANCE

NAME _____ TERMS _____

	DATE	DESCRIPTION	POST. REF.	DEBIT	CREDIT	BALANCE

NAME _____ TERMS _____

	DATE	DESCRIPTION	POST. REF.	DEBIT	CREDIT	BALANCE

NAME _____ TERMS _____

	DATE	DESCRIPTION	POST. REF.	DEBIT	CREDIT	BALANCE

NAME _____ TERMS _____

	DATE	DESCRIPTION	POST. REF.	DEBIT	CREDIT	BALANCE

PROBLEM 8.2A or 8.2B (continued)

Analyze:

EXTRA FORM

PROBLEM 8.3A or 8.3B

PURCHASES JOURNAL

PAGE _____

DATE	PURCHASED FROM	INVOICE NUMBER	INVOICE DATE	TERMS	POST. REF.	ACCOUNTS PAYABLE CREDIT	PURCHASES DEBIT	FREIGHT IN DEBIT

GENERAL JOURNAL

PAGE _____

	DATE	DESCRIPTION	POST. REF.	DEBIT	CREDIT	
1						1
2						2
3						3
4						4
5						5
6						6
7						7
8						8
9						9
10						10
11						11
12						12
13						13
14						14
15						15

PROBLEM 8.3A or 8.3B (continued)

GENERAL LEDGER

ACCOUNT _____ ACCOUNT NO. _____

DATE	DESCRIPTION	POST. REF.	DEBIT	CREDIT	BALANCE	
					DEBIT	CREDIT

ACCOUNT _____ ACCOUNT NO. _____

DATE	DESCRIPTION	POST. REF.	DEBIT	CREDIT	BALANCE	
					DEBIT	CREDIT

ACCOUNT _____ ACCOUNT NO. _____

DATE	DESCRIPTION	POST. REF.	DEBIT	CREDIT	BALANCE	
					DEBIT	CREDIT

ACCOUNT _____ ACCOUNT NO. _____

DATE	DESCRIPTION	POST. REF.	DEBIT	CREDIT	BALANCE	
					DEBIT	CREDIT

_____
_____
_____
_____
_____

PROBLEM 8.3A or 8.3B (continued)

ACCOUNTS PAYABLE SUBSIDIARY LEDGER

NAME _____ TERMS _____

DATE	DESCRIPTION	POST. REF.	DEBIT	CREDIT	BALANCE

NAME _____ TERMS _____

DATE	DESCRIPTION	POST. REF.	DEBIT	CREDIT	BALANCE

NAME _____ TERMS _____

DATE	DESCRIPTION	POST. REF.	DEBIT	CREDIT	BALANCE

NAME _____ TERMS _____

DATE	DESCRIPTION	POST. REF.	DEBIT	CREDIT	BALANCE

NAME _____ TERMS _____

DATE	DESCRIPTION	POST. REF.	DEBIT	CREDIT	BALANCE

PROBLEM 8.3A or 8.3B (continued)

Analyze: _____

_____

EXTRA FORMS

NAME _____ TERMS _____

	DATE	DESCRIPTION	POST. REF.	DEBIT	CREDIT	BALANCE

NAME _____ TERMS _____

	DATE	DESCRIPTION	POST. REF.	DEBIT	CREDIT	BALANCE

PROBLEM 8.4A or 8.4B

PURCHASES JOURNAL   PAGE _____

DATE		PURCHASED FROM	INVOICE NUMBER	INVOICE DATE	TERMS	POST. REF.	ACCOUNTS PAYABLE CREDIT	PURCHASES DEBIT	FREIGHT IN DEBIT

GENERAL JOURNAL   PAGE _____

	DATE		DESCRIPTION	POST. REF.	DEBIT	CREDIT	
1							1
2							2
3							3
4							4
5							5
6							6
7							7
8							8
9							9
10							10
11							11
12							12
13							13
14							14
15							15

PROBLEM 8.4A or 8.4B (continued)

GENERAL LEDGER

ACCOUNT _____ ACCOUNT NO. _____

DATE	DESCRIPTION	POST. REF.	DEBIT	CREDIT	BALANCE	
					DEBIT	CREDIT

ACCOUNT _____ ACCOUNT NO. _____

DATE	DESCRIPTION	POST. REF.	DEBIT	CREDIT	BALANCE	
					DEBIT	CREDIT

ACCOUNT _____ ACCOUNT NO. _____

DATE	DESCRIPTION	POST. REF.	DEBIT	CREDIT	BALANCE	
					DEBIT	CREDIT

ACCOUNT _____ ACCOUNT NO. _____

DATE	DESCRIPTION	POST. REF.	DEBIT	CREDIT	BALANCE	
					DEBIT	CREDIT

Net Delivered Cost of Purchases

_____
_____
_____
_____
_____

PROBLEM 8.4A or 8.4B (continued)

ACCOUNTS PAYABLE SUBSIDIARY LEDGER

NAME _____ TERMS _____

DATE	DESCRIPTION	POST. REF.	DEBIT	CREDIT	BALANCE

NAME _____ TERMS _____

DATE	DESCRIPTION	POST. REF.	DEBIT	CREDIT	BALANCE

NAME _____ TERMS _____

DATE	DESCRIPTION	POST. REF.	DEBIT	CREDIT	BALANCE

NAME _____ TERMS _____

DATE	DESCRIPTION	POST. REF.	DEBIT	CREDIT	BALANCE

NAME _____ TERMS _____

DATE	DESCRIPTION	POST. REF.	DEBIT	CREDIT	BALANCE

PROBLEM 8.4A or 8.4B (continued)

Analyze:

EXTRA FORM

CRITICAL THINKING PROBLEM 8.1

PURCHASES JOURNAL

PAGE _____

DATE	PURCHASED FROM	INVOICE NUMBER	INVOICE DATE	TERMS	POST. REF.	ACCOUNTS PAYABLE CREDIT	PURCHASES DEBIT	FREIGHT IN DEBIT

SALES JOURNAL

PAGE _____

	DATE	SALES SLIP NO.	CUSTOMER'S NAME	POST. REF.	ACCOUNTS RECEIVABLE DEBIT	SALES TAX PAYABLE CREDIT	SALES CREDIT	
1								1
2								2
3								3
4								4
5								5
6								6
7								7
8								8
9								9
10								10
11								11
12								12
13								13
14								14
15								15

CRITICAL THINKING PROBLEM 8.1 (continued)

ACCOUNTS PAYABLE SUBSIDIARY LEDGER

NAME _____ TERMS _____

	DATE	DESCRIPTION	POST. REF.	DEBIT	CREDIT	BALANCE

NAME _____ TERMS _____

	DATE	DESCRIPTION	POST. REF.	DEBIT	CREDIT	BALANCE

NAME _____ TERMS _____

	DATE	DESCRIPTION	POST. REF.	DEBIT	CREDIT	BALANCE

NAME _____ TERMS _____

	DATE	DESCRIPTION	POST. REF.	DEBIT	CREDIT	BALANCE

NAME _____ TERMS _____

	DATE	DESCRIPTION	POST. REF.	DEBIT	CREDIT	BALANCE

NAME _____ TERMS _____

	DATE	DESCRIPTION	POST. REF.	DEBIT	CREDIT	BALANCE

CRITICAL THINKING PROBLEM 8.1 (continued)

ACCOUNTS PAYABLE SUBSIDIARY LEDGER

NAME _____ TERMS _____

DATE	DESCRIPTION	POST. REF.	DEBIT	CREDIT	BALANCE

NAME _____ TERMS _____

DATE	DESCRIPTION	POST. REF.	DEBIT	CREDIT	BALANCE

ACCOUNTS RECEIVABLE SUBSIDIARY LEDGER

NAME _____ TERMS _____

DATE	DESCRIPTION	POST. REF.	DEBIT	CREDIT	BALANCE

NAME _____ TERMS _____

DATE	DESCRIPTION	POST. REF.	DEBIT	CREDIT	BALANCE

NAME _____ TERMS _____

DATE	DESCRIPTION	POST. REF.	DEBIT	CREDIT	BALANCE

CRITICAL THINKING PROBLEM 8.1 (continued)

ACCOUNTS RECEIVABLE SUBSIDIARY LEDGER

NAME _____ TERMS _____

	DATE	DESCRIPTION	POST. REF.	DEBIT	CREDIT	BALANCE	

NAME _____ TERMS _____

	DATE	DESCRIPTION	POST. REF.	DEBIT	CREDIT	BALANCE	

NAME _____ TERMS _____

	DATE	DESCRIPTION	POST. REF.	DEBIT	CREDIT	BALANCE	

NAME _____ TERMS _____

	DATE	DESCRIPTION	POST. REF.	DEBIT	CREDIT	BALANCE	

NAME _____ TERMS _____

	DATE	DESCRIPTION	POST. REF.	DEBIT	CREDIT	BALANCE	

NAME _____ TERMS _____

	DATE	DESCRIPTION	POST. REF.	DEBIT	CREDIT	BALANCE	

CRITICAL THINKING PROBLEM 8.1 (continued)

ACCOUNTS RECEIVABLE SUBSIDIARY LEDGER

NAME _____ TERMS _____

	DATE	DESCRIPTION	POST. REF.	DEBIT	CREDIT	BALANCE

NAME _____ TERMS _____

	DATE	DESCRIPTION	POST. REF.	DEBIT	CREDIT	BALANCE

GENERAL LEDGER

ACCOUNT _____ ACCOUNT NO. _____

	DATE	DESCRIPTION	POST. REF.	DEBIT	CREDIT	BALANCE DEBIT	BALANCE CREDIT

ACCOUNT _____ ACCOUNT NO. _____

	DATE	DESCRIPTION	POST. REF.	DEBIT	CREDIT	BALANCE DEBIT	BALANCE CREDIT

ACCOUNT _____ ACCOUNT NO. _____

	DATE	DESCRIPTION	POST. REF.	DEBIT	CREDIT	BALANCE DEBIT	BALANCE CREDIT

ACCOUNT _____ ACCOUNT NO. _____

	DATE	DESCRIPTION	POST. REF.	DEBIT	CREDIT	BALANCE DEBIT	BALANCE CREDIT

CRITICAL THINKING PROBLEM 8.1 (continued)

GENERAL LEDGER

ACCOUNT _____ ACCOUNT NO. _____

DATE	DESCRIPTION	POST. REF.	DEBIT	CREDIT	BALANCE DEBIT	BALANCE CREDIT

ACCOUNT _____ ACCOUNT NO. _____

DATE	DESCRIPTION	POST. REF.	DEBIT	CREDIT	BALANCE DEBIT	BALANCE CREDIT

CRITICAL THINKING PROBLEM 8.1 (continued)

_____

_____

Analyze: _____

_____

_____

_____

CRITICAL THINKING PROBLEM 8.2

_____

_____

_____

_____

_____

_____

_____

_____

_____

_____

_____

_____

_____

_____

_____

_____

_____

_____

_____

_____

_____

_____

_____

_____

_____

_____

_____

_____

_____

Chapter 8 Practice Test Answer Key

Part A True-False		Part B Exercises
1. F	11. T	1. An Expense.
2. T	12. F	2. Accounts Payable Credit = Purchases Debit + Freight In Debit.
3. T	13. T	3. All Columns.
4. T	14. F	4. It is not recorded in the purchases journal at all; it is entered in the cash payments journal.
5. T	15. F	
6. T	16. T	
7. F	17. T	5. The Accounts Payable Column.
8. T	18. F	6. The General Journal.
9. T	19. T	7. In the Cost of Goods Sold Section.
10. T	20. F	

CHAPTER 9

Cash Receipts, Cash Payments, and Banking Procedures

STUDY GUIDE

Understanding the Chapter

Objectives

1. Record cash receipts in a cash receipts journal. 2. Account for cash short or over. 3. Post from the cash receipts journal to subsidiary and general ledgers. 4. Record cash payments in a cash payments journal. 5. Post from the cash payments journal to subsidiary and general ledgers. 6. Demonstrate a knowledge of procedures for a petty cash fund. 7. Demonstrate a knowledge of internal control routines for cash. 8. Write a check, endorse checks, prepare a bank deposit slip, and maintain a checkbook balance. 9. Reconcile the monthly bank statement. 10. Record any adjusting entries required from the bank reconciliation. 11. Understand how businesses use online banking to manage cash activities. 12. Define accounting terms new to this chapter.

Reading Assignment

Read Chapter 9 in the textbook. Complete the Section Self Review as you finish reading each section of the chapter, and the Comprehensive Self Review at the end of the chapter. Refer to the Chapter 9 Glossary or to the Glossary at the end of the book to find definitions for terms that are not familiar to you.

Activities

❏ **Thinking Critically**   Answer the *Thinking Critically* questions for H&R Block and Managerial Implications

❏ **Discussion Questions**   Answer each assigned review question in Chapter 9.

❏ **Exercises**   Complete each assigned exercise in Chapter 9. Use the forms provided in this SGWP. The objectives covered by an exercise are given after the exercise number. If you need help with an exercise, review the portion of the chapter related to the objective(s) covered.

❏ **Problems A/B**   Complete each assigned problem in Chapter 9. Use the forms provided in this SGWP. The objectives covered by a problem are given after the problem number. If you need help with a problem review the portion of the chapter related to the objective(s) covered.

❏ **Critical Thinking Problems**   Complete the critical thinking problems as assigned. Use the forms provided in this SGWP.

❏ **Business Connections**   Complete the Business Connections activities as assigned to gain a deeper understanding of Chapter 9 concepts.

Practice Tests

Complete the Practice Tests, which cover the main points in your reading assignment. Compare your answers with those in the Practice Test Answer Key for Chapter 9 at the end of this chapter. If you have answered any questions incorrectly, review the related section of the text.

Part A True-False
For each of the following statements, circle T in the answer column if the statement is true or F if the statement is false.

T   F   **1.** Account numbers are recorded below the totals of each column as each summary posting from the cash payments journal is completed.

T   F   **2.** A cash investment by the owner in a business should be recorded in the cash receipts journal.

T   F   **3.** The title of a special journal makes it possible to omit much of the explanation that would be needed in a general journal entry.

T   F   **4.** The **Sales Tax Payable** account represents a liability of the business.

T   F   **5.** **Cash Short or Over** is a general ledger account that normally has a credit balance because cash tends to be short more often than over.

T   F   **6.** Cash received by mail should be deposited by the same person who accepts and lists it.

T   F   **7.** Only checks are listed on the deposit slip.

T   F   **8.** Checks can be identified on a deposit slip by the use of the American Bankers Association transit numbers.

T   F   **9.** Checks made payable to cash or to bearer need not be endorsed when deposited.

T   F   **10.** The money represented by deposited checks becomes available for use as soon as the deposit is made.

T   F   **11.** The best form of endorsement for business purposes is the restrictive endorsement, which limits the use of the check to a stated purpose.

T   F   **12.** Internal controls are not necessary if payments are made by check.

T   F   **13.** Except for petty cash payments, all payments should be made by check.

T   F   **14.** Correct internal control procedures require that the approval for paying all bills, writing all checks, and signing all checks should be the responsibility of the same person.

T   F   **15.** An adequate system of internal control over cash will provide for safeguarding both incoming and outgoing funds.

T   F   **16.** Each petty cash payment is entered separately in the cash payments journal.

T   F   **17.** The petty cash analysis sheet is a memorandum record of petty cash payments rather than a record of original entry.

T   F   **18.** The check to replenish the petty cash fund is written for an amount sufficient to restore the fund to its established balance.

T   F   **19.** When posting from the cash payments journal at the end of the month, the accountant posts the total cash payments as a single credit to cash.

T   F   **20.** The abbreviation "CP5" in the Posting Reference column of a ledger account indicates that the posting was made from the cash payments journal on the fifth day of the month.

T   F   **21.** The Other Accounts Debit column of a cash payments journal is used to record the debits that are to be posted individually.

T   F   **22.** Once created, login information for online bank account access should not be changed.

Part B Matching *For each numbered item, choose the matching term from the box and write the identifying letter in the answer column.*

		Box
_____	1. A check on which payment has been refused because of too few funds in the issuer's account.	**a.** NSF Check
_____	2. The person or firm from whose account a check is to be paid.	**b.** Deposit in Transit
_____	3. The form that contains all the information necessary for journalizing a transaction paid by check.	**c.** Outstanding checks
_____	4. The firm or person designated on the check to receive payment.	**d.** Bank reconciliation
_____	5. The process of determining why a difference exists between the firm's accounting records and the bank records and bringing them into balance.	**e.** Bank statement

a. NSF Check
b. Deposit in Transit
c. Outstanding checks
d. Bank reconciliation
e. Bank statement
f. Stub
g. Payee
h. Drawer
i. Deposit slip
j. Promissory note
k. Summary posting
l. Internal control
m. EFT

_____ 1. A check on which payment has been refused because of too few funds in the issuer's account.

_____ 2. The person or firm from whose account a check is to be paid.

_____ 3. The form that contains all the information necessary for journalizing a transaction paid by check.

_____ 4. The firm or person designated on the check to receive payment.

_____ 5. The process of determining why a difference exists between the firm's accounting records and the bank records and bringing them into balance.

_____ 6. A form on which all cash and cash items are listed before they are placed in the bank.

_____ 7. Checks issued and recorded that have not been paid by the bank.

_____ 8. A form received from the bank showing all transactions recorded in the depositor's account during the month.

_____ 9. Receipts that have been deposited and entered in the firm's accounting records but have not yet been entered on the bank's records.

_____ 10. A written promise to pay a specific amount at a specific time.

_____ 11. A system designed to safeguard assets and to help ensure the accuracy and reliability of accounting records.

_____ 12. The process by which a single amount is posted instead of each entry being posted separately.

_____ 13. An electronic transfer of money from one account to another.

Demonstration Problem

On June 2, 2013, Orange Coast Legal Services received its May bank statement. Enclosed with the bank statement, shown below, was a debit memorandum for $150 for a NSF check issued by James Greene. Additionally, Check No. 177 was correctly drawn for $400 in payment of a utility bill. Orange Coast Legal Services mistakenly recorded the check as $40. The firm's checkbook contained the information shown below about deposits made and checks issued during May. The balance of the **Cash** account and the checkbook on May 31 was $37,425.

Instructions

1. Prepare a bank reconciliation statement for Orange Coast Legal Services as of May 31, 2013.

2. Record general journal entries for any items on the bank reconciliation statement that must be journalized. Date the entries May 31, 2013. Number the journal as page 17.

Checkbook information:

May 1	Balance	$40,592
1	Check 177	40
1	Check 178	800
7	Deposit	2,600
8	Check 179	900
12	Check 180	6,000
17	Check 181	720
19	Deposit	680
22	Check 182	88
23	Check 183	592
26	Deposit	1,748
29	Check 184	160
31	Deposit	925
		$37,245

First California National Bank

Orange Coast Legal Services
4312 Brea Street
Yorba Linda, CA 92885-8714

ACCOUNT NO. 77546798
PERIOD ENDING: May 31, 2013

CHECK NO.	AMOUNT	DATE	DESCRIPTION	BALANCE
			Balance last statement	40,592.00
177	400.00	6/1		40,192.00
178	800.00	6/4		39,392.00
	2,600.00	6/7	Deposit	41,992.00
179	900.00	6/8		41,092.00
180	6,000.00	6/12		35,092.00
	150.00	6/12	Debit Memorandum	34,942.00
181	720.00	6/17		34,222.00
	680.00	6/19	Deposit	34,902.00
182	88.00	6/22		34,814.00
	1,748.00	6/26	Deposit	36,562.00
	15.00	6/29	Service Charge	36,547.00

SOLUTION

Orange Coast Legal Services
Bank Reconciliation Statement
May 31, 2013

Balance on Bank Statement					36 5 4 7 00	
Additions:						
Deposit of May 31 in Transit					9 2 5 00	
					37 4 7 2 00	
Deductions for Outstanding Checks:						
Check 183 of May 23		5 9 2 00				
Check 184 of May 29		1 6 0 00				
Total Checks Outstanding					7 5 2 00	
Adjusted Bank Balance					36 7 2 0 00	
Balance in Books					37 2 4 5 00	
Deductions:						
NSF Check		1 5 0 00				
Recording Error, Check 177		3 6 0 00				
Bank Service Charge		1 5 00			5 2 5 00	
Adjusted Book Balance					36 7 2 0 00	

GENERAL JOURNAL

PAGE ___**17**___

	DATE		DESCRIPTION	POST. REF.	DEBIT	CREDIT	
1	2013						1
2	May	31	Accounts Receivable/James Greene		1 5 0 00		2
3			Cash			1 5 0 00	3
4			To record NSF check returned by bank				4
5							5
6		31	Miscellaneous Expense		1 5 00		6
7			Cash			1 5 00	7
8			To record bank service charge for May				8
9							9

WORKING PAPERS

EXERCISES 9.1, 9.2

EXERCISE 9.1

CASH RECEIPTS JOURNAL

PAGE _____

DATE	DESCRIPTION	POST. REF.	ACCOUNTS RECEIVABLE CREDIT	SALES TAX PAYABLE CREDIT	SALES CREDIT	OTHER ACCOUNTS CREDIT			CASH DEBIT
						ACCOUNT NAME	POST. REF.	AMOUNT	

EXERCISE 9.2

CASH PAYMENTS JOURNAL

PAGE _____

DATE	CK. NO.	DESCRIPTION	POST. REF.	ACCOUNTS PAYABLE DEBIT	OTHER ACCOUNTS DEBIT			PURCHASES DISCOUNT CREDIT	CASH CREDIT
					ACCOUNT NAME	POST. REF.	AMOUNT		

EXERCISES 9.3, 9.4

EXERCISE 9.3

CASH PAYMENTS JOURNAL   PAGE _____

DATE	CK. NO.	DESCRIPTION	POST. REF.	ACCOUNTS PAYABLE DEBIT	OTHER ACCOUNTS DEBIT			PURCHASES DISCOUNT CREDIT	CASH CREDIT
					ACCOUNT NAME	POST. REF.	AMOUNT		

EXERCISE 9.4

CASH PAYMENTS JOURNAL   PAGE _____

DATE	CK. NO.	DESCRIPTION	POST. REF.	ACCOUNTS PAYABLE DEBIT	OTHER ACCOUNTS DEBIT			PURCHASES DISCOUNT CREDIT	CASH CREDIT
					ACCOUNT NAME	POST. REF.	AMOUNT		

EXERCISE 9.5

_____

_____

GENERAL JOURNAL

PAGE _____

	DATE	DESCRIPTION	POST. REF.	DEBIT	CREDIT	
1						1
2						2
3						3
4						4
5						5
6						6
7						7
8						8
9						9
10						10
11						11
12						12
13						13
14						14

EXERCISE 9.6

	Bank Balance	Book Balance	Accounting Entry
1.	_____	_____	_____
2.	_____	_____	_____
3.	_____	_____	_____
4.	_____	_____	_____
5.	_____	_____	_____
6.	_____	_____	_____
7.	_____	_____	_____

EXTRA FORM

_____

_____

GENERAL JOURNAL   PAGE _____

	DATE	DESCRIPTION	POST. REF.	DEBIT	CREDIT	
1						1
2						2
3						3
4						4
5						5
6						6
7						7
8						8
9						9
10						10
11						11
12						12
13						13
14						14

EXERCISE 9.7

EXERCISE 9.7 (continued)

GENERAL JOURNAL   PAGE _____

	DATE		DESCRIPTION	POST. REF.	DEBIT	CREDIT	
1							1
2							2
3							3
4							4
5							5
6							6
7							7
8							8
9							9
10							10
11							11
12							12

EXERCISE 9.8

EXERCISE 9.9

GENERAL JOURNAL   PAGE ___21___

	DATE		DESCRIPTION	POST. REF.	DEBIT	CREDIT	
1							1
2							2
3							3
4							4
5							5
6							6
7							7
8							8
9							9
10							10
11							11
12							12
13							13
14							14

PROBLEM 9.1A or 9.1B

CASH RECEIPTS JOURNAL

DATE	DESCRIPTION	POST. REF.	ACCOUNTS RECEIVABLE CREDIT	SALES TAX PAYABLE CREDIT	SALES CREDIT	OTHER ACCOUNTS CREDIT			CASH DEBIT
						ACCOUNT NAME	POST. REF.	AMOUNT	

PROBLEM 9.1A or 9.1B (continued)

GENERAL LEDGER

ACCOUNT _____   ACCOUNT NO. _____

DATE		DESCRIPTION	POST. REF.	DEBIT	CREDIT	BALANCE	
						DEBIT	CREDIT

ACCOUNT _____   ACCOUNT NO. _____

DATE		DESCRIPTION	POST. REF.	DEBIT	CREDIT	BALANCE	
						DEBIT	CREDIT

ACCOUNT _____   ACCOUNT NO. _____

DATE		DESCRIPTION	POST. REF.	DEBIT	CREDIT	BALANCE	
						DEBIT	CREDIT

ACCOUNT _____   ACCOUNT NO. _____

DATE		DESCRIPTION	POST. REF.	DEBIT	CREDIT	BALANCE	
						DEBIT	CREDIT

ACCOUNT _____   ACCOUNT NO. _____

DATE		DESCRIPTION	POST. REF.	DEBIT	CREDIT	BALANCE	
						DEBIT	CREDIT

PROBLEM 9.1A or 9.1B (continued)

GENERAL LEDGER

ACCOUNT _____ ACCOUNT NO. _____

DATE	DESCRIPTION	POST. REF.	DEBIT	CREDIT	BALANCE	
					DEBIT	CREDIT

ACCOUNT _____ ACCOUNT NO. _____

DATE	DESCRIPTION	POST. REF.	DEBIT	CREDIT	BALANCE	
					DEBIT	CREDIT

ACCOUNT _____ ACCOUNT NO. _____

DATE	DESCRIPTION	POST. REF.	DEBIT	CREDIT	BALANCE	
					DEBIT	CREDIT

ACCOUNT _____ ACCOUNT NO. _____

DATE	DESCRIPTION	POST. REF.	DEBIT	CREDIT	BALANCE	
					DEBIT	CREDIT

Analyze: _____

_____

PROBLEM 9.2A or 9.2B

PAGE _____

CASH PAYMENTS JOURNAL

DATE	CK. NO.	DESCRIPTION	POST. REF.	ACCOUNTS PAYABLE DEBIT	OTHER ACCOUNTS DEBIT			PURCHASES DISCOUNT CREDIT	CASH CREDIT
					ACCOUNT NAME	POST. REF.	AMOUNT		

PROBLEM 9.2A or 9.2B (continued)

PETTY CASH ANALYSIS SHEET

DATE	VOU. NO.	DESCRIPTION	RECEIPTS	PAYMENTS	DISTRIBUTION OF PAYMENTS			OTHER ACCOUNTS DEBIT	
					SUPPLIES DEBIT	DELIVERY EXPENSE DEBIT	MISC. EXPENSE DEBIT	ACCOUNT NAME	AMOUNT

PROBLEM 9.2A or 9.2B (continued)

GENERAL LEDGER

ACCOUNT _____ ACCOUNT NO. _____

DATE	DESCRIPTION	POST. REF.	DEBIT	CREDIT	BALANCE	
					DEBIT	CREDIT

ACCOUNT _____ ACCOUNT NO. _____

DATE	DESCRIPTION	POST. REF.	DEBIT	CREDIT	BALANCE	
					DEBIT	CREDIT

ACCOUNT _____ ACCOUNT NO. _____

DATE	DESCRIPTION	POST. REF.	DEBIT	CREDIT	BALANCE	
					DEBIT	CREDIT

ACCOUNT _____ ACCOUNT NO. _____

DATE	DESCRIPTION	POST. REF.	DEBIT	CREDIT	BALANCE	
					DEBIT	CREDIT

ACCOUNT _____ ACCOUNT NO. _____

DATE	DESCRIPTION	POST. REF.	DEBIT	CREDIT	BALANCE	
					DEBIT	CREDIT

PROBLEM 9.2A or 9.2B (continued)

GENERAL LEDGER

ACCOUNT _____ ACCOUNT NO. _____

DATE	DESCRIPTION	POST. REF.	DEBIT	CREDIT	BALANCE DEBIT	BALANCE CREDIT

ACCOUNT _____ ACCOUNT NO. _____

DATE	DESCRIPTION	POST. REF.	DEBIT	CREDIT	BALANCE DEBIT	BALANCE CREDIT

ACCOUNT _____ ACCOUNT NO. _____

DATE	DESCRIPTION	POST. REF.	DEBIT	CREDIT	BALANCE DEBIT	BALANCE CREDIT

ACCOUNT _____ ACCOUNT NO. _____

DATE	DESCRIPTION	POST. REF.	DEBIT	CREDIT	BALANCE DEBIT	BALANCE CREDIT

ACCOUNT _____ ACCOUNT NO. _____

DATE	DESCRIPTION	POST. REF.	DEBIT	CREDIT	BALANCE DEBIT	BALANCE CREDIT

Name _____

PROBLEM 9.2A or 9.2B (continued)

GENERAL LEDGER

ACCOUNT _____ ACCOUNT NO. _____

	DATE	DESCRIPTION	POST. REF.	DEBIT	CREDIT	BALANCE DEBIT	BALANCE CREDIT

ACCOUNT _____ ACCOUNT NO. _____

	DATE	DESCRIPTION	POST. REF.	DEBIT	CREDIT	BALANCE DEBIT	BALANCE CREDIT

ACCOUNT _____ ACCOUNT NO. _____

	DATE	DESCRIPTION	POST. REF.	DEBIT	CREDIT	BALANCE DEBIT	BALANCE CREDIT

ACCOUNT _____ ACCOUNT NO. _____

	DATE	DESCRIPTION	POST. REF.	DEBIT	CREDIT	BALANCE DEBIT	BALANCE CREDIT

ACCOUNT _____ ACCOUNT NO. _____

	DATE	DESCRIPTION	POST. REF.	DEBIT	CREDIT	BALANCE DEBIT	BALANCE CREDIT

Analyze: _____

_____

PROBLEM 9.3A or 9.3B

PAGE ___

SALES JOURNAL

DATE	INVOICE NO.	CUSTOMER'S NAME	POST. REF.	ACCOUNTS RECEIVABLE DR./ SALES CR.
				1
				2
				3
				4
				5
				6
				7
				8
				9
				10
				11

PAGE ___

CASH RECEIPTS JOURNAL

DATE	DESCRIPTION	POST. REF.	ACCOUNTS RECEIVABLE CREDIT	SALES CREDIT	OTHER ACCOUNTS CREDIT ACCOUNT NAME	POST. REF.	AMOUNT	SALES DISCOUNTS DEBIT	CASH DEBIT

PROBLEM 9.3A or 9.3B (continued)

GENERAL JOURNAL   PAGE _____

	DATE	DESCRIPTION	POST. REF.	DEBIT	CREDIT	
1						1
2						2
3						3
4						4
5						5
6						6
7						7
8						8
9						9
10						10
11						11
12						12

GENERAL LEDGER (PARTIAL)

ACCOUNT _____ ACCOUNT NO. _____

DATE	DESCRIPTION	POST. REF.	DEBIT	CREDIT	BALANCE DEBIT	BALANCE CREDIT

ACCOUNT _____ ACCOUNT NO. _____

DATE	DESCRIPTION	POST. REF.	DEBIT	CREDIT	BALANCE DEBIT	BALANCE CREDIT

ACCOUNT _____ ACCOUNT NO. _____

DATE	DESCRIPTION	POST. REF.	DEBIT	CREDIT	BALANCE DEBIT	BALANCE CREDIT

PROBLEM 9.3A or 9.3B (continued)

GENERAL LEDGER (PARTIAL)

ACCOUNT _____   ACCOUNT NO. _____

DATE	DESCRIPTION	POST. REF.	DEBIT	CREDIT	BALANCE DEBIT	BALANCE CREDIT

ACCOUNT _____   ACCOUNT NO. _____

DATE	DESCRIPTION	POST. REF.	DEBIT	CREDIT	BALANCE DEBIT	BALANCE CREDIT

ACCOUNT _____   ACCOUNT NO. _____

DATE	DESCRIPTION	POST. REF.	DEBIT	CREDIT	BALANCE DEBIT	BALANCE CREDIT

Analyze: _____

PROBLEM 9.4A or 9.4B

PURCHASES JOURNAL

PAGE _____

DATE		PURCHASED FROM	INVOICE NUMBER	INVOICE DATE	TERMS	POST. REF.	PURCHASES DR./ ACCOUNTS PAYABLE CR.

GENERAL JOURNAL

PAGE _____

	DATE		DESCRIPTION	POST. REF.	DEBIT	CREDIT	
1							1
2							2
3							3
4							4
5							5
6							6
7							7
8							8
9							9
10							10
11							11
12							12
13							13
14							14
15							15
16							16
17							17
18							18
19							19
20							20
21							21
22							22
23							23

PROBLEM 9.4A or 9.4B (continued)

CASH PAYMENTS JOURNAL   PAGE _____

DATE	CK. NO.	DESCRIPTION	POST. REF.	ACCOUNTS PAYABLE DEBIT	OTHER ACCOUNTS DEBIT			PURCHASES DISCOUNT CREDIT	CASH CREDIT
					ACCOUNT NAME	POST. REF.	AMOUNT		

PROBLEM 9.4A or 9.4B (continued)

GENERAL LEDGER

ACCOUNT _____ ACCOUNT NO. _____

	DATE	DESCRIPTION	POST. REF.	DEBIT	CREDIT	BALANCE	
						DEBIT	CREDIT

ACCOUNT _____ ACCOUNT NO. _____

	DATE	DESCRIPTION	POST. REF.	DEBIT	CREDIT	BALANCE	
						DEBIT	CREDIT

ACCOUNT _____ ACCOUNT NO. _____

	DATE	DESCRIPTION	POST. REF.	DEBIT	CREDIT	BALANCE	
						DEBIT	CREDIT

ACCOUNT _____ ACCOUNT NO. _____

	DATE	DESCRIPTION	POST. REF.	DEBIT	CREDIT	BALANCE	
						DEBIT	CREDIT

PROBLEM 9.4A or 9.4B (continued)

GENERAL LEDGER

ACCOUNT _____ ACCOUNT NO. _____

DATE	DESCRIPTION	POST. REF.	DEBIT	CREDIT	BALANCE	
					DEBIT	CREDIT

ACCOUNT _____ ACCOUNT NO. _____

DATE	DESCRIPTION	POST. REF.	DEBIT	CREDIT	BALANCE	
					DEBIT	CREDIT

ACCOUNT _____ ACCOUNT NO. _____

DATE	DESCRIPTION	POST. REF.	DEBIT	CREDIT	BALANCE	
					DEBIT	CREDIT

ACCOUNT _____ ACCOUNT NO. _____

DATE	DESCRIPTION	POST. REF.	DEBIT	CREDIT	BALANCE	
					DEBIT	CREDIT

ACCOUNT _____ ACCOUNT NO. _____

DATE	DESCRIPTION	POST. REF.	DEBIT	CREDIT	BALANCE	
					DEBIT	CREDIT

ACCOUNT _____ ACCOUNT NO. _____

DATE	DESCRIPTION	POST. REF.	DEBIT	CREDIT	BALANCE	
					DEBIT	CREDIT

PROBLEM 9.4A or 9.4B (continued)

Analyze:

EXTRA FORM

PROBLEM 9.5A or 9.5B

_____

_____

GENERAL JOURNAL

PAGE _____

	DATE	DESCRIPTION	POST. REF.	DEBIT	CREDIT	
1						1
2						2
3						3
4						4
5						5
6						6
7						7
8						8
9						9
10						10
11						11
12						12
13						13

Analyze: _____

_____

PROBLEM 9.6A or 9.6B

PROBLEM 9.6A or 9.6B (continued)

GENERAL JOURNAL   PAGE _____

	DATE		DESCRIPTION	POST. REF.	DEBIT	CREDIT	
1							1
2							2
3							3
4							4
5							5
6							6
7							7
8							8
9							9
10							10
11							11
12							12
13							13
14							14
15							15
16							16
17							17
18							18
19							19
20							20
21							21
22							22
23							23
24							24
25							25
26							26
27							27
28							28

Analyze: _____

_____

_____

PROBLEM 9.7A or 9.7B

GENERAL JOURNAL

PAGE _____

	DATE	DESCRIPTION	POST. REF.	DEBIT	CREDIT	
1						1
2						2
3						3
4						4
5						5
6						6
7						7
8						8
9						9
10						10
11						11
12						12
13						13

Analyze: _____

PROBLEM 9.8A or 9.8B

_____

_____

PROBLEM 9.8A or 9.8B (continued)

GENERAL JOURNAL   PAGE _____

	DATE	DESCRIPTION	POST. REF.	DEBIT	CREDIT	
1						1
2						2
3						3
4						4
5						5
6						6
7						7
8						8
9						9
10						10
11						11
12						12
13						13
14						14
15						15
16						16
17						17
18						18
19						19
20						20
21						21
22						22
23						23
24						24
25						25
26						26
27						27
28						28

Analyze: _____
_____
_____

CRITICAL THINKING PROBLEM 9.1

SALES JOURNAL

PAGE _____

	DATE	SALES SLIP NO.	CUSTOMER'S NAME	POST. REF.	ACCOUNTS RECEIVABLE DEBIT	SALES TAX PAYABLE CREDIT	SALES CREDIT	
1								1
2								2
3								3
4								4
5								5
6								6
7								7
8								8
9								9
10								10
11								11
12								12
13								13
14								14
15								15
16								16

PURCHASES JOURNAL

PAGE _____

DATE	PURCHASED FROM	INVOICE NUMBER	INVOICE DATE	TERMS	POST. REF.	ACCOUNTS PAYABLE CREDIT	PURCHASES DEBIT	FREIGHT IN DEBIT

CRITICAL THINKING PROBLEM 9.1 (continued)

GENERAL JOURNAL   PAGE _____

	DATE		DESCRIPTION	POST. REF.	DEBIT	CREDIT	
1							1
2							2
3							3
4							4
5							5
6							6
7							7
8							8
9							9
10							10
11							11
12							12
13							13
14							14
15							15
16							16
17							17
18							18
19							19
20							20
21							21
22							22
23							23
24							24
25							25
26							26
27							27
28							28
29							29
30							30
31							31
32							32
33							33
34							34
35							35
36							36
37							37

CRITICAL THINKING PROBLEM 9.1 (continued)

PAGE _____

CASH RECEIPTS JOURNAL

DATE	DESCRIPTION	POST. REF.	ACCOUNTS RECEIVABLE CREDIT	SALES TAX PAYABLE CREDIT	SALES CREDIT	OTHER ACCOUNTS CREDIT			CASH DEBIT
						ACCOUNT NAME	POST. REF.	AMOUNT	

CRITICAL THINKING PROBLEM 9.1 (continued)

CASH PAYMENTS JOURNAL

DATE	CK. NO.	DESCRIPTION	POST. REF.	ACCOUNTS PAYABLE DEBIT	OTHER ACCOUNTS DEBIT			PURCHASES DISCOUNTS CREDIT	CASH CREDIT
					ACCOUNT NAME	POST. REF.	AMOUNT		

CRITICAL THINKING PROBLEM 9.1 (continued)

GENERAL LEDGER

ACCOUNT _____ ACCOUNT NO. _____

DATE	DESCRIPTION	POST. REF.	DEBIT	CREDIT	BALANCE	
					DEBIT	CREDIT

ACCOUNT _____ ACCOUNT NO. _____

DATE	DESCRIPTION	POST. REF.	DEBIT	CREDIT	BALANCE	
					DEBIT	CREDIT

ACCOUNT _____ ACCOUNT NO. _____

DATE	DESCRIPTION	POST. REF.	DEBIT	CREDIT	BALANCE	
					DEBIT	CREDIT

ACCOUNT _____ ACCOUNT NO. _____

DATE	DESCRIPTION	POST. REF.	DEBIT	CREDIT	BALANCE	
					DEBIT	CREDIT

ACCOUNT _____ ACCOUNT NO. _____

DATE	DESCRIPTION	POST. REF.	DEBIT	CREDIT	BALANCE	
					DEBIT	CREDIT

ACCOUNT _____ ACCOUNT NO. _____

DATE	DESCRIPTION	POST. REF.	DEBIT	CREDIT	BALANCE	
					DEBIT	CREDIT

CRITICAL THINKING PROBLEM 9.1 (continued)

GENERAL LEDGER

ACCOUNT _____ ACCOUNT NO. _____

DATE	DESCRIPTION	POST. REF.	DEBIT	CREDIT	BALANCE	
					DEBIT	CREDIT

ACCOUNT _____ ACCOUNT NO. _____

DATE	DESCRIPTION	POST. REF.	DEBIT	CREDIT	BALANCE	
					DEBIT	CREDIT

ACCOUNT _____ ACCOUNT NO. _____

DATE	DESCRIPTION	POST. REF.	DEBIT	CREDIT	BALANCE	
					DEBIT	CREDIT

ACCOUNT _____ ACCOUNT NO. _____

DATE	DESCRIPTION	POST. REF.	DEBIT	CREDIT	BALANCE	
					DEBIT	CREDIT

ACCOUNT _____ ACCOUNT NO. _____

DATE	DESCRIPTION	POST. REF.	DEBIT	CREDIT	BALANCE	
					DEBIT	CREDIT

CRITICAL THINKING PROBLEM 9.1 (continued)

GENERAL LEDGER

ACCOUNT _____ ACCOUNT NO. _____

DATE	DESCRIPTION	POST. REF.	DEBIT	CREDIT	BALANCE DEBIT	BALANCE CREDIT

ACCOUNT _____ ACCOUNT NO. _____

DATE	DESCRIPTION	POST. REF.	DEBIT	CREDIT	BALANCE DEBIT	BALANCE CREDIT

ACCOUNT _____ ACCOUNT NO. _____

DATE	DESCRIPTION	POST. REF.	DEBIT	CREDIT	BALANCE DEBIT	BALANCE CREDIT

ACCOUNT _____ ACCOUNT NO. _____

DATE	DESCRIPTION	POST. REF.	DEBIT	CREDIT	BALANCE DEBIT	BALANCE CREDIT

ACCOUNT _____ ACCOUNT NO. _____

DATE	DESCRIPTION	POST. REF.	DEBIT	CREDIT	BALANCE DEBIT	BALANCE CREDIT

CRITICAL THINKING PROBLEM 9.1 (continued)

GENERAL LEDGER

ACCOUNT _____ ACCOUNT NO. _____

	DATE	DESCRIPTION	POST. REF.	DEBIT	CREDIT	BALANCE	
						DEBIT	CREDIT

ACCOUNT _____ ACCOUNT NO. _____

	DATE	DESCRIPTION	POST. REF.	DEBIT	CREDIT	BALANCE	
						DEBIT	CREDIT

ACCOUNT _____ ACCOUNT NO. _____

	DATE	DESCRIPTION	POST. REF.	DEBIT	CREDIT	BALANCE	
						DEBIT	CREDIT

ACCOUNTS RECEIVABLE SUBSIDIARY LEDGER

NAME _____ TERMS _____

	DATE	DESCRIPTION	POST. REF.	DEBIT	CREDIT	BALANCE

NAME _____ TERMS _____

	DATE	DESCRIPTION	POST. REF.	DEBIT	CREDIT	BALANCE

CRITICAL THINKING PROBLEM 9.1 (continued)

ACCOUNTS RECEIVABLE SUBSIDIARY LEDGER

NAME_____ TERMS _____

	DATE	DESCRIPTION	POST. REF.	DEBIT	CREDIT	BALANCE

NAME_____ TERMS _____

	DATE	DESCRIPTION	POST. REF.	DEBIT	CREDIT	BALANCE

NAME_____ TERMS _____

	DATE	DESCRIPTION	POST. REF.	DEBIT	CREDIT	BALANCE

NAME_____ TERMS _____

	DATE	DESCRIPTION	POST. REF.	DEBIT	CREDIT	BALANCE

NAME_____ TERMS _____

	DATE	DESCRIPTION	POST. REF.	DEBIT	CREDIT	BALANCE

CRITICAL THINKING PROBLEM 9.1 (continued)

ACCOUNTS PAYABLE SUBSIDIARY LEDGER

NAME _____ TERMS _____

	DATE	DESCRIPTION	POST. REF.	DEBIT	CREDIT	BALANCE

NAME _____ TERMS _____

	DATE	DESCRIPTION	POST. REF.	DEBIT	CREDIT	BALANCE

NAME _____ TERMS _____

	DATE	DESCRIPTION	POST. REF.	DEBIT	CREDIT	BALANCE

NAME _____ TERMS _____

	DATE	DESCRIPTION	POST. REF.	DEBIT	CREDIT	BALANCE

CRITICAL THINKING PROBLEM 9.1 (continued)

NAME _____ TERMS _____

	DATE	DESCRIPTION	POST. REF.	DEBIT	CREDIT	BALANCE

NAME _____ TERMS _____

	DATE	DESCRIPTION	POST. REF.	DEBIT	CREDIT	BALANCE

ACCOUNTS PAYABLE SUBSIDIARY LEDGER

NAME _____ TERMS _____

	DATE	DESCRIPTION	POST. REF.	DEBIT	CREDIT	BALANCE

Analyze: _____

_____

CRITICAL THINKING PROBLEM 9.2

CRITICAL THINKING PROBLEM 9.2 (continued)

_____

_____

_____

_____

_____

_____

_____

_____

_____

_____

_____

_____

_____

_____

_____

_____

_____

_____

_____

_____

Chapter 9 Practice Test Answer Key

Part A True-False		Part B Matching
1. T	12. F	1. a
2. T	13. T	2. h
3. T	14. F	3. f
4. T	15. T	4. g
5. F	16. F	5. d
6. F	17. T	6. i
7. F	18. T	7. c
8. T	19. T	8. e
9. F	20. F	9. b
10. F	21. T	10. j
11. T	22. F	11. l
		12. k
		13. m

Payroll Computations, Records, and Payment

STUDY GUIDE

Understanding the Chapter

Objectives	**1.** Explain the major federal laws relating to employee earnings and withholding. **2.** Compute gross earnings of employees. **3.** Determine employee deductions for social security taxes. **4.** Determine employee deductions for Medicare taxes. **5.** Determine employee deductions for income taxes. **6.** Enter gross earnings, deductions, and net pay in the payroll register. **7.** Journalize payroll transactions in the general journal. **8.** Maintain an earnings record for each employee. **9.** Define the accounting terms new to this chapter.
Reading Assignment	Read Chapter 10 in the textbook. Complete the Section Self Review as you finish reading each section of the chapter, and the Comprehensive Self Review at the end of the chapter. Refer to the Chapter 10 Glossary or to the Glossary at the end of the book to find definitions for terms that are not familiar to you.

Activities

❏ **Thinking Critically**	Answer the *Thinking Critically* questions for Clif Bar and Managerial Implications.
❏ **Discussion Questions**	Answer each assigned review question in Chapter 10.
❏ **Exercises**	Complete each assigned exercise in Chapter 10. Use the forms provided in this SGWP. The objectives covered by an exercise are given after the exercise number. If you need help with an exercise, review the portion of the chapter related to the objective(s) covered.
❏ **Problems A/B**	Complete each assigned problem in Chapter 10. Use the forms provided in this SGWP. The objectives covered by a problem are given after the problem number. If you need help with a problem, review the portion of the chapter related to the objective(s) covered.
❏ **Critical Thinking Problems**	Complete the critical thinking problems as assigned. Use the forms provided in this SGWP.
❏ **Business Connections**	Complete the Business Connections activities as assigned to gain a deeper understanding of Chapter 10 concepts.

Practice Tests

Complete the Practice Tests, which cover the main points in your reading assignment. Compare your answers with those in the Practice Test Answer Key for Chapter 10 at the end of this chapter. If you have answered any questions incorrectly, review the related section of the text.

Part A True-False *For each of the following statements, circle T in the answer column if the statement is true or F if the statement is false.*

T   F   **1.** Payroll taxes apply to salaries and wages paid employees and to amounts paid independent contractors.

T   F   **2.** The Fair Labor Standards Act fixes a minimum wage for supervisory employees paid a monthly salary.

T   F   **3.** Employees can choose whether they want to be covered by the social security laws.

T   F   **4.** Most employers determine the amount of income tax to be withheld from the employee's pay by using withholding tables.

T   F   **5.** The Medicare tax is included in the social security tax (FICA).

T   F   **6.** The employee's marital status, number of exemptions, earnings for the pay period, and length of pay period are all factors in determining the amount of social security tax to be withheld.

T   F   **7.** The employer is required to contribute the same amount of federal unemployment tax as the amount withheld from the employee's earnings.

T   F   **8.** The state unemployment tax rate can be reduced by the rate charged by the federal government in the federal unemployment tax program.

T   F   **9.** The workers' compensation program is a federal program.

T   F   **10.** The payroll register provides all the information required to make a general journal entry to record the payroll.

T   F   **11.** An employee worked 48 hours during the week. Her regular hourly pay is $10 per hour. Her gross pay for the week is $480.00.

T   F   **12.** A company hires Michael Santori, CPA, to prepare monthly financial statements. Santori comes to the company's office, reviews source documents, and later returns the statements. Sestini would be classified as an employee.

Part B Matching

For each numbered item, choose the matching term from the box and write the identifying letter in the answer column.

_____ 1. A record for each employee showing the person's earnings and deductions for the period, along with cumulative data.

_____ 2. Deductions to pay for medical benefits for retired persons.

_____ 3. A tax levied on the employer to provide benefits to employees who lose their jobs.

_____ 4. A government publication containing withholding tables for employee taxes.

_____ 5. Wages before deductions.

_____ 6. Wages paid in a year above the base amount subject to a tax.

_____ 7. A columnar record that shows each employee's earnings, deductions, and net pay.

_____ 8. Time worked in excess of 40 hours per week.

_____ 9. Provides for funding of retirement and disability benefits.

_____ 10. The form that employees file in order to claim the number of allowances to which they are entitled.

a. Employee earnings record
b. Payroll register
c. Exempt wages
d. Workers' compensation insurance
e. Overtime
f. Circular E
g. Medicare premiums
h. Unemployment tax
i. Federal Insurance Contributions Act
j. Employee's Withholding Allowance Certificate Form W4
k. Gross pay

Demonstration Problem

Los Olivos Consulting Company pays its employees monthly. Payments made by the company on November 30, 2013, follow. Cumulative amounts paid to the persons named prior to November 30 are also given.

1. John Arciero, President, gross monthly salary of $17,000; gross earnings prior to November 30, $170,000.

2. Virginia Richey, Vice President, gross monthly salary of $14,000; gross earnings paid prior to November 30, $140,000.

3. Kathryn Price, independent accountant who audits the company's accounts, $17,500; gross amounts paid prior to November 30, $5,000.

4. Evelyn Wu, Treasurer, gross monthly salary of $10,060; gross earnings prior to November 30, $100,000.

5. Payment to Hankins Research Services for monthly services of Robert Hankins, a tax consultant, $7,000; amount paid to Hankins Research Services prior to November 30, $24,000.

Instructions

1. Use an earnings ceiling of $106,800, and a tax rate of 6.2 percent for social security taxes and a tax rate of 1.45 percent on all earnings for medicare taxes. Prepare a schedule showing:

   a. Each employee's cumulative earnings prior to November 30.

   b. Each employee's gross earnings for November.

   c. The amounts to be withheld for each payroll tax from each employee's earnings; the employee's income tax withholdings are Arciero, $5,500; Richey, $3,250; Wu, $1,250.

   d. The net amount due each employee.

   e. The total gross earnings, the total of each payroll tax deduction, and the total net amount payable to employees.

2. Give the general journal entry to record the company's payroll on November 30. Use journal page 34. Omit description.

3. Give the general journal entry to record payments to employees on November 30.

SOLUTION

EARNINGS SCHEDULE

EMPLOYEE NAME	CUMULATIVE EARNINGS	MONTHLY PAY	SOCIAL SECURITY	MEDICARE	EMPLOYEE INCOME TAX WITHHOLDING	NET PAY
John Arciero	$170,000.00	$17,000.00	—	$246.50	$5,500.00	$11,253.50
Virginia Richey	140,000.00	14,000.00	—	203.00	3,250.00	10,547.00
Evelyn Wu	100,000.00	10,000.00	421.60	145.00	1,250.00	8,183.40
Totals	$410,000.00	$41,000.00	$421.60	$594.50	$10,000.00	$29,983.90

<u>**Kathryn Price and Robert Hankins are not employees of Los Olivos Consulting Company.**</u>

GENERAL JOURNAL

PAGE __34__

	DATE		DESCRIPTION	POST. REF.	DEBIT	CREDIT	
1	2013						1
2	Nov.	30	Salaries Expense		41 0 0 0 00		2
3			Social Security Tax Payable			4 2 1 60	3
4			Medicare Tax Payable			5 9 4 50	4
5			Employee Income Tax Payable			10 0 0 0 00	5
6			Salaries Payable			29 9 8 3 90	6
7							7
8		30	Salaries Payable		29 9 8 3 90		8
9			Cash			29 9 8 3 90	9
10							10

WORKING PAPERS

Name _____

EXERCISE 10.1

EMPLOYEE NO.	HOURLY RATE	HOURS WORKED	GROSS EARNINGS
_____	_____	_____	_____
_____	_____	_____	_____
_____	_____	_____	_____
_____	_____	_____	_____

EXERCISE 10.2

HOURLY RATE	OVERTIME RATE	REGULAR HOURS WORKED	OVERTIME HOURS WORKED	REGULAR PAY	OVERTIME PAY	GROSS PAY
_____	_____	_____	_____	_____	_____	_____
_____	_____	_____	_____	_____	_____	_____
_____	_____	_____	_____	_____	_____	_____
_____	_____	_____	_____	_____	_____	_____

EXERCISE 10.3

EMPLOYEE NO.	DECEMBER SALARY	YEAR TO DATE EARNINGS THROUGH NOVEMBER 30	SOC. SEC. TAXABLE EARNINGS- DECEMBER	SOCIAL SECURITY TAX 6.20%
_____	_____	_____	_____	_____
_____	_____	_____	_____	_____
_____	_____	_____	_____	_____

EXERCISE 10.4

EMPLOYEE NO.	DECEMBER SALARY	MEDICARE TAXABLE EARNINGS- DECEMBER	MEDICARE TAX 1.45%
_____	_____	_____	_____
_____	_____	_____	_____
_____	_____	_____	_____

EXERCISE 10.5

EMPLOYEE NO.	MARITAL STATUS	WITHHOLDING ALLOWANCES	WEEKLY SALARY	INCOME TAX WITHHOLDING
_____	_____	_____	_____	_____
_____	_____	_____	_____	_____
_____	_____	_____	_____	_____

EXERCISE 10.6

GENERAL JOURNAL

PAGE _____

	DATE		DESCRIPTION	POST. REF.	DEBIT	CREDIT	
1							1
2							2
3							3
4							4
5							5
6							6
7							7
8							8
9							9
10							10
11							11
12							12
13							13
14							14
15							15

EXERCISE 10.7

GENERAL JOURNAL

PAGE _____

	DATE		DESCRIPTION	POST. REF.	DEBIT	CREDIT	
1							1
2							2
3							3
4							4
5							5
6							6
7							7
8							8
9							9
10							10
11							11
12							12
13							13
14							14
15							15

PROBLEM 10.1A or 10.1B

EMPLOYEE NO.	REGULAR HOURS, HOURLY RATE	HOURS WORKED	REGULAR TIME EARNINGS	OVERTIME EARNINGS	GROSS EARNINGS
_____	_____	_____	_____	_____	_____
_____	_____	_____	_____	_____	_____
_____	_____	_____	_____	_____	_____

Gross Pay _____

Social Security Tax _____

Medicare Tax _____

Income Tax Withholding _____

Health & Disability _____

United Way _____

U.S. Savings Bond _____

Net Pay _____

GENERAL JOURNAL   PAGE _____

	DATE	DESCRIPTION	POST. REF.	DEBIT	CREDIT	
1						1
2						2
3						3
4						4
5						5

Analyze: _____

_____

_____

_____

_____

_____

_____

PROBLEM 10.2A or 10.2B

PAYROLL REGISTER ___ **WEEK BEGINNING** ___

NAME	NO. OF ALLOW.	MARITAL STATUS	CUMULATIVE EARNINGS	NO. OF HRS.	RATE	REGULAR TIME EARNINGS	EARNINGS OVERTIME EARNINGS	GROSS AMOUNT	CUMULATIVE EARNINGS

AND ENDING ___ **PAID** ___

TAXABLE WAGES SOCIAL SECURITY	MEDICARE	FUTA	DEDUCTIONS SOCIAL SECURITY	MEDICARE	INCOME TAX	NET AMOUNT	DISTRIBUTION CHECK NO.	WAGES EXPENSE

PROBLEM 10.2A or 10.2B (continued)

GENERAL JOURNAL   PAGE _____

	DATE		DESCRIPTION	POST. REF.	DEBIT	CREDIT	
1							1
2							2
3							3
4							4
5							5
6							6
7							7
8							8
9							9
10							10
11							11
12							12
13							13
14							14
15							15
16							16
17							17
18							18
19							19
20							20
21							21
22							22
23							23
24							24
25							25
26							26
27							27
28							28
29							29
30							30
31							31
32							32
33							33
34							34

Analyze: _____

_____

PROBLEM 10.3A or 10.3B

PAYROLL REGISTER   WEEK BEGINNING

NAME	NO. OF ALLOW.	MARITAL STATUS	CUMULATIVE EARNINGS	NO. OF HRS.	RATE	EARNINGS REGULAR TIME EARNINGS	EARNINGS OVERTIME EARNINGS	GROSS AMOUNT	CUMULATIVE EARNINGS

AND ENDING   PAID

TAXABLE WAGES SOCIAL SECURITY	TAXABLE WAGES MEDICARE	FUTA	DEDUCTIONS SOCIAL SECURITY	DEDUCTIONS MEDICARE	INCOME TAX	NET AMOUNT	CHECK NO.	DISTRIBUTION OFFICE WAGES	DELIVERY WAGES

PROBLEM 10.3A or 10.3B (continued)

GENERAL JOURNAL   PAGE _____

DATE	DESCRIPTION	POST. REF.	DEBIT	CREDIT	
1					1
2					2
3					3
4					4
5					5
6					6
7					7
8					8
9					9
10					10
11					11
12					12
13					13
14					14
15					15
16					16
17					17
18					18
19					19
20					20
21					21
22					22
23					23
24					24
25					25
26					26
27					27
28					28
29					29
30					30
31					31
32					32
33					33
34					34

Analyze: _____

_____

PROBLEM 10.4A or 10.4B

EMPLOYEE NAME	CUMULATIVE EARNINGS	MONTHLY PAY	SOCIAL SECURITY	MEDICARE	EMPLOYEE INCOME TAX WITHHOLDING	NET PAY
Totals						

GENERAL JOURNAL

PAGE _____

	DATE	DESCRIPTION	POST. REF.	DEBIT	CREDIT	
1						1
2						2
3						3
4						4
5						5
6						6
7						7
8						8
9						9
10						10
11						11
12						12
13						13
14						14
15						15
16						16
17						17
18						18
19						19
20						20
21						21
22						22
23						23
24						24
25						25
26						26

Analyze: _____
_____
_____

CRITICAL THINKING PROBLEM 10.1

EMPLOYEE NAME	CUMULATIVE EARNINGS	MONTHLY PAY	SOCIAL SECURITY	MEDICARE	EMPLOYEE INCOME TAX WITHHOLDING	NET PAY

GENERAL JOURNAL   PAGE _____

	DATE	DESCRIPTION	POST. REF.	DEBIT	CREDIT	
1						1
2						2
3						3
4						4
5						5
6						6
7						7
8						8
9						9
10						10
11						11
12						12
13						13
14						14
15						15

Analyze: _____

CRITICAL THINKING PROBLEM 10.2

_____

_____

_____

_____

_____

_____

_____

_____

_____

_____

_____

_____

_____

_____

_____

_____

_____

_____

_____

_____

_____

_____

Chapter 10 Practice Test Answer Key

Part A True-False	Part B Matching
1. F	1. a
2. F	2. g
3. F	3. h
4. T	4. f
5. F	5. k
6. F	6. c
7. F	7. b
8. F	8. e
9. F	9. i
10. T	10. j
11. F	
12. F	

CHAPTER 11 — Payroll Taxes, Deposits, and Reports

STUDY GUIDE

Understanding the Chapter

Objectives

1. Explain how and when payroll taxes are paid to the government. 2. Compute and record the employer's social security and Medicare taxes. 3. Record deposit of social security, Medicare, and employee income taxes. 4. Prepare an Employer's Quarterly Federal Tax Return, Form 941. 5. Prepare Wage and Tax Statement (Form W-2) and Annual Transmittal of Wage and Tax Statements (Form W-3). 6. Compute and record liability for federal and state unemployment taxes and record payment of the taxes. 7. Prepare an Employer's Federal Unemployment Tax Return, Form 940 or 940-EZ. 8. Compute and record workers' compensation insurance premiums. 9. Define the accounting terms new to this chapter.

Reading Assignment

Read Chapter 11 in the textbook. Complete the textbook Section Self Review as you finish reading each section of the chapter, and Comprehensive Self Review at the end of the chapter. Refer to the Chapter 11 Glossary or to the Glossary at the end of the book to find definitions for terms that are not familiar to you.

Activities

❑ **Thinking Critically**   Answer the *Thinking Critically* questions for New Castle Hotels and Resorts and Managerial Implications.

❑ **Discussion Questions**   Answer each assigned discussion question in Chapter 11.

❑ **Exercises**   Complete each assigned exercise in Chapter 11. Use the forms provided in this SGWP. The objectives covered by an exercise are given after the exercise number. If you need help with an exercise, review the portion of the chapter related to the objective(s) covered.

❑ **Problems A/B**   Complete each assigned problem in Chapter 11. Use the forms provided in this SGWP. The objectives covered by a problem are given after the problem number. If you need help with a problem, review the portion of the chapter related to the objective(s) covered.

❑ **Critical Thinking Problems**   Complete the critical thinking problems as assigned. Use the forms provided in this SGWP.

❑ **Business Connections**   Complete the Business Connections activities as assigned to gain a deeper understanding of Chapter 11 concepts.

Practice Tests

Complete the Practice Tests, which cover the main points in your reading assignment. Compare your answers with those in the Practice Test Answer Key for Chapter 11 at the end of this chapter. If you have answered any questions incorrectly, review the related section of the text.

Part A True-False

For each of the following statements, circle T in the answer column if the statement is true or F if the statement is false.

T F **1.** Employers with a small number of employees are frequently required to deposit the entire amount of estimated workers' compensation insurance premiums early in the year.

T F **2.** The credit against the federal unemployment tax is the amount actually paid to the state under its unemployment compensation insurance program.

T F **3.** The premium on workers' compensation insurance is based on the federal unemployment tax.

T F **4.** Premiums on workers' compensation insurance vary with the type of work performed by employees.

T F **5.** The federal unemployment tax for the year is based on an audit of the payroll for the year.

T F **6.** Under a typical state plan, the federal government actually receives 0.8 percent of the taxable wages because the employer is allowed credits for payments made to the state.

T F **7.** The federal government grants a lower federal unemployment rate under an experience rating system to those employers who provide stable employment.

T F **8.** Most states allow a credit against the FUTA for amounts paid to the federal government as SUTA.

T F **9.** The employer's payroll taxes are usually recorded at the end of each payroll period, even though the cash will not be paid out until later.

T F **10.** A business firm pays income tax withholding at the same rate and on the same taxable wages as employees.

T F **11.** During the month immediately following the close of each calendar quarter, an employer is required to file a quarterly tax report and pay in or deposit any balance owed for social security and Medicare taxes and employees' income tax withheld.

T F **12.** On each date of payment of an employee's wages, the employer must provide the employee with a statement, on Form W-2, of earnings and taxes withheld.

T F **13.** Employees' individual earnings records provide much of the information needed to prepare the Employer's Quarterly Federal Tax Return, Form 941.

T F **14.** Only the amount of each employee's earnings up to $7,000 each year is subject to the social security tax.

T F **15.** Payments of social security tax, Medicare tax, and employee income tax withheld may be deposited, without penalty, in an authorized depository at any time up to January 31 of the following year.

T F **16.** The employee must attach a Form W-3 to his or her federal income tax return.

T F **17.** Each employer subject to the Federal Unemployment Compensation Tax Act must file an annual return on Form 940 by January 15 of the following year.

T F **18.** Social security taxes are paid by the employer but not the employee.

Part B Matching

For each number item, choose the matching term from the box and write the identifying letter in the answer column.

_____	**1.** A tax borne equally by the employer and employee.
_____	**2.** A tax paid solely by the employer.
_____	**3.** An IRS publication containing tax rates and other information about payroll taxes.
_____	**4.** Plan providing benefits to employees who are injured or become ill on the job.
_____	**5.** A plan under which the SUTA is adjusted to reflect the unemployment experience of the employer.
_____	**6.** A yearly form sent to the U.S. government summarizing earnings and payroll taxes withheld for the year.
_____	**7.** A statement of earnings and deductions for each employee.
_____	**8.** A deposit "coupon" accompanying the employer's deposit of taxes in a commercial bank.
_____	**9.** An annual report to the federal government summarizing the employer's unemployment compensation tax for the year.
_____	**10.** A quarterly report to the federal government summarizing taxable wages and payroll taxes due for the quarter.

a. Workers' compensation

b. Form 8109

c. Form 941

d. Form 940

e. Form W-3

f. Form W-2

g. Experience rating system

h. Publication 15, Circular E

i. Federal unemployment tax

j. Medicare tax

Demonstration Problem

The payroll register of the Express Printing and Copy Center showed employee earnings of $15,560 for the month ended January 31, 2013. Employee income tax withholding was $3,900. Use a social security rate of 6.2%, Medicare rate of 1.45% FUTA rate of 0.8% and SUTA rate of 5.4%. Assure all earnings are subject to these taxes.

Instructions

1. Compute the employees' social security and Medicare taxes.

2. Record the payroll for January in the general journal, page 3.

3. Compute the employer's payroll taxes for the period.

4. Prepare a general journal entry to record the employer's payroll taxes for the period.

5. Prepare a general journal entry to record the February 4 deposit of the social security, Medicare, and employee income taxes for the month.

SOLUTION

CALCULATION OF EMPLOYEE TAXES

Social security: 0.062 × $15,560	$964.72
Medicare: 0.0145 × $15,560	225.62
	$1,190.34

CALCULATION OF EMPLOYER TAXES

Social security: 0.062 × $15,560	$964.72
Medicare: 0.0145 × $15,560	225.62
FUTA: 0.008 × $15,560	124.48
SUTA: 0.054 × $15,560	840.24
	$2,155.06

SOLUTION (continued)

GENERAL JOURNAL   PAGE ___3___

	DATE		DESCRIPTION	POST. REF.	DEBIT	CREDIT	
1	2013						1
2	Jan.	31	Salaries Expense		15 5 6 0 00		2
3			Social Security Tax Payable			9 6 4 72	3
4			Medicare Tax Payable			2 2 5 62	4
5			Employee Income Tax Payable			3 9 0 0 00	5
6			Salaries Payable			10 4 6 9 66	6
7			Payroll for January				7
8							8
9		31	Payroll Tax Expense		2 1 5 5 06		9
10			Social Security Tax Payable			9 6 4 72	10
11			Medicare Tax Payable			2 2 5 62	11
12			Federal Unemployment Tax Payable			1 2 4 48	12
13			State Unemployment Tax Payable			8 4 0 24	13
14			Payroll for January				14
15							15
16	Feb.	4	Social Security Tax Payable		1 9 2 9 44		16
17			Medicare Tax Payable		4 5 1 24		17
18			Employee Income Tax Payable		3 9 0 0 00		18
19			Cash			6 2 8 0 68	19
20			Deposit of payroll taxes withholding				20
21							21
22							22
23							23
24							24
25							25
26							26
27							27
28							28
29							29
30							30
31							31
32							32
33							33
34							34
35							35
36							36
37							37
38							38

WORKING PAPERS

Name _____

EXERCISE 11.1

_____
_____
_____
_____
_____

EXERCISE 11.2

GENERAL JOURNAL

PAGE _____

	DATE		DESCRIPTION	POST. REF.	DEBIT	CREDIT	
1							1
2							2
3							3
4							4
5							5
6							6
7							7

EXERCISE 11.3

TAX	BASE	RATE	AMOUNT
_____	_____	_____	_____
_____	_____	_____	_____
_____	_____	_____	_____
_____	_____	_____	_____

EXERCISE 11.4

GENERAL JOURNAL

PAGE _____

	DATE		DESCRIPTION	POST. REF.	DEBIT	CREDIT	
1							1
2							2
3							3
4							4
5							5
6							6
7							7

EXERCISE 11.5

_____

_____

_____

EXERCISE 11.6

GENERAL JOURNAL   PAGE _____

	DATE	DESCRIPTION	POST. REF.	DEBIT	CREDIT	
1						1
2						2
3						3
4						4
5						5
6						6
7						7

EXERCISE 11.7

_____

_____

_____

_____

EXERCISE 11.8

WORK CLASSIFICATION	ESTIMATED EARNINGS	RATE	ESTIMATED PREMIUM
_____	_____	_____	_____
_____	_____	_____	_____
_____	_____	_____	_____

PROBLEM 11.1A or 11.1B

TAX	BASE	RATE	AMOUNT
_____	_____	_____	_____
_____	_____	_____	_____
_____	_____	_____	_____
_____	_____	_____	_____
_____	_____	_____	_____

GENERAL JOURNAL

PAGE __28__

	DATE	DESCRIPTION	POST. REF.	DEBIT	CREDIT	
1						1
2						2
3						3
4						4
5						5
6						6
7						7
8						8
9						9
10						10
11						11
12						12

Analyze: _____

PROBLEM 11.2A or 11.2B

GENERAL JOURNAL   PAGE _____

	DATE		DESCRIPTION	POST. REF.	DEBIT	CREDIT	
1							1
2							2
3							3
4							4
5							5
6							6
7							7
8							8
9							9
10							10
11							11
12							12
13							13
14							14
15							15
16							16
17							17
18							18
19							19
20							20
21							21
22							22
23							23
24							24
25							25
26							26
27							27
28							28
29							29
30							30
31							31
32							32
33							33

Analyze: _____

_____

PROBLEM 11.3A or 11.3B

GENERAL JOURNAL   PAGE _____

	DATE		DESCRIPTION	POST. REF.	DEBIT	CREDIT	
1							1
2							2
3							3
4							4
5							5
6							6
7							7
8							8
9							9
10							10
11							11
12							12
13							13
14							14
15							15
16							16
17							17
18							18
19							19
20							20
21							21
22							22
23							23
24							24
25							25
26							26
27							27
28							28
29							29
30							30
31							31
32							32
33							33

Analyze: _____

_____

PROBLEM 11.3A or 11.3B (continued)

Form **941 for 2013:** Employer's Quarterly Federal Tax Return

9901

(Rev. January 2005)

Department of the Treasury — Internal Revenue Service

OMB No. 1545-0029

Employer identification number ☐☐ – ☐☐☐☐☐☐☐

Name (not your trade name) _____

Trade name (if any) _____

Address _____

| Number | Street | | Suite or room number |

| City | | State | ZIP code |

Report for this Quarter ...
(Check one.)

☐ **1:** January, February, March

☒ **2:** April, May, June

☐ **3:** July, August, September

☐ **4:** October, November, December

Read the separate instructions before you fill out this form. Please type or print within the boxes.

Part 1: Answer these questions for this quarter.

1 Number of employees who received wages, tips, or other compensation for the pay period including: *Mar. 12* (Quarter 1), *June 12* (Quarter 2), *Sept. 12* (Quarter 3), *Dec. 12* (Quarter 4) **1** ☐

2 Wages, tips, and other compensation . . . . **2** ☐ .

3 Total income tax withheld from wages, tips, and other compensation . . . . . **3** ☐ .

4 If no wages, tips, and other compensation are subject to social security or Medicare tax . ☐ Check and go to line 6.

5 Taxable social security and Medicare wages and tips:

	Column 1		Column 2
5a Taxable social security wages	☐ .	$\times$ .124 =	☐ .
5b Taxable social security tips	☐ .	$\times$ .124 =	☐ .
5c Taxable Medicare wages & tips	☐ .	$\times$ .029 =	☐ .

5d Total social security and Medicare taxes (*Column 2*, lines 5a + 5b + 5c = line 5d) . **5d** ☐ .

6 Total taxes before adjustments (lines 3 + 5d = line 6) . . . . **6** ☐ .

7 Tax adjustments (If your answer is a negative number, write it in brackets.):

7a Current quarter's fractions of cents . . . . ☐ .

7b Current quarter's sick pay . . . . ☐ .

7c Current quarter's adjustments for tips and group-term life insurance ☐ .

7d Current year's income tax withholding (Attach Form 941c) . . ☐ .

7e Prior quarters' social security and Medicare taxes (Attach Form 941c) ☐ .

7f Special additions to federal income tax (reserved use) . . . . ☐ .

7g Special additions to social security and Medicare (reserved use) ☐ .

7h Total adjustments (Combine all amounts: lines 7a through 7g.) . . . . . . **7h** ☐ .

8 Total taxes after adjustments (Combine lines 6 and 7h.) . . . . **8** ☐ .

9 Advance earned income credit (EIC) payments made to employees . . . . . . **9** ☐ .

10 Total taxes after adjustment for advance EIC (lines 8 – 9 = line 10) . . . . . **10** ☐ .

11 Total deposits for this quarter, including overpayment applied from a prior quarter . . **11** ☐ .

12 Balance due (lines 10 – 11 = line 12) Make checks payable to the *United States Treasury* . **12** ☐ .

13 Overpayment (If line 11 is more than line 10, write the difference here.) ☐ . Check one ☐ Apply to next return.
☐ Send a refund.

Next ➡

For Privacy Act and Paperwork Reduction Act Notice, see the back of the Payment Voucher.

Cat. No. 17001Z   Form **941**

PROBLEM 11.3A or 11.3B (continued)

9902

Name (not your trade name)	Employer identification number

Part 2: Tell us about your deposit schedule for this quarter.

If you are unsure about whether you are a monthly schedule depositor or a semiweekly schedule depositor, see *Pub. 15 (Circular E)*, section 11.

14 ☐☐ Write the state abbreviation for the state where you made your deposits OR write "MU" if you made your deposits in *multiple* states.

15 Check one: ☐ Line 10 is less than $2,500. Go to Part 3.

☐ You were a monthly schedule depositor for the entire quarter. Fill out your tax liability for each month. Then go to Part 3.

Tax liability: Month 1 [_____ . __]

Month 2 [_____ . __]

Month 3 [_____ . __]

Total [_____ . __] Total must equal line 10.

☐ You were a semiweekly schedule depositor for any part of this quarter. Fill out *Schedule B (Form 941): Report of Tax Liability for Semiweekly Schedule Depositors*, and attach it to this form.

Part 3: Tell us about your business. If a question does NOT apply to your business, leave it blank.

16 If your business has closed and you do not have to file returns in the future . . . . ☐ Check here, and

enter the final date you paid wages [___ / ___ / ___] .

17 If you are a seasonal employer and you do not have to file a return for every quarter of the year . ☐ Check here.

Part 4: May we contact your third-party designee?

Do you want to allow an employee, a paid tax preparer, or another person to discuss this return with the IRS? See the instructions for details.

☐ Yes. Designee's name [_____]

Phone (___) ___ – ___ Personal Identification Number (PIN) ☐☐☐☐☐

☐ No.

Part 5: Sign here

Under penalties of perjury, I declare that I have examined this return, including accompanying schedules and statements, and to the best of my knowledge and belief, it is true, correct, and complete.

X

Sign your name here [_____]

Print name and title [_____]

Date [___ / ___ / ___] Phone (___) ___ – ___

Part 6: For paid preparers only (optional)

Preparer's signature [_____]

Firm's name [_____]

Address [_____] EIN [_____]

[_____] ZIP code [_____]

Date [___ / ___ / ___] Phone (___) ___ – ___ SSN/PTIN [_____]

☐ Check if you are self-employed.

Page **2**

Form **941**

PROBLEM 11.4A or 11.4B

_____

_____

_____

GENERAL JOURNAL

PAGE _____

	DATE	DESCRIPTION	POST. REF.	DEBIT	CREDIT	
1						1
2						2
3						3
4						4
5						5
6						6
7						7
8						8
9						9
10						10
11						11
12						12
13						13
14						14
15						15
16						16
17						17
18						18
19						19
20						20
21						21
22						22
23						23
24						24
25						25
26						26
27						27
28						28
29						29

Analyze: _____

_____

PROBLEM 11.5A or 11.5B

GENERAL JOURNAL

PAGE _____

	DATE		DESCRIPTION	POST. REF.	DEBIT	CREDIT	
1							1
2							2
3							3
4							4
5							5
6							6
7							7
8							8
9							9
10							10
11							11
12							12
13							13
14							14
15							15
16							16
17							17
18							18
19							19
20							20
21							21
22							22
23							23
24							24
25							25
26							26
27							27
28							28
29							29
30							30
31							31
32							32
33							33
34							34

Analyze: _____

_____

Name _____

Form **940-EZ**	**Employer's Annual Federal Unemployment (FUTA) Tax Return**	OMB No. 1545-1110
Department of the Treasury Internal Revenue Service	▶ See the separate Instructions for Form 940-EZ for information on completing this form.	**2013**

	T	
	FF	
	FD	
	FP	
	I	
	T	

You must complete this section. ▶

Name (as distinguished from trade name)	Calendar year
Trade name, if any	Employer identification number (EIN)
Address (number and street)	City, state, and ZIP code

*Answer the questions under **Who May Use Form 940-EZ** on page 2. If you cannot use Form 940-EZ, you must use Form 940.*

A Enter the amount of contributions paid to your state unemployment fund (see the separate instructions) . ▶ $ _____ |

B (1) Enter the name of the state where you have to pay contributions . . . . ▶ _____
  (2) Enter your state reporting number as shown on your state unemployment tax return ▶

If you will not have to file returns in the future, check here (see Who Must File in separate instructions) **and complete and sign the return.** ▶ ☐

If this is an Amended Return, check here (see Amended Returns in the separate instructions) . . . . ▶ ☐

Part I Taxable Wages and FUTA Tax

1	Total payments (including payments shown on lines 2 and 3) during the calendar year for services of employees	**1**	
2	Exempt payments. (Explain all exempt payments, attaching additional sheets if necessary.) ▶ _____ _____	**2**	
3	Payments of more than $7,000 for services. Enter only amounts over the first $7,000 paid to each employee **(see the separate instructions)**	**3**	
4	Add lines 2 and 3	**4**	
5	**Total taxable wages** (subtract line 4 from line 1) . . . . ▶	**5**	
6	**FUTA tax.** Multiply the wages on line 5 by .008 and enter here. **(If the result is over $100, also complete Part II.)**	**6**	
7	Total FUTA tax deposited for the year, including any overpayment applied from a prior year	**7**	
8	**Balance due** (subtract line 7 from line 6). Pay to the "United States Treasury." . . . . ▶	**8**	
	If you owe more than $100, see **Depositing FUTA tax** in the separate instructions.		
9	**Overpayment** (subtract line 6 from line 7). Check if it is to be: ☐ **Applied to next return** or ☐ **Refunded** ▶	**9**	

Part II Record of Quarterly Federal Unemployment Tax Liability (Do not include state liability.) Complete only if line 6 is over $100.

Quarter	First (Jan. 1 – Mar. 31)	Second (Apr. 1 – June 30)	Third (July 1 – Sept. 30)	Fourth (Oct. 1 – Dec. 31)	Total for year
Liability for quarter					

Third–Party Designee	Do you want to allow another person to discuss this return with the IRS (see the separate instructions)? ☐ **Yes.** Complete the following. ☐ **No**

| Designee's name ▶ | Phone no. ▶ ( ) | Personal identification number (PIN) ▶ | | | | | |

Under penalties of perjury, I declare that I have examined this return, including accompanying schedules and statements, and, to the best of my knowledge and belief, it is true, correct, and complete, and that no part of any payment made to a state unemployment fund claimed as a credit was, or is to be, deducted from the payments to employees.

Signature ▶ _____ Title (Owner, etc.) ▶ _____ Date ▶ _____

▼ **DETACH HERE** ▼   Cat. No. 10983G   Form **940-EZ**

- -

Form **940-V(EZ)**	**Payment Voucher**	OMB No. 1545-1110
Department of the Treasury Internal Revenue Service	Use this voucher only when making a payment with your return.	**2013**

Complete boxes 1, 2, and 3. Do not send cash, and do not staple your payment to this voucher. Make your check or money order payable to the "United States Treasury." Be sure to enter your employer identification number (EIN), "Form 940-EZ," and "2004" on your payment.

1 Enter your employer identification number (EIN).	2 **Enter the amount of your payment.** ▶	Dollars	Cents
	3 Enter your business name (individual name for sole proprietors).		
	Enter your address.		
	Enter your city, state, and ZIP code.		

PROBLEM 11.6A or 11.6B

WORK CLASSIFICATION	ESTIMATED EARNINGS	INSURANCE RATE	ESTIMATED PREMIUMS

WORK CLASSIFICATION	ACTUAL EARNINGS	INSURANCE RATE	ACTUAL PREMIUMS

PROBLEM 11.6A or 11.6B (continued)

GENERAL JOURNAL   PAGE _____

	DATE		DESCRIPTION	POST. REF.	DEBIT	CREDIT	
1							1
2							2
3							3
4							4
5							5
6							6
7							7
8							8
9							9
10							10
11							11
12							12
13							13
14							14
15							15
16							16
17							17
18							18
19							19

Analyze: _____

_____

CRITICAL THINKING PROBLEM 11.1

1. _____

_____

2. _____

_____

3. _____

4. _____

_____

5. _____

_____

Analyze: _____

_____

CRITICAL THINKING PROBLEM 11.2

1. _____

_____

_____

_____

2.   YEARLY COST—CURRENT SYSTEM

_____

_____

_____

_____

_____

_____

_____

_____

_____

_____

_____

_____

_____

CRITICAL THINKING PROBLEM 11.2 (continued)

YEARLY COST—PROPOSED SYSTEM

_____

_____

_____

_____

_____

_____

_____

_____

_____

_____

_____

_____

_____

_____

3. _____

_____

_____

_____

_____

Chapter 11 Practice Test Answer Key

Part A True-False		Part B Matching
1. T	10. F	1. j
2. F	11. T	2. i
3. F	12. F	3. h
4. T	13. T	4. a
5. F	14. F	5. g
6. T	15. F	6. e
7. F	16. F	7. f
8. F	17. F	8. b
9. T	18. F	9. d
		10. c

STUDY GUIDE

Understanding the Chapter

Objectives	**1.** Determine the adjustment for merchandise inventory and enter the adjustment on the worksheet. **2.** Compute adjustments for accrued and prepaid expense items and enter the adjustments on the worksheet. **3.** Compute adjustments for accrued and deferred income items and enter the adjustments on the worksheet. **4.** Complete a ten-column worksheet. **5.** Define the accounting terms new to this chapter.
Reading Assignment	Read Chapter 12 in the textbook. Complete the textbook Section Self Review as you finish reading each section of the chapter, and the Comprehensive Self Review at the end of the chapter. Refer to the Chapter 12 Glossary or to the Glossary at the end of the book to find definitions for terms that are not familiar to you.

Activities

❏ **Thinking Critically**	Answer the *Thinking Critically* questions for Urban Outfitters and Managerial Implications.
❏ **Discussion Questions**	Answer each assigned discussion question in Chapter 12.
❏ **Exercises**	Complete each assigned exercise in Chapter 12. Use the forms provided in this SGWP. The objectives covered by an exercise are given after the exercise number. If you need help with an exercise, review the portion of the chapter related to the objective(s) covered.
❏ **Problems A/B**	Complete each assigned problem in Chapter 12. Use the forms provided in this SGWP. The objectives covered by a problem are given after the problem number. If you need help with a problem, review the portion of the chapter related to the objective(s) covered.
❏ **Critical Thinking Problems**	Complete the critical thinking problems as assigned. Use the forms provided in this SGWP.
❏ **Business Connections**	Complete the Business Connections activities as assigned to gain a deeper understanding of Chapter 12 concepts.

Practice Tests

Complete the Practice Tests, which cover the main points in your reading assignment. Compare your answers with those in the Practice Test Answer Key for Chapter 12 at the end of this chapter. If you have answered any questions incorrectly, review the related section of the text.

T   F   **1.** After the amounts shown in the Adjusted Trial Balance section have been extended, the difference between the total debits and total credits in the balance sheet section represents the net income or loss for the period.

T   F   **2.** The Adjusted Trial Balance column of the worksheet tests only the arithmetic accuracy of the worksheet to that point in the worksheet and statement preparation process.

T   F   **3.** The accountant completes the worksheet and prepares the financial statements as soon as all adjustments have been entered on the worksheet.

T   F   **4.** The net income for the business is entered as a debit entry in the Balance Sheet section and as a credit entry in the Income Statement section of the worksheet.

T   F   **5.** Office or store supplies that have been paid for in cash do not need any adjusting entries.

T   F   **6.** An adjustment for depreciation results in an entry debiting the **Depreciation Expense** account and crediting the **Equipment** account.

T   F   **7.** On the trial balance, the **Store Supplies** account shows a debit balance of $300. A physical count showed supplies on hand of $80. The adjusting entry includes a debit of $80 to the **Store Supplies Expense** account.

T   F   **8.** At the end of an accounting period, an adjustment is needed to record as an expense any part of the balance in an asset account that has been used up or has expired.

T   F   **9.** The unadjusted trial balance figures for accumulated depreciation accounts do not include depreciation for the current period.

T   F   **10.** The **Unearned Subscriptions Income** account will appear in the Liabilities section of the balance sheet.

T   F   **11.** In the "adjustments" column of the worksheet, the **Merchandise Inventory** is debited for the amount of ending inventory and credited for the amount of beginning inventory.

T   F   **12.** Under the accrual basis of accounting, purchases are recorded after the purchase has been paid.

T   F   **13.** The **Interest Expense** account must be adjusted if an interest-bearing note payable is outstanding at the end of the fiscal period and interest has not been paid on that date.

T   F   **14.** In most cases, **Prepaid Interest Expense** will be classified in the Assets section on the balance sheet.

T   F   **15.** **Interest Receivable** is usually classified as a revenue account.

T   F   **16.** The entry to record accrued interest on notes payable is a debit to **Interest Expense** and a credit to **Interest Receivable.**

T   F   **17.** Deferred income has been earned but not recorded, while accrued income has been recorded but not earned.

T   F   **18.** Adjusting entries are recorded in the general journal after the worksheet and the financial statements are completed.

T   F   **19.** The beginning merchandise inventory does not appear in the Adjusted Trial Balance.

T   F   **20.** The **Drawing** account balance is extended to the Debit column in the Income Statement section.

T   F   **21.** The statement of owner's equity should be prepared after the income statement is prepared.

T   F   **22.** The financial statements are prepared directly from the worksheet.

T   F   **23.** In preparing financial statements, it is unnecessary to make adjustments for relatively small items because they are immaterial and will not affect the statements.

T   F   **24.** A prepaid expense incorrectly charged to expense in an accounting period results in an understatement of net income in that period and an overstatement of net income in the following period.

T   F   **25.** The accounts should be adjusted when preparing monthly or quarterly statements.

Part B Exercise *In each of the following independent cases give the general journal entry to adjust the accounts for the year on December 31, 2013. Omit the descriptions.*

1. Store supplies costing $1,600 were purchased during the year and were charged to the **Store Supplies** account. At the end of the year, supplies costing $400 were on hand.

GENERAL JOURNAL   PAGE _____

	DATE	DESCRIPTION	POST. REF.	DEBIT	CREDIT	
1						1
2						2

2. On December 1, 2013 the company gave a $4,000 note payable to a supplier. The note bears interest at 6 percent.

GENERAL JOURNAL   PAGE _____

	DATE	DESCRIPTION	POST. REF.	DEBIT	CREDIT	
1						1
2						2

3. On October 1, 2013, the company received a four-month, 8 percent note for $3,500 from settlement of an overdue account. No interest has been recorded on the note.

GENERAL JOURNAL   PAGE _____

	DATE	DESCRIPTION	POST. REF.	DEBIT	CREDIT	
1						1
2						2

4. On November 1, 2013, the company purchased a one-year insurance policy for $2,400. The amount was charged to **Prepaid Insurance.**

GENERAL JOURNAL   PAGE _____

	DATE	DESCRIPTION	POST. REF.	DEBIT	CREDIT	
1						1
2						2

5. During 2013, the Irvine Quakes minor league hockey team received $900,000 from the sale of season tickets for 20 home games. The Unearned Season Tickets Income account was credited upon receipt of the cash. As of December 31, 8 home games had been played.

GENERAL JOURNAL   PAGE _____

	DATE	DESCRIPTION	POST. REF.	DEBIT	CREDIT	
1						1
2						2

Demonstration Problem

The trial balance for Pietro's Imports on December 31, 2013, the end of its accounting period, is shown on the worksheet.

Instructions

1. Complete the worksheet for the year, using the following information:

   a-b. Ending merchandise inventory, $108,570.

   c. Uncollectible accounts expense, $1,900.

   d. Supplies on hand December 31, $680.

   e. Depreciation on store equipment, $8,100.

   f. Depreciation on office equipment, $3,050.

   g. Accrued sales salaries, $4,000; accrued office salaries, $750.

   h. Tax on accrued salaries: social security, $294.50; Medicare, $68.88.

2. Journalize the adjusting entries on page 16 of the general journal.

SOLUTION

Pietro's Imports

Worksheet

December 31, 2013

	ACCOUNT NAME	TRIAL BALANCE DEBIT	TRIAL BALANCE CREDIT	ADJUSTMENTS DEBIT	ADJUSTMENTS CREDIT
1	Cash	39 810 00			
2	Accounts Receivable	32 340 00			
3	Allowance for Doubtful Accounts		5 060 00		(c) 1 900 00
4	Merchandise Inventory	116 780 00		(b)108 570 00	(a)116 780 00
5	Supplies	10 600 00			(d) 9 920 00
6	Store Equipment	84 000 00			
7	Accumulated Depreciation—Store Equip.		16 590 00		(e) 8 100 00
8	Office Equipment	25 700 00			
9	Accumulated Depreciation—Office Equip.		7 033 00		(f) 3 050 00
10	Accounts Payable		22 560 00		
11	Salaries Payable				(g) 4 750 00
12	Social Security Tax Payable				(h) 2 94 50
13	Medicare Tax Payable				(h) 6 88
14	Pietro Canzone, Capital		230 764 00		
15	Pietro Canzone, Drawing	26 000 00			
16	Income Summary			(a)116 780 00	(b)108 570 00
17	Sales		424 642 00		
18	Sales Returns and Allowances	8 155 00			
19	Purchases	197 534 00			
20	Purchase Returns and Allowances		1 200 00		
21	Purchase Discounts		600 00		
22	Freight In	12 260 00			
23	Sales Salaries Expense	94 580 00		(g) 4 000 00	
24	Rent Expense	31 000 00			
25	Advertising Expense	12 045 00			
26	Supplies Expense			(d) 9 920 00	
27	Depreciation Expense—Store Equipment			(e) 8 100 00	
28	Office Salaries Expense	17 645 00		(g) 750 00	
29	Payroll Taxes Expense			(h) 3 63 38	
30	Depreciation Expense—Office Equipment			(f) 3 050 00	
31	Uncollectible Accounts Expense			(c) 1 900 00	
32		708 449 00	708 449 00	253 433 38	253 433 38
33	Net Income				
34					
35					

SOLUTION (continued)

ADJUSTED TRIAL BALANCE DEBIT	ADJUSTED TRIAL BALANCE CREDIT	INCOME STATEMENT DEBIT	INCOME STATEMENT CREDIT	BALANCE SHEET DEBIT	BALANCE SHEET CREDIT	
39 8 1 0 00				39 8 1 0 00		1
32 3 4 0 00				32 3 4 0 00		2
	6 9 6 0 00				6 9 6 0 00	3
108 5 7 0 00				108 5 7 0 00		4
6 8 0 00				6 8 0 00		5
84 0 0 0 00				84 0 0 0 00		6
	24 6 9 0 00				24 6 9 0 00	7
25 7 0 0 00				25 7 0 0 00		8
	10 0 8 3 00				10 0 8 3 00	9
	22 5 6 0 00				22 5 6 0 00	10
	4 7 5 0 00				4 7 5 0 00	11
	2 9 4 50				2 9 4 50	12
	6 8 88				6 8 88	13
	230 7 6 4 00				230 7 6 4 00	14
26 0 0 0 00				26 0 0 0 00		15
116 7 8 0 00	108 5 7 0 00	116 7 8 0 00	108 5 7 0 00			16
	424 6 4 2 00		424 6 4 2 00			17
8 1 5 5 00		8 1 5 5 00				18
197 5 3 4 00		197 5 3 4 00				19
	1 2 0 0 00		1 2 0 0 00			20
	6 0 0 00		6 0 0 00			21
12 2 6 0 00		12 2 6 0 00				22
98 5 8 0 00		98 5 8 0 00				23
31 0 0 0 00		31 0 0 0 00				24
12 0 4 5 00		12 0 4 5 00				25
9 9 2 0 00		9 9 2 0 00				26
8 1 0 0 00		8 1 0 0 00				27
18 3 9 5 00		18 3 9 5 00				28
3 6 3 38		3 6 3 38				29
3 0 5 0 00		3 0 5 0 00				30
1 9 0 0 00		1 9 0 0 00				31
835 1 8 2 38	835 1 8 2 38	518 0 8 2 38	535 0 1 2 00	317 1 0 0 00	300 1 7 0 38	32
		16 9 2 9 62			16 9 2 9 62	33
		535 0 1 2 00	535 0 1 2 00	317 1 0 0 00	317 1 0 0 00	34
						35

SOLUTION (continued)

GENERAL JOURNAL

	DATE		DESCRIPTION	POST. REF.	DEBIT	CREDIT	
1	2013						1
2			(a)				2
3	Dec.	31	Income Summary		116 7 8 0 00		3
4			Merchandise Inventory			116 7 8 0 00	4
5			Close beginning merchandise inventory				5
6			(b)				6
7		31	Merchandise Inventory		108 5 7 0 00		7
8			Income Summary			108 5 7 0 00	8
9			Record ending merchandise inventory				9
10			(c)				10
11		31	Uncollectible Accounts Expense		1 9 0 0 00		11
12			Allowance for Doubtful Accounts			1 9 0 0 00	12
13			Record estimated uncollectible accounts expense				13
14			(d)				14
15		31	Supplies Expense		9 9 2 0 00		15
16			Supplies			9 9 2 0 00	16
17			Record supplies used during year				17
18			(e)				18
19		31	Depreciation Expense—Store Equipment		8 1 0 0 00		19
20			Accumulated Depreciation—Store Equipment			8 1 0 0 00	20
21			Record depreciation on store equipment for year				21
22			(f)				22
23		31	Depreciation Expense—Office Equipment		3 0 5 0 00		23
24			Accumulated Depreciation—Office Equipment			3 0 5 0 00	24
25			Record depreciation on office equipment for year				25
26			(g)				26
27		31	Sales Salaries Expense		4 0 0 0 00		27
28			Office Salaries Expense		7 5 0 00		28
29			Salaries Payable			4 7 5 0 00	29
30			Record accrued salaries				30
31			(h)				31
32		31	Payroll Taxes Expense		3 6 3 38		32
33			Social Security Tax Payable			2 9 4 50	33
34			Medicare Tax Payable			6 8 88	34
35			Record accrued payroll taxes				35
36							36

WORKING PAPERS

Name _____

EXERCISE 12.1

GENERAL JOURNAL

PAGE _____

	DATE	DESCRIPTION	POST. REF.	DEBIT	CREDIT	
1						1
2						2
3						3
4						4
5						5
6						6
7						7

EXERCISE 12.2

_____

_____

_____

EXERCISE 12.3

GENERAL JOURNAL

PAGE _____

	DATE	DESCRIPTION	POST. REF.	DEBIT	CREDIT	
1						1
2						2
3						3
4						4
5						5
6						6
7						7
8						8
9						9
10						10
11						11
12						12
13						13
14						14
15						15
16						16
17						17
18						18

EXERCISE 12.4

GENERAL JOURNAL   PAGE _____

	DATE	DESCRIPTION	POST. REF.	DEBIT	CREDIT	
1						1
2						2
3						3
4						4
5						5
6						6
7						7
8						8
9						9
10						10
11						11
12						12
13						13

EXERCISE 12.5

GENERAL JOURNAL   PAGE _____

	DATE	DESCRIPTION	POST. REF.	DEBIT	CREDIT	
1						1
2						2
3						3
4						4
5						5
6						6
7						7
8						8

EXERCISE 12.6

GENERAL JOURNAL   PAGE _____

	DATE	DESCRIPTION	POST. REF.	DEBIT	CREDIT	
1						1
2						2
3						3
4						4

EXERCISE 12.7

GENERAL JOURNAL

PAGE _____

	DATE		DESCRIPTION	POST. REF.	DEBIT	CREDIT	
1							1
2							2
3							3
4							4
5							5
6							6
7							7
8							8
9							9
10							10
11							11
12							12
13							13

PROBLEM 12.1A or 12.1B

GENERAL JOURNAL

PAGE _____

	DATE	DESCRIPTION	POST. REF.	DEBIT	CREDIT	
1						1
2						2
3						3
4						4
5						5
6						6
7						7
8						8
9						9
10						10
11						11
12						12
13						13
14						14
15						15
16						16
17						17
18						18
19						19
20						20
21						21
22						22
23						23
24						24
25						25
26						26
27						27
28						28
29						29
30						30
31						31
32						32
33						33
34						34
35						35
36						36
37						37

PROBLEM 12.1A or 12.1B (continued)

GENERAL JOURNAL   PAGE _____

	DATE		DESCRIPTION	POST. REF.	DEBIT	CREDIT	
1							1
2							2
3							3
4							4
5							5
6							6
7							7
8							8
9							9
10							10
11							11
12							12
13							13
14							14
15							15
16							16
17							17
18							18
19							19
20							20
21							21
22							22
23							23
24							24
25							25
26							26
27							27
28							28
29							29
30							30
31							31
32							32
33							33
34							34

Analyze: _____

_____

PROBLEM 12.2A or 12.2B

GENERAL JOURNAL

	DATE		DESCRIPTION	POST. REF.	DEBIT	CREDIT	
1							1
2							2
3							3
4							4
5							5
6							6
7							7
8							8
9							9
10							10
11							11
12							12
13							13
14							14
15							15
16							16
17							17
18							18
19							19
20							20
21							21
22							22
23							23
24							24
25							25
26							26
27							27
28							28
29							29
30							30
31							31
32							32
33							33
34							34
35							35
36							36
37							37

PROBLEM 12.2A or 12.2B (continued)

	GENERAL JOURNAL			PAGE __2__

	DATE	DESCRIPTION	POST. REF.	DEBIT	CREDIT	
1						1
2						2
3						3
4						4
5						5
6						6
7						7
8						8
9						9
10						10
11						11
12						12
13						13
14						14
15						15
16						16
17						17
18						18
19						19
20						20
21						21
22						22
23						23
24						24
25						25
26						26
27						27
28						28
29						29
30						30
31						31
32						32
33						33
34						34

Analyze: _____

_____

PROBLEM 12.3A or 12.3B

	ACCOUNT NAME	TRIAL BALANCE		ADJUSTMENTS	
		DEBIT	CREDIT	DEBIT	CREDIT
1					
2					
3					
4					
5					
6					
7					
8					
9					
10					
11					
12					
13					
14					
15					
16					
17					
18					
19					
20					
21					
22					
23					
24					
25					
26					
27					
28					
29					
30					
31					
32					

PROBLEM 12.3A or 12.3B (continued)

		ADJUSTED TRIAL BALANCE				INCOME STATEMENT				BALANCE SHEET			
		DEBIT		CREDIT		DEBIT		CREDIT		DEBIT		CREDIT		
														1
														2
														3
														4
														5
														6
														7
														8
														9
														10
														11
														12
														13
														14
														15
														16
														17
														18
														19
														20
														21
														22
														23
														24
														25
														26
														27
														28
														29
														30
														31
														32

Analyze: _____

_____

PROBLEM 12.4A or 12.4B

	ACCOUNT NAME	TRIAL BALANCE		ADJUSTMENTS	
		DEBIT	CREDIT	DEBIT	CREDIT
1					
2					
3					
4					
5					
6					
7					
8					
9					
10					
11					
12					
13					
14					
15					
16					
17					
18					
19					
20					
21					
22					
23					
24					
25					
26					
27					
28					
29					
30					
31					
32					
33					
34					

PROBLEM 12.4A or 12.4B (continued)

ADJUSTED TRIAL BALANCE		INCOME STATEMENT		BALANCE SHEET		
DEBIT	CREDIT	DEBIT	CREDIT	DEBIT	CREDIT	
						1
						2
						3
						4
						5
						6
						7
						8
						9
						10
						11
						12
						13
						14
						15
						16
						17
						18
						19
						20
						21
						22
						23
						24
						25
						26
						27
						28
						29
						30
						31
						32
						33
						34

PROBLEM 12.4A or 12.4B (continued)

ACCOUNT NAME	TRIAL BALANCE		ADJUSTMENTS	
	DEBIT	CREDIT	DEBIT	CREDIT
1				
2				
3				
4				
5				
6				
7				
8				
9				
10				
11				
12				
13				
14				
15				
16				
17				
18				
19				
20				
21				
22				
23				
24				
25				
26				
27				
28				
29				
30				
31				
32				

PROBLEM 12.4A or 12.4B (continued)

	ADJUSTED TRIAL BALANCE		INCOME STATEMENT		BALANCE SHEET		
	DEBIT	CREDIT	DEBIT	CREDIT	DEBIT	CREDIT	
							1
							2
							3
							4
							5
							6
							7
							8
							9
							10
							11
							12
							13
							14
							15
							16
							17
							18
							19
							20
							21
							22
							23
							24
							25
							26
							27
							28
							29
							30
							31
							32

Analyze: _____

PROBLEM 12.5A or 12.5B

	ACCOUNT NAME	TRIAL BALANCE		ADJUSTMENTS	
		DEBIT	CREDIT	DEBIT	CREDIT
1					
2					
3					
4					
5					
6					
7					
8					
9					
10					
11					
12					
13					
14					
15					
16					
17					
18					
19					
20					
21					
22					
23					
24					
25					
26					
27					
28					
29					
30					
31					
32					
33					
34					

PROBLEM 12.5A or 12.5B (continued)

	ADJUSTED TRIAL BALANCE		INCOME STATEMENT		BALANCE SHEET		
	DEBIT	CREDIT	DEBIT	CREDIT	DEBIT	CREDIT	
							1
							2
							3
							4
							5
							6
							7
							8
							9
							10
							11
							12
							13
							14
							15
							16
							17
							18
							19
							20
							21
							22
							23
							24
							25
							26
							27
							28
							29
							30
							31
							32
							33
							34

PROBLEM 12.5A or 12.5B (continued)

	ACCOUNT NAME	TRIAL BALANCE		ADJUSTMENTS	
		DEBIT	CREDIT	DEBIT	CREDIT
1					
2					
3					
4					
5					
6					
7					
8					
9					
10					
11					
12					
13					
14					
15					
16					
17					
18					
19					
20					
21					
22					
23					
24					
25					
26					
27					
28					
29					
30					
31					
32					

PROBLEM 12.5A or 12.5B (continued)

_____

_____

	ADJUSTED TRIAL BALANCE		INCOME STATEMENT		BALANCE SHEET		
	DEBIT	CREDIT	DEBIT	CREDIT	DEBIT	CREDIT	
							1
							2
							3
							4
							5
							6
							7
							8
							9
							10
							11
							12
							13
							14
							15
							16
							17
							18
							19
							20
							21
							22
							23
							24
							25
							26
							27
							28
							29
							30
							31
							32

Analyze: _____

_____

PROBLEM 12.6A or 12.6B

	ACCOUNT NAME	TRIAL BALANCE		ADJUSTMENTS	
		DEBIT	CREDIT	DEBIT	CREDIT
1					
2					
3					
4					
5					
6					
7					
8					
9					
10					
11					
12					
13					
14					
15					
16					
17					
18					
19					
20					
21					
22					
23					
24					
25					
26					
27					
28					
29					
30					
31					
32					
33					
34					
35					

PROBLEM 12.6A or 12.6B (continued)

ADJUSTED TRIAL BALANCE		INCOME STATEMENT		BALANCE SHEET		
DEBIT	CREDIT	DEBIT	CREDIT	DEBIT	CREDIT	
						1
						2
						3
						4
						5
						6
						7
						8
						9
						10
						11
						12
						13
						14
						15
						16
						17
						18
						19
						20
						21
						22
						23
						24
						25
						26
						27
						28
						29
						30
						31
						32
						33
						34
						35

CRITICAL THINKING PROBLEM 12.1

_____
_____

	ACCOUNT NAME	TRIAL BALANCE		ADJUSTMENTS	
		DEBIT	CREDIT	DEBIT	CREDIT
1					
2					
3					
4					
5					
6					
7					
8					
9					
10					
11					
12					
13					
14					
15					
16					
17					
18					
19					
20					
21					
22					
23					
24					
25					
26					
27					
28					
29					
30					
31					
32					
33					

CRITICAL THINKING PROBLEM 12.1 (continued)

_____

_____

ADJUSTED TRIAL BALANCE		INCOME STATEMENT		BALANCE SHEET		
DEBIT	CREDIT	DEBIT	CREDIT	DEBIT	CREDIT	
						1
						2
						3
						4
						5
						6
						7
						8
						9
						10
						11
						12
						13
						14
						15
						16
						17
						18
						19
						20
						21
						22
						23
						24
						25
						26
						27
						28
						29
						30
						31
						32
						33

CRITICAL THINKING PROBLEM 12.1 (continued)

	ACCOUNT NAME	TRIAL BALANCE		ADJUSTMENTS	
		DEBIT	CREDIT	DEBIT	CREDIT
1					
2					
3					
4					
5					
6					
7					
8					
9					
10					
11					
12					
13					
14					
15					
16					
17					
18					
19					
20					
21					
22					
23					
24					
25					
26					
27					
28					
29					
30					
31					
32					

CRITICAL THINKING PROBLEM 12.1 (continued)

ADJUSTED TRIAL BALANCE		INCOME STATEMENT		BALANCE SHEET		
DEBIT	CREDIT	DEBIT	CREDIT	DEBIT	CREDIT	
						1
						2
						3
						4
						5
						6
						7
						8
						9
						10
						11
						12
						13
						14
						15
						16
						17
						18
						19
						20
						21
						22
						23
						24
						25
						26
						27
						28
						29
						30
						31
						32

CRITICAL THINKING PROBLEM 12.1 (continued)

GENERAL JOURNAL

PAGE ___30___

	DATE	DESCRIPTION	POST. REF.	DEBIT	CREDIT	
1						1
2						2
3						3
4						4
5						5
6						6
7						7
8						8
9						9
10						10
11						11
12						12
13						13
14						14
15						15
16						16
17						17
18						18
19						19
20						20
21						21
22						22
23						23
24						24
25						25
26						26
27						27
28						28
29						29
30						30
31						31
32						32
33						33
34						34
35						35
36						36
37						37

CRITICAL THINKING PROBLEM 12.1 (continued)

GENERAL JOURNAL

	DATE		DESCRIPTION	POST. REF.	DEBIT	CREDIT	
1							1
2							2
3							3
4							4
5							5
6							6
7							7
8							8
9							9
10							10
11							11
12							12
13							13
14							14
15							15
16							16
17							17
18							18
19							19
20							20
21							21
22							22
23							23
24							24
25							25
26							26
27							27
28							28
29							29
30							30
31							31
32							32
33							33
34							34
35							35
36							36
37							37

CRITICAL THINKING PROBLEM 12.1 (continued)

a. Net Sales

_____

_____

_____

b. Net Delivered
Cost of Purchases

_____

_____

_____

_____

_____

_____

_____

c. Cost of Goods Sold

_____

_____

_____

_____

_____

d. Net Income
(from worksheet)

_____

_____

e. Capital,
December 31

_____

_____

_____

_____

Analyze: _____

_____

CRITICAL THINKING PROBLEM 12.2

1. _____

_____

_____

_____

2. _____

_____

_____

_____

_____

_____

_____

_____

_____

_____

_____

_____

_____

_____

_____

_____

_____

_____

_____

swer Key

	F
21.	T
22.	T
23.	F
24.	T
25.	T
	T

Part B Exercises

GENERAL JOURNAL

PAGE _____

	DATE		DESCRIPTION	POST. REF.	DEBIT	CREDIT	
1			**Adjusting Entries**				1
2	2013		(Adjustment 1)				2
3	Dec.	31	Supplies Expense		1 2 0 0 00		3
4			Store Supplies			1 2 0 0 00	4
5			(Adjustment 2)				5
6		31	Interest Expense		2 0 00		6
7			Interest Payable			2 0 00	7
8			(Adjustment 3)				8
9		31	Interest Receivable		7 0 00		9
10			Interest Income			7 0 00	10
11			(Adjustment 4)				11
12		31	Insurance Expense		4 0 0 00		12
13			Prepaid Insurance			4 0 0 00	13
14							14
15			(Adjustment 5)				15
		31	Unearned Season Tickets Income		360 0 0 0 00		
			Season Tickets Income			360 0 0 0 00	

Financial Statemen
and Closing
Procedures

STUDY GUIDE

Understanding the Chapter

Objectives	**1.** Prepare a classified income statement from the worksheet. **2.** Prepare a statement of owner's equity from the worksheet. **3.** Prepare a classified balance sheet from the worksheet. **4.** Journalize and post the adjusting entries. **5.** Journalize and post the closing entries. **6.** Prepare a postclosing trial balance. **7.** Journalize and post reversing entries. **8.** Define the accounting terms new to this chapter.
Reading Assignment	Read Chapter 13 in the textbook. Complete the textbook Section Self Review as you finish reading each section of the chapter, and the Comprehensive Self Review at the end of the chapter. Refer to the Chapter 13 Glossary or to the Glossary at the end of the book to find definitions for terms that are not familiar to you.

Activities

❏ **Thinking Critically**	Answer the *Thinking Critically* questions for Whole Foods Market and Managerial Implications.
❏ **Discussion Questions**	Answer each assigned discussion question in Chapter 13.
❏ **Exercises**	Complete each assigned exercise in Chapter 13. Use the forms provided in this SGWP. The objectives covered by an exercise are given after the exercise number. If you need help with an exercise, review the portion of the chapter related to the objective(s) covered.
❏ **Problems A/B**	Complete each assigned problem in Chapter 13. Use the forms provided in this SGWP. The objectives covered by a problem are given after the problem number. If you need help with a problem review the portion of the chapter related to the objective(s) covered.
❏ **Critical Thinking Problems**	Complete the critical thinking problems as assigned. Use the forms provided in this SGWP.
❏ **Business Connections**	Complete the Business Connections activities as assigned to gain a deeper understanding of Chapter 13 concepts.

Practice Tests

Complete the Practice Tests, which cover the main points in your reading assignment. Compare your answers with those in the Practice Test Answer Key for Chapter 13 at the end of this chapter. If you have answered any questions incorrectly, review the related section of text.

For each of the following statements, circle T in the answer column if the ~~rue~~ *or F if the statement is false.*

ported net sales of $1,000,000 and cost of goods sold of $600,000. The
ercentage is 60%.

counts adjusted in the Adjustment columns of the worksheet do not require
ing entry.

erest Payable** and **Depreciation Expense** are typical of accounts that do not
equire reversing entries.

. Cash, accounts receivable, merchandise inventory, and equipment are classified as
current assets.

5. Reversing entries are not required, but are highly recommended in order to improve
efficiency and reduce errors.

F   **6.** In closing the **Income Summary** account, the net income or loss is closed into the
owner's capital account.

T   **F**   **7.** Closing journal entries for December 31, 2013 should be reversed on January 1, 2014.

T   **F**   **8. Income Summary** is credited for the total of the expenses and the beginning inventory.

T   **F**   **9.** The ending merchandise inventory is recorded in the accounting records by an
adjusting entry.

T   **F**   **10.** Adjustments are posted from the worksheet to the general ledger accounts.

T   **F**   **11.** The depreciation expense for the store equipment appears in the Plant and
Equipment section of the classified balance sheet.

T   **F**   **12.** The net income or loss from operations shown on the classified income statement is
the difference between gross profit on sales and total operating expenses.

T   **F**   **13.** The Cost of Goods Sold section of the classified income statement includes
information about the beginning and ending merchandise inventory and the
purchases and net sales made during the year.

T   **F**   **14.** Current liabilities are debts that are due for payment after one year from the balance
sheet date.

T   **F**   **15.** The gross profit on sales shown on the classified income statement is the difference
between the net sales and the operating expenses.

T   **F**   **16.** Short-term notes receivable, cash, accounts receivable, merchandise inventory and
prepaid expense items appear in the Current Assets section of the classified balance sheet.

T   **F**   **17.** The postclosing trial balance shows essentially the same account balances that appear
in the balance sheet.

T   **F**   **18.** It is desirable to prepare a postclosing trial balance after the adjusting and closing
entries have been journalized and posted.

T   **F**   **19.** The **Income Summary** account is closed at the end of the period.

| T | F | **20.** | Asset, liability, and owner's capital accounts are the only accounts carried forward from one year to the next. |

| T | F | **21.** | The information needed to close the revenue and expense accounts is taken directly from the ledger accounts to ensure accuracy. |

| T | F | **22.** | The revenue and expense accounts are the only accounts carried forward from one year to the next. |

| T | F | **23.** | After all adjustments have been journalized and posted, the ledger account balances should be the same as the post-closing trial balance amounts. |

| T | F | **24.** | After completing the worksheet and the financial statements, adjustments are entered in the general journal. |

| T | F | **25.** | The drawing account is closed into the **Income Summary** account as one of the last closing entries. |

Demonstration Problem

A partial worksheet showing the end-of-year operating results for Sports Warehouse for 2013 follows.

Instructions

1. Prepare a classified income statement. Sports Warehouse does not classify its operating expenses as selling and administrative expenses.

2. Prepare a statement of owner's equity. No additional investments were made during the period.

3. Prepare a classified balance sheet as of December 31, 2013. All notes payable are due within one year.

4. Journalize the closing entries on page 45 of the general journal.

5. Compute the gross profit percentage for the year ended December 31, 2013. Round your answer to one decimal.

6. Compute the current ratio at December 31, 2013. Round your answer to two decimal places.

7. Compute the inventory turnover ratio for the year ended December 31, 2013. Round your answer to two decimal places.

Sports Warehouse

Worksheet (Partial)

Year Ended December 31, 2013

	ACCOUNT NAME	INCOME STATEMENT		BALANCE SHEET	
		DEBIT	CREDIT	DEBIT	CREDIT
1	Cash			24 2 8 5 00	
2	Accounts Receivable			61 2 5 8 00	
3	Allowance for Doubtful Accounts				5 9 3 0 00
4	Merchandise Inventory			197 2 1 4 00	
5	Supplies			3 5 1 2 00	
6	Prepaid Insurance			37 0 0 0 00	
7	Equipment			83 2 9 0 00	
8	Accumulated Depreciation—Equipment				24 3 3 0 00
9	Notes Payable				47 5 0 0 00
10	Accounts Payable				44 8 6 0 00
11	Social Security Tax Payable				2 6 8 3 00
12	Medicare Tax Payable				8 4 5 00
13	Salaries Payable				7 5 3 0 00
14	Interest Payable				3 6 6 0 00
15	Raul Flores, Capital				260 7 3 0 00
16	Raul Flores, Drawing			50 0 0 0 00	
17	Income Summary	201 3 4 5 00	197 2 1 4 00		
18	Sales		625 6 9 0 00		
19	Sales Returns and Allowances	11 9 5 0 00			
20	Purchases	280 1 7 4 00			
21	Purchases Returns and Allowances		10 4 4 0 00		
22	Freight In	11 4 1 0 00			
23	Purchases Discounts		11 9 2 1 00		
24	Telephone Expense	4 1 7 1 00			
25	Salaries Expense	241 3 8 0 00			
26	Payroll Tax Expense	13 1 0 4 00			
27	Supplies Expense	6 0 6 0 00			
28	Insurance Expense	5 0 0 0 00			
29	Depreciation Expense—Equipment	7 4 2 0 00			
30	Uncollectible Accounts Expense	2 6 0 0 00			
31	Interest Expense	2 1 6 0 00			
32	Totals	786 7 7 4 00	845 2 6 5 00	456 5 5 9 00	398 0 6 8 00
33	Net Income	58 4 9 1 00			58 4 9 1 00
34		845 2 6 5 00	845 2 6 5 00	456 5 5 9 00	456 5 5 9 00
35					

SOLUTION

(1.)

Sports Warehouse

Income Statement

Year Ended December 31, 2013

Operating Revenue					
Sales					625 6 9 0 00
Less Sales Returns and Allowances					11 9 5 0 00
Net Sales					613 7 4 0 00
Cost of Goods Sold					
Merchandise Inventory, Jan. 1, 2013				201 3 4 5 00	
Purchases		280 1 7 4 00			
Freight In		11 4 1 0 00			
Delivered Cost of Purchases		291 5 8 4 00			
Less Purchase Returns and Allow.	10 4 4 0 00				
Purchase Discounts	11 9 2 1 00	22 3 6 1 00			
Net Delivered Cost of Purchases				269 2 2 3 00	
Total Merchandise Available for Sale				470 5 6 8 00	
Less Merchandise Inv., Dec. 31, 2013				197 2 1 4 00	
Cost of Goods Sold					273 3 5 4 00
Gross Profit on Sales					340 3 8 6 00
Operating Expenses					
Telephone Expense				4 1 7 1 00	
Salaries Expense				241 3 8 0 00	
Payroll Tax Expense				13 1 0 4 00	
Supplies Expense				6 0 6 0 00	
Insurance Expense				5 0 0 0 00	
Depreciation Expense—Equipment				7 4 2 0 00	
Uncollectible Accounts Expense				2 6 0 0 00	
Total Operating Expenses					279 7 3 5 00
Income from Operations					60 6 5 1 00
Other Expenses					
Interest Expense					2 1 6 0 00
Net Income for Year					58 4 9 1 00

SOLUTION (continued)

(2.)

Sports Warehouse

Statement of Owner's Equity

Year Ended December 31, 2013

Raul Flores, Capital, Jan. 1, 2013		260 730 00
Net Income for Year	58 491 00	
Less Withdrawals for the Year	50 000 00	
Increase in Capital		8 491 00
Raul Flores, Capital, Dec. 31, 2013		269 221 00

(3.)

Sports Warehouse

Balance Sheet

December 31, 2013

Assets		
Current Assets		
Cash		24 285 00
Accounts Receivable	61 258 00	
Less Allowance for Doubtful Accounts	5 930 00	55 328 00
Merchandise Inventory		197 214 00
Prepaid Expenses		
Supplies	3 512 00	
Prepaid Insurance	37 000 00	40 512 00
Total Current Assets		317 339 00
Plant and Equipment		
Equipment	83 290 00	
Less Accumulated Depreciation	24 330 00	
Total Plant and Equipment		58 960 00
Total Assets		376 299 00
Liabilities and Owner's Equity		
Current Liabilities		
Notes Payable	47 500 00	
Accounts Payable	44 860 00	
Interest Payable	3 660 00	
Social Security Tax Payable	2 683 00	
Medicare Tax Payable	845 00	
Salaries Payable	7 530 00	
Total Current Liabilities		107 078 00
Owner's Equity		
Raul Flores, Capital		269 221 00
Total Liabilities and Owner's Equity		376 299 00

326 ■ Chapter 13

SOLUTION (continued)

(4.)

	DATE		DESCRIPTION	POST. REF.	DEBIT	CREDIT	
1			**Closing Entries**				1
2	**2010**						2
3	Dec.	31	Sales		625 6 9 0 00		3
4			Purchase Returns and Allowances		10 4 4 0 00		4
5			Purchases Discounts		11 9 2 1 00		5
6			Income Summary			648 0 5 1 00	6
7							7
8		31	Income Summary		585 4 2 9 00		8
9			Sales Returns and Allowances			11 9 5 0 00	9
10			Purchases			280 1 7 4 00	10
11			Freight In			11 4 1 0 00	11
12			Telephone Expense			4 1 7 1 00	12
13			Salaries Expense			241 3 8 0 00	13
14			Payroll Taxes Expense			13 1 0 4 00	14
15			Supplies Expense			6 0 6 0 00	15
16			Insurance Expense			5 0 0 0 00	16
17			Depreciation Expense—Equipment			7 4 2 0 00	17
18			Uncollectible Accounts Expense			2 6 0 0 00	18
19			Interest Expense			2 1 6 0 00	19
20							20
21		31	Income Summary		58 4 9 1 00		21
22			Raul Flores, Capital			58 4 9 1 00	22
23							23
24		31	Raul Flores, Capital		50 0 0 0 00		24
25			Raul Flores, Drawing			50 0 0 0 00	25
26							26
27							27
28							28
29							29
30							30
31							31
32							32
33							33
34							34
35							35

(5.) The gross profit percentage for the year ended December 31, 2013 is 55.5% ($340,386/$613,740).

(6.) The current ratio at December 31, 2013 is 2.96 ($317,339/$107,078).

(7.) The inventory turnover ratio for the year ended December 31, 2013 is 3.08 ($613,740/$199,279.50).

WORKING PAPERS

Name _____

EXERCISE 13.1

1. Purchases Returns
   and Allowances _____

2. Telephone Expense _____

3. Sales Returns and Allowances _____

4. Purchases _____

5. Interest Income _____

6. Merchandise Inventory _____

7. Interest Expense _____

8. Sales _____

9. Depreciation Expense—
   Store Equipment _____

10. Rent Expense _____

EXERCISE 13.2x

1. Accounts Receivable _____

2. Delivery Van _____

3. Prepaid Insurance _____

4. Notes Payable, due 2014 _____

5. Store Supplies _____

6. Accounts Payable _____

7. Merchandise Inventory _____

8. Ray Lynch, Capital _____

9. Cash _____

10. Unearned Subscription Income _____

EXERCISE 13.3

(continued)

Name

EXERCISE 13.3 (continued)

EXERCISE 13.4

EXERCISE 13.5

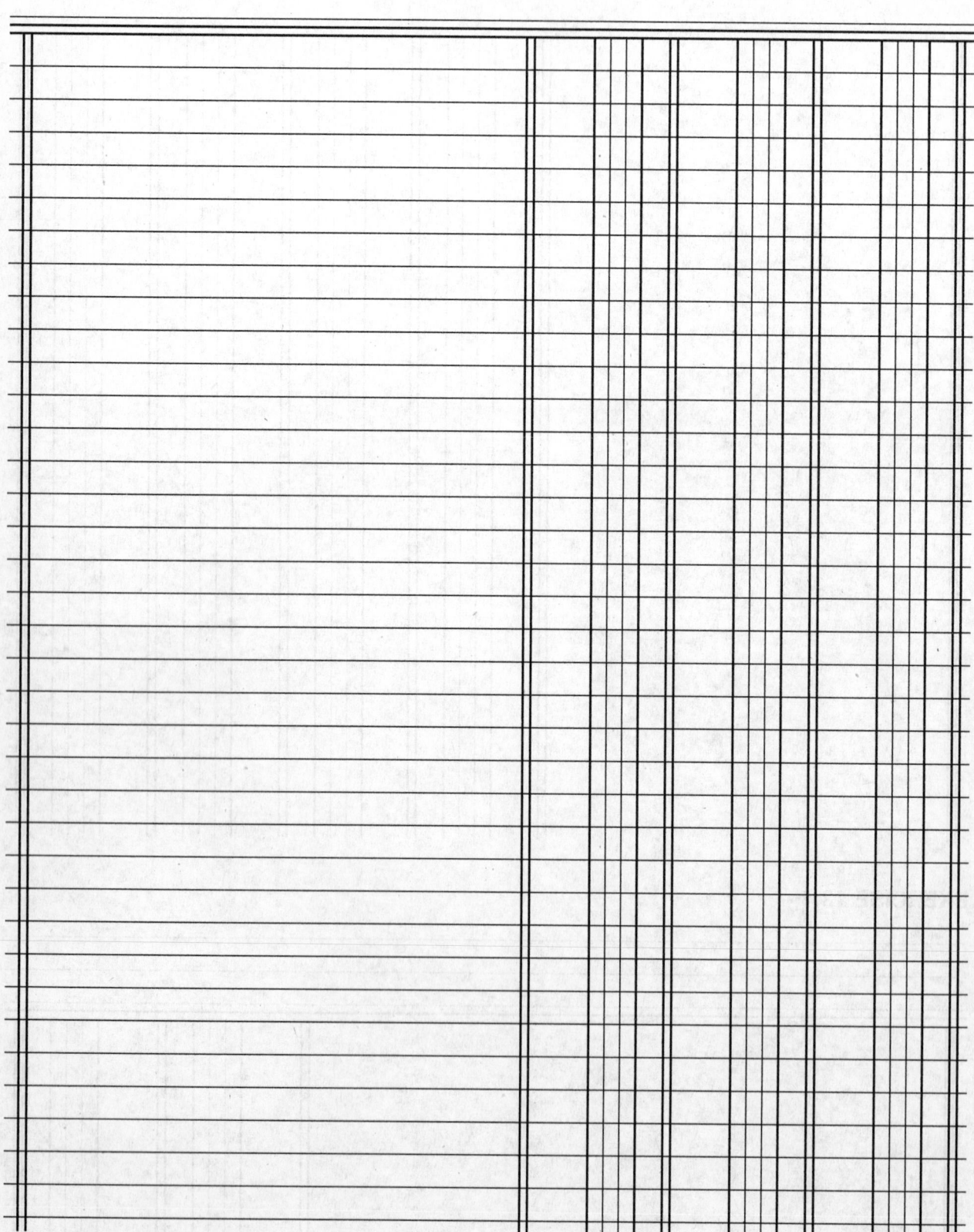

EXERCISE 13.6

GENERAL JOURNAL

PAGE _____

	DATE	DESCRIPTION	POST. REF.	DEBIT	CREDIT	
1						1
2						2
3						3
4						4
5						5
6						6
7						7
8						8
9						9
10						10
11						11
12						12
13						13
14						14
15						15
16						16
17						17
18						18
19						19
20						20
21						21
22						22
23						23
24						24
25						25
26						26
27						27
28						28
29						29
30						30
31						31
32						32
33						33
34						34
35						35
36						36
37						37

EXERCISE 13.7

GENERAL JOURNAL

PAGE _____

	DATE		DESCRIPTION	POST. REF.	DEBIT	CREDIT	
1							1
2							2
3							3
4							4
5							5
6							6
7							7
8							8
9							9
10							10
11							11
12							12
13							13
14							14
15							15
16							16
17							17
18							18
19							19
20							20
21							21
22							22
23							23
24							24
25							25
26							26
27							27
28							28
29							29
30							30
31							31
32							32
33							33
34							34
35							35
36							36
37							37

EXERCISE 13.8

ACCOUNT NAME	DEBIT	CREDIT

EXERCISE 13.9

a. Net Sales is _____

_____

_____

Gross profit is _____

_____

_____

The gross profit percentage is _____

_____

b. Current assets are _____

_____

_____

_____

_____

_____

_____

_____

Current liabilities are _____

_____

_____

_____

Working capital is _____

_____

_____

_____

_____

_____

_____

EXERCISE 13.9 (continued)

c. The current ratio is _____

_____

d. The inventory
turnover is _____

_____

_____

_____

_____

_____

_____

_____

_____

_____

_____

_____

PROBLEM 13.1A or 13.1B

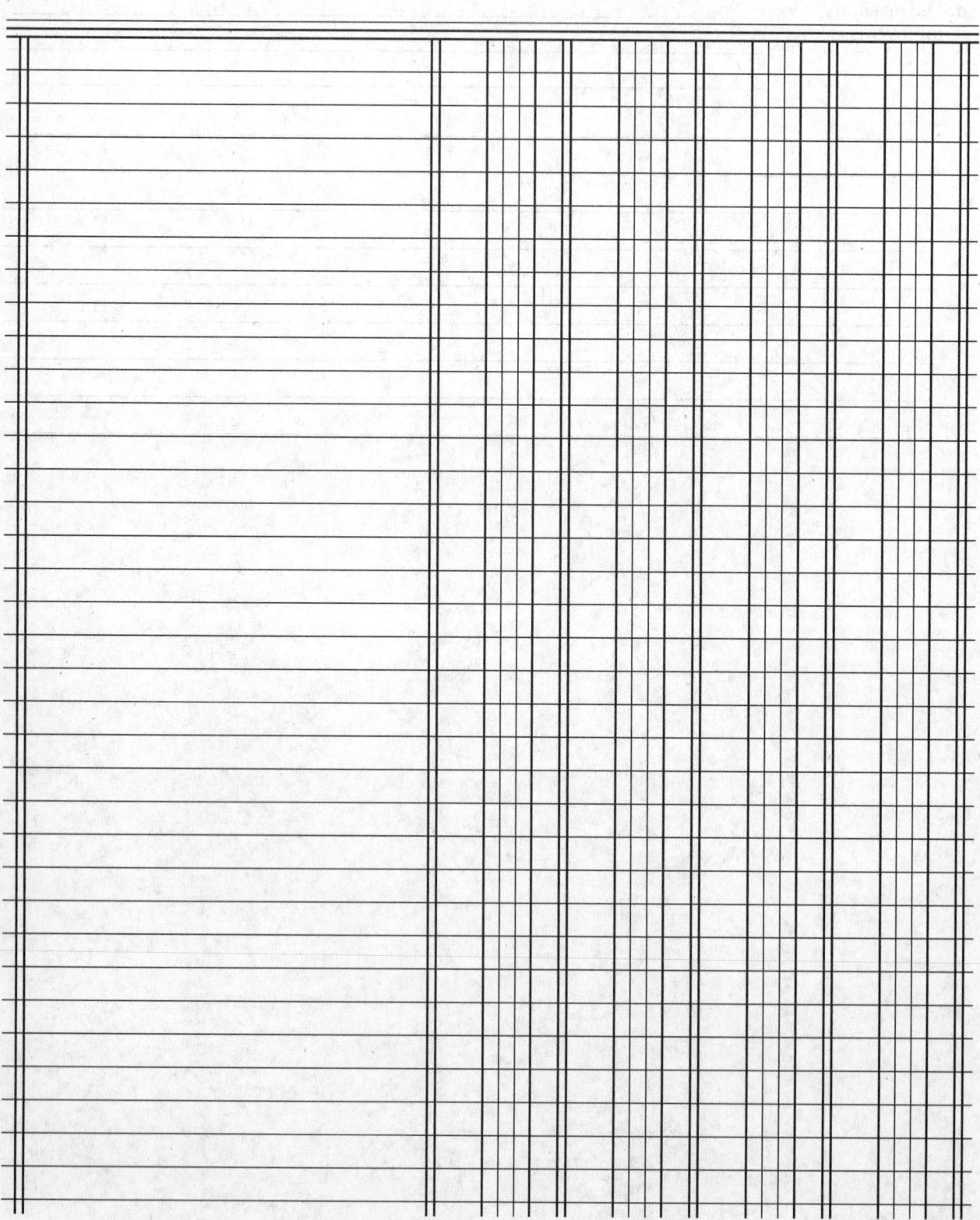

(continued)

PROBLEM 13.1A or 13.1B (continued)

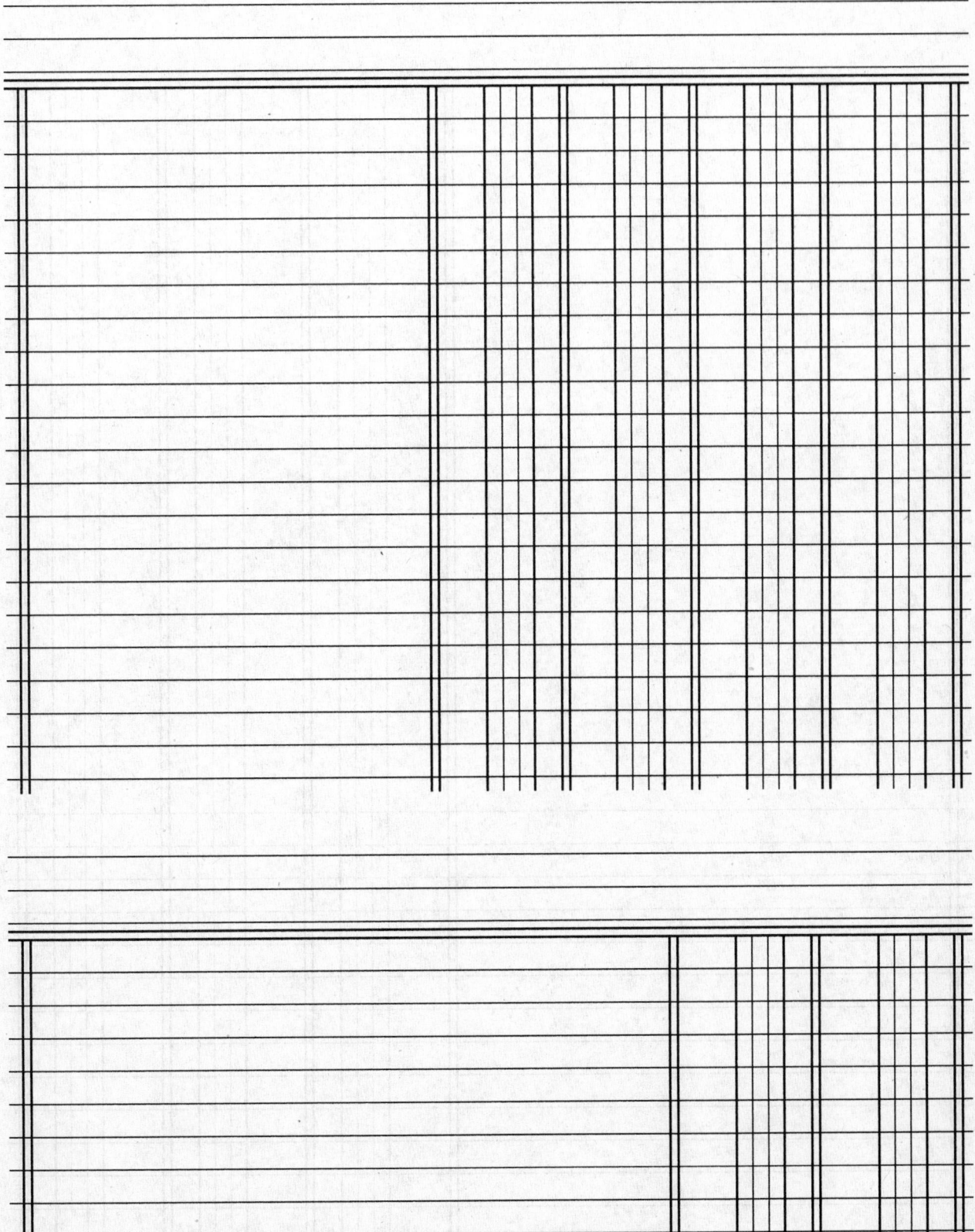

PROBLEM 13.1A or 13.1B (continued)

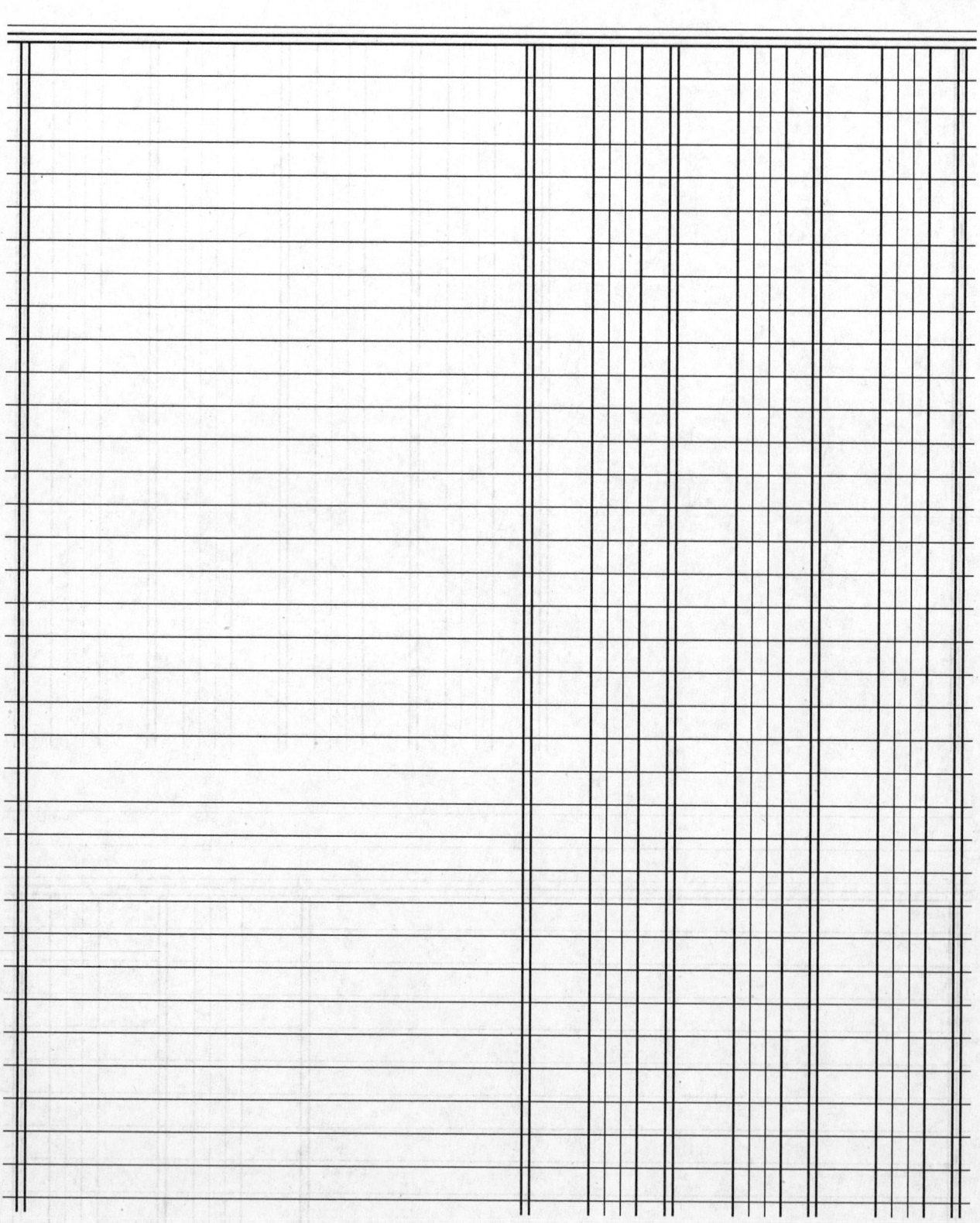

(continued)

PROBLEM 13.1A or 13.1B (continued)

Analyze: _____

PROBLEM 13.2A or 13.2B

_____
_____
_____

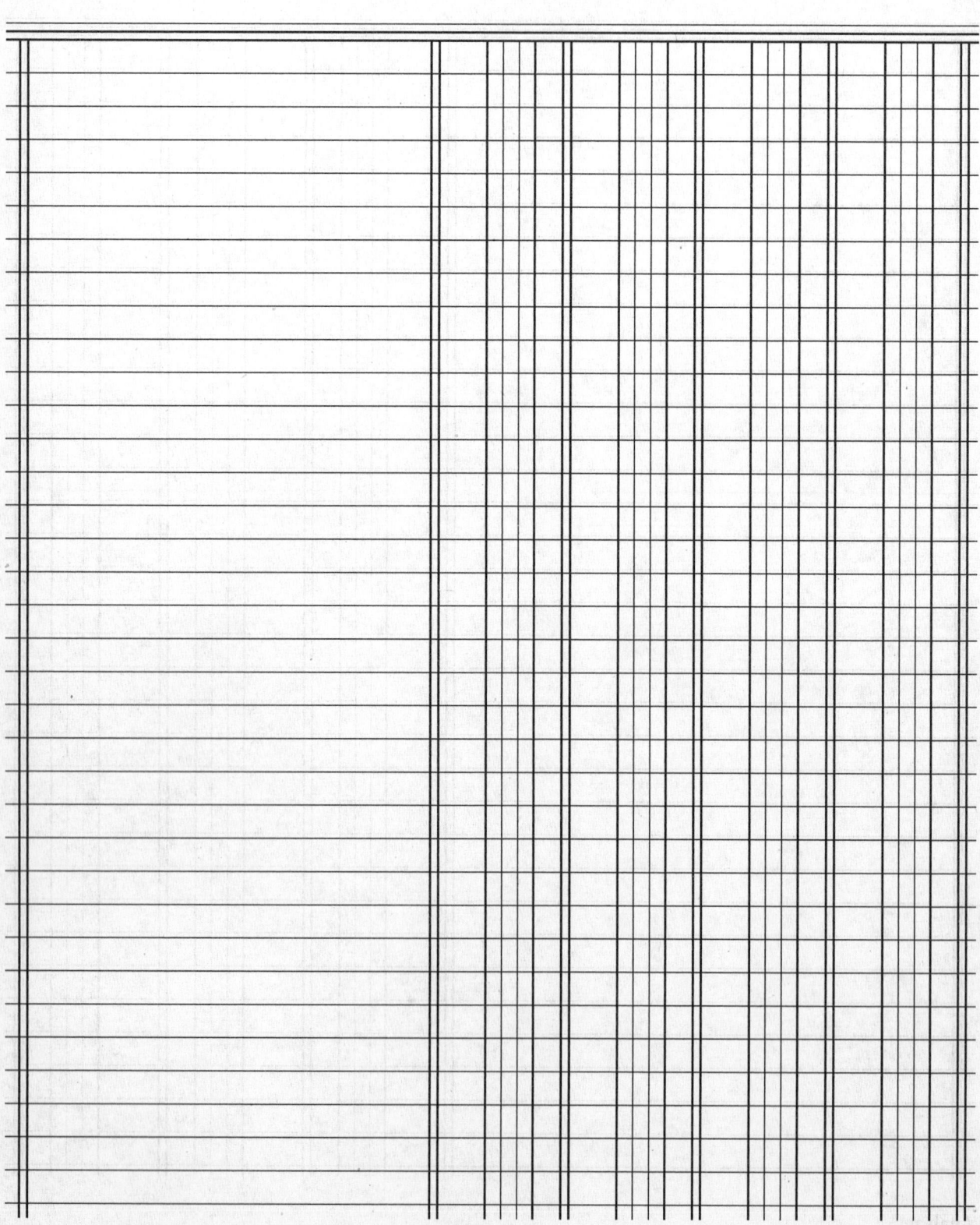

(continued)

Name

PROBLEM 13.2A or 13.2B (continued)

PROBLEM 13.2A or 13.2B (continued)

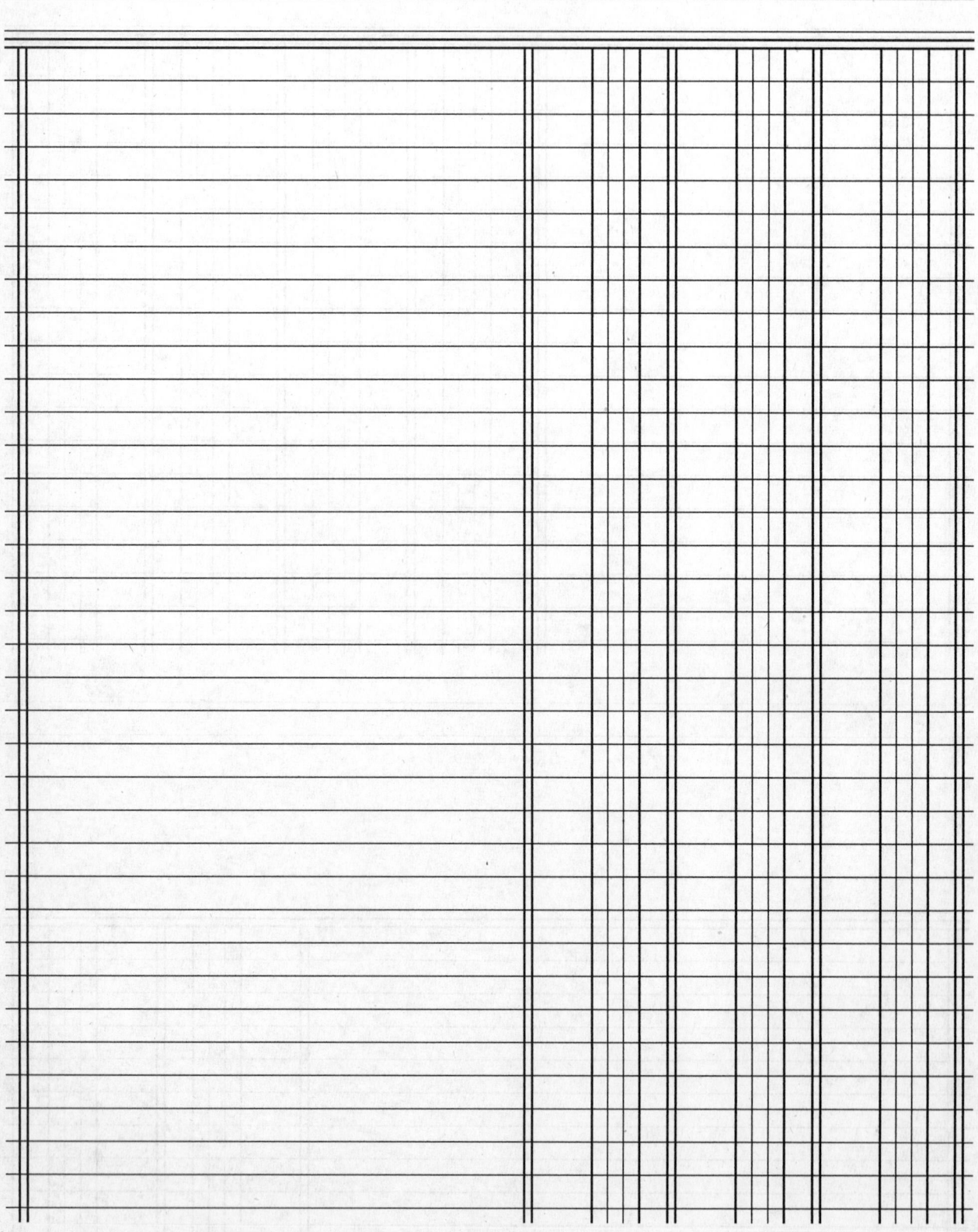

(continued)

PROBLEM 13.2A or 13.2B (continued)

Analyze: _____

PROBLEM 13.3A or 13.3B

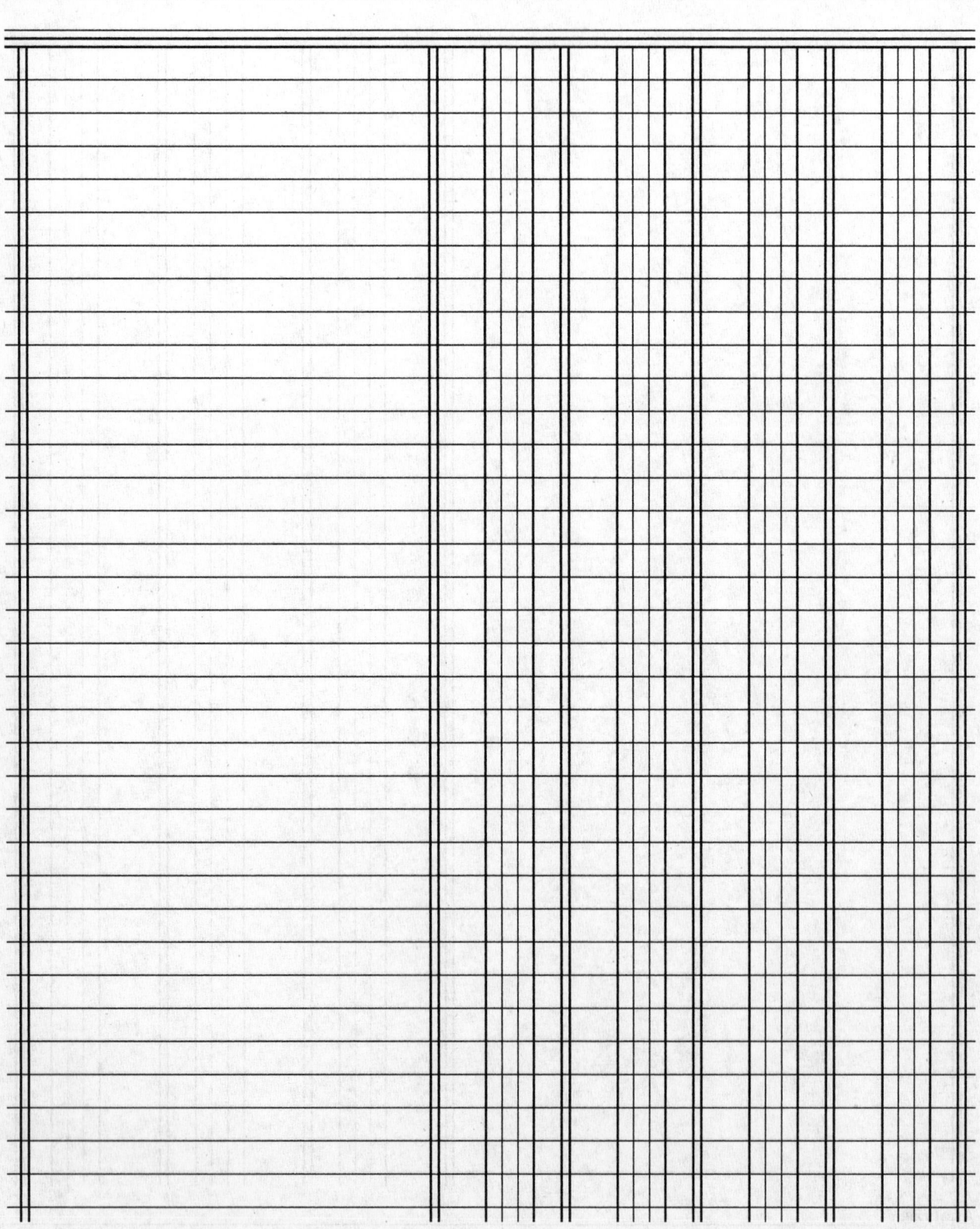

(continued)

PROBLEM 13.3A or 13.3B (continued)

PROBLEM 13.3A or 13.3B (continued)

PROBLEM 13.3A or 13.3B (continued)

Analyze: _____

PROBLEM 13.4A or 13.4B

GENERAL JOURNAL

PAGE _____

	DATE	DESCRIPTION	POST. REF.	DEBIT	CREDIT	
1						1
2						2
3						3
4						4
5						5
6						6
7						7
8						8
9						9
10						10
11						11
12						12
13						13
14						14
15						15
16						16
17						17
18						18
19						19
20						20
21						21
22						22
23						23
24						24
25						25
26						26
27						27
28						28
29						29
30						30
31						31
32						32
33						33
34						34
35						35
36						36
37						37

GENERAL JOURNAL   PAGE _____

	DATE	DESCRIPTION	POST. REF.	DEBIT	CREDIT	
1						1
2						2
3						3
4						4
5						5
6						6
7						7
8						8
9						9
10						10
11						11
12						12
13						13
14						14
15						15
16						16
17						17
18						18
19						19
20						20
21						21
22						22
23						23
24						24
25						25
26						26
27						27
28						28
29						29
30						30
31						31
32						32
33						33
34						34
35						35
36						36
37						37

PROBLEM 13.4A or 13.4B (continued)

GENERAL JOURNAL   PAGE _____

	DATE		DESCRIPTION	POST. REF.	DEBIT	CREDIT	
1							1
2							2
3							3
4							4
5							5
6							6
7							7
8							8
9							9
10							10
11							11
12							12
13							13
14							14
15							15
16							16
17							17
18							18
19							19
20							20
21							21
22							22
23							23
24							24
25							25
26							26
27							27
28							28
29							29
30							30
31							31
32							32
33							33
34							34
35							35
36							36
37							37

PROBLEM 13.4A or 13.4B (continued)

GENERAL JOURNAL   PAGE _____

	DATE		DESCRIPTION	POST. REF.	DEBIT	CREDIT	
1							1
2							2
3							3
4							4
5							5
6							6
7							7
8							8
9							9
10							10
11							11
12							12
13							13
14							14
15							15
16							16
17							17
18							18
19							19
20							20
21							21
22							22
23							23
24							24
25							25

Analyze: _____
_____

PAGE _____

	DATE		DESCRIPTION	POST. REF.	DEBIT	CREDIT	
1							1
2							2
3							3
4							4
5							5
6							6

PROBLEM 13.5A or 13.5B

GENERAL JOURNAL   PAGE _____

	DATE		DESCRIPTION	POST. REF.	DEBIT	CREDIT	
1							1
2							2
3							3
4							4
5							5
6							6
7							7
8							8
9							9
10							10
11							11
12							12
13							13
14							14
15							15
16							16
17							17
18							18
19							19
20							20
21							21
22							22
23							23
24							24
25							25
26							26
27							27
28							28
29							29
30							30
31							31
32							32
33							33
34							34
35							35
36							36

PROBLEM 13.5A or 13.5B (continued)

GENERAL JOURNAL

PAGE _____

	DATE	DESCRIPTION	POST. REF.	DEBIT	CREDIT	
1						1
2						2
3						3
4						4
5						5
6						6
7						7
8						8
9						9
10						10
11						11
12						12
13						13
14						14
15						15
16						16

Analyze: _____

_____

EXTRA FORM

GENERAL JOURNAL

PAGE _____

	DATE	DESCRIPTION	POST. REF.	DEBIT	CREDIT	
1						1
2						2
3						3
4						4
5						5
6						6
7						7
8						8
9						9
10						10
11						11
12						12
13						13

CRITICAL THINKING PROBLEM 13.1

	ACCOUNT NAME	TRIAL BALANCE		ADJUSTMENTS	
		DEBIT	CREDIT	DEBIT	CREDIT
1					
2					
3					
4					
5					
6					
7					
8					
9					
10					
11					
12					
13					
14					
15					
16					
17					
18					
19					
20					
21					
22					
23					
24					
25					
26					
27					
28					
29					
30					
31					
32					
33					
34					
35					
36					

CRITICAL THINKING PROBLEM 13.1 (continued)

ADJUSTED TRIAL BALANCE		INCOME STATEMENT		BALANCE SHEET		
DEBIT	CREDIT	DEBIT	CREDIT	DEBIT	CREDIT	
						1
						2
						3
						4
						5
						6
						7
						8
						9
						10
						11
						12
						13
						14
						15
						16
						17
						18
						19
						20
						21
						22
						23
						24
						25
						26
						27
						28
						29
						30
						31
						32
						33
						34
						35
						36

CRITICAL THINKING PROBLEM 13.1 (continued)

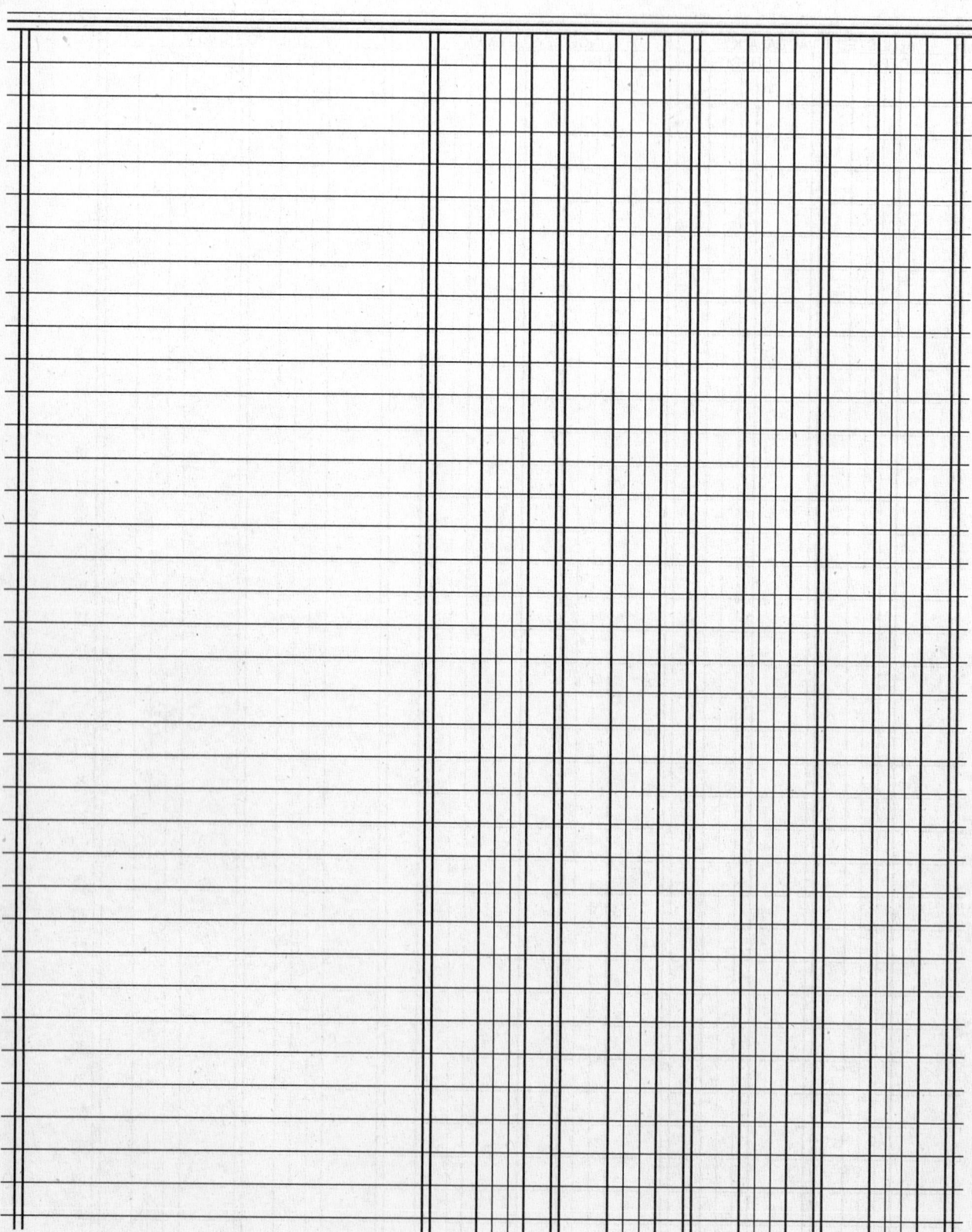

CRITICAL THINKING PROBLEM 13.1 (continued)

EXTRA FORM

CRITICAL THINKING PROBLEM 13.1 (continued)

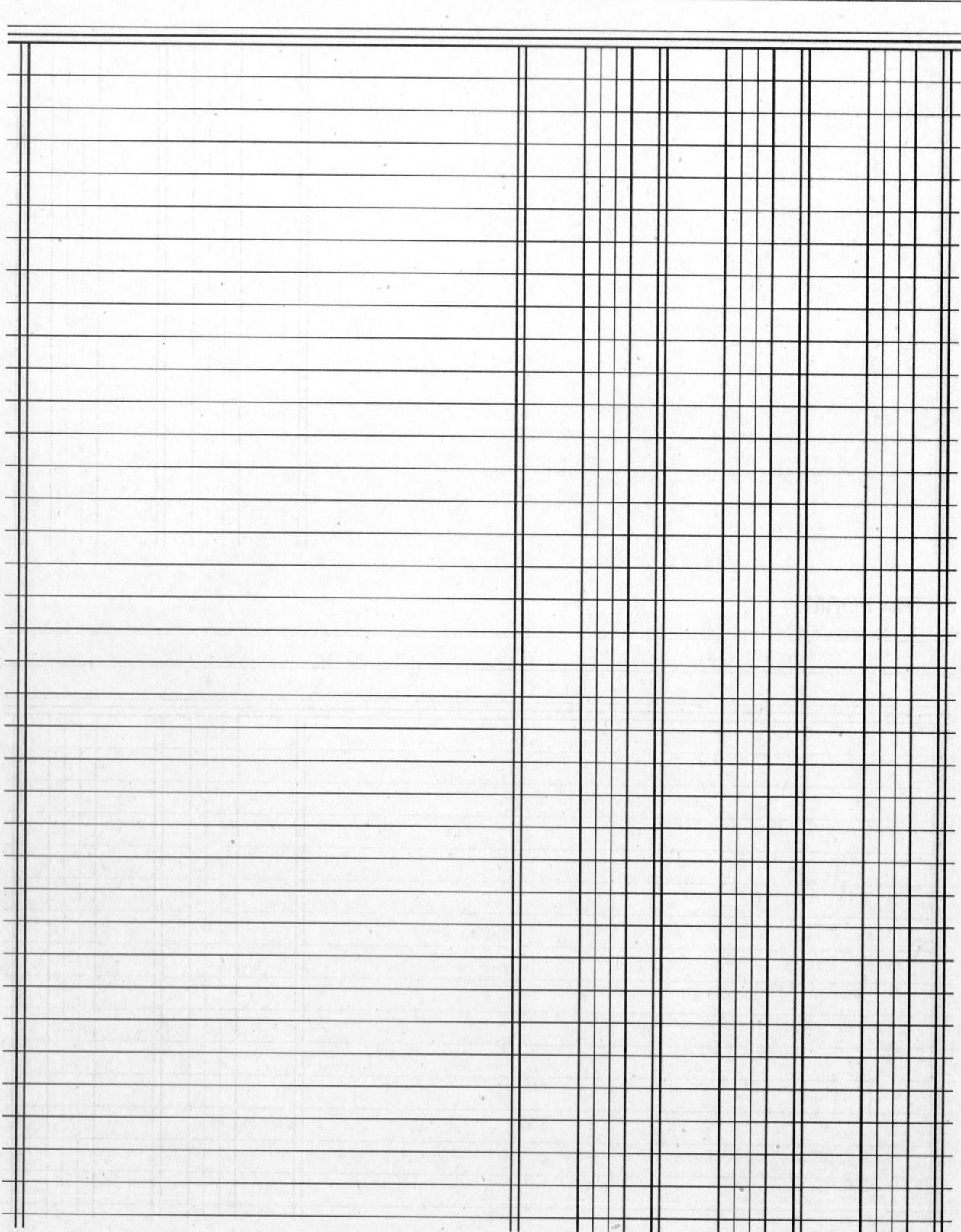

CRITICAL THINKING PROBLEM 13.1 (continued)

GENERAL JOURNAL   PAGE _____

	DATE		DESCRIPTION	POST. REF.	DEBIT	CREDIT	
1							1
2							2
3							3
4							4
5							5
6							6
7							7
8							8
9							9
10							10
11							11
12							12
13							13
14							14
15							15
16							16
17							17
18							18
19							19
20							20
21							21
22							22
23							23
24							24
25							25
26							26
27							27
28							28
29							29
30							30
31							31
32							32
33							33
34							34
35							35
36							36
37							37

CRITICAL THINKING PROBLEM 13.1 (continued)

GENERAL JOURNAL   PAGE _____

	DATE		DESCRIPTION	POST. REF.	DEBIT	CREDIT	
1							1
2							2
3							3
4							4
5							5
6							6
7							7
8							8
9							9
10							10
11							11
12							12
13							13
14							14
15							15
16							16
17							17
18							18
19							19
20							20
21							21
22							22
23							23
24							24
25							25
26							26
27							27
28							28
29							29
30							30
31							31
32							32
33							33
34							34
35							35
36							36
37							37

CRITICAL THINKING PROBLEM 13.1 (continued)

GENERAL JOURNAL   PAGE _____

	DATE	DESCRIPTION	POST. REF.	DEBIT	CREDIT	
1						1
2						2
3						3
4						4
5						5
6						6
7						7
8						8
9						9
10						10
11						11
12						12
13						13
14						14
15						15
16						16
17						17
18						18
19						19
20						20
21						21
22						22
23						23
24						24
25						25
26						26
27						27
28						28
29						29
30						30
31						31
32						32
33						33
34						34
35						35
36						36
37						37

CRITICAL THINKING PROBLEM 13.1 (continued)

GENERAL JOURNAL   PAGE _____

	DATE	DESCRIPTION	POST. REF.	DEBIT	CREDIT	
1						1
2						2
3						3
4						4
5						5
6						6
7						7
8						8
9						9
10						10
11						11
12						12
13						13
14						14
15						15
16						16
17						17
18						18
19						19
20						20
21						21
22						22
23						23
24						24
25						25
26						26
27						27
28						28
29						29
30						30
31						31
32						32
33						33
34						34

Analyze: _____

_____

CRITICAL THINKING PROBLEM 13.2

1.

2. _____
_____
_____
_____
_____

CHAPTER 13 CRITICAL THINKING PROBLEM (continued)

3. _____

Chapter 13 Practice Test Answer Key

Part A True-False

1. F	6. T	11. F	16. T	21. F
2. T	7. F	12. T	17. T	22. F
3. F	8. F	13. F	18. T	23. T
4. F	9. T	14. F	19. T	24. T
5. T	10. F	15. F	20. T	25. F

Name _____

MINI-PRACTICE SET 2

Merchandising Business Accounting Cycle

SALES JOURNAL

PAGE _____

	DATE	SALES SLIP NO.	CUSTOMER'S NAME	POST. REF.	ACCOUNTS RECEIVABLE DEBIT	SALES TAX PAYABLE CREDIT	SALES CREDIT	
1								1
2								2
3								3
4								4
5								5
6								6
7								7
8								8
9								9
10								10
11								11
12								12
13								13
14								14

PURCHASES JOURNAL

PAGE _____

DATE	PURCHASED FROM	INVOICE NUMBER	INVOICE DATE	TERMS	POST. REF.	PURCHASES DR./ ACCOUNTS PAYABLE CREDIT

PAGE _____

CASH RECEIPTS JOURNAL

DATE	DESCRIPTION	POST. REF.	ACCOUNTS RECEIVABLE CREDIT	SALES TAX PAYABLE CREDIT	SALES CREDIT	OTHER ACCOUNTS CREDIT			CASH DEBIT
						ACCOUNT NAME	POST. REF.	AMOUNT	

CASH PAYMENTS JOURNAL   PAGE ____

DATE	CK. NO.	DESCRIPTION	POST. REF.	ACCOUNTS PAYABLE DEBIT	OTHER ACCOUNTS DEBIT			PURCHASES DISCOUNTS CREDIT	CASH CREDIT
					ACCOUNT NAME	POST. REF.	AMOUNT		

Name _____

GENERAL JOURNAL

PAGE _____

	DATE		DESCRIPTION	POST. REF.	DEBIT	CREDIT	
1							1
2							2
3							3
4							4
5							5
6							6
7							7
8							8
9							9
10							10
11							11
12							12
13							13
14							14
15							15
16							16
17							17
18							18
19							19
20							20
21							21
22							22
23							23
24							24
25							25
26							26
27							27
28							28
29							29
30							30
31							31
32							32
33							33
34							34
35							35
36							36
37							37
38							38

GENERAL JOURNAL   PAGE _____

	DATE	DESCRIPTION	POST. REF.	DEBIT	CREDIT	
1						1
2						2
3						3
4						4
5						5
6						6
7						7
8						8
9						9
10						10
11						11
12						12
13						13
14						14
15						15
16						16
17						17
18						18
19						19
20						20
21						21
22						22
23						23
24						24
25						25
26						26
27						27
28						28
29						29
30						30
31						31
32						32
33						33
34						34
35						35
36						36
37						37
38						38

Name _____

GENERAL JOURNAL

PAGE _____

	DATE		DESCRIPTION	POST. REF.	DEBIT	CREDIT	
1							1
2							2
3							3
4							4
5							5
6							6
7							7
8							8
9							9
10							10
11							11
12							12
13							13
14							14
15							15
16							16
17							17
18							18
19							19
20							20
21							21
22							22
23							23
24							24
25							25
26							26
27							27
28							28
29							29
30							30
31							31
32							32
33							33
34							34
35							35
36							36
37							37
38							38

GENERAL LEDGER

ACCOUNT _____   ACCOUNT NO. _____

DATE	DESCRIPTION	POST. REF.	DEBIT	CREDIT	BALANCE	
					DEBIT	CREDIT

ACCOUNT _____   ACCOUNT NO. _____

DATE	DESCRIPTION	POST. REF.	DEBIT	CREDIT	BALANCE	
					DEBIT	CREDIT

ACCOUNT _____   ACCOUNT NO. _____

DATE	DESCRIPTION	POST. REF.	DEBIT	CREDIT	BALANCE	
					DEBIT	CREDIT

ACCOUNT _____   ACCOUNT NO. _____

DATE	DESCRIPTION	POST. REF.	DEBIT	CREDIT	BALANCE	
					DEBIT	CREDIT

Name _____

GENERAL LEDGER

ACCOUNT _____ ACCOUNT NO. _____

DATE	DESCRIPTION	POST. REF.	DEBIT	CREDIT	BALANCE DEBIT	BALANCE CREDIT

ACCOUNT _____ ACCOUNT NO. _____

DATE	DESCRIPTION	POST. REF.	DEBIT	CREDIT	BALANCE DEBIT	BALANCE CREDIT

ACCOUNT _____ ACCOUNT NO. _____

DATE	DESCRIPTION	POST. REF.	DEBIT	CREDIT	BALANCE DEBIT	BALANCE CREDIT

ACCOUNT _____ ACCOUNT NO. _____

DATE	DESCRIPTION	POST. REF.	DEBIT	CREDIT	BALANCE DEBIT	BALANCE CREDIT

ACCOUNT _____ ACCOUNT NO. _____

DATE	DESCRIPTION	POST. REF.	DEBIT	CREDIT	BALANCE DEBIT	BALANCE CREDIT

GENERAL LEDGER

ACCOUNT _____ ACCOUNT NO. _____

DATE	DESCRIPTION	POST. REF.	DEBIT	CREDIT	BALANCE	
					DEBIT	CREDIT

ACCOUNT _____ ACCOUNT NO. _____

DATE	DESCRIPTION	POST. REF.	DEBIT	CREDIT	BALANCE	
					DEBIT	CREDIT

ACCOUNT _____ ACCOUNT NO. _____

DATE	DESCRIPTION	POST. REF.	DEBIT	CREDIT	BALANCE	
					DEBIT	CREDIT

ACCOUNT _____ ACCOUNT NO. _____

DATE	DESCRIPTION	POST. REF.	DEBIT	CREDIT	BALANCE	
					DEBIT	CREDIT

Name _____

GENERAL LEDGER

ACCOUNT _____ ACCOUNT NO. _____

DATE	DESCRIPTION	POST. REF.	DEBIT	CREDIT	BALANCE DEBIT	BALANCE CREDIT

ACCOUNT _____ ACCOUNT NO. _____

DATE	DESCRIPTION	POST. REF.	DEBIT	CREDIT	BALANCE DEBIT	BALANCE CREDIT

ACCOUNT _____ ACCOUNT NO. _____

DATE	DESCRIPTION	POST. REF.	DEBIT	CREDIT	BALANCE DEBIT	BALANCE CREDIT

ACCOUNT _____ ACCOUNT NO. _____

DATE	DESCRIPTION	POST. REF.	DEBIT	CREDIT	BALANCE DEBIT	BALANCE CREDIT

ACCOUNT _____ ACCOUNT NO. _____

DATE	DESCRIPTION	POST. REF.	DEBIT	CREDIT	BALANCE DEBIT	BALANCE CREDIT

GENERAL LEDGER

ACCOUNT _____ ACCOUNT NO. _____

	DATE	DESCRIPTION	POST. REF.	DEBIT	CREDIT	BALANCE DEBIT	BALANCE CREDIT

ACCOUNT _____ ACCOUNT NO. _____

	DATE	DESCRIPTION	POST. REF.	DEBIT	CREDIT	BALANCE DEBIT	BALANCE CREDIT

ACCOUNT _____ ACCOUNT NO. _____

	DATE	DESCRIPTION	POST. REF.	DEBIT	CREDIT	BALANCE DEBIT	BALANCE CREDIT

ACCOUNT _____ ACCOUNT NO. _____

	DATE	DESCRIPTION	POST. REF.	DEBIT	CREDIT	BALANCE DEBIT	BALANCE CREDIT

Name

GENERAL LEDGER

ACCOUNT _____ ACCOUNT NO. _____

DATE	DESCRIPTION	POST. REF.	DEBIT	CREDIT	BALANCE	
					DEBIT	CREDIT

ACCOUNT _____ ACCOUNT NO. _____

DATE	DESCRIPTION	POST. REF.	DEBIT	CREDIT	BALANCE	
					DEBIT	CREDIT

ACCOUNT _____ ACCOUNT NO. _____

DATE	DESCRIPTION	POST. REF.	DEBIT	CREDIT	BALANCE	
					DEBIT	CREDIT

ACCOUNT _____ ACCOUNT NO. _____

DATE	DESCRIPTION	POST. REF.	DEBIT	CREDIT	BALANCE	
					DEBIT	CREDIT

ACCOUNT _____ ACCOUNT NO. _____

DATE	DESCRIPTION	POST. REF.	DEBIT	CREDIT	BALANCE	
					DEBIT	CREDIT

GENERAL LEDGER

ACCOUNT _____   ACCOUNT NO. _____

DATE	DESCRIPTION	POST. REF.	DEBIT	CREDIT	BALANCE DEBIT	BALANCE CREDIT

ACCOUNT _____   ACCOUNT NO. _____

DATE	DESCRIPTION	POST. REF.	DEBIT	CREDIT	BALANCE DEBIT	BALANCE CREDIT

ACCOUNT _____   ACCOUNT NO. _____

DATE	DESCRIPTION	POST. REF.	DEBIT	CREDIT	BALANCE DEBIT	BALANCE CREDIT

ACCOUNT _____   ACCOUNT NO. _____

DATE	DESCRIPTION	POST. REF.	DEBIT	CREDIT	BALANCE DEBIT	BALANCE CREDIT

ACCOUNT _____   ACCOUNT NO. _____

DATE	DESCRIPTION	POST. REF.	DEBIT	CREDIT	BALANCE DEBIT	BALANCE CREDIT

GENERAL LEDGER

ACCOUNT _____   ACCOUNT NO. _____

DATE	DESCRIPTION	POST. REF.	DEBIT	CREDIT	BALANCE DEBIT	CREDIT

ACCOUNT _____   ACCOUNT NO. _____

DATE	DESCRIPTION	POST. REF.	DEBIT	CREDIT	BALANCE DEBIT	CREDIT

ACCOUNT _____   ACCOUNT NO. _____

DATE	DESCRIPTION	POST. REF.	DEBIT	CREDIT	BALANCE DEBIT	CREDIT

ACCOUNT _____   ACCOUNT NO. _____

DATE	DESCRIPTION	POST. REF.	DEBIT	CREDIT	BALANCE DEBIT	CREDIT

ACCOUNT _____   ACCOUNT NO. _____

DATE	DESCRIPTION	POST. REF.	DEBIT	CREDIT	BALANCE DEBIT	CREDIT

ACCOUNTS RECEIVABLE SUBSIDIARY LEDGER

NAME _____   TERMS _____

	DATE	DESCRIPTION	POST. REF.	DEBIT	CREDIT	BALANCE

NAME _____   TERMS _____

	DATE	DESCRIPTION	POST. REF.	DEBIT	CREDIT	BALANCE

NAME _____   TERMS _____

	DATE	DESCRIPTION	POST. REF.	DEBIT	CREDIT	BALANCE

NAME _____   TERMS _____

	DATE	DESCRIPTION	POST. REF.	DEBIT	CREDIT	BALANCE

NAME _____   TERMS _____

	DATE	DESCRIPTION	POST. REF.	DEBIT	CREDIT	BALANCE

ACCOUNTS RECEIVABLE SUBSIDIARY LEDGER

NAME _____ TERMS _____

DATE	DESCRIPTION	POST. REF.	DEBIT	CREDIT	BALANCE

NAME _____ TERMS _____

DATE	DESCRIPTION	POST. REF.	DEBIT	CREDIT	BALANCE

ACCOUNTS PAYABLE SUBSIDIARY LEDGER

NAME _____ TERMS _____

DATE	DESCRIPTION	POST. REF.	DEBIT	CREDIT	BALANCE

NAME _____ TERMS _____

DATE	DESCRIPTION	POST. REF.	DEBIT	CREDIT	BALANCE

Name _____

ACCOUNTS PAYABLE SUBSIDIARY LEDGER

NAME _____ TERMS _____

	DATE		DESCRIPTION	POST. REF.	DEBIT	CREDIT	BALANCE

	ACCOUNT NAME	TRIAL BALANCE		ADJUSTMENTS	
		DEBIT	CREDIT	DEBIT	CREDIT
1					
2					
3					
4					
5					
6					
7					
8					
9					
10					
11					
12					
13					
14					
15					
16					
17					
18					
19					
20					
21					
22					
23					
24					
25					
26					
27					
28					
29					
30					
31					
32					
33					
34					
35					
36					

ADJUSTED TRIAL BALANCE		INCOME STATEMENT		BALANCE SHEET		
DEBIT	CREDIT	DEBIT	CREDIT	DEBIT	CREDIT	
						1
						2
						3
						4
						5
						6
						7
						8
						9
						10
						11
						12
						13
						14
						15
						16
						17
						18
						19
						20
						21
						22
						23
						24
						25
						26
						27
						28
						29
						30
						31
						32
						33
						34
						35
						36

_____

	ACCOUNT NAME	TRIAL BALANCE		ADJUSTMENTS	
		DEBIT	CREDIT	DEBIT	CREDIT
1					
2					
3					
4					
5					
6					
7					
8					
9					
10					
11					
12					
13					
14					
15					
16					
17					
18					
19					
20					
21					
22					
23					
24					
25					
26					
27					
28					
29					
30					
31					
32					
33					
34					
35					
36					

ADJUSTED TRIAL BALANCE		INCOME STATEMENT		BALANCE SHEET		
DEBIT	CREDIT	DEBIT	CREDIT	DEBIT	CREDIT	
						1
						2
						3
						4
						5
						6
						7
						8
						9
						10
						11
						12
						13
						14
						15
						16
						17
						18
						19
						20
						21
						22
						23
						24
						25
						26
						27
						28
						29
						30
						31
						32
						33
						34
						35
						36

ACCOUNT NAME	DEBIT	CREDIT

	ACCOUNT NAME	TRIAL BALANCE		ADJUSTMENTS	
		DEBIT	CREDIT	DEBIT	CREDIT
1					
2					
3					
4					
5					
6					
7					
8					
9					
10					
11					
12					
13					
14					
15					
16					
17					
18					
19					
20					
21					
22					
23					
24					
25					
26					
27					
28					
29					
30					
31					
32					
33					
34					

ADJUSTED TRIAL BALANCE		INCOME STATEMENT		BALANCE SHEET		
DEBIT	CREDIT	DEBIT	CREDIT	DEBIT	CREDIT	
						1
						2
						3
						4
						5
						6
						7
						8
						9
						10
						11
						12
						13
						14
						15
						16
						17
						18
						19
						20
						21
						22
						23
						24
						25
						26
						27
						28
						29
						30
						31
						32
						33
						34

EXTRA FORM

GENERAL JOURNAL   PAGE _____

	DATE		DESCRIPTION	POST. REF.	DEBIT	CREDIT	
1							1
2							2
3							3
4							4
5							5
6							6
7							7
8							8
9							9
10							10
11							11
12							12
13							13
14							14
15							15
16							16
17							17
18							18
19							19
20							20
21							21
22							22
23							23
24							24
25							25
26							26
27							27
28							28
29							29
30							30
31							31
32							32
33							33
34							34
35							35
36							36
37							37

CHAPTER 14 Accounting Principles and Reporting Standards

STUDY GUIDE

Understanding the Chapter

Objectives

1. Understand the process used to develop generally accepted accounting principles. 2. Identify the major accounting standards-setting bodies and their roles in the standards-setting process. 3. Describe the users and uses of financial reports. 4. Identify and explain the qualitative characteristics of accounting information. 5. Describe and explain the basic assumptions about accounting reports. 6. Explain and apply the basic principles of accounting. 7. Describe and apply the modifying constraints on accounting principles. 8. Define the accounting terms new to this chapter.

Reading Assignment

Read Chapter 14 in the textbook. Complete the textbook Section Self Review as you finish reading each section of the chapter, and the Comprehensive Self Review at the end of the chapter. Refer to the Chapter 14 Glossary or to the Glossary at the end of the book to find definitions for terms that are not familiar to you.

Activities

❏ **Thinking Critically**

Answer the *Thinking Critically* questions for Green Mountain Coffee Roasters and Managerial Implications.

❏ **Discussion Questions**

Answer each assigned discussion question in Chapter 14.

❏ **Exercises**

Complete each assigned exercise in Chapter 14. Use the forms provided in this SGWP. The objectives covered by an exercise are given after the exercise number. If you need help with an exercise, review the portion of the chapter related to the objective(s) covered.

❏ **Problems A/B**

Complete each assigned problem in Chapter 14. Use the forms provided in this SGWP. The objectives covered by a problem are given after the problem number. If you need help with a problem, review the portion of the chapter related to the objective(s) covered.

❏ **Critical Thinking Problems**

Complete the critical thinking problems as assigned. Use the forms provided in this SGWP.

❏ **Business Connections**

Complete the Business Connections activities as assigned to gain a deeper understanding of Chapter 14 concepts.

Practice Tests

Complete the Practice Tests, which cover the main points in your reading assignment. Compare your answers with those in the Practice Test Answer Key for Chapter 14 at the end of this chapter. If you have answered any questions incorrectly, review the related section of the text.

Part A True-False *For each of the following statements, circle T in the answer column if the statement is true or F if the statement is false.*

T   F   **1.** There is only one accepted method of accounting for each transaction.

T   F   **2.** The Financial Accounting Standards Board is a governmental organization.

T   F   **3.** For convenience, accountants assume that the value of money is stable or that changes in its value are insignificant.

T   F   **4.** Revenue should not be recognized until cash is received.

T   F   **5.** Statement users have the right to assume that the figures in audited statements are objective and are based on verifiable evidence.

T   F   **6.** The "constraints" serve to modify basic principles of accounting.

T   F   **7.** An overstatement of an expense account in one accounting period results in an understatement of profit in the succeeding period or periods.

T   F   **8.** There is a conflict between the "going concern" concept and the historical cost principle.

T   F   **9.** In order for information to be reliable, it must be verifiable.

T   F   **10.** Adjusting entries are necessary because of the matching principle.

T   F   **11.** The matching principle requires that all known costs be charged to the current period of operations.

T   F   **12.** The "stable monetary unit" assumption simplifies accounting records.

T   F   **13.** The SEC discourages disclosures outside the financial statements.

T   F   **14.** The traits of objectivity and verifiability reduce subjective decisions.

T   F   **15.** The Conceptual Framework assumes that readers of financial reports know little about accounting and financial reporting.

T   F   **16.** Long-term assets are usually carried in the accounts at market value, less depreciation, until used up or disposed of.

T   F   **17.** The Sarbanes-Oxley Act reaffirms the SEC's option to depend on a private sector organization in developing accounting principles and standards and the SEC has chosen the FASB as that organization.

T   F   **18.** Because of the separate entity assumption, the personal activities of the owner of a sole proprietorship should be combined with his or her business activities in the accounting records.

T   F   **19.** The Securities and Exchange Commission has little power to dictate accounting methods used by companies whose stocks are traded on the stock exchanges.

T   F   **20.** The International Accounting Standards Board sets GAAP for US Companies.

Part B Completion *In the answer column, supply the missing word or words needed to complete each of the following statements.*

_____ 1. The idea that the same accounting principles should be followed each year is called the _____ characteristic.

_____ 2. Matching revenues and expenses of specific fiscal periods is called the _____ basis of accounting.

_____ 3. If the accounting records are kept on the accrual basis, income is recognized in the period in which it has been _____ and _____.

_____ 4. The notes to the financial statements illustrate application of the principle of _____.

_____ 5. Under the modifying convention of _____, assets are sometimes stated at a lower amount than they might be stated if other principles could be logically applied under GAAP.

_____ 6. The _____ constraint may make it possible for a transaction with small value to be exempt from GAAP.

_____ 7. The _____ assumption permits carrying forward the un-depreciated cost of assets to be charged against future operations.

_____ 8. The _____ quality of financial statements permits the reports of different entities to be compared meaningfully with one another.

_____ 9. The _____ assumption implies that an enterprise's economic activities can be divided into time periods.

_____ 10. The organization that has the authority to monitor CPA firms that audit publicly held companies is the _____.

_____ 11. Before the FASB was established, the _____ was recognized as the private sector source of GAAP.

_____ 12. _____ refers to the significance of an item in relation to other items in the financial statements.

_____ 13. The business enterprise is normally thought of by the accountant as a _____ entity.

_____ 14. The international body that was established to develop accounting rules that might be followed on a world-wide basis is the _____ _____.

_____ 15. The agency with statutory authority to establish accounting standards for publicly-held corporations is the _____.

_____ 16. The assumption that permits the cost of assets acquired to be included in the same account is the _____ assumption.

Part C Exercise

Answer each of the following in the space provided. Make your answers complete but as brief as possible.

1. Does the separate entity assumption conform to the legal obligations of a sole proprietor? Explain.

_____

_____

_____

_____

_____

_____

2. In its accounting, ABC Company (a non-public US company) has been following US GAAP for years. It discovers in November 2013 that the International Accounting Standards Board has issued a "Standard" with greatly different reporting requirements from those of US GAAP. What must ABC Company do?

_____

_____

_____

_____

_____

_____

3. Explain why the accountant assumes continuity in the operation of the business.

_____

_____

_____

_____

_____

4. Explain the tests that must be met for revenue to be recognized.

_____

_____

_____

_____

_____

_____

5. Explain the role of the FASB's conceptual framework of accounting.

_____

_____

_____

_____

_____

_____

_____

Demonstration Problem

You are an independent CPA performing audits of financial statements. In your work you encounter the independent situations described in items 1–6. For each situation, indicate which accounting assumption, principle or constraint is most relevant. If the treatment described conforms to GAAP, explain why. If the treatment does not conform, explain which concept is violated and how the situation should be reported.

1. Quoren Company has been sued in court by customers for defective products. The company's attorney expects a liability of $5 million is reasonably possible. In the statements, the lawsuits are not mentioned.

2. BTC Inc. has an income statement that shows only sales, cost of sales, total expenses and net profit.

3. Your Holidays spends a large sum on sales promotions during this year. Management thinks the advertising will generate revenues for three years, so has charged to expense only one-third of the amount spent this year. The remainder will be charged off in equal amounts in the next two years.

4. Black Company occupies a building purchased 7 years ago. Because the value of the building has increased each year, no depreciation has been taken.

5. During 2013, James received and reported as income $1 million in deposits accompanying orders for products to be manufactured and delivered in 2014.

6. Future Labs Co. has constructed special-purpose equipment designed for research use. The equipment may be used for several different research projects in the future. Because of its special use, this equipment has virtually no resale value to any other company. Therefore, Future Labs charged the entire cost to build the equipment, $5,000,000, to expense in the year it was put into service.

SOLUTION

1. **Full disclosure.** Assuming that this is a material amount, disclosure of the lawsuits should be given in the footnotes to the financial statements. It probably is not reasonable to expect the company to reveal the attorney's attitude toward the case. However, disclosure of the amount of the suit, with some indication of the impact of a decision in favor of the plaintiffs should be made.

2. **Full disclosure.** The disclosure of such few items does not provide the user with information needed. The components of the net income are important to users who are trying to evaluate the business, and in this instance the disclosures should take the form of inclusion in the income statement. Even though it is appropriate to make a summary of income and costs in the income statement, without all the details, the procedure being followed is not satisfactory.

3. **Objectivity and verifiability.** To defer a cost such as advertising, there must be verification that a future benefit has been created and it must be possible to objectively measure the benefit. Neither of these factors appears to be present, so the costs should be charged to expense in the year incurred.

4. **Matching. Historical cost principle.** The cost of the building should be depreciated over its useful life. This is also part of the historical cost framework of accounting.

5. **Revenue recognition and matching.** Revenue should be reported only if it has been realized (which it has) and earned (which it has not). The revenue should be deferred and matched against costs to be incurred in the next year.

6. **Going concern, matching and historical cost concepts.** The accounting concept framework assumes a going concern. Therefore historical cost of an asset is entered in the accounts and depreciated over the useful life of the asset. There is no intent to sell the asset, but to use it in the business. There is no indication that the asset has lost its usefulness or even that its usefulness has decreased.

EXTRA FORM

WORKING PAPERS

Name _____

EXERCISE 14.1

1. _____
_____
_____
_____
_____

2. _____
_____
_____
_____
_____

3. _____
_____
_____
_____
_____

EXERCISE 14.2

1. _____
_____
_____
_____
_____
_____
_____

2. _____
_____
_____
_____

3. _____
_____
_____
_____
_____

EXERCISE 14.3

1. _____

_____

_____

_____

_____

2. _____

_____

_____

_____

3. _____

_____

_____

_____

_____

EXERCISE 14.4

1. _____

_____

_____

_____

_____

2. _____

_____

_____

_____

_____

3. _____

_____

_____

_____

_____

_____

EXERCISE 14.5

_____
_____
_____
_____
_____
_____

EXERCISE 14.6

_____
_____
_____
_____
_____
_____

EXTRA FORM

_____
_____
_____
_____
_____
_____
_____
_____
_____
_____
_____
_____
_____
_____
_____

PROBLEM 14.1A or 14.1B

1. _____
2. _____
3. _____
4. _____
5. _____
6. _____
7. _____
8. _____
9. _____
10. _____

EXTRA FORM

_____
_____
_____
_____
_____
_____
_____
_____
_____
_____
_____
_____
_____
_____
_____
_____
_____
_____
_____
_____
_____
_____

PROBLEM 14.2A or 14.2B

Handled Properly?	Basic Concept	Proper Presentation
1. _____	_____	_____
	_____	_____
	_____	_____
	_____	_____
2. _____	_____	_____
	_____	_____
	_____	_____
	_____	_____
3. _____	_____	_____
	_____	_____
	_____	_____
	_____	_____
4. _____	_____	_____
	_____	_____
	_____	_____
	_____	_____
5. _____	_____	_____
	_____	_____
	_____	_____
	_____	_____
6. _____	_____	_____
	_____	_____
	_____	_____
	_____	_____

Analyze: _____

_____

PROBLEM 14.3A or 14.3B

PROBLEM 14.3A or 14.3B (continued)

COMPUTATIONS

_____ _____

_____ _____

_____ _____

_____ _____

_____ _____

_____ _____

_____ _____

_____ _____

_____ _____

_____ _____

_____ _____

_____ _____

_____ _____

_____ _____

_____ _____

_____ _____

_____ _____

_____ _____

_____ _____

_____ _____

_____ _____

_____ _____

_____ _____

_____ _____

_____ _____

_____ _____

_____ _____

_____ _____

_____ _____

Analyze: _____

_____

PROBLEM 14.4A or 14.4B

PROBLEM 14.4A or 14.4B (continued)

NOTES

_____
_____
_____
_____
_____
_____
_____
_____
_____
_____
_____
_____
_____
_____
_____
_____
_____
_____
_____
_____
_____
_____
_____
_____
_____

Analyze: _____
_____
_____

PROBLEM 14.5A or 14.5B

_____

_____

_____

_____

_____

_____

_____

_____

_____

_____

_____

_____

_____

_____

_____

_____

_____

_____

_____

_____

_____

_____

_____

_____

_____

_____

_____

_____

_____

_____

_____

_____

_____

Analyze: _____

_____

CRITICAL THINKING PROBLEM 14.1

Analyze:

CRITICAL THINKING PROBLEM 14.2

Chapter 14 Practice Test Answer Key

Part A True-False

1. F	8. F	15. F
2. F	9. T	16. F
3. T	10. T	17. T
4. F	11. F	18. F
5. T	12. T	19. F
6. T	13. F	20. F
7. F	14. T	

Part B Completion

1. consistency
2. accrual
3. earned and realized
4. full disclosure
5. conservatism
6. cost-benefit
7. going concern
8. comparability
9. periodicity of income
10. Public Company Accounting Oversight Board (PCAOB)
11. American Institute of CPAs (Accounting Principles Board)
12. materiality
13. separate
14. International Accounting Standards Board
15. Securities and Exchange Commission
16. stable monetary unit

Part C Exercise

1. No. The owner of a sole proprietorship is generally legally liable for the debts and other obligations of the business as well as for personal debts.

2. ABC must use US GAAP since it has no international reporting requirements.

3. If continuity were not assumed, the accounting records would have to be kept on the assumption that the business is about to liquidate—presumably reflecting estimated value.

4. For revenue to be recognized, it must have been (1) realized (cash or other assets must have been received or debts liquidated) and (2) earned, which means that goods or services have been delivered and the costs related to the revenue have been incurred.

5. The conceptual framework is designed to provide a sound basis for developing accounting standards and rules. It permits development of a coherent set of standards based on the same assumptions, basic principles, and constraints.

Accounts Receivable and Uncollectible Accounts

STUDY GUIDE

Understanding the Chapter

Objectives

1. Record the estimated expense from uncollectible accounts receivable using the allowance method. 2. Charge off uncollectible accounts using the allowance method. 3. Record the collection of accounts previously written off using the allowance method. 4. Record losses from uncollectible accounts using the direct charge-off method. 5. Record the collection of accounts previously written off using the direct charge-off method. 6. Recognize common internal controls for accounts receivable. 7. Define the accounting terms new to this chapter.

Reading Assignment

Read Chapter 15 in the textbook. Complete the textbook Section Self Review as you finish reading each section of the chapter, and the Comprehensive Self Review at the end of the chapter. Refer to the Chapter 15 Glossary or to the Glossary at the end of the book to find definitions for terms that are not familiar to you.

Activities

❑ **Thinking Critically**
Answer the *Thinking Critically* questions for FedEx Corporation and Managerial Implications.

❑ **Discussion Questions**
Answer each assigned discussion question in Chapter 15.

❑ **Exercises**
Complete each assigned exercise in Chapter 15. Use the forms provided in this SGWP. The objectives covered by an exercise are given after the exercise number. If you need help with an exercise, review the portion of the chapter related to the objective(s) covered.

❑ **Problems A/B**
Complete each assigned problem in Chapter 15. Use the forms provided in this SGWP. The objectives covered by a problem are given after the problem number. If you need help with a problem, review the portion of the chapter related to the objective(s) covered.

❑ **Critical Thinking Problems**
Complete the critical thinking problems as assigned. Use the forms provided in this SGWP.

❑ **Business Connections**
Complete the Business Connections activities as assigned to gain a deeper understanding of Chapter 15 concepts.

Practice Tests

Complete the Practice Tests, which cover the main points in your reading assignment. Compare your answers with those in the Practice Test Answer Key for Chapter 15 at the end of this chapter. If you have answered any questions incorrectly, review the related section of the text.

Part A True-False

For each of the following statements, circle T in the answer column if the answer is true or F if the statement is false.

T　F　**1.** When there is a partial collection of a balance previously written off, only the amount expected to be recoverable should be reversed in the creditor's accounting records.

T　F　**2.** If the provision for estimated losses from uncollectible accounts is based on a percent of net sales, the balance of the allowance account is adjusted so that it equals the product of the percentage of net sales.

T　F　**3.** When a part of an account previously written off is collected, an entry should be made reversing the original write-off of the entire amount written off if the allowance method is being used.

T　F　**4.** Given that the direct charge-off method is being used, if an account is charged off in 2013, but is recovered in 2014, the credit entry to reinstate the customer's account should be to **Uncollectible Accounts Expense.**

T　F　**5.** Uncollectible Accounts Expense should be deducted from the Sales account in the Revenue section of the income statement.

T　F　**6.** When losses from uncollectible accounts are recorded using the direct charge-off method, **Uncollectible Accounts Expense** is debited and **Allowance for Doubtful Accounts** and the customers' accounts are credited.

T　F　**7.** In the balance sheet, the balance of Allowance for Doubtful Accounts is deducted from the Accounts Receivable account balance to arrive at the net value of the firm's receivables.

T　F　**8.** Allowance for Doubtful Accounts is a liability account.

T　F　**9.** Generally, as accounts receivable get older a lower percent of the receivables will be uncollectible.

T　F　**10.** Losses resulting from uncollectible accounts should be considered when evaluating the operating efficiency of a firm's credit department.

T　F　**11.** Basing the estimated uncollectible accounts on net credit sales is the method for estimating uncollectible accounts that emphasizes the valuation of assets.

T　F　**12.** Allowance for Doubtful Accounts is called a valuation account.

T　F　**13.** **The Allowance for Doubtful Accounts** increases during the year as individual accounts receivable are deemed to be uncollectible and written off.

T　F　**14.** Providing for losses from uncollectible accounts before they occur permits the seller to match the estimated amount of uncollectible accounts against the sales revenue earned during the same accounting period.

T　F　**15.** The experience of other firms in the same line of business may be used in estimating losses from uncollectible accounts for a new firm.

T　F　**16.** Aging the accounts receivable will provide useful information for determining the estimated loss from uncollectible accounts.

T　F　**17.** The direct charge-off method of recording losses from uncollectible accounts is required by generally accepted accounting principles.

T　F　**18.** The collection of an account previously written off is recorded in the general journal and the cash receipts journal.

T　F　**19.** Under the allowance method, the entry to record estimated expenses from uncollectible accounts is a debit to **Uncollectible Accounts Expense** and a credit to **Accounts Receivable.**

Part B Exercise I   *Determining the amount of uncollectible accounts expense using the allowance method.*

In each of the following cases, compute the amount of the adjusting entry to be debited to **Uncollectible Accounts Expense** and enter the amount in the space provided. Round all calculations to the nearest dollar.

The balance of the Accounts Receivable account on December 31 is $150,000. Total sales for the year were $1.5 million. Total sales returns and allowances were $35,000. Gross credit sales were $990,000, and returns of credit sales were $23,000.

_____
1. **Allowance for Doubtful Accounts** has a credit balance of $100. Losses from uncollectible accounts are estimated as nine-tenths of one percent of net credit sales.

_____
2. **Allowance for Doubtful Accounts** has a debit balance of $100. Losses from uncollectible accounts are estimated to be nine-tenths of 1 percent of net credit sales.

_____
3. **Allowance for Doubtful Accounts** has a credit balance of $100. It is estimated that 4 percent of **Accounts Receivable** are uncollectible.

_____
4. Allowance for Doubtful Accounts has a debit balance of $100. It is estimated that 4 percent of Accounts Receivable are uncollectible.

Part C Exercise II   *Prepare a schedule of accounts receivable by age, based on the information that follows. Use the form provided.*

At the end of its first year of operations, on December 31, 2013, Network Distributors had accounts receivable totaling $34,300. The accounts and amounts outstanding are shown below. Sales terms are 2/10, net 30 days.

John Anderson
Invoice of 10/3	$3,500
Invoice of 12/04	3,000
Total	$6,500

Kim Duong
Invoice of 9/15	$4,500
Invoice of 10/25	1,500
Total	$6,000

Ken Graham
Invoice of 12/08	$7,000

John Maus
Invoice of 11/12	$4,800
Invoice of 11/19	2,000
Total	$6,800

Andrew Tang
Invoice of 12/15	$8,000

Instructions: Prepare an aging schedule for the accounts receivable, using the form provided below.

ACCOUNT	BALANCE	CURRENT	PAST DUE—DAYS		
			1–30	31–60	OVER 60
Anderson, John					
Duong, Kim					
Graham, Ken					
Maus, John					
Tang, Andrew					

Demonstration Problem

Executive clubs is a retailer of golf clubs and other golf accessories. In 2013, its net credit sales were $30,860,000. The company's trial balance for December 31, contained the following account balances.

Accounts Receivable	$3,137,000
Allowance for Doubtful Accounts (credit)	5,200

In preparing the trial balance, the following additional accounts were identified as being uncollectible and should be charged off.

Don Brown	$1,849
Mike Chin	2,408

Instructions

(Omit explanations in journal entries. Round your entries to the nearest dollar.)

1. Record the general journal entry to charge off the two accounts identified as being uncollectible. Number the journal as page 6.

2. Assume that the company uses the percentage of sales method to estimate uncollectible accounts expense. Historical data shows that approximately 0.50 percent of net credit sales prove uncollectible. Enter the necessary adjusting journal entry to record estimated uncollectible accounts expense. Round the amount of the journal entry to the nearest dollar.

3. Assume that the company bases its estimated uncollectible accounts on accounts receivable. The company estimates that approximately three percent of accounts receivable will be uncollectible. Prepare the general journal entry to adjust the accounts on that basis. Round the amount of the journal entry to the nearest dollar.

4. Assume that the company uses the aging of accounts receivable method to estimate uncollectible accounts. Using the following information, calculate the estimated uncollectible amount on December 31, 2013, and prepare the general journal entry to adjust the accounts. Round the amount of the journal entry to the nearest dollar.

Receivable Category	Estimated Loss Rate	Amount in Receivables
Current	0.5%	$2,315,000
1–30 days past due	3.5%	543,400
31–60 days past due	16.0%	195,370
Over 60 days past due	40.0%	78,973
		$3,132,743

5. Assume that on February 8, 2014, Don Brown, whose account was charged off on December 31, 2013 (Instruction 1), sent a check for the entire amount of his account. Give the entries, in general journal form to account for this event.

SOLUTION

	DATE		DESCRIPTION	POST. REF.	DEBIT	CREDIT	
1	2013		(1)				1
2	Dec.	31	Allowance for Doubtful Accounts		4 2 5 7 00		2
3			Accounts Receivable/Don Brown			1 8 4 9 00	3
4			Accounts Receivable/Mike Chin			2 4 0 8 00	4
5			(2)				5
6		31	Uncollectible Accounts Expense		154 3 0 0 00		6
7			Allowance for Doubtful Accounts			154 3 0 0 00	7
8			(3)				8
9		31	Uncollectible Accounts Expense		93 0 3 9 00		9
10			Allowance for Doubtful Accounts			93 0 3 9 00	10
11			(4)				11
12		31	Uncollectible Accounts Expense		92 4 9 9 00		12
13			Allowance for Doubtful Accounts			92 4 9 9 00	13
14							14
15	2014		(5)				15
16	Feb.	8	Accounts Receivable/Don Brown		1 8 4 9 00		16
17			Allowance for Doubtful Accounts			1 8 4 9 00	17
18							18
19		8	Cash		1 8 4 9 00		19
20			Accounts Receivable/Don Brown			1 8 4 9 00	20
21							21
22							22
23							23
24							24

WORKING PAPERS

Name _____

EXERCISE 15.1

_____
_____
_____
_____
_____

GENERAL JOURNAL

PAGE _____

	DATE	DESCRIPTION	POST. REF.	DEBIT	CREDIT	
1						1
2						2
3						3
4						4
5						5
6						6
7						7
8						8
9						9

EXERCISE 15.2

_____
_____
_____
_____
_____

GENERAL JOURNAL

PAGE _____

	DATE	DESCRIPTION	POST. REF.	DEBIT	CREDIT	
1						1
2						2
3						3
4						4
5						5
6						6
7						7
8						8
9						9
10						10
11						11
12						12

EXERCISE 15.3

_____

_____

_____

_____

_____

GENERAL JOURNAL   PAGE _____

	DATE		DESCRIPTION	POST. REF.	DEBIT	CREDIT	
1							1
2							2
3							3
4							4
5							5
6							6
7							7
8							8

EXERCISE 15.4

GENERAL JOURNAL   PAGE _____

	DATE		DESCRIPTION	POST. REF.	DEBIT	CREDIT	
1							1
2							2
3							3
4							4
5							5
6							6
7							7
8							8

EXERCISE 15.5

GENERAL JOURNAL

PAGE _____

	DATE		DESCRIPTION	POST. REF.	DEBIT	CREDIT	
1							1
2							2
3							3
4							4
5							5
6							6
7							7
8							8
9							9
10							10
11							11

EXERCISE 15.6

GENERAL JOURNAL

PAGE _____

	DATE		DESCRIPTION	POST. REF.	DEBIT	CREDIT	
1							1
2							2
3							3
4							4
5							5
6							6
7							7
8							8
9							9
10							10

EXERCISE 15.7

GENERAL JOURNAL   PAGE _____

	DATE		DESCRIPTION	POST. REF.	DEBIT	CREDIT	
1							1
2							2
3							3
4							4
5							5
6							6
7							7
8							8
9							9
10							10
11							11
12							12
13							13
14							14
15							15

EXERCISE 15.8

GENERAL JOURNAL   PAGE _____

	DATE		DESCRIPTION	POST. REF.	DEBIT	CREDIT	
1							1
2							2
3							3
4							4
5							5
6							6
7							7
8							8
9							9
10							10
11							11
12							12
13							13
14							14
15							15

EXERCISE 15.9

GENERAL JOURNAL

PAGE _____

	DATE		DESCRIPTION	POST. REF.	DEBIT	CREDIT	
1							1
2							2
3							3
4							4
5							5
6							6
7							7
8							8
9							9
10							10
11							11
12							12
13							13
14							14
15							15

PROBLEM 15.1A or 15.1B

_____
_____
_____

GENERAL JOURNAL   PAGE _____

	DATE		DESCRIPTION	POST. REF.	DEBIT	CREDIT	
1			(2)				1
2							2
3							3
4							4
5							5
6							6
7			(4)				7
8							8
9							9
10							10
11							11
12			(5)				12
13							13
14							14
15							15
16							16
17							17
18							18

Analyze: _____
_____

PROBLEM 15.2A or 15.2B

ESTIMATE OF UNCOLLECTIBLE ACCOUNTS

_____

_____

_____

_____

ADJUSTMENT FOR ESTIMATED UNCOLLECTIBLE ACCOUNTS

_____

_____

_____

GENERAL JOURNAL   PAGE _____

	DATE	DESCRIPTION	POST. REF.	DEBIT	CREDIT	
1		(3)				1
2						2
3						3
4						4
5						5
6						6
7		(4)				7
8						8
9						9
10						10
11		(5)				11
12						12
13						13
14						14
15						15
16						16
17						17
2						2
3						3
4						4
5						5
6						6
7						7

Analyze: _____

PROBLEM 15.3A or 15.3B

1. a. _____

_____

_____

_____

_____

_____

b. _____

_____

_____

_____

_____

_____

2. a. _____

_____

_____

_____

_____

_____

b. _____

_____

_____

_____

_____

Analyze: _____

_____

PROBLEM 15.4A or 15.4B

GENERAL JOURNAL

PAGE _____

	DATE		DESCRIPTION	POST. REF.	DEBIT	CREDIT	
1							1
2							2
3							3
4							4
5							5
6							6
7							7
8							8
9							9
10							10
11							11
12							12
13							13
14							14
15							15
16							16
17							17
18							18
19							19
20							20
21							21
22							22
23							23
24							24
25							25
26							26
27							27
28							28
29							29
30							30
31							31
32							32
33							33
34							34
35							35

Analyze: _____

CRITICAL THINKING PROBLEM 15.1

GENERAL JOURNAL

PAGE _____

	DATE	DESCRIPTION	POST. REF.	DEBIT	CREDIT	
1						1
2						2
3						3
4						4
5						5
6						6
7						7
8						8
9						9
10						10
11						11
12						12
13						13
14						14
15						15
16						16
17						17
18						18
19						19
20						20
21						21

ESTIMATE OF UNCOLLECTIBLE ACCOUNTS

_____

_____

_____

_____

_____

_____

Allowance for Doubtful Accounts   **Accounts Receivable**

CRITICAL THINKING PROBLEM 15.1 (continued)

_____

_____

_____

_____

_____

_____

_____

_____

_____

_____

_____

_____

_____

_____

_____

_____

_____

_____

_____

_____

_____

_____

_____

_____

_____

_____

_____

_____

_____

Analyze: _____

_____

_____

_____

Name _____

GENERAL JOURNAL   PAGE _____

	DATE	DESCRIPTION	POST. REF.	DEBIT	CREDIT	
1						1
2						2
3						3
4						4
5						5
6						6
7						7
8						8
9						9
10						10
11						11
12						12
13						13
14						14
15						15
16						16
17						17
18						18
19						19
20						20
21						21
22						22
23						23
24						24
25						25
26						26
27						27
28						28

ESTIMATED UNCOLLECTIBLE ACCOUNTS

_____

_____

_____

_____

CRITICAL THINKING PROBLEM 15.2 (continued)

GENERAL JOURNAL   PAGE _____

	DATE		DESCRIPTION	POST. REF.	DEBIT	CREDIT	
1							1
2							2
3							3
4							4
5							5
6							6
7							7
8							8
9							9
10							10
11							11

Allowance for Doubtful Accounts

ANALYSIS BY TERRITORY

EXTRA FORM

GENERAL JOURNAL

PAGE _____

	DATE	DESCRIPTION	POST. REF.	DEBIT	CREDIT	
1						1
2						2
3						3
4						4
5						5
6						6
7						7
8						8
9						9
10						10
11						11
12						12
13						13
14						14
15						15
16						16
17						17
18						18
19						19
20						20

GENERAL JOURNAL

PAGE _____

	DATE	DESCRIPTION	POST. REF.	DEBIT	CREDIT	
1						1
2						2
3						3
4						4
5						5
6						6
7						7
8						8
9						9
10						10
11						11
12						12

Chapter 15 Practice Test Answer Key

Part A True-False		Part B Exercise I	
1. T	**18.** T	**1.** $8,703	**3.** $5,900
2. F	**19.** F	**2.** $8,703	**4.** $6,100
3. F			
4. F			
5. F			
6. F			
7. T			
8. F			
9. F			
10. T			
11. F			
12. T			
13. F			
14. T			
15. T			
16. T			
17. F			

Part C Exercise II

NETWORK DISTRIBUTORS
Schedule of Accounts Receivable by Age
December 31, 2013

ACCOUNT	BALANCE	CURRENT	PAST DUE—DAYS 1–30	PAST DUE—DAYS 31–60	PAST DUE—DAYS OVER 60
Anderson, John	$ 6,500	$ 3,000		$3,500	
Duong, Kim	6,000			1,500	$4,500
Graham, Ken	7,000	7,000			
Maus, John	6,800		$6,800		
Tang, Andrew	8,000	8,000			
Totals	$34,300	$18,000	$6,800	$5,000	$4,500

CHAPTER 16 / Notes Payable and Notes Receivable

STUDY GUIDE

Understanding the Chapter

Objectives

1. Determine whether an instrument meets all the requirements of negotiability. **2.** Calculate the interest on a note. **3.** Determine the maturity date of a note. **4.** Record routine notes payable transactions. **5.** Record discounted notes payable transactions. **6.** Record routine notes receivable transactions. **7.** Compute the proceeds from a discounted note receivable and record transactions related to discounting of notes receivable. **8.** Understand how to use bank drafts and trade acceptances and how to record transactions related to those instruments. **9.** Define the accounting terms new to this chapter.

Reading Assignment

Read Chapter 16 in the textbook. Complete the textbook Section Self Review as you finish reading each section of the chapter, and the Comprehensive Self Review at the end of the chapter. Refer to the Chapter 16 Glossary or to the Glossary at the end of the book to find definitions for terms that are not familiar to you.

Activities

❑ **Thinking Critically**

Answer the *Thinking Critically* questions for Bank of America and Managerial Implications.

❑ **Discussion Questions**

Answer each assigned discussion question in Chapter 16.

❑ **Exercises**

Complete each assigned exercise in Chapter 16. Use the forms provided in this SGWP. The objectives covered by an exercise are given after the exercise number. If you need help with an exercise, review the portion of the chapter related to the objective(s) covered.

❑ **Problems A/B**

Complete each assigned problem in Chapter 16. Use the forms provided in this SGWP. The objectives covered by a problem are given after the problem number. If you need help with a problem, review the portion of the chapter related to the objective(s) covered.

❑ **Critical Thinking Problems**

Complete the critical thinking problems as assigned. Use the forms provided in this SGWP.

❑ **Business Connections**

Complete the Business Connections activities as assigned to gain a deeper understanding of Chapter 16 concepts.

Practice Tests

Complete the Practice Tests, which cover the main points in your reading assignment. Compare your answers with those in the Practice Test Answer Key for Chapter 16 at the end of this chapter. If you have answered any questions incorrectly, review the related section of the text.

Part A True-False *For each of the following statements, circle T in the answer column if the statement is true, F if the statement is false.*

1. To be negotiable, an instrument must:

T   F   **a.** Be payable only to a named person

T   F   **b.** Be signed by the maker or drawer

T   F   **c.** Be payable on demand or at a future time that is fixed or that can be determined

T   F   **d.** Contain an unconditional promise to pay a definite sum

T   F   **e.** Be written on a standard note form

T   F   **f.** Name or identify any drawee mentioned in the instrument

T   F   **2.** Interest = Principal × Rate × Time

T   F   **3.** In computing interest, a "bankers' year" of 365 days is normally used.

T   F   **4.** The maturity value of a note is the amount of principal less any interest that is payable on the due date of the note.

T   F   **5.** Banks deduct interest in advance when discounting a note payable.

T   F   **6.** Notes Payable may appear in the Current Assets section or in the Long-Term Assets section of the balance sheet.

T   F   **7.** The payment of a promissory note results in a debit to Notes Receivable and a credit to Notes Payable.

T   F   **8.** The methods used in computing maturity dates and interest on a note receivable are the same as those used for a note payable.

T   F   **9.** The discounting of a note receivable involves a credit to Cash.

T   F   **10.** Short-term notes receivable are listed in the Current Assets section on the balance sheet.

T   F   **11. The Notes Receivable—Discounted** account is a liability account.

T   F   **12.** A bank draft is a draft written by a bank on its own funds.

13. The Elmore Company receives a $2,000 note from a customer. The note is dated July 31, matures four months later, and bears interest at 6 percent.

T   F   **a.** The maturity date of the note is December 1.

T   F   **b.** The maturity value of the note is $2,120.

T   F   **c.** If the note is discounted on November 1 at a discount rate of 10 percent, the proceeds will be $2,013.08.

T   F   **d.** If the customer dishonors the note at maturity and the bank charges a protest fee of $25, the total amount to be charged to Elmore's account by the bank will be $2,025.

Part B Exercises *Complete each of the following in the spaces provided.*

1. Fill in the blanks in each case below.

	Date of Note	Face Amount	Length of Note	Maturity Date	Interest Rate	Total Interest	Maturity Value
a.	3/8/13	$12,000	3 months	_____	9%	$_____	$_____
b.	6/10/13	$ 4,800	60 days	_____	_____	$ 48.00	_____

2. The maturity value of a note receivable is $3,600. The holder of the note discounts it at the bank with 30 days left until its maturity date. The bank charges a discount rate of 10 percent. Compute the proceeds of the note.

_____

_____

_____

3. Give the general journal entries to record the following transactions. Omit the description.

Jack Walls borrowed $24,000 from Northern Bank on April 10, 2013, signing a 60-day, 8 percent, interest-bearing note for that amount. On the maturity date, Walls paid the note.

GENERAL JOURNAL   PAGE _____

	DATE	DESCRIPTION	POST. REF.	DEBIT	CREDIT	
1						1
2						2
3						3
4						4
5						5
6						6

Demonstration Problem

Compute each of the amounts called for in the situations described below. Show all your computations.

1. Compute the maturity value of a $8,400 note payable. The note carries interest of 6 percent and is payable 60 days from February 27, 2013, the date of the note.

2. What is the amount of a bank's discount on a 120-day note for $18,000, discounted at 7 percent?

3. What is the maturity value of a $8,000, 6-month note receivable, bearing interest at 9 percent?

4. On July 31, 2013, Porter discounted a $10,000 note payable at the bank. The discount rate was 10 percent. The term is three months. Give the journal entry to record the transaction.

5. Tom Lee is late paying his account of $8,000 at your business. Lee signs a note for that amount with interest at 7 percent. The note is due 60 days from July 31, the date of signing.
   a. Give the general journal entry to record this transaction. Omit descriptions. Number the journal as page 12.
   b. Give the general journal entry to record payment in full on the note's maturity date.
   c. Suppose, instead, that the note holder discounted Lee's note at the bank with 45 days remaining on the note. The bank charged a discount rate of 9 percent. Give the general journal to record discounting of this note receivable.

SOLUTION

1. Maturity Value = Principal + Interest

= $8,400 + ($8,400 × .06 × 60/360)

= $8,400 + $84.00

= $8,484.00

2. Discount   = $18,000 × 0.07 × 120/360

= $420.00

3. Maturity Value = Principal + Interest

= $8,000 + ($8,000 × .09 × 6/12)

= $8,000 + $360

= $8,360

4. Discount   = ($10,000 × .10 × 3/12)

= $250

Proceeds   = $10,000 − $250

= $9,750

GENERAL JOURNAL

PAGE _____

	DATE		DESCRIPTION	POST. REF.	DEBIT	CREDIT	
1	2013						1
2	July	31	Cash		9 7 5 0 00		2
3			Interest Expense		2 5 0 00		3
4			Notes Payable			10 0 0 0 00	4
5							5

5. **a.** Notes Receivable = Amount of account balance = $8,000

b. Maturity Value   = $8,000 + ($8,000 × 0.07 × 60/360)

= $8,000 + $93.33

= $8,093.33

c. Proceeds = Maturity Value − Discount

= $8,093.33 − ($8,093.33 × 0.09 × 45/360)

= $8,093.33 − $91.05

= $8,002.28

GENERAL JOURNAL

PAGE ___**12**___

	DATE		DESCRIPTION	POST. REF.	DEBIT	CREDIT	
1	2013						1
2	a. July	31	Notes Receivable		8 0 0 0 00		2
3			Accounts Receivable/Tom Lee			8 0 0 0 00	3
4							4
5	b. Sept.	29	Cash		8 0 9 3 33		5
6			Interest Income			9 3 33	6
7			Notes Receivable			8 0 0 0 00	7
8							8
9	c. Aug.	15	Cash		8 0 0 2 28		9
10			Notes Receivable Discounted			8 0 0 0 00	10
11			Interest Income			2 28	11

WORKING PAPERS

Name _____

EXERCISE 16.1

1. _____
2. _____
3. _____

EXERCISE 16.2

1. _____
_____
_____
_____

2. _____
_____
_____

EXERCISE 16.3

1. _____
_____
_____

2. _____
_____
_____
_____

EXERCISE 16.4

GENERAL JOURNAL   PAGE _____

	DATE	DESCRIPTION	POST. REF.	DEBIT	CREDIT	
1						1
2						2
3						3
4						4
5						5
6						6
7						7
8						8
9						9
10						10
11						11
12						12
13						13
14						14
15						15

(continued)

EXERCISE 16.4 (continued)

GENERAL JOURNAL PAGE _____

	DATE		DESCRIPTION	POST. REF.	DEBIT	CREDIT	
1							1
2							2
3							3
4							4
5							5
6							6

EXERCISE 16.5

GENERAL JOURNAL PAGE _____

	DATE		DESCRIPTION	POST. REF.	DEBIT	CREDIT	
1							1
2							2
3							3
4							4
5							5
6							6

EXERCISE 16.6

GENERAL JOURNAL PAGE _____

	DATE		DESCRIPTION	POST. REF.	DEBIT	CREDIT	
1							1
2							2
3							3
4							4
5							5
6							6
7							7
8							8
9							9
10							10
11							11
12							12
13							13
14							14

EXERCISE 16.7

GENERAL JOURNAL
PAGE _____

	DATE	DESCRIPTION	POST. REF.	DEBIT	CREDIT	
1						1
2						2
3						3
4						4

EXERCISE 16.8

GENERAL JOURNAL
PAGE _____

	DATE	DESCRIPTION	POST. REF.	DEBIT	CREDIT	
1						1
2						2
3						3
4						4
5						5
6						6
7						7

EXTRA FORM

GENERAL JOURNAL
PAGE _____

	DATE	DESCRIPTION	POST. REF.	DEBIT	CREDIT	
1						1
2						2
3						3
4						4
5						5
6						6
7						7
8						8
9						9
10						10
11						11
12						12
13						13
14						14
15						15
16						16

PROBLEM 16.1A or 16.1B

1. _____

_____

_____

2. _____

_____

3. _____

_____

Analyze: _____

_____

PROBLEM 16.2A or 16.2B

GENERAL JOURNAL   PAGE _____

	DATE	DESCRIPTION	POST. REF.	DEBIT	CREDIT	
1						1
2						2
3						3
4						4
5						5
6						6
7						7
8						8
9						9
10						10
11						11
12						12
13						13
14						14
15						15
16						16
17						17
18						18
19						19
20						20
21						21

Analyze: _____

_____

PROBLEM 16.3A or 16.3B

_____

_____

_____

_____

_____

_____

_____

_____

Analyze: _____

_____

PROBLEM 16.4A or 16.4B

_____

_____

_____

_____

_____

_____

_____

_____

_____

_____

_____

_____

_____

_____

_____

_____

_____

_____

Analyze: _____

_____

PROBLEM 16.5A or 16.5B

GENERAL JOURNAL

PAGE _____

	DATE		DESCRIPTION	POST. REF.	DEBIT	CREDIT	
1							1
2							2
3							3
4							4
5							5
6							6
7							7
8							8
9							9
10							10
11							11
12							12
13							13
14							14
15							15
16							16
17							17
18							18
19							19
20							20

Analyze: _____

CRITICAL THINKING PROBLEM 16.1

_____
_____
_____
_____
_____
_____
_____
_____
_____

CRITICAL THINKING PROBLEM 16.2

Omit descriptions

GENERAL JOURNAL

PAGE _____

	DATE		DESCRIPTION	POST. REF.	DEBIT	CREDIT	
1							1
2							2
3							3
4							4
5							5
6							6
7							7
8							8
9							9
10							10
11							11
12							12
13							13
14							14
15							15
16							16
17							17
18							18
19							19
20							20
21							21
22							22
23							23

CRITICAL THINKING PROBLEM 16.2 (continued)

Omit descriptions   GENERAL JOURNAL   PAGE _____

	DATE	DESCRIPTION	POST. REF.	DEBIT	CREDIT	
1						1
2						2
3						3
4						4
5						5
6						6
7						7
8						8
9						9
10						10
11						11
12						12
13						13
14						14
15						15
16						16
17						17
18						18
19						19
20						20
21						21
22						22

Analyze: _____

_____

Chapter 16 Practice Test Answer Key

Part A True-False

1. a. F	3.	F	10.	T	
b. T	4.	F	11.	F	
c. T	5.	T	12.	F	
d. T	6.	F	13. a. T		
e. F	7.	F	b. F		
f. T	8.	T	c. F		
2. T	9.	F	d. F		

Part B Exercises

1. **a.** Maturity date,   6/8/13
   Total interest, $ 270
   Maturity value, $12,270
   b. Maturity date,   8/9/13
   Interest rate   6%
   Maturity value $4,848
2. Discount = $3,600 × .10 × 30/360 = $30
   Proceeds = $3,600 − $30 = $3,570
3. 2013

		Debit	Credit
Apr. 10	Cash	24,000.00	
	Notes Payable—Bank		24,000.00
June 9	Notes Payable—Bank	24,000.00	
	Interest Expense	320.00	
	Cash		24,320.00

CHAPTER 17 Merchandise Inventory

STUDY GUIDE

Understanding the Chapter

Objectives	**1.** Compute inventory cost by applying four commonly used costing methods. **2.** Compare the different methods of inventory costing. **3.** Compute inventory value under the lower of cost or market rule. **4.** Estimate inventory cost using the gross profit method. **5.** Estimate inventory cost using the retail method. **6.** Define the accounting terms new to this chapter.
Reading Assignment	Read Chapter 17 in the textbook. Complete the textbook Section Self Review as you finish reading each section of the chapter, and the Comprehensive Self Review at the end of the chapter. Refer to the Chapter 17 Glossary or to the Glossary at the end of the book to find definitions for terms that are not familiar to you.

Activities

❏ **Thinking Critically**	Answer the *Thinking Critically* questions for Best Buy and Managerial Implications.
❏ **Discussion Questions**	Answer each assigned discussion question in Chapter 17.
❏ **Exercises**	Complete each assigned exercise in Chapter 17. Use the forms provided in this SGWP. The objectives covered by an exercise are given after the exercise number. If you need help with an exercise, review the portion of the chapter related to the objective(s) covered.
❏ **Problems A/B**	Complete each assigned problem in Chapter 17. Use the forms provided in this SGWP. The objectives covered by a problem are given after the problem number. If you need help with a problem, review the portion of the chapter related to the objective(s) covered.
❏ **Critical Thinking Problems**	Complete the critical thinking problems as assigned. Use the forms provided in this SGWP.
❏ **Business Connections**	Complete the Business Connections activities as assigned to gain a deeper understanding of Chapter 17 concepts.

Practice Tests

Complete the Practice Tests, which cover the main points in your reading assignment. Compare your answers with those in the Practice Test Answer Key for Chapter 17 at the end of this chapter. If you have answered any questions incorrectly, review the related section of the text.

Part A True-False
For each of the following statements, circle T in the answer column if the statement is true or F if the statement is false.

T   **F**   **1.** LIFO inventory costing parallels the actual flow of goods in most businesses.

T   **F**   **2.** The valuation of the ending inventory has a direct effect on the net income for a period.

T   **F**   **3.** As used in inventory valuation, market price is the price at which an item can be bought at the inventory date through the usual channels and in the usual quantities.

T   **F**   **4.** During a period of falling prices, the FIFO method of inventory valuation will result in a higher reported net income than the LIFO method.

T   **F**   **5.** The gross profit method of estimating inventory and the retail method utilize the same basic concept—the relation between sales price of inventory and its cost.

T   **F**   **6.** Applying the lower of cost or market rule on the basis of total cost and total market will generally result in a higher value than its application on the basis of individual items or groups of items.

T   **F**   **7.** The average cost method of inventory valuation will usually result in the lowest reported net income of the valuation methods that may be used.

T   **F**   **8.** A decline in the market value of inventory to less than its cost should be reflected in the financial statements of the period in which the decline occurs.

T   **F**   **9.** Under the perpetual inventory system, the cost of goods on hand at any given time can be determined.

T   **F**   **10.** Ending Merchandise Inventory appears on both the balance sheet and the income statement.

T   **F**   **11.** It is necessary to count the goods on hand to estimate the inventory cost under the retail method.

T   **F**   **12.** The most conservative method of applying the lower of cost or market rule is to apply it to inventory items on a group by group basis.

T   **F**   **13.** During a period of rising prices, the FIFO method will yield a lower ending inventory cost than the LIFO method.

Part B Matching

For each of the numbered items, choose the matching term from the box and write the identifying letter in the answer column.

a. Average cost
b. First in, first out
c. Last in, first out
d. Markdown
e. Markup
f. Retail method
g. Specific identification

_____ 1. Reduction of an originally established selling price.

_____ 2. The inventory valuation method that attempts to match the current cost of goods purchased with current sales.

_____ 3. The difference between the cost and the initial retail selling price of merchandise.

_____ 4. An inventory valuation method that assumes the oldest items of inventory are sold first.

_____ 5. The inventory valuation method in which the actual cost of each individual item is determined.

_____ 6. Determining the sales value of the goods on hand and computing the approximate cost by applying the ratio of cost to the selling price during the accounting period.

_____ 7. The cost of all like items available for sale during a period are averaged to determine a unit cost in valuing the ending inventory.

Demonstration Problem

The Rest at Ease Security Company has three types of electronic security systems in its electronics department. Group S, Group U and Group V. The following data relates to January 2013 inventory transactions for the three groups.

Inventory, January 1, 2013:

Group S   8 @ $125.00
Group U   16 @ $130.00
Group V   8 @ $175.00

Purchases

Date	Group	Units	Unit Cost	Total
Jan. 7	S	31	$110.00	$3,410.00
	U	22	120.00	2,640.00
	V	33	205.00	6,765.00
Jan. 18	S	25	115.00	2,875.00
	U	26	125.00	3,250.00
	V	23	210.00	4,830.00
Jan. 29	S	19	120.00	2,280.00
	U	19	130.00	2,470.00
	V	12	220.00	2,640.00

The company uses the LIFO method of determining cost of inventory.
Sales for the month were as follows:

Group S   76 units
Group U   45 units
Group V   41 units

1. What is the cost of goods sold during the month?
2. What is the cost of the ending inventory?

SOLUTION

1. Cost of Goods Sold:

Group S	19 units @ $120.00	=	$ 2,280.00
	25 units @ $115.00	=	2,875.00
	31 units @ $110.00	=	3,410.00
	1 unit @ $125.00	=	125.00
	Total, Group S		$ 8,690.00
Group U	19 units @ $130.00	=	$ 2,470.00
	26 units @ $125.00	=	3,250.00
	Total, Group U		$ 5,720.00
Group V	12 units @ $220.00	=	$ 2,640.00
	23 units @ $210.00	=	4,830.00
	6 units @ $205.00	=	1,230.00
	Total, Group V		$ 8,700.00
Total Cost of Goods Sold			**$23,110.00**

2. Cost of Ending Inventory

Group S	7 units @ $125.00	=	$ 875.00
	Total, Group S	=	$ 875.00
Group U	22 units @ $120.00	=	$ 2,640.00
	16 units @ $130.00	=	2,080.00
	Total, Group U		$ 4,720.00
Group V	27 units @ $205.00	=	$ 5,535.00
	8 units @ $175.00	=	1,400.00
	Total, Group V		$ 6,935.00
Total Ending Inventory			**$12,530.00**

WORKING PAPERS

Name _____

EXERCISE 17.1

Description	Number of Units	Unit Cost	Total Cost
_____	_____	_____	_____
_____	_____	_____	_____
_____	_____	_____	_____
_____	_____	_____	_____
_____	_____	_____	_____
_____	_____	_____	_____
_____	_____	_____	_____

1. Average Cost Method

_____	_____	_____	_____
_____	_____	_____	_____
_____	_____	_____	_____
_____	_____	_____	_____

2. FIFO Method

_____	_____	_____	_____
_____	_____	_____	_____
_____	_____	_____	_____

3. LIFO Method

_____	_____	_____	_____
_____	_____	_____	_____
_____	_____	_____	_____

EXERCISE 17.2

Description	Quantity	Unit Cost	Market Value	Total Cost	Total Market
1. Item by Item					
_____	_____	_____	_____	_____	_____
_____	_____	_____	_____	_____	_____
_____	_____	_____	_____	_____	_____
_____	_____	_____	_____	_____	_____
_____	_____	_____	_____	_____	_____
_____	_____	_____	_____	_____	_____
_____	_____	_____	_____	_____	_____

2. Total Cost or Total Market Value of Ending Inventory

3. By Groups

EXERCISE 17.3

EXERCISE 17.4

EXERCISE 17.5

ESTIMATED INVENTORY COST

	Cost	Retail
_____	_____	_____
_____	_____	_____
_____	_____	_____
_____	_____	_____
_____	_____	_____
_____	_____	_____
_____	_____	_____
_____	_____	_____
_____	_____	_____
_____	_____	_____
_____	_____	_____
_____	_____	_____
_____	_____	_____
_____	_____	_____
_____	_____	_____
_____	_____	_____
_____	_____	_____
_____	_____	_____
_____	_____	_____
_____	_____	_____
_____	_____	_____
_____	_____	_____
_____	_____	_____
_____	_____	_____
_____	_____	_____
_____	_____	_____
_____	_____	_____
_____	_____	_____

PROBLEM 17.1A or 17.1B

Description	Number of Units	Unit Cost	Total Cost
_____	_____	_____	_____
_____	_____	_____	_____
_____	_____	_____	_____
_____	_____	_____	_____
_____	_____	_____	_____
_____	_____	_____	_____
_____	_____	_____	_____
_____	_____	_____	_____

a. Average Cost Method

_____	_____	_____	_____
_____	_____	_____	_____
_____	_____	_____	_____
_____	_____	_____	_____

b. FIFO Method

_____	_____	_____	_____
_____	_____	_____	_____
_____	_____	_____	_____
_____	_____	_____	_____

c. LIFO Method

_____	_____	_____	_____
_____	_____	_____	_____
_____	_____	_____	_____
_____	_____	_____	_____
_____	_____	_____	_____

Analyze: _____

_____

PROBLEM 17.2A or 17.2B

1.

Description	Number of Units	Unit Cost	Total Cost
_____	_____	_____	_____
_____	_____	_____	_____
_____	_____	_____	_____
_____	_____	_____	_____
_____	_____	_____	_____
_____	_____	_____	_____

Description	Number of Units	Unit Cost	Inventory Valuation	Cost of Goods Sold

a. FIFO Method

_____	_____	_____	_____	_____
_____	_____	_____	_____	_____
_____	_____	_____	_____	_____
_____	_____	_____	_____	_____
_____	_____	_____	_____	_____

b. LIFO Method

_____	_____	_____	_____	_____
_____	_____	_____	_____	_____
_____	_____	_____	_____	_____
_____	_____	_____	_____	_____
_____	_____	_____	_____	_____

c. Average Cost Method

_____	_____	_____	_____	_____
_____	_____	_____	_____	_____
_____	_____	_____	_____	_____

2.

Method	Number of Units	Valuation Based On: Cost	Market	Valuation Basis	Lower of Cost or Market
a. FIFO	_____	_____	_____	_____	_____
b. LIFO	_____	_____	_____	_____	_____
c. Average Cost	_____	_____	_____	_____	_____

Analyze: _____

_____

PROBLEM 17.3A or 17.3B

Description	Quantity	Unit Cost	Market Value	Total Cost	Total Market	Lower of Cost or Market
_____	_____	_____	_____	_____	_____	_____
_____	_____	_____	_____	_____	_____	_____
_____	_____	_____	_____	_____	_____	_____
_____	_____	_____	_____	_____	_____	_____
_____	_____	_____	_____	_____	_____	_____
_____	_____	_____	_____	_____	_____	_____
_____	_____	_____	_____	_____	_____	_____
_____	_____	_____	_____	_____	_____	_____

Inventory Valuations   **Lower of Cost or Market**

_____   _____

_____   _____

_____   _____

_____   _____

_____   _____

_____   _____

_____   _____

Analyze: _____

_____

PROBLEM 17.4A or 17.4B

_____   _____

_____   _____

_____   _____

_____   _____

_____   _____

_____   _____

_____   _____

_____   _____

Analyze: _____

PROBLEM 17.5A or 17.5B

Estimated Inventory	Cost	Retail
_____	_____	_____
_____	_____	_____
_____	_____	_____
_____	_____	_____
_____	_____	_____
_____	_____	_____
_____	_____	_____
_____	_____	_____
_____	_____	_____
_____	_____	_____
_____	_____	_____
_____	_____	_____

Analyze: _____

_____

PROBLEM 17.6A or 17.6B

_____

_____

_____

_____

Item	Cost
_____	_____
_____	_____
_____	_____
_____	_____
_____	_____
_____	_____
_____	_____
_____	_____

Analyze: _____

_____

CRITICAL THINKING PROBLEM 17.1

_____
_____
_____

Estimated Inventory	Cost	Retail
_____	_____	_____
_____	_____	_____
_____	_____	_____
_____	_____	_____
_____	_____	_____
_____	_____	_____
_____	_____	_____
_____	_____	_____

Analyze: _____
_____

CRITICAL THINKING PROBLEM 17.2

_____
_____
_____
_____
_____
_____
_____
_____
_____

Chapter 17 Practice Test Answer Key

Part A True-False

1. F	6. T	11. F
2. T	7. F	12. F
3. T	8. T	13. F
4. F	9. T	
5. T	10. T	

Part B Matching

1. d	5. g
2. c	6. f
3. e	7. a
4. b	

CHAPTER 18 Property, Plant, and Equipment

STUDY GUIDE

Understanding the Chapter

Objectives

1. Determine the amount to record as an asset's cost. 2. Compute and record depreciation of property, plant, and equipment by commonly used methods. 3. Apply the Modified Accelerated Cost Recovery System (MACRS) for federal income tax purposes. 4. Record sales of plant and equipment. 5. Record asset trade-ins using the financial accounting rules and income tax requirements. 6. Compute and record depletion of natural resources. 7. Recognize asset impairment and understand the general concepts of accounting for impairment. 8. Compute and record amortization and impairment of intangible assets. 9. Define the accounting terms new to this chapter.

Reading Assignment

Read Chapter 18 in the textbook. Complete the textbook Section Self Review as you finish reading each section of the chapter, and the Comprehensive Self Review at the end of the chapter. Refer to the Chapter 18 Glossary or to the Glossary at the end of the book to find definitions for terms that are not familiar to you.

Activities

❏ **Thinking Critically**

Answer the *Thinking Critically* questions for The Coca-Cola Company and Managerial Implications.

❏ **Discussion Questions**

Answer each assigned discussion question in Chapter 18.

❏ **Exercises**

Complete each assigned exercise in Chapter 18. Use the forms provided in this SGWP. The objectives covered by an exercise are given after the exercise number. If you need help with an exercise, review the portion of the chapter related to the objective(s) covered.

❏ **Problems A/B**

Complete each assigned problem in Chapter 18. Use the forms provided in this SGWP. The objectives covered by a problem are given after the problem number. If you need help with a problem, review the portion of the chapter related to the objective(s) covered.

❏ **Critical Thinking Problems**

Complete the critical thinking problems as assigned. Use the forms provided in this SGWP.

❏ **Business Connections**

Complete the Business Connections activities as assigned to gain a deeper understanding of Chapter 18 concepts.

Practice Tests

Complete the Practice Tests, which cover the main points in your reading assignment. Compare your answers with those in the Practice Test Answer Key for Chapter 18 at the end of this chapter. If you have answered any questions incorrectly, review the related section of the text.

Part A True-False *For each of the following statements, circle T in the answer column if the statement is true or F if the statement is false.*

T F **1.** Depreciation should be debited to expense and credited to the asset account.

T F **2.** Salvage value is ignored under the units-of-output method.

T F **3.** If the trade-in allowance for an old asset is greater than its book value, for financial accounting purposes, a gain should be recognized on the trade-in.

T F **4.** Neither gain nor loss is recognized for income tax purposes on the exchange or trade-in of like assets.

T F **5.** Under GAAP, a loss on the trade-in of an old asset of like kind must be recognized.

T F **6.** The declining-balance method should be used in computing depletion on the cost of mineral deposits.

T F **7.** Under GAAP, most R & D costs must be charged to expense when incurred.

T F **8.** Amortization of the costs of amortizable intangibles is charged to an expense account and credited directly to the asset account.

T F **9.** Costs of intangible assets having limited lives, such as patents and copyrights, should be amortized over the legal life of the intangible or its useful life, whichever is shorter.

T F **10.** Purchased intangibles with unlimited lives, such as goodwill, are not amortized, but are subject to an impairment test each year.

T F **11.** The cost of paving a parking lot for a business is debited to the land account on which the lot is located.

T F **12.** At the end of an accounting period, current depreciation or depletion is debited to an expense account and credited to a contra-asset account.

T F **13. Prepaid Insurance** is included in plant and equipment.

T F **14.** A building under construction is an example of an intangible asset.

T F **15.** The cost of installing or modifying a new asset should be charged to expense.

T F **16.** If the declining-balance depreciation method is used, salvage is ignored until that time at which the accumulated depreciation equals estimated salvage. From that point forward, no further depreciation is recorded.

T F **17.** The sum-of-the-years'-digits method is an accelerated method of depreciation.

T F **18.** Salvage is ignored if the sum-of-years'-digits method of depreciation is used.

T F **19.** A business must use the same depreciation method for all its assets.

T F **20.** The decline in market value of an asset each period is generally a satisfactory measure of depreciation of the asset for that period.

Part B Matching *For each numbered item, choose the matching term from the box and write the identifying letter in the answer column.*

_____ 1. A method of computing depreciation in which the same amount is recorded for each accounting period over the useful life of an asset.

_____ 2. The term used to describe the periodic transfer of acquisition costs to expense when natural resources such as ores or oil are physically removed by production.

_____ 3. The term used to describe the situation when an asset is determined to have a market value or value-in-use less than its book value.

_____ 4. The transfer of cost of an intangible asset with a fixed life to expense.

_____ 5. The value of a business in excess of its net identifiable assets.

_____ 6. A means of computing annual depreciation by applying a constant percentage to the book value of an asset at the beginning of the year.

a. Amortization
b. Book value
c. Declining balance method
d. Depletion
e. Depreciation
f. Goodwill
g. Impairment
h. Intangibles
i. Straight-line method
j. Unit-of-production methods

_____ 7. A method of computing annual depreciation by dividing the depreciable cost of the asset by the expected units of production and multiplying that rate by the units produced during the year.

_____ 8. Assets such as patents, goodwill, trademarks and copyrights.

_____ 9. The term used to describe the periodic transfer of capitalized costs of plant and equipment to expense.

_____ 10. The difference between the capitalized costs of an asset and the accumulated depreciation for the asset.

Part C Exercise

On January 1, 2013, a business acquired at a cost of $44,000 new office equipment with an estimated useful life of 8 years. Estimated salvage value at the end of that time is $4,000. Compute depreciation for 2013 and 2014 using the following methods. (Round all computations to nearest whole dollar.)

a. straight-line method.

b. the sum-of-years'-digits method.

c. double-declining-balance method.

Demonstration Problem

Discovery Company was formed in January 2013 to operate a research laboratory.

1. In January it acquired a tract of land at a cost of $102,000. In connection with the purchase, Discovery paid closing costs of $8,000. The company immediately began preparations for constructing the new laboratory. This included costs of $3,000 to demolish a shed located on the land, $2,000 to have the debris removed, $10,000 for leveling the building site, $4,000 for "clean-up of the property" required as condition of purchase, and $3,500 for drainage of low areas of land. The owners paid $46,200 for design and engineering of the building, $4,000 for legal fees associated with the building permit, and $3,000 for the city permit fee. Erecting a fence along the rear of the property cost $51,600. A parking lot was paid at a cost of $110,000 and a new building constructed at a cost of $950,000. The building was completed in December, 2013. Determine the total cost of each asset involved. Show the details of cost of each.

SOLUTION

Land:	
Purchase price	$102,000
Closing costs	8,000
Shed demolition	3,000
Debris removal	2,000
Property clean-up	4,000
Leveling site	10,000
Drainage	3,500
Land total	$132,500

Land Improvements:	
Paving parking lot	$ 110,000
Erect fence	51,600
Improvements total	$161,600

Building:	
Design and engineering	$ 46,200
Legal fees—permit	4,000
City permit fee	3,000
Construction contract	950,000
Building total	$1,003,200

2. Discovery completed the building at the end of 2013 and placed it in use on January 2, 2014. Its useful life is estimated as 30 years, with estimated net salvage value of $53,000. Three chemical research "vats," the items of equipment to be used, were installed and were put into operation on January 2, 2014. The three units are quite different in use and in physical characteristics.

   a. Vat one cost $240,000 and has an estimated life of five years, and estimated net salvage value of $24,000. Because of high operating cost as the unit is used, Discovery decided to use the double-declining-balance method of depreciation on the asset.

   b. Vat two cost $150,000 and has an estimated useful life of 10 years, with expected net salvage of $15,000. Because its operating costs and the hours of use are expected to be fairly constant, straight-line depreciation is used.

   c. Vat three cost $350,000 and is expected to have a salvage value of $30,000, with an expected useful life of 8 years. It is decided to apply the sum-of-years'-digits method to this asset.

   Compute depreciation on the building and each of these three vats for 2014 and 2015. (Round all amounts to nearest whole dollar.)

SOLUTION

<u>Building:</u>

2014 depreciation ($1,003,200 − $53,000) ÷ 30 years =	$31,673	
2015 depreciation ($1,003,200 − $53,000) ÷ 30 years =	$31,673	

<u>Vat 1:</u>

2013 depreciation ($240,000 × .40)	=	$96,000
2014 depreciation ($240,000 − $96,000) × .40	=	$57,600

<u>Vat 2:</u>

2013 depreciation ($150,000 − $15,000) × .10	=	$13,500
2014 depreciation ($150,000 − $15,000) × .10	=	$13,500

<u>Vat 3:</u>

2013 depreciation ($350,000 − $30,000) × 8/36	=	$71,111
2014 depreciation ($350,000 − $30,000) × 7/36	=	$62,222

3. On March 31, 2014, Discovery realized that Vat 2 was inadequate and traded it on a new vat (Vat 4) with a fair value and list price of $250,000. Discovery received a trade-in allowance of $65,000 for Vat 2 and paid the difference of $185,000 in cash.

a. What amount of depreciation will be recorded on March 31 on Vat 2?
b. Will gain or loss be recorded on the trade-in? If so, which? If so, how much?
c. What amount will be recorded in the asset account for Vat 4?

SOLUTION

a. Depreciation for three months = [($150,000 − $15,000) × .10 × 3/12] = $3,375.

b. Losses, but not gains, are recognized. In this case the loss is $54,625:

Trade-in allowance received	$ 65,000
Less: book value of old asset (150,000 − $16,875)	133,125
= Loss on trade-in	$ 68,125

c. Vat 4 cost is deemed to be cash paid ($185,000) + trade-in allowance ($65,000) = $250,000. This is also the fair market value of the new asset.

WORKING PAPERS

Name _____

EXERCISE 18.1

	Land	Warehouse
_____	_____	_____
_____	_____	_____
_____	_____	_____
_____	_____	_____
_____	_____	_____
_____	_____	_____
_____	_____	_____

EXERCISE 18.2

_____

_____

_____

_____

_____

_____

EXERCISE 18.3

GENERAL JOURNAL

PAGE _____

	DATE	DESCRIPTION	POST. REF.	DEBIT	CREDIT	
1						1
2						2
3						3
4						4
5						5
6						6
7						7

EXTRA FORM

GENERAL JOURNAL

PAGE _____

	DATE	DESCRIPTION	POST. REF.	DEBIT	CREDIT	
1						1
2						2
3						3
4						4
5						5

EXERCISE 18.4

STRAIGHT-LINE METHOD

Year	Acquisition Cost	Salvage Value	Useful Life	Depreciation	Accumulated Depreciation
_____	_____	_____	_____	_____	_____
_____	_____	_____	_____	_____	_____

DOUBLE-DECLINING-BALANCE METHOD

Year	Beginning Book Value	Rate	Depreciation	Accumulated Depreciation
_____	_____	_____	_____	_____
_____	_____	_____	_____	_____

SUM-OF-THE-YEARS'-DIGITS METHOD

Year	Fraction	Cost Less Salvage	Depreciation	Accumulated Depreciation
_____	_____	_____	_____	_____
_____	_____	_____	_____	_____

EXERCISE 18.5

EXERCISE 18.6

_____
_____
_____
_____
_____
_____
_____
_____

EXERCISE 18.7

GENERAL JOURNAL

PAGE _____

	DATE	DESCRIPTION	POST. REF.	DEBIT	CREDIT	
1						1
2						2
3						3
4						4
5						5
6						6
7						7
8						8
9						9
10						10
11						11
12						12
13						13

EXERCISE 18.8

_____
_____
_____
_____
_____
_____
_____

EXERCISE 18.8 (continued)

GENERAL JOURNAL   PAGE _____

	DATE		DESCRIPTION	POST. REF.	DEBIT	CREDIT	
1							1
2							2
3							3
4							4
5							5
6							6
7							7
8							8
9							9
10							10
11							11
12							12
13							13

EXERCISE 18.9

1. _____

2. _____

_____

_____

_____

_____

_____

_____

_____

EXERCISE 18.10

_____

_____

_____

_____

_____

EXERCISE 18.11

a. _____

_____

_____

b. _____

_____

_____

_____

_____

EXERCISE 18.12

1. _____

_____

_____

_____

2. _____

_____

_____

_____

_____

_____

_____

_____

_____

_____

_____

PROBLEM 18.1A or 18.1B

1. _____ _____

_____ _____

_____ _____

_____ _____

_____ _____

2. _____ _____

_____ _____

_____ _____

_____ _____

_____ _____

_____ _____

_____ _____

_____ _____

_____ _____

_____ _____

_____ _____

_____ _____

_____ _____

3. _____ _____

_____ _____

_____ _____

Analyze: _____ _____

_____ _____

_____ _____

_____ _____

PROBLEM 18.2A or 18.2B

STRAIGHT-LINE METHOD

Year	Acquisition Cost	Salvage Value	Useful Life	Annual Depreciation	Accumulated Depreciation
_____	_____	_____	_____	_____	_____
_____	_____	_____	_____	_____	_____
_____	_____	_____	_____	_____	_____

SUM-OF-THE-YEARS'-DIGITS METHOD

Year	Fraction	Cost Less Salvage	Annual Depreciation	Accumulated Depreciation
_____	_____	_____	_____	_____
_____	_____	_____	_____	_____
_____	_____	_____	_____	_____

DOUBLE-DECLINING-BALANCE METHOD

Year	Beginning Book Value	Rate	Annual Depreciation	Accumulated Depreciation
_____	_____	_____	_____	_____
_____	_____	_____	_____	_____
_____	_____	_____	_____	_____

Analyze: _____

_____

PROBLEM 18.3A or 18.3B

STRAIGHT-LINE METHOD

Year	Acquisition Cost	Salvage Value	Useful Life	Annual Depreciation	Accumulated Depreciation
_____	_____	_____	_____	_____	_____
_____	_____	_____	_____	_____	_____
_____	_____	_____	_____	_____	_____

UNITS-OF-PRODUCTION METHOD

Year	Acquisition Cost	Salvage Value	Total Expected Units of Production	Actual Units of Production	Cost per Unit	Annual Depreciation	Accumulated Depreciation
_____	_____	_____	_____	_____	_____	_____	_____
_____	_____	_____	_____	_____	_____	_____	_____
_____	_____	_____	_____	_____	_____	_____	_____

Analyze: _____

_____

PROBLEM 18.4A or 18.4B

1. _____

2. _____

3. _____

4. _____

Analyze: _____

PROBLEM 18.5A or 18.5B

GENERAL JOURNAL PAGE _____

	DATE	DESCRIPTION	POST. REF.	DEBIT	CREDIT	
1						1
2						2
3						3
4						4
5						5
6						6
7						7
8						8
9						9
10						10
11						11
12						12
13						13
14						14
15						15
16						16
17						17
18						18
19						19
20						20
21						21
22						22
23						23
24						24
25						25
26						26
27						27
28						28
29						29
30						30
31						31
32						32
33						33
34						34
35						35
36						36

Analyze: _____

PROBLEM 18.5A or 18.5B (continued)

GENERAL JOURNAL

PAGE _____

	DATE	DESCRIPTION	POST. REF.	DEBIT	CREDIT	
1						1
2						2
3						3
4						4
5						5
6						6
7						7
8						8
9						9
10						10
11						11
12						12
13						13
14						14
15						15
16						16
17						17
18						18
19						19
20						20
21						21
22						22
23						23
24						24
25						25
26						26
27						27
28						28
29						29
30						30
31						31
32						32
33						33
34						34
35						35
36						36

Analyze: _____

PROBLEM 18.6A or 18.6B

GENERAL JOURNAL   PAGE _____

	DATE		DESCRIPTION	POST. REF.	DEBIT	CREDIT	
1							1
2							2
3							3
4							4
5							5
6							6
7							7
8							8
9							9
10							10
11							11
12							12
13							13
14							14
15							15
16							16
17							17
18							18
19							19
20							20
21							21
22							22
23							23
24							24
25							25
26							26
27							27
28							28
29							29
30							30
31							31
32							32
33							33
34							34
35							35
36							36
37							37

PROBLEM 18.6A or 18.6B (continued)

GENERAL JOURNAL   PAGE _____

	DATE		DESCRIPTION	POST. REF.	DEBIT	CREDIT	
1							1
2							2
3							3
4							4
5							5
6							6
7							7
8							8
9							9
10							10
11							11
12							12
13							13
14							14
15							15
16							16
17							17
18							18
19							19
20							20
21							21
22							22
23							23
24							24
25							25
26							26
27							27
28							28
29							29
30							30
31							31
32							32
33							33
34							34
35							35
36							36

Analyze: _____

PROBLEM 18.7A or 18.7B

1. _____

_____

_____

_____

_____

_____

_____

_____

2. a. _____

_____

b. _____

c. _____

_____

_____

_____

_____

_____

_____

d. _____

_____

_____

Analyze: _____

_____

_____

_____

_____

_____

PROBLEM 18.8A or 18.8B

1. _____

_____

_____

_____

2. _____

3. _____

_____

4. _____

_____

_____

_____

Analyze: _____

_____

_____

_____

_____

_____

_____

_____

_____

_____

_____

_____

_____

PROBLEM 18.9A or 18.9B

GENERAL JOURNAL   PAGE _____

	DATE		DESCRIPTION	POST. REF.	DEBIT	CREDIT	
1							1
2							2
3							3
4							4
5							5
6							6
7							7
8							8
9							9
10							10
11							11
12							12
13							13
14							14
15							15
16							16
17							17
18							18
19							19
20							20
21							21
22							22
23							23
24							24
25							25
26							26
27							27
28							28
29							29
30							30
31							31
32							32
33							33
34							34
35							35
36							36
37							37

PROBLEM 18.9A or 18.9B (continued)

GENERAL JOURNAL   PAGE _____

	DATE	DESCRIPTION	POST. REF.	DEBIT	CREDIT	
1						1
2						2
3						3
4						4
5						5
6						6
7						7
8						8
9						9
10						10
11						11
12						12
13						13
14						14
15						15
16						16
17						17
18						18
19						19
20						20
21						21
22						22
23						23
24						24
25						25
26						26
27						27
28						28
29						29
30						30
31						31
32						32
33						33

Analyze: _____

_____

CRITICAL THINKING PROBLEM 18.1

1. _____
   _____
   _____
   _____
   _____
   _____

2. _____
   _____
   _____
   _____
   _____
   _____
   _____
   _____
   _____
   _____
   _____
   _____
   _____
   _____

3. _____
   _____
   _____
   _____
   _____

4. _____
   _____
   _____
   _____
   _____
   _____

CRITICAL THINKING PROBLEM 18.2

GENERAL JOURNAL

PAGE _____

	DATE	DESCRIPTION	POST. REF.	DEBIT	CREDIT	
1						1
2						2
3						3
4						4
5						5
6						6
7						7
8						8
9						9
10						10
11						11
12						12
13						13
14						14
15						15
16						16
17						17
18						18
19						19
20						20
21						21
22						22
23						23
24						24
25						25
26						26

2. a. _____

_____

_____

b. _____

CRITICAL THINKING PROBLEM 18.2 (continued)

3. _____

_____

_____

_____

_____

_____

4. _____

_____

_____

_____

_____

Chapter 18 Practice Test Answer Key

Part A True-False

1. F	8. T	15. F
2. F	9. T	16. T
3. T	10. T	17. T
4. T	11. F	18. F
5. T	12. T	19. F
6. F	13. F	20. F
7. T	14. F	

Part B Matching

1. i	6. c
2. d	7. j
3. g	8. h
4. a	9. e
5. f	10. b

Part C Exercise

1. Depreciation for 2013 = ($44,000 − $4,000) ÷ 8 years = $5,000
   Depreciation for 2014 = ($44,000 − $4,000) ÷ 8 years = $5,000

2. Depreciation for 2013 = ($44,000 − $4,000) × 8/36 = $8,888
   Depreciation for 2014 = ($44,000 − $4,000) × 7/36 = $7,778

3. Depreciation for 2013 = $44,000 × .25 = $11,000
   Depreciation for 2014 = ($44,000 − $11,000) × .25 = $8,250

CHAPTER 19 Accounting for Partnerships

STUDY GUIDE

Understanding the Chapter

Objectives

1. Explain the major advantages and disadvantages of a partnership. **2.** State the important provisions that should be included in every partnership agreement. **3.** Account for the formation of a partnership. **4.** Compute and record the division of net income or net loss between partners in accordance with the partnership agreement. **5.** Prepare a statement of partners' equities. **6.** Account for the revaluation of assets and liabilities prior to the dissolution of a partnership. **7.** Account for the sale of a partnership interest. **8.** Account for the investment of a new partner in an existing partnership. **9.** Account for the withdrawal of a partner from a partnership. **10.** Define the accounting terms new to this chapter.

Reading Assignment

Read Chapter 19 in the textbook. Complete the textbook Section Self Review as you finish reading each section of the chapter, and the Comprehensive Self Review at the end of the chapter. Refer to the Chapter 19 Glossary or to the Glossary at the end of the book to find definitions for terms that are not familiar to you.

Activities

❑ **Thinking Critically**

Answer the *Thinking Critically* questions for Healthcare Venture Professionals, L.L.C. and Managerial Implications.

❑ **Discussion Questions**

Answer each assigned discussion question in Chapter 19.

❑ **Exercises**

Complete each assigned exercise in Chapter 19. Use the forms provided in this SGWP. The objectives covered by an exercise are given after the exercise number. If you need help with an exercise, review the portion of the chapter related to the objective(s) covered.

❑ **Problems A/B**

Complete each assigned problem in Chapter 19. Use the forms provided in this SGWP. The objectives covered by a problem are given after the problem number. If you need help with a problem, review the portion of the chapter related to the objective(s) covered.

❑ **Critical Thinking Problems**

Complete the critical thinking problems as assigned. Use the forms provided in this SGWP.

❑ **Business Connections**

Complete the Business Connections activities as assigned to gain a deeper understanding of Chapter 19 concepts.

Practice Tests

Complete the Practice Tests, which cover the main points in your reading assignment. Compare your answers with those in the Practice Test Answer Key for Chapter 19 at the end of this chapter. If you have answered any questions incorrectly, review the related section of the text.

Part A True-False   *For each of the following statements, circle T in the answer column if the statement is true or F if the statement is false.*

T   F   **1.** Each partner should have a drawing account and a capital account.

T   F   **2.** Salary allowances to partners are considered in dividing net income or loss, even though the partnership may have a loss for the period.

T   F   **3.** A salary may be allowed to one partner, even though other partners do not receive salary allowances.

T   F   **4.** Salaries allowed a partner must be deducted in arriving at the partnership's net profit or loss for the year.

T   F   **5.** The partnership's accounting records should reflect the sales price of an existing partnership interest to a new partner.

T   F   **6.** If a new partner purchases an interest from an old partner, no cash comes into the partnership, and the only entry necessary is one to record the transfer between the capital accounts.

T   F   **7.** A gain or loss on revaluation of assets should be allocated to the partners in accordance with the ratio of the balance of the partners' capital accounts.

T   F   **8.** If a new partner's investment is greater than the corresponding partnership equity, it may be said that a bonus has been allowed the original partners.

T   F   **9.** A major advantage of the partnership form of business entity is that it does not pay federal income taxes.

T   F   **10.** Unless the partnership agreement states otherwise, partners share profits and losses equally among the partners.

T   F   **11.** General partners have personal liability for all debts of the partnership.

T   F   **12.** Limited partners do not, generally, have a voice in operating decisions.

T   F   **13.** Unless otherwise stated in the partnership agreement, a partnership has a life of 28 years.

T   F   **14.** A legal partnership may exist without a written partnership agreement.

T   F   **15.** Unless the partnership agreement provides otherwise, profits and losses are shared in proportion to average balances in their capital accounts during the year.

T   F   **16.** When the assets and liabilities of an existing sole proprietorship are transferred to a partnership, they are recorded on the partnership books at their fair market values.

T   F   **17.** Salary allowances to partners are deducted in arriving at net income for financial accounting purposes; however they are not deductible in determining net income for federal income tax purposes.

T   F   **18.** If fixed assets are transferred from an existing sole proprietorship to a partnership, the accumulated balance of the **Allowance for Depreciation** account should be brought forward to the partnership books.

Part B Matching

For each numbered item, choose the matching term from the box and write the identifying letter in the answer column.

_____ 1. The rule that one partner's actions can bind all other partners.

_____ 2. The adjustment of asset and liability accounts to reflect current value.

_____ 3. The situation in which all assets are sold and cash is distributed to partners.

_____ 4. The situation in which a business continues even though an owner dies or transfers ownership to someone else.

_____ 5. The value placed on the partnership interest of a partner who dies.

_____ 6. A factor that may be used in dividing profits and losses.

_____ 7. A legal contract between the partners creating the partnership.

_____ 8. A characteristic of partnerships under which a partner is responsible for all debts of the partnership.

_____ 9. The account that is debited for salary payments to a partner.

_____ 10. A partner who has general liability for losses and debts of a partnership without being limited to that partner's investment in the partnership.

_____ 11. The amount that may be credited to the old partners' accounts when the amount invested by a new partner is greater than that partner's share of total equity.

> **a.** Bonus
> **b.** Business continuity
> **c.** Dissolution value
> **d.** General partner
> **e.** Liquidation
> **f.** Mutual agency
> **g.** Partner's Drawing
> **h.** Partnership agreement
> **i.** Revaluation
> **j.** Salary allowance
> **k.** Unlimited liability

Part C Completion

In the answer column, supply the missing word or words needed to complete each of the following statements.

_____ 1. The _____ is a written contract between the partners containing the major provisions of their agreement.

_____ 2. _____ partners have liability for debts of the partnership only to the extent of their investments.

_____ 3. Articles of Partnership are commonly referred to as the _____.

_____ 4. A partnership is said to lack _____ because the partnership is terminated if a partner dies or is incapacitated.

_____ 5. The _____ (partnership, partners) must pay federal income tax on a partnership's profits.

_____ 6. Assets transferred to a partnership by a sole proprietor in return for a partnership interest should be recorded in the partnership's records at their _____.

_____ 7. A partnership _____ occurs when the partnership is completely terminated and the business ceases to exist.

_____ 8. Payments of salaries to a partner should be charged to the _____ account.

_____ 9. At the end of the period, each partner's drawing account is closed into each partner's _____ account.

_____ 10. If an incoming partner invests less than the book value of his or her interest, the _____ partner(s) can be said to have received a bonus.

Demonstration Problem

For several years, Beatrice Wilson has operated the Wilson Hardware Store (there are actually three stores) as a sole proprietor. Near the end of 2013, she agreed to form a partnership with Elnora Jones to operate the stores under the name Wilson Stores, effective January 1, 2014. Pertinent terms of the partnership agreement follow:

1. Beatrice Wilson is to withdraw all cash from her business on December 31, 2013. She is to transfer to the partnership the accounts receivable, merchandise inventory, furniture and equipment, and all liabilities of the sole proprietorship in return for a partnership interest of 60 percent of the partnership capital. Wilson Hardware Store assets are to be appraised and transferred to the partnership at the appraised values.

   Balances in the relevant accounts of Wilson's sole proprietorship at the close of business on December 31, 2013, were:

Accounts Receivable	$126,800 Dr.
Allowance for Doubtful Accounts	8,400 Cr.
Merchandise Inventory	213,000 Dr.
Furniture and Equipment	88,000 Dr.
Allowance for Depreciation of	
Furniture and Equipment	10,000 Cr.
Accounts Payable	70,000 Cr.

2. The two parties agreed there are $2,000 of additional unrecorded accounts payable and unrecorded accrued expenses of $1,500. They also agreed that $4,000 of the accounts receivable were definitely uncollectible and should not be transferred to the partnership and that the balance for **Allowance for Doubtful Accounts** should be $6,000. The appraised values of the other assets were: Merchandise Inventory, $198,000, and Furniture and Equipment, $108,000.

3. In return for a 40 percent interest in partnership capital, Jones is to invest cash in an amount equal to 65% of Wilson's net investment.

4. Each partner is to be allowed a salary, payable on the 15th day of each month. Wilson's salary is to be $8,000 per month and Jones is to be $6,000 per month.

5. The partners are to be allowed interest of 10 percent of their beginning Capital balances.

6. The balance of profit or loss after salary and interest allowance is to be divided equally between the two partners.

7. Revenues for 2014 were $2,060,000, expenses were $528,000, and cost of goods sold was $1,292,000. Payments for salary allowances were charged to the Drawing accounts.

Instructions

1. Record the general journal entries for the following transactions. Omit descriptions.

   a. Receipt by the partnership of assets and liabilities from Wilson on January 1, 2013.

   b. Investment of cash by Jones on January 1, 2014.

   c. Summary of cash withdrawals for salaries for the two partners during the year (date entry as December 31, 2014.)

2. Prepare a schedule showing the division of net income to the partners as it would appear on the income statement for 2014.

3. Prepare journal entries to record the following factors related to distribution of net income or loss for the year:

   a. Entry to record salary allowances

   b. Entry to record interest allowances

   c. Entry to close balance of **Income Summary** account

SOLUTION

1.

	DATE		DESCRIPTION	POST. REF.	DEBIT	CREDIT	
1	2014		a.				1
2	Jan.	1	Accounts Receivable		122 800 00		2
3			Merchandise Inventory		198 000 00		3
4			Furniture and Equipment		108 000 00		4
5			Allowance for Doubtful Accounts			6 000 00	5
6			Accounts Payable			72 000 00	6
7			Accrued Expenses			1 500 00	7
8			Beatrice Wilson, Capital			349 300 00	8
9							9
10			b.				10
11		1	Cash		227 045 00		11
12			Elnora Jones, Capital			227 045 00	12
13							13
14			c.				14
15	Dec.	31	Beatrice Wilson, Drawing		96 000 00		15
16			Elnora Jones, Drawing		72 000 00		16
17			Cash			168 000 00	17
18							18
19							19
20							20
21							21
22							22
23							23
24							24
25							25
26							26
27							27
28							28
29							29
30							30
31							31
32							32
33							33
34							34
35							35
36							36
37							37

SOLUTION (continued)

2.

Wilson Stores

Income Statement (Partial)

Year Ended December 31, 2014

	Wilson	Jones	
Net Income for Year			240 0 0 0 00
Salary Allowance	96 0 0 0 00	72 0 0 0 00	168 0 0 0 00
Interest Allowance	34 9 3 0 00	22 7 0 4 50	57 6 3 4 50
Remainder in 50:50 Ratio	7 1 8 2 75	7 1 8 2 75	14 3 6 5 50
	138 1 1 2 75	101 8 8 7 25	240 0 0 0 00

3.

GENERAL JOURNAL   PAGE _____

	DATE		DESCRIPTION	POST. REF.	DEBIT	CREDIT	
1	2014		a.				1
2	Dec.	31	Income Summary		168 0 0 0 00		2
3			Beatrice Wilson, Capital			96 0 0 0 00	3
4			Elnora Jones, Capital			72 0 0 0 00	4
5							5
6			b.				6
7		31	Income Summary		57 6 3 4 50		7
8			Beatrice Wilson, Capital			34 9 3 0 00	8
9			Elnora Jones, Capital			22 7 0 4 50	9
10							10
11			c.				11
12		31	Income Summary		14 3 6 5 50		12
13			Beatrice Wilson, Capital			7 1 8 2 75	13
14			Elnora Jones, Capital			7 1 8 2 75	14
15							15
16							16
17							17

WORKING PAPERS

Name _____

EXERCISE 19.1

GENERAL JOURNAL

PAGE _____

	DATE	DESCRIPTION	POST. REF.	DEBIT	CREDIT	
1						1
2						2
3						3
4						4

EXERCISE 19.2

GENERAL JOURNAL

PAGE _____

	DATE	DESCRIPTION	POST. REF.	DEBIT	CREDIT	
1						1
2						2
3						3
4						4
5						5
6						6
7						7
8						8
9						9

EXERCISE 19.3

EXERCISE 19.4

EXERCISE 19.5

EXERCISE 19.6

EXERCISE 19.7

GENERAL JOURNAL

PAGE _____

	DATE		DESCRIPTION	POST. REF.	DEBIT	CREDIT	
1							1
2							2
3							3
4							4
5							5
6							6
7							7
8							8
9							9
10							10
11							11
12							12

EXERCISE 19.8

GENERAL JOURNAL

PAGE _____

	DATE		DESCRIPTION	POST. REF.	DEBIT	CREDIT	
1							1
2							2
3							3
4							4
5							5
6							6

EXERCISE 19.9

_____

_____

_____

EXERCISE 19.10

_____

_____

_____

_____

_____

_____

EXERCISE 19.10 (continued)

GENERAL JOURNAL

PAGE _____

	DATE		DESCRIPTION	POST. REF.	DEBIT	CREDIT	
1							1
2							2
3							3
4							4
5							5
6							6

EXERCISE 19.11

GENERAL JOURNAL

PAGE _____

	DATE		DESCRIPTION	POST. REF.	DEBIT	CREDIT	
1							1
2							2
3							3
4							4

EXERCISE 19.12

PROBLEM 19.1A or 19.1B

GENERAL JOURNAL   PAGE _____

	DATE		ACCOUNTS	POST. REF.	DEBIT	CREDIT	
1							1
2							2
3							3
4							4
5							5
6							6
7							7
8							8
9							9
10							10
11							11
12							12
13							13
14							14

Analyze: _____

PROBLEM 19.2A or 19.2B

GENERAL JOURNAL

	DATE	DESCRIPTION	POST. REF.	DEBIT	CREDIT	
1						1
2						2
3						3
4						4
5						5
6						6
7						7
8						8
9						9
10						10
11						11
12						12
13						13
14						14

Analyze: _____

_____

PROBLEM 19.3A or 19.3B

GENERAL JOURNAL   PAGE _____

	DATE		ACCOUNTS	POST. REF.	DEBIT	CREDIT	
1							1
2							2
3							3
4							4
5							5
6							6
7							7
8							8
9							9
10							10
11							11
12							12
13							13
14							14
15							15
16							16
17							17
18							18
19							19
20							20
21							21
22							22
23							23
24							24
25							25
26							26
27							27
28							28
29							29
30							30
31							31
32							32
33							33
34							34
35							35

Analyze: _____

_____

PROBLEM 19.4A or 19.4B

GENERAL JOURNAL   PAGE _____

	DATE		ACCOUNTS	POST. REF.	DEBIT	CREDIT	
1							1
2							2
3							3
4							4
5							5
6							6
7							7
8							8
9							9
10							10
11							11
12							12
13							13
14							14
15							15
16							16
17							17
18							18
19							19
20							20
21							21
22							22
23							23
24							24
25							25
26							26
27							27
28							28
29							29
30							30
31							31
32							32
33							33
34							34
35							35
36							36
37							37

PROBLEM 19.4A or 19.4B (continued)

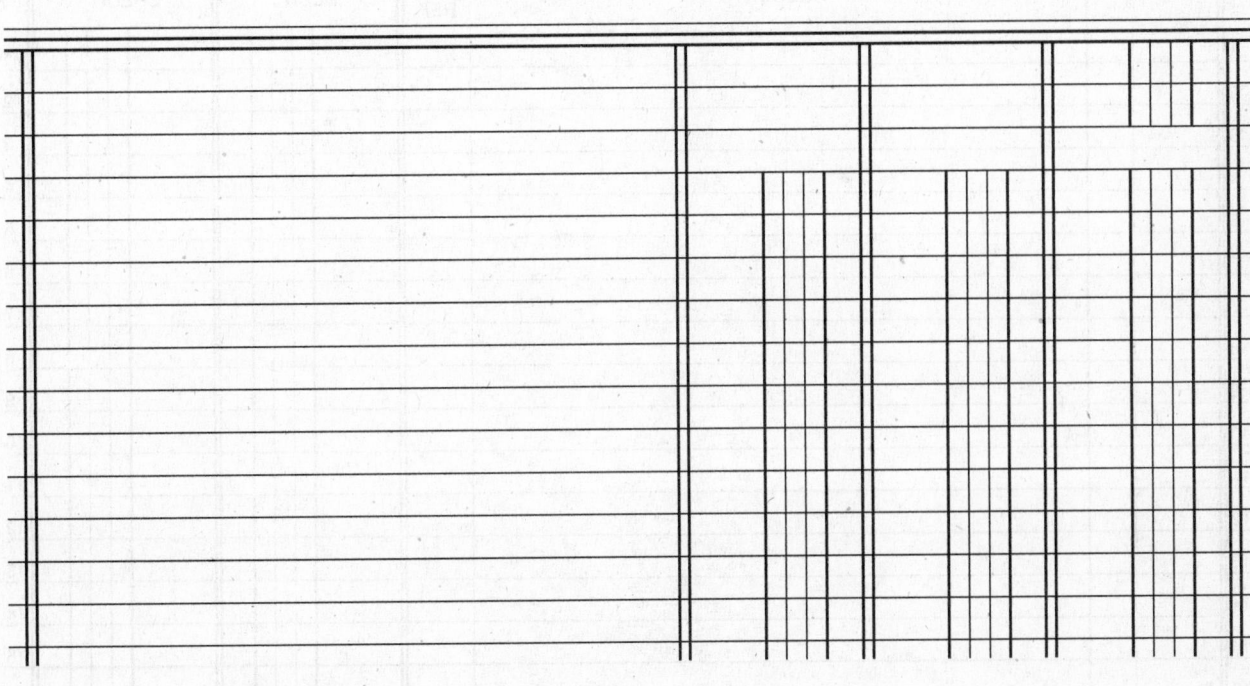

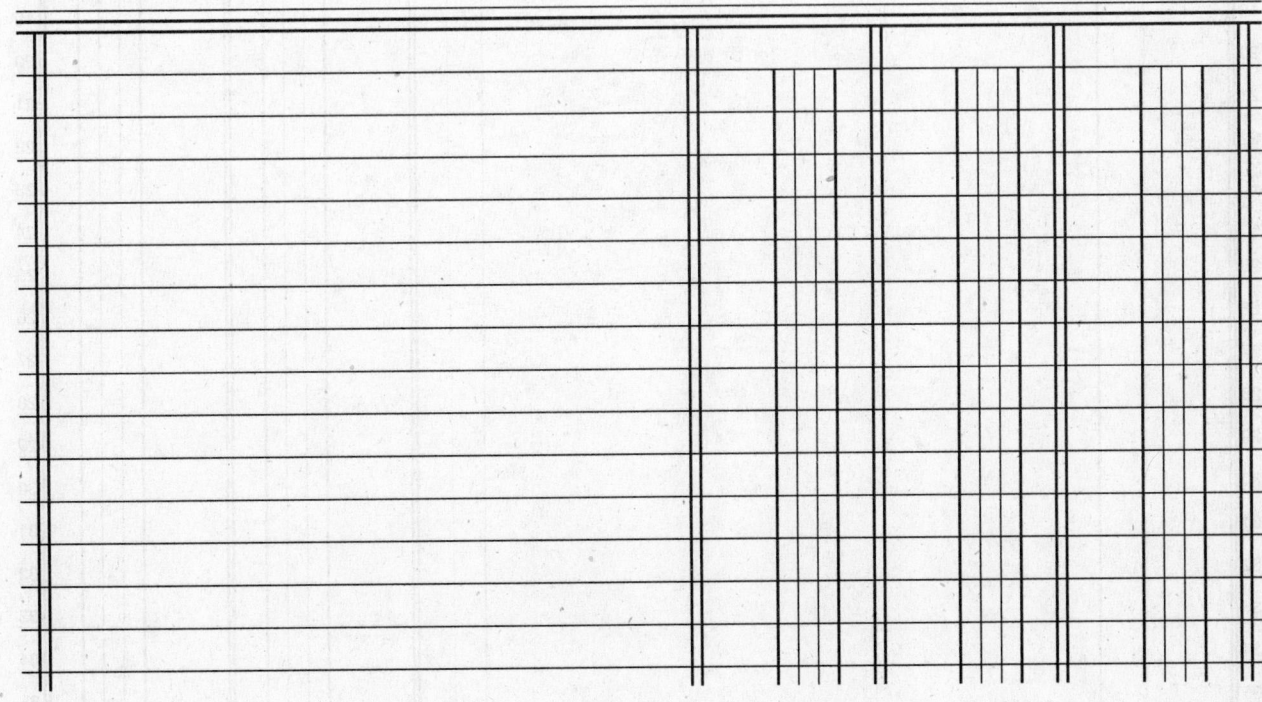

Analyze: _____

PROBLEM 19.5A or 19.5B

GENERAL JOURNAL

PAGE _____

	DATE		ACCOUNTS	POST. REF.	DEBIT	CREDIT	
1							1
2							2
3							3
4							4
5							5
6							6
7							7
8							8
9							9
10							10
11							11
12							12
13							13
14							14
15							15
16							16
17							17
18							18
19							19
20							20
21							21
22							22
23							23
24							24
25							25
26							26
27							27
28							28
29							29
30							30
31							31
32							32
33							33
34							34
35							35
36							36
37							37

PROBLEM 19.5A or 19.5B (continued)

GENERAL JOURNAL   PAGE _____

	DATE		DESCRIPTION	POST. REF.	DEBIT	CREDIT	
1							1
2							2
3							3
4							4
5							5
6							6
7							7
8							8
9							9
10							10
11							11
12							12
13							13
14							14
15							15
16							16
17							17
18							18
19							19
20							20
21							21
22							22
23							23
24							24
25							25
26							26
27							27
28							28
29							29
30							30
31							31
32							32
33							33
34							34
35							35
36							36

Analyze: _____

PROBLEM 19.6A or 19.6B

GENERAL JOURNAL

PAGE _____

	DATE	ACCOUNTS	POST. REF.	DEBIT	CREDIT	
1						1
2						2
3						3
4						4
5						5
6						6
7						7
8						8
9						9
10						10
11						11
12						12
13						13
14						14
15						15
16						16
17						17
18						18
19						19
20						20
21						21
22						22
23						23
24						24
25						25
26						26
27						27
28						28
29						29
30						30
31						31
32						32
33						33
34						34

Analyze: _____

_____

498 ■ Chapter 19

CRITICAL THINKING PROBLEM 19.1

_____
_____
_____
_____
_____
_____
_____
_____
_____
_____
_____
_____
_____
_____
_____
_____
_____
_____
_____
_____
_____
_____
_____
_____
_____
_____
_____
_____

CRITICAL THINKING PROBLEM 19.2

GENERAL JOURNAL

PAGE _____

	DATE	ACCOUNTS	POST. REF.	DEBIT	CREDIT	
1						1
2						2
3						3
4						4
5						5
6						6
7						7
8						8
9						9
10						10
11						11
12						12

CRITICAL THINKING PROBLEM 19.2 (continued)

GENERAL JOURNAL   PAGE _____

	DATE		ACCOUNTS	POST. REF.	DEBIT	CREDIT	
1							1
2							2
3							3
4							4
5							5
6							6
7							7
8							8
9							9
10							10
11							11
12							12
13							13
14							14
15							15
16							16
17							17
18							18
19							19
20							20
21							21
22							22
23							23
24							24
25							25
26							26
27							27
28							28
29							29
30							30
31							31
32							32
33							33
34							34

CRITICAL THINKING PROBLEM 19.2 (continued)

GENERAL LEDGER

ACCOUNT _____ ACCOUNT NO. _____

DATE	DESCRIPTION	POST. REF.	DEBIT	CREDIT	BALANCE	
					DEBIT	CREDIT

ACCOUNT _____ ACCOUNT NO. _____

DATE	DESCRIPTION	POST. REF.	DEBIT	CREDIT	BALANCE	
					DEBIT	CREDIT

CRITICAL THINKING PROBLEM 19.2 (continued)

GENERAL JOURNAL   PAGE _____

	DATE	ACCOUNTS	POST. REF.	DEBIT	CREDIT	
1						1
2						2
3						3
4						4
5						5
6						6
7						7
8						8
9						9
10						10

Analyze: _____

Chapter 19 Practice Test Answer Key

Part A True-False

1. T	7. F	13. F
2. T	8. T	14. T
3. T	9. T	15. F
4. F	10. T	16. T
5. T	11. T	17. T
6. T	12. T	18. F

Part B Matching

1. f	7. h
2. i	8. k
3. e	9. g
4. b	10. d
5. c	11. a
6. j	

Part C Completion

1. partnership agreement
2. limited
3. partnership agreement
4. continuity
5. partners
6. market values
7. liquidation
8. partners' drawing
9. capital
10. incoming

CHAPTER 20

Corporations: Formation and Capital Stock Transactions

STUDY GUIDE

Understanding the Chapter

Objectives	1. Explain the characteristics of a corporation. 2. Describe special "hybrid" organizations that have some characteristics of partnerships and some characteristics of corporations. 3. Describe the different types of stock. 4. Compute the number of shares of common stock to be issued on the conversion of convertible preferred stock. 5. Compute dividends payable on stock. 6. Record the issuance of capital stock at par value. 7. Prepare a balance sheet for a corporation. 8. Record organization costs. 9. Record stock issued at a premium and stock with no par value. 10. Record transactions for stock subscriptions. 11. Describe the capital stock records for a corporation. 12. Define the accounting terms new to this chapter.
Reading Assignment	Read Chapter 20 in the textbook. Complete the textbook Section Self Review as you finish reading each section of the chapter, and the Comprehensive Self Review at the end of the chapter. Refer to the Chapter 20 Glossary or to the Glossary at the end of the book to find definitions for terms that are not familiar to you.

Activities

❏ **Thinking Critically**	Answer the *Thinking Critically* questions for ConAgra Foods and Managerial Implications.
❏ **Discussion Questions**	Answer each assigned discussion question in Chapter 20.
❏ **Exercises**	Complete each assigned exercise in Chapter 20. Use the forms provided in this SGWP. The objectives covered by an exercise are given after the exercise number. If you need help with an exercise, review the portion of the chapter related to the objective(s) covered.
❏ **Problems A/B**	Complete each assigned problem in Chapter 20. Use the forms provided in this SGWP. The objectives covered by a problem are given after the problem number. If you need help with a problem, review the portion of the chapter related to the objective(s) covered.
❏ **Critical Thinking Problems**	Complete the critical thinking problems as assigned. Use the forms provided in this SGWP.
❏ **Business Connections**	Complete the Business Connections activities as assigned to gain a deeper understanding of Chapter 20 concepts.

Practice Tests

Complete the Practice Tests, which cover the main points in your reading assignment. Compare your answers with those in the Practice Test Answer Key for Chapter 20 at the end of this chapter. If you have answered any questions incorrectly, review the related section of the text.

Part A True-False *For each of the following statements, circle T in the answer column if the answer is true or F if the answer is false.*

T   F   **1.** The preemptive right gives the stockholders the right to receive dividends when declared by the directors.

T   F   **2.** The conversion ratio establishes the number of shares of common stock into which a share of convertible preferred stock can be converted.

T   F   **3.** Callable preferred stock may be reacquired by the corporation from the stockholders at the option of the corporation, provided pre-established conditions are met.

T   F   **4.** Organization costs are now usually charged to expense when incurred.

T   F   **5.** The stock certificate is usually issued as soon as the stock subscription is recorded.

T   F   **6.** If common stock has a par value, the Common Stock account should be debited for the par value of all common stock issued.

T   F   **7.** Preferred stock must have the same par value as the corporation's common stock.

T   F   **8.** Convertible preferred stock must have the same par value as nonconvertible preferred stock.

T   F   **9.** Convertible preferred stock is redeemable for cash by the owner.

T   F   **10.** A shareholder generally has the right to sell the shares he or she owns without prior approval of the corporation.

T   F   **11.** It is necessary to obtain a charter from the United States government before a corporation can commence business.

T   F   **12.** A corporation is a legal entity, separate and apart from its owners.

T   F   **13.** Owners of stock of a corporation are usually personally liable for the corporation's debts.

T   F   **14.** Stockholders are empowered to act for the corporation in most circumstances.

T   F   **15.** Most preferred stock does not have a par value.

T   F   **16.** Usually a corporation must pay federal income taxes on its net income.

T   F   **17.** If dividends on participating preferred stock are not paid in one year, they must be paid in the following year before any dividends can be paid on common stock.

T   F   **18.** If only one class of stock is issued by a corporation, it is referred to as *normal* stock.

T   F   **19.** A corporate charter specifies the classes and number of shares of stock authorized.

Part B Completion   *In the answer column, supply the missing word or words needed to complete each of the following statements.*

_____ 1. The figure shown in the corporate charter to establish a face value for each share of stock is known as _____.

_____ 2. Stock that may have prior claims on profits or on assets in case of liquidation is known as _____ stock.

_____ 3. An amount known as _____ may be set by the board of directors to be credited to the Capital Stock account for each share.

_____ 4. A state government issues a _____, which establishes or creates a corporation.

_____ 5. If preferred stock is _____, dividends stated must be paid to preferred stockholders for the current year and all prior years before any dividend can be paid on common stock.

_____ 6. The transfer of stock between shareholders is recorded in the _____ journal.

_____ 7. The amount above par value or stated value at which stock is issued is the _____.

_____ 8. The paper that serves as evidence of ownership of stock is the _____.

_____ 9. The _____ contains a record of all meetings of stockholders and directors.

_____ 10. A record of the number of shares owned by each shareholder is kept in the _____.

_____ 11. A corporation that is generally taxed as a partnership is a(an) _____ corporation.

Demonstration Problem

Just after its formation on July 1, 2013, the ledger accounts of the Fralicks Athletics Corporation showed the following balances.

Accrued Expenses	$ 48,000	Merchandise Inventory	139,000
Accounts Payable	160,000	Notes Payable—Short-Term	88,000
Accounts Receivable	144,000	Paid-in Capital in Excess of Par—Common	137,200
Allowance for Doubtful Accounts	28,000	Paid-in Capital in Excess of Par—Preferred	43,000
Building	800,000	Preferred Stock (8%, $25 Par)	200,000
Cash	150,000	Preferred Stock Subscribed	80,000
Common Stock ($50 Par)	800,000	Subscriptions Receivable—Common	35,200
Common Stock Subscribed	32,000	Subscriptions Receivable—Preferred	80,000
Furniture and Fixtures	268,000		

The corporation is authorized to issue 200,000 shares of $50 par common stock and 40,000 shares of 8 percent, $25 par noncumulative and nonparticipating preferred stock.

Instructions

Answer the questions that follow.

1. How many shares of common stock are outstanding?

2. How many shares of common stock are subscribed?

3. How many shares of preferred stock are outstanding?

4. How many shares of preferred stock are subscribed?

5. At what average price has common stock been subscribed or issued?

6. Assume that no dividends are paid in the first year of the corporation's existence. What are the rights of the preferred stockholders?

7. Assuming that all paid-in capital in excess of par on common stock was applicable to the shares of common stock that have been subscribed but not yet issued, what is the subscription price per share of the common stock subscribed?

8. Assuming that the board of directors declared no dividends in 2013, what amount would have to be paid to preferred stockholders in 2014 before any dividend could be paid to common stockholders?

9. Prepare a classified balance sheet for Fralicks Athletics Corporation just after its formation on July 1, 2013.

SOLUTION

1. $800,000 ÷ $50 = 16,000 shares of common stock

2. $ 32,000 ÷ $50 = 640 shares

3. $200,000 ÷ $25 = 8,000 shares

4. $ 80,000 ÷ $25 = 3,200 shares

5.

Common Stock	$800,000
Common Stock Subscribed	32,000
Paid-in Capital in Excess of Par—Common	137,200
Total	$969,200

$969,200 ÷ 16,640 shares = $58.25 per share

6. None. The preferred stock is noncumulative.

7. ($32,000 + $137,200 = $169,200) ÷ 640 = $264.38 per share

8. $2.00 dividend per share must be paid to preferred stockholders ($25 × 0.08)

SOLUTION (continued)

Fralicks Athletics Corporation

Balance Sheet

July 1, 2013

Assets									
Current Assets									
Cash						150	0	0	0	00
Accounts Receivable	144	0	0	0	00				
Less Allowance for Doubtful Accounts	28	0	0	0	00	116	0	0	0	00
Subscriptions Receivable—Common						35	2	0	0	00
Subscriptions Receivable—Preferred						80	0	0	0	00
Merchandise Inventory						139	0	0	0	00
Total Current Assets						520	2	0	0	00
Property, Plant, and Equipment									
Building	800	0	0	0	00				
Furniture and Fixtures	268	0	0	0	00				
Total Property, Plant, and Equipment						1,068	0	0	0	00
Total Assets						1,588	2	0	0	00

Liabilities and Stockholders' Equity									
Current Liabilities									
Accrued Expenses	48	0	0	0	00				
Accounts Payable	160	0	0	0	00				
Notes Payable—Short-Term	88	0	0	0	00				
Total Liabilities						296	0	0	0	00
Stockholders' Equity									
Preferred Stock (8%, $25 par, 40,000 sh auth., 8,000 sh iss. and out.)	200	0	0	0	00				
Preferred Stock Subscribed (3,200 shares)	80	0	0	0	00				
Paid-in Capital in Excess of Par—Preferred	43	0	0	0	00	323	0	0	0	00
Common Stock ($50 par, 200,000 shares authorized, 16,000 sh. iss. and out.)	800	0	0	0	00				
Common Stock Subscribed (640 shares)	32	0	0	0	00				
Paid-in Capital in Excess of Par—Common	137	2	0	0	00	969	2	0	0	00
Total Stockholders' Equity						1,292	2	0	0	00
Total Liabilities and Stockholders' Equity						1,588	2	0	0	00

WORKING PAPERS

EXERCISE 20.1

_____
_____
_____
_____

EXERCISE 20.2

1. _____
_____
_____
_____
_____
_____

2. _____
_____
_____
_____
_____
_____
_____
_____
_____
_____
_____
_____
_____
_____
_____
_____
_____
_____
_____
_____
_____
_____
_____
_____
_____

EXERCISE 20.3

1. _____
_____
_____
_____
_____
_____
_____
_____
_____

2. _____
_____
_____
_____
_____
_____
_____
_____
_____
_____
_____
_____
_____

EXERCISE 20.4

_____
_____

EXERCISE 20.5

_____
_____
_____

EXERCISE 20.6

_____
_____
_____
_____

EXERCISE 20.7

GENERAL JOURNAL   PAGE _____

	DATE		DESCRIPTION	POST. REF.	DEBIT	CREDIT	
1							1
2							2
3							3
4							4
5							5
6							6
7							7
8							8

EXERCISE 20.8

GENERAL JOURNAL   PAGE _____

	DATE		DESCRIPTION	POST. REF.	DEBIT	CREDIT	
1							1
2							2
3							3
4							4
5							5
6							6
7							7
8							8

EXERCISE 20.9

GENERAL JOURNAL   PAGE _____

	DATE		DESCRIPTION	POST. REF.	DEBIT	CREDIT	
1							1
2							2
3							3
4							4
5							5
6							6
7							7
8							8
9							9
10							10

EXERCISE 20.10

GENERAL JOURNAL   PAGE _____

	DATE		DESCRIPTION	POST. REF.	DEBIT	CREDIT	
1							1
2							2
3							3
4							4
5							5
6							6
7							7
8							8
9							9
10							10
11							11
12							12
13							13
14							14
15							15
16							16
17							17
18							18
19							19
20							20
21							21
22							22
23							23
24							24
25							25
26							26
27							27
28							28
29							29
30							30
31							31
32							32
33							33
34							34
35							35
36							36
37							37

PROBLEM 20.1A or 20.1B

	Year	Total Dividends	Preferred Stock		Common Stock	
			Total	Per Share	Total	Per Share
_____	____	_____	_____	_____	_____	_____
_____	____	_____	_____	_____	_____	_____
_____	____	_____	_____	_____	_____	_____
_____	____	_____	_____	_____	_____	_____
_____	____	_____	_____	_____	_____	_____
_____	____	_____	_____	_____	_____	_____
_____	____	_____	_____	_____	_____	_____
_____	____	_____	_____	_____	_____	_____
_____	____	_____	_____	_____	_____	_____
_____	____	_____	_____	_____	_____	_____
_____	____	_____	_____	_____	_____	_____
_____	____	_____	_____	_____	_____	_____
_____	____	_____	_____	_____	_____	_____
_____	____	_____	_____	_____	_____	_____
_____	____	_____	_____	_____	_____	_____
_____	____	_____	_____	_____	_____	_____

Analyze: _____

PROBLEM 20.2A or 20.2B

PART I

PROBLEM 20.2A or 20.2B (continued)

PART II

_____

_____

_____

_____

_____

_____

_____

_____

_____

_____

Analyze: _____

PROBLEM 20.3A or 20.3B

GENERAL JOURNAL   PAGE _____

	DATE	DESCRIPTION	POST. REF.	DEBIT	CREDIT	
1						1
2						2
3						3
4						4
5						5
6						6
7						7
8						8
9						9
10						10
11						11
12						12
13						13
14						14
15						15
16						16
17						17
18						18
19						19
20						20
21						21
22						22

Analyze: _____

PROBLEM 20.4A or 20.4B

GENERAL JOURNAL

PAGE _____

	DATE		DESCRIPTION	POST. REF.	DEBIT	CREDIT	
1							1
2							2
3							3
4							4
5							5
6							6
7							7
8							8
9							9
10							10
11							11
12							12
13							13
14							14
15							15
16							16
17							17
18							18
19							19
20							20
21							21
22							22
23							23
24							24
25							25
26							26
27							27
28							28
29							29
30							30
31							31
32							32
33							33
34							34
35							35
36							36

PROBLEM 20.4A or 20.4B (continued)

Analyze:

PROBLEM 20.5A or 20.5B

GENERAL JOURNAL

PAGE _____

	DATE		DESCRIPTION	POST. REF.	DEBIT	CREDIT	
1							1
2							2
3							3
4							4
5							5
6							6
7							7
8							8
9							9
10							10
11							11
12							12
13							13
14							14
15							15
16							16
17							17
18							18
19							19
20							20
21							21
22							22
23							23
24							24
25							25
26							26
27							27
28							28
29							29
30							30
31							31
32							32
33							33
34							34
35							35
36							36
37							37

Name _____

PROBLEM 20.5A or 20.5B (continued)

GENERAL JOURNAL   PAGE _____

	DATE	DESCRIPTION	POST. REF.	DEBIT	CREDIT	
1						1
2						2
3						3
4						4
5						5
6						6
7						7
8						8
9						9
10						10
11						11
12						12
13						13
14						14
15						15
16						16
17						17
18						18
19						19
20						20
21						21
22						22

GENERAL LEDGER

ACCOUNT _____ ACCOUNT NO. _____

DATE	DESCRIPTION	POST. REF.	DEBIT	CREDIT	BALANCE DEBIT	BALANCE CREDIT

PROBLEM 20.5A or 20.5B (continued)

GENERAL LEDGER

ACCOUNT _____ ACCOUNT NO. _____

DATE	DESCRIPTION	POST. REF.	DEBIT	CREDIT	BALANCE DEBIT	CREDIT

ACCOUNT _____ ACCOUNT NO. _____

DATE	DESCRIPTION	POST. REF.	DEBIT	CREDIT	BALANCE DEBIT	CREDIT

ACCOUNT _____ ACCOUNT NO. _____

DATE	DESCRIPTION	POST. REF.	DEBIT	CREDIT	BALANCE DEBIT	CREDIT

ACCOUNT _____ ACCOUNT NO. _____

DATE	DESCRIPTION	POST. REF.	DEBIT	CREDIT	BALANCE DEBIT	CREDIT

ACCOUNT _____ ACCOUNT NO. _____

DATE	DESCRIPTION	POST. REF.	DEBIT	CREDIT	BALANCE DEBIT	CREDIT

PROBLEM 20.5A or 20.5B (continued)

GENERAL LEDGER

ACCOUNT _____ ACCOUNT NO. _____

DATE	DESCRIPTION	POST. REF.	DEBIT	CREDIT	BALANCE DEBIT	BALANCE CREDIT

ACCOUNT _____ ACCOUNT NO. _____

DATE	DESCRIPTION	POST. REF.	DEBIT	CREDIT	BALANCE DEBIT	BALANCE CREDIT

ACCOUNT _____ ACCOUNT NO. _____

DATE	DESCRIPTION	POST. REF.	DEBIT	CREDIT	BALANCE DEBIT	BALANCE CREDIT

Analyze: _____

_____

CRITICAL THINKING PROBLEM 20.1

1. _____

_____

_____

_____

_____

_____

_____

_____

_____

_____

_____

_____

_____

_____

_____

_____

_____

_____

_____

_____

_____

_____

_____

_____

_____

_____

_____

_____

_____

_____

_____

_____

_____

_____

_____

_____

CRITICAL THINKING PROBLEM 20.1 (continued)

2. _____

Analyze: _____

CRITICAL THINKING PROBLEM 20.2

(blank ruled lines)

Chapter 20 Practice Test Answer Key

Part A True-False		Part B Completion
1. F	11. F	1. par value
2. T	12. T	2. preferred stock
3. T	13. F	3. stated value
4. T	14. F	4. charter
5. F	15. F	5. cumulative
6. F	16. T	6. capital stock transfer
7. F	17. F	7. premium
8. F	18. F	8. stock certificate
9. F	19. T	9. minute book
10. T		10. capital stock ledger
		11. Subchapter S (or "S")

STUDY GUIDE

Understanding the Chapter

Objectives

1. Estimate the federal corporate income tax and prepare related journal entries. 2. Complete a worksheet for a corporation. 3. Record corporate adjusting and closing entries. 4. Prepare an income statement for a corporation. 5. Record the declaration and payment of cash dividends. 6. Record the declaration and issuance of stock dividends. 7. Record stock splits. 8. Record appropriations of retained earnings. 9. Record a corporation's receipt of donated assets. 10. Record treasury stock transactions. 11. Prepare financial statements for a corporation. 12. Define the accounting terms new to this chapter.

Reading Assignment

Read Chapter 21 in the textbook. Complete the textbook Section Self Review as you finish reading each section of the chapter, and the Comprehensive Self Review at the end of the chapter. Refer to the Chapter 21 Glossary or to the Glossary at the end of the book to find definitions for terms that are not familiar to you.

Activities

❑ **Thinking Critically**

Answer the *Thinking Critically* questions for McDonald's Corporation and Managerial Implications.

❑ **Discussion Questions**

Answer each assigned discussion question in Chapter 21.

❑ **Exercises**

Complete each assigned exercise in Chapter 21. Use the forms provided in this SGWP. The objectives covered by an exercise are given after the exercise number. If you need help with an exercise, review the portion of the chapter related to the objective(s) covered.

❑ **Problems A/B**

Complete each assigned problem in Chapter 21. Use the forms provided in this SGWP. The objectives covered by a problem are given after the problem number. If you need help with a problem, review the portion of the chapter related to the objective(s) covered.

❑ **Critical Thinking Problems**

Complete the critical thinking problems as assigned. Use the forms provided in this SGWP.

❑ **Business Connections**

Complete the Business Connections activities as assigned to gain a deeper understanding of Chapter 21 concepts.

Practice Tests

Complete the Practice Tests, which cover the main points in your reading assignment. Compare your answers with those in the Practice Test Answer Key for Chapter 21 at the end of this chapter. If you have answered any questions incorrectly, review the related section of the text.

Part A True-False *For each of the following statements, circle T in the answer column if the statement is true or F if the statement is false.*

T   F   **1.** Property received as a gift should be recorded at its fair market value and credited to an account such as **Donated Capital.**

T   F   **2.** When a stock dividend is declared, the **Retained Earnings** account is debited for the par value of the stock to be issued.

T   F   **3.** The **Treasury Stock** account is debited for the market value of treasury stock purchased.

T   F   **4.** Extraordinary gains and losses are commonly shown "net of tax."

T   F   **5.** Corporate income taxes may be shown as operating expenses or as a final deduction to arrive at "net income after taxes."

T   F   **6.** The issuance of a stock dividend decreases the total stockholders' equity of the corporation.

T   F   **7.** Cash dividends are credited to the **Retained Earnings** account.

T   F   **8.** Extraordinary gains and losses should be classified as Other Income or Other Deductions in the income statement.

T   F   **9.** A stock dividend decreases the Paid-in Capital of the corporation.

T   F   **10.** The entry to record a stock dividend is made on the declaration date.

T   F   **11.** Appropriated retained earnings represents cash set aside for specific purposes.

T   F   **12.** Appropriations of retained earnings may reflect contractual requirements or may be purely discretionary.

T   F   **13.** When a stock split is declared, the **Retained Earnings** account is debited for the estimated market value of the stock to be issued.

T   F   **14.** The statement of retained earnings shows all changes in the corporate capital during the year.

T   F   **15.** Treasury stock should be shown as a liability on the balance sheet.

Part B Matching *For each numbered item, choose the matching term from the box and write the identifying letter in the answer column.*

_____ **1.** An example of an appropriation of retained earnings for a specific project.

_____ **2.** The issuance of new shares to shareholders with a debit to **Retained Earnings,** a credit to **Paid-in Capital** and **Stock Dividends Distributable.**

_____ **3.** The section of a balance sheet that contains paid-in capital and retained earnings.

_____ **4.** The term used to describe the accumulated net income of a corporation.

_____ **5.** Stock that has been issued and reacquired.

_____ **6.** The account credited when a gift of property is received by a corporation.

_____ **7.** An analysis of the equity accounts of a corporation.

> **a.** Donated Capital
>
> **b.** Retained Earnings
>
> **c.** Stockholders' equity
>
> **d.** Statement of stockholders' equity
>
> **e.** Treasury Stock
>
> **f.** Retained Earnings Appropriated for Plant Expansion
>
> **g.** Stock dividend

Part C Exercises

1. Prior to a 10 percent stock dividend, the total stockholders' equity of the Fall Corporation consists of $300,000 of common stock (30,000 shares of $10 par value, issued and outstanding) plus retained earnings of $450,000. Assets are $850,000 and liabilities, $100,000. The estimated market value of the stock to be issued is $25 per share. Compute the book value per share before and after the dividend is declared.

2. The Western Corporation has 1,000 shares of $20 par value, 10 percent, cumulative, nonparticipating preferred stock authorized and issued. On December 15, 2013, the directors declare a dividend on preferred stock payable on January 12, 2014, to stockholders of record on December 31, 2013. The dividend is the regular dividend for the current year and the dividends in arrears. (No dividend was paid in 2012.) Record the general journal entry for the dividend declaration.

GENERAL JOURNAL   PAGE _____

	DATE	DESCRIPTION	POST. REF.	DEBIT	CREDIT	
1						1
2						2
3						3
4						4
5						5

Demonstration Problem

The stockholders' equity section of the balance sheets of the Vandy Landscaping Corporation on December 31, 2012, and December 31, 2013, plus other selected account balances, follows (some information is omitted). During 2013 the following transactions, other than net income or loss after taxes, affected stockholders' equity.

1. A stock dividend was declared on common stock and issued in March. No other common stock was issued during the year.

2. A cash dividend of $5 a share was declared and paid on common stock in December 2013.

3. Preferred treasury stock was purchased at par value in January.

4. Additional preferred stock was issued for cash in April 2013.

5. The yearly cash dividend of $5 per share was declared and paid on preferred stock outstanding as of December 2013.

Partial Balance Sheets

Stockholders' Equity	2013	2012
Paid-in Capital		
Preferred Stock (5%, $100 par, 10,000 shares authorized)	$ 100,000	$ 80,000
Paid-in Capital in Excess of Par—Preferred	10,000	–0–
Common Stock ($10 par value, 100,000 shares authorized)	550,000	500,000
Paid-In Capital in Excess of Par—Common	10,000	–0–
Total Paid-in Capital	$ 670,000	$ 580,000
Retained Earnings		
Appropriated for Plant Expansion	200,000	100,000
Unappropriated	700,000	500,000
Total Retained Earnings	900,000	600,000
	$1,570,000	$1,180,000
Less Treasury Stock, Preferred	10,000	–0–
Total Stockholders' Equity	$1,560,000	$1,180,000

Instructions

Answer these questions.

1. How many shares of preferred stock were outstanding on December 31, 2013?
2. How many shares of common stock were issued as a stock dividend during 2013?
3. How many shares of preferred stock were purchased as treasury stock?
4. How many shares of preferred stock were issued for cash during 2013?
5. What was the sales price per share of the preferred stock issued during the year?
6. What was the total cash dividend on preferred stock during the year?
7. What was the total cash dividend on common stock?
8. What was the corporation's net income or loss after taxes during 2013?

SOLUTION

1. $100,000 ÷ $100 = 1,000 shares issued; 1,000 shares issued − 100 shares treasury stock ($10,000 ÷ $100) = 900 shares outstanding

2. $550,000 − $500,000 = $50,000; $50,000 ÷ $10 = 5,000 shares

3. $10,000 ÷ $100 = 100 shares of treasury stock purchased

4. $100,000 − $80,000 = $20,000; ($20,000 + $10,000) ÷ $100 = 300 shares

5. $100,000 − $80,000 = $20,000; $20,000 ÷ $100 per share = 200 shares; $20,000 + $10,000 paid-in capital = $30,000; $30,000 ÷ 200 shares = $150 per share

6. 1,000 shares preferred stock − 100 shares treasury stock = 900 shares for dividends; 900 × $5 = $4,500 in dividends

7. $550,000 ÷ $10 = 55,000 shares of common stock; 55,000 × $5 = $275,000 in dividends

8.

Increase in retained earnings, unappropriated	$200,000
Stock dividend	50,000
Cash dividend, common stock	275,000
Cash dividend, preferred stock	4,500
Increase in appropriation for plant expansion	100,000
Income for year	$629,500

WORKING PAPERS

Name _____

EXERCISE 21.1

_____
_____
_____
_____
_____
_____

EXERCISE 21.2

GENERAL JOURNAL

PAGE _____

	DATE	DESCRIPTION	POST. REF.	DEBIT	CREDIT	
1						1
2						2
3						3
4						4
5						5
6						6

EXERCISE 21.3

a. _____
_____

b. _____
_____

c. _____
_____

EXERCISE 21.4

GENERAL JOURNAL

PAGE _____

	DATE	DESCRIPTION	POST. REF.	DEBIT	CREDIT	
1						1
2						2
3						3
4						4
5						5
6						6

EXERCISE 21.5

GENERAL JOURNAL   PAGE _____

	DATE		DESCRIPTION	POST. REF.	DEBIT	CREDIT	
1							1
2							2
3							3
4							4
5							5
6							6
7							7
8							8

EXERCISE 21.6

GENERAL JOURNAL   PAGE _____

	DATE		DESCRIPTION	POST. REF.	DEBIT	CREDIT	
1							1
2							2
3							3
4							4
5							5
6							6
7							7
8							8
9							9

EXERCISE 21.7

GENERAL JOURNAL   PAGE _____

	DATE		DESCRIPTION	POST. REF.	DEBIT	CREDIT	
1							1
2							2
3							3
4							4
5							5

EXERCISE 21.8

GENERAL JOURNAL   PAGE _____

	DATE		DESCRIPTION	POST. REF.	DEBIT	CREDIT	
1							1
2							2
3							3
4							4

EXERCISE 21.9

GENERAL JOURNAL   PAGE _____

	DATE	DESCRIPTION	POST. REF.	DEBIT	CREDIT	
1						1
2						2
3						3
4						4
5						5
6						6

EXERCISE 21.10

GENERAL JOURNAL   PAGE _____

	DATE	DESCRIPTION	POST. REF.	DEBIT	CREDIT	
1						1
2						2
3						3
4						4
5						5

EXERCISE 21.11

GENERAL JOURNAL   PAGE _____

	DATE	DESCRIPTION	POST. REF.	DEBIT	CREDIT	
1						1
2						2
3						3
4						4
5						5

EXERCISE 21.12

PROBLEM 21.1A or 21.1B

GENERAL JOURNAL　　　　　　　　　PAGE _____

	DATE		DESCRIPTION	POST. REF.	DEBIT	CREDIT	
1							1
2							2
3							3
4							4
5							5
6							6
7							7
8							8
9							9
10							10
11							11
12							12
13							13
14							14
15							15
16							16
17							17
18							18
19							19
20							20
21							21
22							22
23							23
24							24
25							25
26							26
27							27
28							28
29							29
30							30
31							31
32							32
33							33
34							34
35							35
36							36
37							37
38							38

PROBLEM 21.1A or 21.1B (continued)

GENERAL JOURNAL   PAGE _____

	DATE		DESCRIPTION	POST. REF.	DEBIT	CREDIT	
1							1
2							2
3							3
4							4
5							5
6							6
7							7
8							8
9							9
10							10
11							11
12							12
13							13
14							14
15							15
16							16
17							17
18							18
19							19
20							20
21							21
22							22
23							23
24							24
25							25
26							26
27							27
28							28
29							29
30							30
31							31
32							32
33							33
34							34

Analyze: _____

_____

PROBLEM 21.2A or 21.2B

_____

_____

_____

	ACCOUNT NAME	TRIAL BALANCE		ADJUSTMENTS	
		DEBIT	CREDIT	DEBIT	CREDIT
1					
2					
3					
4					
5					
6					
7					
8					
9					
10					
11					
12					
13					
14					
15					
16					
17					
18					
19					
20					
21					
22					
23					
24					
25					
26					
27					
28					
29					
30					
31					
32					
33					
34					
35					

PROBLEM 21.2A or 21.2B (continued)

INCOME STATEMENT		BALANCE SHEET		
DEBIT	CREDIT	DEBIT	CREDIT	
				1
				2
				3
				4
				5
				6
				7
				8
				9
				10
				11
				12
				13
				14
				15
				16
				17
				18
				19
				20
				21
				22
				23
				24
				25
				26
				27
				28
				29
				30
				31
				32
				33
				34
				35

PROBLEM 21.2A or 21.2B (continued)

PROBLEM 21.2A or 21.2B (continued)

(continued)

PROBLEM 21.2A or 21.2B (continued)

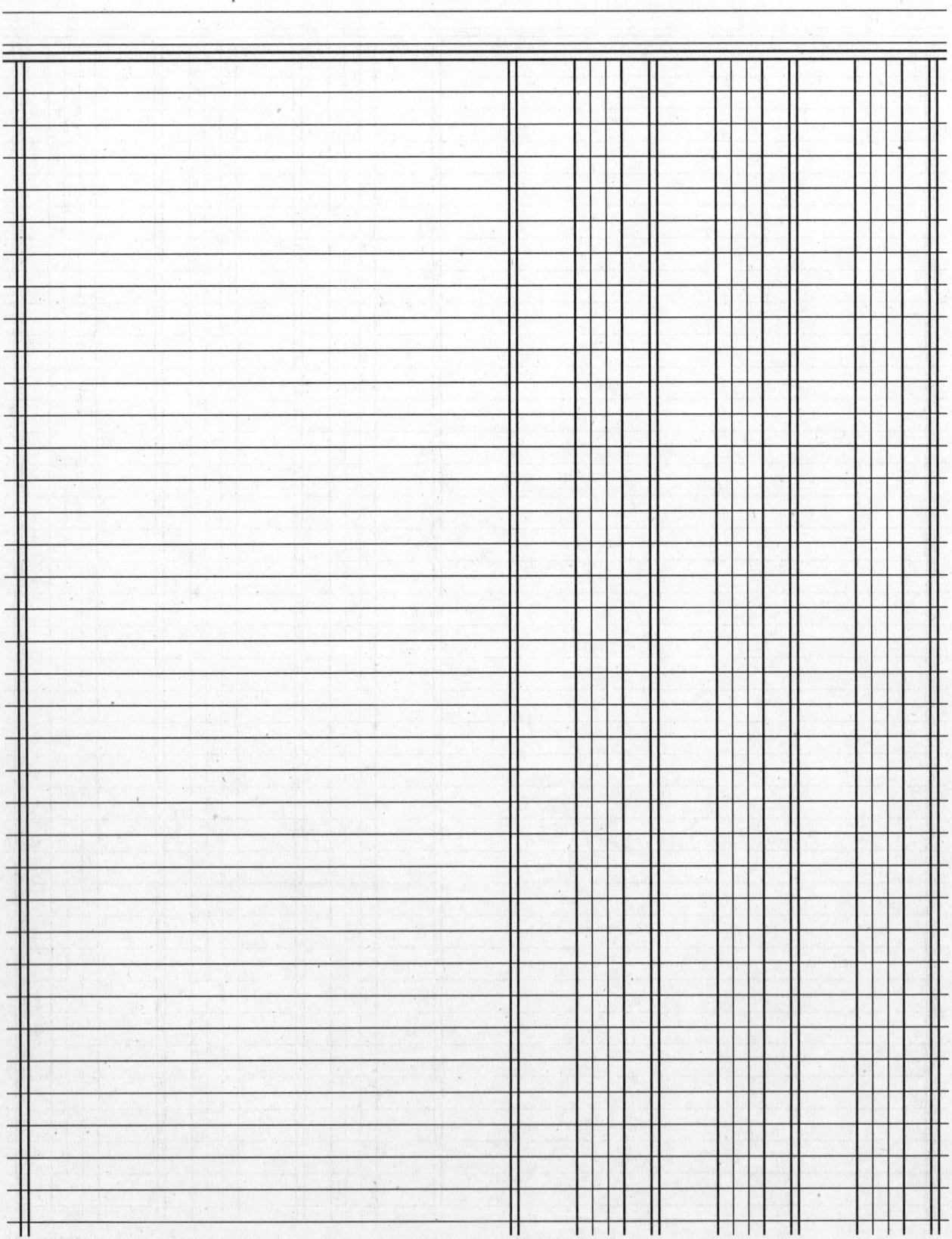

PROBLEM 21.2A or 21.2B (continued)

GENERAL JOURNAL   PAGE _____

	DATE	DESCRIPTION	POST. REF.	DEBIT	CREDIT	
1						1
2						2
3						3
4						4
5						5
6						6
7						7
8						8
9						9
10						10
11						11
12						12
13						13
14						14
15						15
16						16
17						17
18						18
19						19
20						20
21						21
22						22
23						23
24						24
25						25
26						26
27						27
28						28
29						29
30						30
31						31
32						32
33						33
34						34
35						35
36						36
37						37

PROBLEM 21.2A or 21.2B (continued)

GENERAL JOURNAL   PAGE _____

	DATE		DESCRIPTION	POST. REF.	DEBIT	CREDIT	
1							1
2							2
3							3
4							4
5							5
6							6
7							7
8							8
9							9
10							10
11							11
12							12
13							13
14							14
15							15
16							16
17							17
18							18
19							19
20							20
21							21
22							22
23							23
24							24
25							25
26							26
27							27
28							28
29							29
30							30
31							31
32							32
33							33
34							34

Analyze: _____

_____

PROBLEM 21.3A or 21.3B

GENERAL JOURNAL   PAGE _____

	DATE		DESCRIPTION	POST. REF.	DEBIT	CREDIT	
1							1
2							2
3							3
4							4
5							5
6							6
7							7
8							8
9							9
10							10
11							11
12							12
13							13
14							14
15							15
16							16
17							17
18							18
19							19
20							20
21							21
22							22
23							23
24							24
25							25
26							26
27							27
28							28
29							29
30							30
31							31
32							32
33							33
34							34
35							35
36							36
37							37

PROBLEM 21.3A or 21.3B (continued)

GENERAL LEDGER

ACCOUNT _____ ACCOUNT NO. ___**381**___

DATE	DESCRIPTION	POST. REF.	DEBIT	CREDIT	BALANCE	
					DEBIT	CREDIT

Analyze: _____

PROBLEM 21.4A or 21.4B

GENERAL JOURNAL

PAGE _____

	DATE		DESCRIPTION	POST. REF.	DEBIT	CREDIT	
1							1
2							2
3							3
4							4
5							5
6							6
7							7
8							8
9							9
10							10
11							11
12							12
13							13
14							14
15							15
16							16
17							17
18							18
19							19
20							20
21							21
22							22
23							23
24							24
25							25
26							26
27							27
28							28
29							29
30							30
31							31
32							32
33							33
34							34
35							35
36							36
37							37

PROBLEM 21.4A or 21.4B (continued)

GENERAL JOURNAL   PAGE _____

	DATE		DESCRIPTION	POST. REF.	DEBIT	CREDIT	
1							1
2							2
3							3
4							4
5							5
6							6
7							7
8							8
9							9
10							10
11							11
12							12
13							13
14							14
15							15
16							16
17							17
18							18
19							19
20							20
21							21
22							22

GENERAL LEDGER

ACCOUNT __10% Preferred Stock, $10 Par__   ACCOUNT NO. ____301__

DATE	DESCRIPTION	POST. REF.	DEBIT	CREDIT	BALANCE	
					DEBIT	CREDIT

ACCOUNT __Paid-in Capital in Excess of Par Value—Preferred__   ACCOUNT NO. ____305__

DATE	DESCRIPTION	POST. REF.	DEBIT	CREDIT	BALANCE	
					DEBIT	CREDIT

PROBLEM 21.4A or 21.4B (continued)

GENERAL LEDGER

ACCOUNT __Common Stock, No-Par, Stated Value, $50__   ACCOUNT NO. ___311___

DATE	DESCRIPTION	POST. REF.	DEBIT	CREDIT	BALANCE DEBIT	BALANCE CREDIT

ACCOUNT __Paid-in Capital in Excess of Stated Value—Common__   ACCOUNT NO. ___315___

DATE	DESCRIPTION	POST. REF.	DEBIT	CREDIT	BALANCE DEBIT	BALANCE CREDIT

ACCOUNT __Donated Capital__   ACCOUNT NO. ___371___

DATE	DESCRIPTION	POST. REF.	DEBIT	CREDIT	BALANCE DEBIT	BALANCE CREDIT

ACCOUNT __Treasury Stock—Preferred__   ACCOUNT NO. ___372___

DATE	DESCRIPTION	POST. REF.	DEBIT	CREDIT	BALANCE DEBIT	BALANCE CREDIT

ACCOUNT __Retained Earnings__   ACCOUNT NO. ___381___

DATE	DESCRIPTION	POST. REF.	DEBIT	CREDIT	BALANCE DEBIT	BALANCE CREDIT

PROBLEM 21.4A or 21.4B (continued)

GENERAL LEDGER

ACCOUNT __Retained Earnings Appropriated for Treasury Stock__   ACCOUNT NO. ____382____

DATE	DESCRIPTION	POST. REF.	DEBIT	CREDIT	BALANCE	
					DEBIT	CREDIT

Analyze: _____

_____

CRITICAL THINKING PROBLEM 21.1

_____

_____

_____

_____

_____

_____

_____

_____

_____

_____

_____

_____

_____

_____

_____

_____

_____

_____

_____

_____

_____

_____

_____

_____

_____

_____

_____

_____

_____

_____

_____

_____

_____

_____

Analyze: _____

_____

CRITICAL THINKING PROBLEM 21.2

Chapter 21 Practice Test Answer Key

Part A True-False

1. T		9. F	
2. F		10. T	
3. T		11. F	
4. T		12. T	
5. T		13. F	
6. F		14. F	
7. F		15. F	
8. F			

Part B Matching

1. f
2. g
3. c
4. b
5. e
6. a
7. d

Part C Exercises

1. Book value **before** stock dividend:

   Stockholders' equity, $750,000 ÷ 30,000 shares = $25.00 per share

   Book value **after** stock dividend:

   Stockholders' equity, $750,000 ÷ 33,000 shares = $22.72 per share.

2. Entry to record dividend declaration:

2014			
Dec. 15	Retained Earnings	4,000.00	
	Preferred Stock Dividend Payable		4,000.00
	To record dividends payable on		
	cumulative preferred stock for 2012		
	and 2013. Payable on January 12, 2014		
	to holders of record on December 31, 2013.		

STUDY GUIDE

Understanding the Chapter

Objectives

1. Name and define the various types of bonds. **2.** Explain the advantages and disadvantages of using bonds as a method of financing. **3.** Record the issuance of bonds. **4.** Record the payment of interest on bonds. **5.** Record the accrual of interest on bonds. **6.** Compute and record the periodic amortization of a bond premium. **7.** Compute and record the periodic amortization of a bond discount. **8.** Record the transactions of a bond sinking fund investment. **9.** Record an increase or decrease in retained earnings appropriated for bond retirement. **10.** Record retirement of bonds payable. **11.** Define the accounting terms new to this chapter.

Reading Assignment

Read Chapter 22 in the textbook. Complete the textbook Section Self Review as you finish reading each section of the chapter, and the Comprehensive Self Review at the end of the chapter. Refer to the Chapter 22 Glossary or to the Glossary at the end of the book to find definitions for terms that are not familiar to you.

Activities

❑ **Thinking Critically**   Answer the *Thinking Critically* questions for H. J. Heinz and Managerial Implications.

❑ **Discussion Questions**   Answer each assigned discussion question in Chapter 22.

❑ **Exercises**   Complete each assigned exercise in Chapter 22. Use the forms provided in this SGWP. The objectives covered by an exercise are given after the exercise number. If you need help with an exercise, review the portion of the chapter related to the objective(s) covered.

❑ **Problems A/B**   Complete each assigned problem in Chapter 22. Use the forms provided in this SGWP. The objectives covered by a problem are given after the problem number. If you need help with a problem, review the portion of the chapter related to the objective(s) covered.

❑ **Critical Thinking Problems**   Complete the critical thinking problems as assigned. Use the forms provided in this SGWP.

❑ **Business Connections**   Complete the Business Connections activities as assigned to gain a deeper understanding of Chapter 22 concepts.

Practice Tests

Complete the Practice Tests, which cover the main points in your reading assignment. Compare your answers with those in the Practice Test Answer Key for Chapter 22 at the end of this chapter. If you have answered any questions incorrectly, review the related section of the text.

Part A True-False
For each of the following statements, circle T in the answer column if the statement is true and F if the statement is false.

T   F   **1.** In case of liquidation of a corporation, the claims of stockholders take priority over the claims of bondholders.

T   F   **2.** Interest paid on bonds payable is not deductible for federal income tax purposes.

T   F   **3.** The issuance of bonds payable is a method for raising cash.

T   F   **4.** Bonds cannot be issued at a price greater than their par value.

T   F   **5.** The interest on coupon bonds is paid when the bondholders detach the interest coupons from the bonds and submit them for payment.

T   F   **6.** The interest on registered bonds is usually paid by check made payable to the bondholder.

T   F   **7.** Amortization of bond discount increases the bond interest expense.

T   F   **8.** The **Discount on Bonds Payable** is shown on the balance sheet as a current liability.

T   F   **9.** A premium on bonds payable is amortized over the remaining life of the bond.

T   F   **10.** At the end of the year, an adjusting entry is made to record amortization of discount or premium since the last interest payment.

T   F   **11.** When bonds are sold between interest payment dates, the purchaser pays the seller for any interest accrued on the bonds.

T   F   **12.** The **Premium on Bonds Payable** account has a debit balance and should be shown on the income statement as an expense.

T   F   **13.** The bond sinking fund represents assets put aside to be used to retire outstanding bonds.

T   F   **14.** A bond sinking fund is another name for retained earnings appropriated for bond retirement.

T   F   **15.** Bond issue costs may be offset against the premium or added to the discount.

Part B Matching
For each numbered item, choose the matching term from the box and write the identifying letter in the answer column.

_____ **1.** Bonds whose ownership may be transferred by delivery.

_____ **2.** The amount by which the par value of bonds exceeds their issue price.

_____ **3.** A contract covering the issuance of bonds.

_____ **4.** Bonds issued upon pledge of property.

_____ **5.** Cash or other assets set aside for the retirement of bonds.

_____ **6.** Bonds whose ownership is recorded on the books of the corporation.

_____ **7.** Bonds issued on the general credit of the corporation.

_____ **8.** The amount by which the issue price of bonds exceeds par.

_____ **9.** Bonds secured by the pledge of stocks or bonds of other corporations.

_____ **10.** A method of financing for an intermediate period of more than one year, and usually less than five years.

_____ **11.** Loans for an extended period, secured by notes given as part of the purchase price of land, building, or equipment.

a. Debenture bonds

b. Registered bonds

c. Secured bonds

d. Bond indenture

e. Premium

f. Bond sinking fund

g. Discount

h. Long-term notes

i. Collateral trust bonds

j. Unregistered bonds

k. Mortgage loans

Demonstration Problem

On December 31, 2013, the equity accounts of GRAC Inc. contained these balances:

Common Stock ($1 par value, 500,000 shares authorized)

100,000 shares issued and outstanding	$100,000
Retained Earnings	400,000

For the year 2013, the corporation had net income before income taxes of $350,000, income taxes of $87,500, and net income after taxes of $262,500. The corporation's tax rate is 25 percent.

Construction of a new plant at a cost of $1,000,000 is planned. The corporation's president estimates that the new plant will generate additional net income of approximately $200,000 before interest and taxes. The financial vice-president is less optimistic and forecasts an increase in net income of about $150,000 before interest and taxes.

Management is considering two possibilities for financing the project:

1. Issuance of 200,000 additional shares of common stock for $5 per share.

2. Issuance of $1,000,000 face amount, 10-year, 5 percent bonds payable, secured by a mortgage lien on the plant.

Instructions

1. Assuming that profits from existing operations will remain the same and that the president's estimate of net income from the new plant is correct, prepare a table with two columns to show the cumulative effect of each financing plan for the items listed below.

   a. Total net income before interest and taxes

   b. Total bond interest

   c. Total income tax

   d. Total income after taxes

   e. Present income after taxes

   f. Increase (decrease) in total income after bond interest and taxes

   g. Present earnings per share of common stock (compute earnings per share by dividing net income after taxes by the shares of common stock outstanding)

   h. Estimated earnings per share of common stock under the proposed plans

   i. Ratio of net income, after income taxes for 2013 to total stockholders' equity on December 31, 2013 (divide net income by total stockholders' equity on December 31, 2013)

   j. Ratio of net income after income taxes to total stockholders' equity if the plant is constructed

2. Prepare a similar table assuming the financial vice-president's estimate of earnings is correct.

SOLUTION

		STOCK	BONDS
1. a. $350,000 + $200,000		$550,000	$550,000
b. $1,000,000 × 0.05		–0–	50,000
		$550,000	$500,000
c. Stock $87,500 + (0.25 tax rate × $200,000)		137,500	
Bonds $200,000 − $50,000 = $150,000 (increase in income before tax)			
$87,500 + (0.25 × $150,000)			125,000
d.		$412,500	$375,000
e.		262,500	262,500
f.		$150,000	$112,500
g. $262,500 ÷ 100,000 shares		$ 2.62	
h. $412,500 ÷ 300,000 shares; $375,000 ÷ 100,000 shares		$ 1.38	$ 3.75
i. $262,500 ÷ $500,000		52.5%	
j. $412,500 ÷ $1,500,000 ($500,000 + $1,000,000)		27.5%	
$375,000 ÷ $500,000			75.0%

		STOCK	BONDS
2. a. $325,000 + $150,000		$500,000	$500,000
b. $1,000,000 × 0.05			50,000
		$500,000	$450,000
c. Stock $87,500 + (0.25 × $150,000)		125,000	
Bonds $150,000 − $50,000 = $100,000 (increase in income before tax)			
$87,500 + (0.25 × $100,000)			112,500
d.		$375,000	$337,500
e.		262,500	262,500
f.		$112,500	$ 75,000
g. $262,500 ÷ 100,000 shares		$ 2.62	
h. $375,000 ÷ 300,000; $337,500 ÷ 100,000 shares		$ 1.25	$ 3.37
i. $262,500 ÷ $500,000		52.5%	
j. $375,000 ÷ $1,500,000 ($500,000 + $1,000,000)		25.0%	
$337,500 ÷ $500,000			67.5%

WORKING PAPERS

Name _____

EXERCISE 22.1

GENERAL JOURNAL

PAGE _____

	DATE	DESCRIPTION	POST. REF.	DEBIT	CREDIT	
1						1
2						2
3						3
4						4
5						5

EXERCISE 22.2

GENERAL JOURNAL

PAGE _____

	DATE	DESCRIPTION	POST. REF.	DEBIT	CREDIT	
1						1
2						2
3						3
4						4
5						5

EXERCISE 22.3

GENERAL JOURNAL

PAGE _____

	DATE	DESCRIPTION	POST. REF.	DEBIT	CREDIT	
1						1
2						2
3						3
4						4
5						5

EXERCISE 22.4

GENERAL JOURNAL

PAGE _____

	DATE	DESCRIPTION	POST. REF.	DEBIT	CREDIT	
1						1
2						2
3						3
4						4
5						5
6						6

EXERCISE 22.5

GENERAL JOURNAL   PAGE _____

	DATE	DESCRIPTION	POST. REF.	DEBIT	CREDIT	
1						1
2						2
3						3
4						4
5						5
6						6

EXERCISE 22.6

GENERAL JOURNAL   PAGE _____

	DATE	DESCRIPTION	POST. REF.	DEBIT	CREDIT	
1						1
2						2
3						3
4						4
5						5
6						6
7						7

EXERCISE 22.7

GENERAL JOURNAL   PAGE _____

	DATE	DESCRIPTION	POST. REF.	DEBIT	CREDIT	
1						1
2						2
3						3
4						4
5						5
6						6
7						7
8						8
9						9
10						10
11						11
12						12
13						13

EXERCISE 22.8

GENERAL JOURNAL   PAGE _____

	DATE	DESCRIPTION	POST. REF.	DEBIT	CREDIT	
1						1
2						2
3						3
4						4
5						5

EXERCISE 22.9

GENERAL JOURNAL   PAGE _____

	DATE	DESCRIPTION	POST. REF.	DEBIT	CREDIT	
1						1
2						2
3						3
4						4
5						5
6						6
7						7
8						8
9						9
10						10
11						11
12						12
13						13

EXTRA FORM

GENERAL JOURNAL   PAGE _____

	DATE	DESCRIPTION	POST. REF.	DEBIT	CREDIT	
1						1
2						2
3						3
4						4
5						5
6						6
7						7
8						8

PROBLEM 22.1A or 22.1B

GENERAL JOURNAL

	DATE	DESCRIPTION	POST. REF.	DEBIT	CREDIT	
1						1
2						2
3						3
4						4
5						5
6						6
7						7
8						8
9						9
10						10
11						11
12						12
13						13
14						14
15						15
16						16
17						17
18						18
19						19
20						20
21						21
22						22
23						23
24						24
25						25
26						26
27						27
28						28
29						29
30						30
31						31
32						32
33						33
34						34
35						35
36						36
37						37

PROBLEM 22.1A or 22.1B (continued)

GENERAL JOURNAL   PAGE _____

	DATE	DESCRIPTION	POST. REF.	DEBIT	CREDIT	
1						1
2						2
3						3
4						4
5						5
6						6
7						7
8						8
9						9
10						10
11						11
12						12
13						13
14						14
15						15
16						16
17						17
18						18
19						19
20						20
21						21
22						22
23						23
24						24
25						25
26						26
27						27
28						28
29						29
30						30
31						31
32						32
33						33
34						34

Analyze: _____

PROBLEM 22.2A or 22.2B

GENERAL JOURNAL

PAGE _____

	DATE		DESCRIPTION	POST. REF.	DEBIT	CREDIT	
1							1
2							2
3							3
4							4
5							5
6							6
7							7
8							8
9							9
10							10
11							11
12							12
13							13
14							14
15							15
16							16
17							17
18							18
19							19
20							20
21							21
22							22
23							23
24							24
25							25
26							26
27							27
28							28
29							29
30							30
31							31
32							32
33							33
34							34
35							35
36							36
37							37

PROBLEM 22.2A or 22.2B (continued)

Analyze: _____

EXTRA FORM

PROBLEM 22.3A or 22.3B

GENERAL JOURNAL   PAGE _____

	DATE		DESCRIPTION	POST. REF.	DEBIT	CREDIT	
1							1
2							2
3							3
4							4
5							5
6							6
7							7
8							8
9							9
10							10
11							11
12							12
13							13
14							14
15							15
16							16
17							17
18							18
19							19
20							20
21							21
22							22
23							23
24							24
25							25
26							26
27							27
28							28
29							29
30							30
31							31
32							32
33							33
34							34
35							35
36							36
37							37

PROBLEM 22.3A or 22.3B (continued)

Analyze: _____

PROBLEM 22.4A or 22.4B

GENERAL JOURNAL

PAGE _____

	DATE		DESCRIPTION	POST. REF.	DEBIT	CREDIT	
1							1
2							2
3							3
4							4
5							5
6							6
7							7
8							8
9							9
10							10
11							11
12							12
13							13
14							14
15							15
16							16
17							17
18							18
19							19
20							20
21							21
22							22
23							23
24							24

PROBLEM 22.4A or 22.4B (continued)

Analyze: _____

PROBLEM 22.5A or 22.5B

GENERAL JOURNAL

PAGE _____

	DATE	DESCRIPTION	POST. REF.	DEBIT	CREDIT	
1						1
2						2
3						3
4						4
5						5
6						6
7						7
8						8
9						9
10						10
11						11
12						12
13						13
14						14
15						15

Analyze: _____

CRITICAL THINKING PROBLEM 22.1

1. _____
_____
_____
_____
_____
_____
_____
_____
_____

2. _____
_____
_____
_____
_____
_____
_____
_____
_____
_____
_____
_____

CRITICAL THINKING PROBLEM 22.2

	Issuing Common Stock	Issuing Bonds Payable
1. **President's estimated net income**		
before interest and taxes =		
a. Net income before interest and taxes		
b. Total bond interest		
Taxable income		
c. Total income tax		
d. Total income after tax		
e. Present income after tax		
f. Increase in net income		
g. Present EPS		
h. Proposed EPS		

CRITICAL THINKING PROBLEM 22.2 (continued)

	Issuing Common Stock	Issuing Bonds Payable
2. Financial VP's estimate of net income before interest and taxes =		
a. Net income before interest and taxes		
b. Total bond interest		
Taxable income		
c. Total income tax		
d. Total income after tax		
e. Present income after tax		
f. Increase in net income		
g. Present EPS		
h. Proposed EPS		

3. _____
_____
_____
_____
_____
_____

Analyze: _____
_____
_____
_____
_____

Chapter 22 Practice Test Answer Key

Part A True-False	Part B Matching
1. F	1. j
2. F	2. g
3. T	3. d
4. F	4. c
5. T	5. f
6. T	6. b
7. T	7. a
8. F	8. e
9. T	9. i
10. T	10. h
11. T	11. k
12. F	
13. T	
14. F	
15. T	

MINI-PRACTICE SET 3

Corporation Accounting Cycle

The Kansas Company

Name _____

GENERAL JOURNAL   PAGE ____1____

	DATE	DESCRIPTION	POST. REF.	DEBIT	CREDIT	
1						
2						2
3						3
4						4
5						5
6						6
7						7
8						8
9						9
10						10
11						11
12						12
13						13
14						14
15						15
16						16
17						17
18						18
19						19
20						20
21						21
22						22
23						23
24						24
25						25
26						26
27						27
28						28
29						29
30						30
31						31
32						32
33						33
34						34
35						35

Name _____

GENERAL JOURNAL PAGE ____2____

	DATE		DESCRIPTION	POST. REF.	DEBIT	CREDIT	
1							1
2							2
3							3
4							4
5							5
6							6
7							7
8							8
9							9
10							10
11							11
12							12
13							13
14							14
15							15
16							16
17							17
18							18
19							19
20							20
21							21
22							22
23							23
24							24
25							25
26							26
27							27
28							28
29							29
30							30
31							31
32							32
33							33
34							34
35							35
36							36
37							37
38							38
39							39

GENERAL JOURNAL   PAGE ___3___

	DATE	DESCRIPTION	POST. REF.	DEBIT	CREDIT	
1						1
2						2
3						3
4						4
5						5
6						6
7						7
8						8
9						9
10						10
11						11
12						12
13						13
14						14
15						15
16						16
17						17
18						18
19						19
20						20
21						21
22						22
23						23
24						24
25						25
26						26
27						27
28						28
29						29
30						30
31						31
32						32
33						33
34						34
35						35
36						36
37						37
38						38
39						39

Name _____

GENERAL JOURNAL

PAGE ___4___

	DATE		DESCRIPTION	POST. REF.	DEBIT	CREDIT	
1							1
2							2
3							3
4							4
5							5
6							6
7							7
8							8
9							9
10							10
11							11
12							12
13							13
14							14
15							15
16							16
17							17
18							18
19							19
20							20
21							21
22							22
23							23
24							24
25							25
26							26
27							27
28							28
29							29
30							30
31							31
32							32
33							33
34							34
35							35
36							36
37							37

GENERAL JOURNAL   PAGE ___5___

	DATE		DESCRIPTION	POST. REF.	DEBIT	CREDIT	
1							1
2							2
3							3
4							4
5							5
6							6
7							7
8							8
9							9
10							10
11							11
12							12
13							13
14							14
15							15
16							16
17							17
18							18
19							19
20							20
21							21
22							22
23							23
24							24
25							25
26							26
27							27
28							28
29							29
30							30
31							31
32							32
33							33
34							34
35							35
36							36
37							37

Name _____

GENERAL LEDGER

ACCOUNT __Cash__ _____ ACCOUNT NO. ____101____

DATE	DESCRIPTION	POST. REF.	DEBIT	CREDIT	BALANCE	
					DEBIT	CREDIT

ACCOUNT __Accounts Receivable__ _____ ACCOUNT NO. ____103____

DATE	DESCRIPTION	POST. REF.	DEBIT	CREDIT	BALANCE	
					DEBIT	CREDIT

ACCOUNT __Allowance for Doubtful Accounts__ _____ ACCOUNT NO. ____104____

DATE	DESCRIPTION	POST. REF.	DEBIT	CREDIT	BALANCE	
					DEBIT	CREDIT

MINI-PRACTICE SET 3 (continued)   Name _____

GENERAL LEDGER

ACCOUNT __Subscriptions Receivable—Common Stock__   ACCOUNT NO. __105__

DATE	DESCRIPTION	POST. REF.	DEBIT	CREDIT	BALANCE DEBIT	BALANCE CREDIT

ACCOUNT __Interest Receivable__   ACCOUNT NO. __121__

DATE	DESCRIPTION	POST. REF.	DEBIT	CREDIT	BALANCE DEBIT	BALANCE CREDIT

ACCOUNT __Merchandise Inventory__   ACCOUNT NO. __131__

DATE	DESCRIPTION	POST. REF.	DEBIT	CREDIT	BALANCE DEBIT	BALANCE CREDIT

ACCOUNT __Land__   ACCOUNT NO. __141__

DATE	DESCRIPTION	POST. REF.	DEBIT	CREDIT	BALANCE DEBIT	BALANCE CREDIT

ACCOUNT __Buildings__   ACCOUNT NO. __151__

DATE	DESCRIPTION	POST. REF.	DEBIT	CREDIT	BALANCE DEBIT	BALANCE CREDIT

GENERAL LEDGER

ACCOUNT __Accumulated Depreciation—Buildings__   ACCOUNT NO. ____152____

DATE	DESCRIPTION	POST. REF.	DEBIT	CREDIT	BALANCE	
					DEBIT	CREDIT

ACCOUNT __Furniture and Equipment__   ACCOUNT NO. ____161____

DATE	DESCRIPTION	POST. REF.	DEBIT	CREDIT	BALANCE	
					DEBIT	CREDIT

ACCOUNT __Accumulated Depreciation—Furniture and Equipment__   ACCOUNT NO. ____162____

DATE	DESCRIPTION	POST. REF.	DEBIT	CREDIT	BALANCE	
					DEBIT	CREDIT

ACCOUNT __Organization Costs__   ACCOUNT NO. ____181____

DATE	DESCRIPTION	POST. REF.	DEBIT	CREDIT	BALANCE	
					DEBIT	CREDIT

ACCOUNT __Accounts Payable__   ACCOUNT NO. ____202____

DATE	DESCRIPTION	POST. REF.	DEBIT	CREDIT	BALANCE	
					DEBIT	CREDIT

GENERAL LEDGER

ACCOUNT __Interest Payable__   ACCOUNT NO. ____203____

DATE	DESCRIPTION	POST. REF.	DEBIT	CREDIT	BALANCE DEBIT	BALANCE CREDIT

ACCOUNT __Estimated Income Taxes Payable__   ACCOUNT NO. ____205____

DATE	DESCRIPTION	POST. REF.	DEBIT	CREDIT	BALANCE DEBIT	BALANCE CREDIT

ACCOUNT __Dividends Payable—Preferred Stock__   ACCOUNT NO. ____206____

DATE	DESCRIPTION	POST. REF.	DEBIT	CREDIT	BALANCE DEBIT	BALANCE CREDIT

ACCOUNT __Dividends Payable—Common Stock__   ACCOUNT NO. ____207____

DATE	DESCRIPTION	POST. REF.	DEBIT	CREDIT	BALANCE DEBIT	BALANCE CREDIT

ACCOUNT __10-Year, 10% Bonds Payable__   ACCOUNT NO. ____211____

DATE	DESCRIPTION	POST. REF.	DEBIT	CREDIT	BALANCE DEBIT	BALANCE CREDIT

Name _____

GENERAL LEDGER

ACCOUNT ___Premium on Bonds Payable_____ ACCOUNT NO. ___212___

DATE	DESCRIPTION	POST. REF.	DEBIT	CREDIT	BALANCE DEBIT	BALANCE CREDIT

ACCOUNT ___5% Preferred Stock ($100 par, 10,000 shares authorized)_____ ACCOUNT NO. ___301___

DATE	DESCRIPTION	POST. REF.	DEBIT	CREDIT	BALANCE DEBIT	BALANCE CREDIT

ACCOUNT ___Paid-in Capital in Excess of Par—Preferred Stock_____ ACCOUNT NO. ___302___

DATE	DESCRIPTION	POST. REF.	DEBIT	CREDIT	BALANCE DEBIT	BALANCE CREDIT

ACCOUNT ___Common Stock ($10 par, 100,000 shares authorized)_____ ACCOUNT NO. ___303___

DATE	DESCRIPTION	POST. REF.	DEBIT	CREDIT	BALANCE DEBIT	BALANCE CREDIT

ACCOUNT ___Paid-in Capital in Excess of Par—Common Stock_____ ACCOUNT NO. ___304___

DATE	DESCRIPTION	POST. REF.	DEBIT	CREDIT	BALANCE DEBIT	BALANCE CREDIT

GENERAL LEDGER

ACCOUNT __Common Stock Subscribed__   ACCOUNT NO. ____305____

DATE	DESCRIPTION	POST. REF.	DEBIT	CREDIT	BALANCE DEBIT	BALANCE CREDIT

ACCOUNT __Common Stock Dividend Distributable__   ACCOUNT NO. ____306____

DATE	DESCRIPTION	POST. REF.	DEBIT	CREDIT	BALANCE DEBIT	BALANCE CREDIT

ACCOUNT __Retained Earnings Appropriated__   ACCOUNT NO. ____311____

DATE	DESCRIPTION	POST. REF.	DEBIT	CREDIT	BALANCE DEBIT	BALANCE CREDIT

ACCOUNT __Retained Earnings Unappropriated__   ACCOUNT NO. ____312____

DATE	DESCRIPTION	POST. REF.	DEBIT	CREDIT	BALANCE DEBIT	BALANCE CREDIT

ACCOUNT __Treasury Stock—Preferred__   ACCOUNT NO. ____343____

DATE	DESCRIPTION	POST. REF.	DEBIT	CREDIT	BALANCE DEBIT	BALANCE CREDIT

Name _____

GENERAL LEDGER

ACCOUNT __Income Summary_____ ACCOUNT NO. ___399___

DATE	DESCRIPTION	POST. REF.	DEBIT	CREDIT	BALANCE	
					DEBIT	CREDIT

ACCOUNT __Sales_____ ACCOUNT NO. ___401___

DATE	DESCRIPTION	POST. REF.	DEBIT	CREDIT	BALANCE	
					DEBIT	CREDIT

ACCOUNT __Purchases_____ ACCOUNT NO. ___501___

DATE	DESCRIPTION	POST. REF.	DEBIT	CREDIT	BALANCE	
					DEBIT	CREDIT

ACCOUNT __Operating Expenses_____ ACCOUNT NO. ___601___

DATE	DESCRIPTION	POST. REF.	DEBIT	CREDIT	BALANCE	
					DEBIT	CREDIT

GENERAL LEDGER

ACCOUNT __Interest Income__   ACCOUNT NO. ____701

DATE	DESCRIPTION	POST. REF.	DEBIT	CREDIT	BALANCE DEBIT	BALANCE CREDIT

ACCOUNT __Gain on Early Retirement of Bonds Payable__   ACCOUNT NO. ____711

DATE	DESCRIPTION	POST. REF.	DEBIT	CREDIT	BALANCE DEBIT	BALANCE CREDIT

ACCOUNT __Interest Expense__   ACCOUNT NO. ____751

DATE	DESCRIPTION	POST. REF.	DEBIT	CREDIT	BALANCE DEBIT	BALANCE CREDIT

ACCOUNT __Amortization of Organization Costs__   ACCOUNT NO. ____753

DATE	DESCRIPTION	POST. REF.	DEBIT	CREDIT	BALANCE DEBIT	BALANCE CREDIT

ACCOUNT __Income Tax Expense__   ACCOUNT NO. ____801

DATE	DESCRIPTION	POST. REF.	DEBIT	CREDIT	BALANCE DEBIT	BALANCE CREDIT

	ACCOUNT NAME	TRIAL BALANCE		ADJUSTMENTS	
		DEBIT	CREDIT	DEBIT	CREDIT
1	Cash				
2	Accounts Receivable				
3	Allowance for Doubtful Accounts				
4	Subscriptions Receivable—Common Stock				
5	Merchandise Inventory				
6	Land				
7	Buildings				
8	Accumulated Depreciation—Bldg				
9	Furniture and Equipment				
10	Accum. Depreciation—Furn. and Equip.				
11	Organization Costs				
12	Accounts Payable				
13	Interest Payable				
14	Estimated Income Tax Payable				
15	Dividends Payable—Preferred Stock				
16	Dividends Payable—Common Stock				
17	10-Year, 10% Bonds Payable				
18	Premium on Bonds Payable				
19	5% Preferred Stock				
20	Paid-in Cap. in Excess of Par—Pref. Stock				
21	Common Stock				
22	Paid-in Cap. in Excess of Par—Com. Stock				
23	Common Stock Subscribed				
24	Common Stock Dividend Distrib.				
25	Retained Earnings Appropriated				
26	Retained Earnings Unappropriated				
27	Treasury Stock—Preferred				
28	Income Summary				
29	Sales				
30	Purchases				
31	Operating Expenses				
32					
33					
34	Totals Carried Forward				
35					

ADJUSTED TRIAL BALANCE		INCOME STATEMENT		BALANCE SHEET		
DEBIT	CREDIT	DEBIT	CREDIT	DEBIT	CREDIT	
						1
						2
						3
						4
						5
						6
						7
						8
						9
						10
						11
						12
						13
						14
						15
						16
						17
						18
						19
						20
						21
						22
						23
						24
						25
						26
						27
						28
						29
						30
						31
						32
						33
						34
						35

_____

_____

	ACCOUNT NAME	TRIAL BALANCE		ADJUSTMENTS	
		DEBIT	CREDIT	DEBIT	CREDIT
1					
2	Totals Brought Forward				
3	Gain on Early Retirement of Bonds Payable				
4	Interest Expense				
5	Amortization of Organization Costs				
6	Income Tax Expense				
7	Totals				
8	Net Income After Tax				
9	Totals				
10					
11					
12					
13					
14					
15					
16					
17					
18					
19					
20					
21					
22					
23					
24					
25					
26					
27					
28					
29					
30					
31					
32					

ADJUSTED TRIAL BALANCE		INCOME STATEMENT		BALANCE SHEET		
DEBIT	CREDIT	DEBIT	CREDIT	DEBIT	CREDIT	
						1
						2
						3
						4
						5
						6
						7
						8
						9
						10
						11
						12
						13
						14
						15
						16
						17
						18
						19
						20
						21
						22
						23
						24
						25
						26
						27
						28
						29
						30
						31
						32

Summary Income Statement

Statement of Retained Earnings

Balance Sheet

(continued)

Name _____

Balance Sheet (continued)

CHAPTER 23 — Financial Statement Analysis

STUDY GUIDE

Understanding the Chapter

Objectives

1. Use vertical analysis techniques to analyze a comparative income statement and balance sheet. 2. Use horizontal analysis techniques to analyze a comparative income statement and balance sheet. 3. Use trend analysis to evaluate financial statements. 4. Interpret the results of the statement analysis by comparison with industry averages. 5. Compute and interpret financial ratios that measure profitability, operating results, and efficiency. 6. Compute and interpret financial ratios that measure financial strength. 7. Compute and interpret financial ratios that measure liquidity. 8. Recognize shortcomings in financial statement analysis. 9. Define the accounting terms new to this chapter.

Reading Assignment

Read Chapter 23 in the textbook. Complete the textbook Section Self Review as you finish reading each section of the chapter, and the Comprehensive Self Review at the end of the chapter. Refer to the Chapter 23 Glossary or to the Glossary at the end of the book to find definitions for terms that are not familiar to you.

Activities

❑ **Thinking Critically**

Answer the *Thinking Critically* questions for Teva Pharmaceuticals and Managerial Implications.

❑ **Discussion Questions**

Answer each assigned discussion question in Chapter 23.

❑ **Exercises**

Complete each assigned exercise in Chapter 23. Use the forms provided in this SGWP. The objectives covered by an exercise are given after the exercise number. If you need help with an exercise, review the portion of the chapter related to the objective(s) covered.

❑ **Problems A/B**

Complete each assigned problem in Chapter 23. Use the forms provided in this SGWP. The objectives covered by a problem are given after the problem number. If you need help with a problem, review the portion of the chapter related to the objective(s) covered.

❑ **Critical Thinking Problems**

Complete the critical thinking problems as assigned. Use the forms provided in this SGWP.

❑ **Business Connections**

Complete the Business Connections activities as assigned to gain a deeper understanding of Chapter 23 concepts.

Practice Tests

Complete the Practice Tests, which cover the main points in your reading assignment. Compare your answers with those in the Practice Test Answer Key for Chapter 23 at the end of this chapter. If you have answered any questions incorrectly, review the related section of the text.

Part A True-False

For each of the following statements, circle T if the statement is true or F if the statement is false.

T   F   **1.** In general, a period of two years is adequate for comparing figures such as net sales.

T   F   **2.** The earlier period is considered to be the base period in the horizontal analysis of statements.

T   F   **3.** A lender will be more interested in net income than in the acid-test ratio.

T   F   **4.** In statement analysis, a small percentage change in a large dollar amount may be more important than a large percentage change in a small dollar amount.

T   F   **5.** The rate of return on total assets is affected by the source of financing used to acquire assets.

T   F   **6.** Common-size statements are statements of companies that sold approximately the same product.

T   F   **7.** In horizontal analysis, the items on each line of the statements for two periods are compared to determine the change in dollar amounts and percentages.

T   F   **8.** In vertical analysis of the balance sheet, each liability item is usually expressed as a percent of total liabilities.

T   F   **9.** Current ratio and acid-test ratio are the same ratio.

T   F   **10.** In general, the lower the rate of inventory turnover, the better.

T   F   **11.** The net sales figure of a business is normally used as the base, or 100%, for vertical analysis comparisons on the income statement.

T   F   **12.** The interpretation phase of statement analysis is composed primarily of computing percentages and ratios.

T   F   **13.** In vertical analysis, the percentages may be added and subtracted.

T   F   **14.** The analyst is interested in both the amount of change and the percent of change in an item from year to year.

T   F   **15.** Having an accounts receivable collection period that exceeds 30 days will have no effect on your cash flow planning for the business.

Part B Matching

For each of the transactions below, decide the effect (or effects) the transaction would have on the corporation's financial statements or ratios. In the space provided, enter the letter or letters corresponding to all effects that apply. If there is no appropriate response among the effects listed, write "none".

Transaction	Effect
_____ **1.** Purchased a new office desk for cash.	**a.** Increases working capital
_____ **2.** Declared a cash dividend due in one month.	**b.** Reduces working capital
_____ **3.** Omitted the payment of a dividend.	**c.** Increases the current ratio
_____ **4.** Declared and paid an ordinary cash dividend.	**d.** Decreases the current ratio
_____ **5.** Issued new common stock shares on a 4 for 1 stock split.	**e.** Increases the dollar amount of the total capital stock
_____ **6.** Issued long-term notes payable for cash.	**f.** Decreases the dollar amount of the total capital stock
	g. Increases total retained earnings
	h. Decreases total retained earnings
	i. Reduces the book value of each share of common stock
	j. Reduces the book value of each common shareholder's interest

Demonstration Problem

A condensed income statement for Far Out Corporation, for the years 2013 and 2012, follows. This report has been condensed and simplified from the corporation's annual Form 10K for 2013, filed with the U.S. Securities and Exchange Commission. Amounts given are in millions of dollars.

Instructions

1. Prepare a combined horizontal and vertical analysis of the comparative income statement of Far Out Corporation.

2. Analyze the data on the Far Out Corporation. What conclusions might be drawn from the following increases or decreases?

   a. Sales
   b. Cost of goods sold
   c. Inventory
   d. Operating expenses
   e. Net income after income taxes

SOLUTION

1.

Far Out Corporation
Comparative Income Statement
Years Ended December 31, 2013 and 2012

	AMOUNTS 2013	AMOUNTS 2012	PERCENT OF NET SALES 2013	PERCENT OF NET SALES 2012	INCREASE OR (DECREASE) AMOUNT	INCREASE OR (DECREASE) PERCENT
Revenue:						
Sales	575000	500000	100.4	100.6	75000	15.0
Less Sales Returns and Allowances	2500	3000	0.4	0.6	-500	-16.7
Net Sales	572500	497000	100.0	100.0	75500	15.2
Cost of Goods Sold						
Merchandise Inventory, January 1	40000	38000	7.0	7.6	2000	5.3
Net Purchases	120000	100000	21.0	20.1	20000	20.0
Total Merchandise Available for Sale	160000	138000	27.9	27.8	22000	15.9
Less Merchandise Inventory, December 31	36000	40000	6.3	8.0	-4000	-10.0
Cost of Goods Sold	124000	98000	21.7	19.7	26000	26.5
Gross Profit on Sales	448500	399000	78.3	80.3	49500	12.4
Operating Expenses						
Selling Expenses						
Sales Salaries Expense	100000	79000	17.5	15.9	21000	26.6
Payroll Tax Expenses-Selling	10000	7900	1.7	1.6	2100	26.6
Other Selling Expenses	25800	15200	4.5	3.1	10600	69.7
Total Selling Expense	135800	102100	23.7	20.5	33700	33.0
General and Administrative Expenses						
Officers Salaries Expense	150000	125000	26.2	25.2	25000	20.0
Payroll Tax Expense-Administrative	15000	12500	2.6	2.5	2500	20.0
Depreciation Expense	8250	8250	1.4	1.7	0	0.0
Other General and Administrative Expense	12000	7000	2.1	1.4	5000	71.4
Total General and Administrative Expense	185250	152750	32.4	30.7	32500	21.3
Total Operating Expenses	321050	254850	56.1	51.3	66200	26.0
Net Income Before Income Taxes	127450	144150	22.3	29.0	-16700	-11.6
Income Tax Expense	38235	43245	6.7	8.7	-5010	-11.6
Net Income After Income Taxes	89215	100905	15.6	20.3	-11690	-11.6

SOLUTION (continued)

2.   Several items on the comparative balance sheet of Far Out Corporation merit additional investigation.

   a. The nice increase in sales was accompanied by other expense increases-you should expect this.

   b. The percentage increase of Cost of Goods Sold should be examined. Increases in sales cannot totally compensate for higher increases of the cost of goods.

   c. The reduction of ending inventory is a nice indicator. Efforts should be encouraged to keep this trend continuing.

   d. As sales increase, management should anticipate these expenses to increase. The 26% increase is probably reasonable considering the 15% increase in sales.

   e. The large increase in sales is not reflected in the net income after income taxes. If the owners are involved in the company and the increases in sales salaries and officers' salaries expense are benefiting the owners, they are probably ok with results. However, the net income after taxes in 2013 is lower primarily because of the increased operating expenses.

WORKING PAPERS

Name _____

EXERCISE 23.1

	2013		2012	

EXERCISE 23.2

	2013		2012	

EXERCISE 23.3

	2013	2012	Change	Percent

EXTRA FORM

EXERCISE 23.4

	2013	2012	Difference	Percent

EXERCISE 23.5

2013   2012

_____

_____

EXERCISE 23.6

2013   2012

_____

_____

EXERCISE 23.7

2013   2012

_____

_____

EXERCISE 23.8

2013   2012

_____

_____

EXERCISE 23.9

2013   2012

_____

_____

EXERCISE 23.10

2013   2012

_____

_____

EXERCISE 23.11

2013   2012

_____

_____

EXERCISE 23.12

2013   2012

_____

_____

PROBLEM 23.1A or 23.1B

Comparative Income Statement

1.

	AMOUNTS		PERCENT OF NET SALES		INCREASE OR (DECREASE)	
	2013	2012	2013	2012	AMOUNT	PERCENT

PROBLEM 23.1A or 23.1B (continued)

Comparative Income Statement (continued)

		AMOUNTS		PERCENT OF NET SALES		INCREASE OR (DECREASE)	
		2013	2012	2013	2012	AMOUNT	PERCENT

PROBLEM 23.1A or 23.1B (continued)

Comparative Balance Sheet

	AMOUNTS		PERCENT OF TOTAL ASSETS		INCREASE OR (DECREASE)	
	2013	2012	2013	2012	AMOUNT	PERCENT

PROBLEM 23.1A or 23.1B (continued)

Comparative Balance Sheet (continued)

	AMOUNTS		PERCENT OF TOTAL ASSETS		INCREASE OR (DECREASE)	
	2013	2012	2013	2012	AMOUNT	PERCENT

2.

Analyze:

PROBLEM 23.2A or 23.2B

PART I

2012

2013

1.

2.

3.

4.

5.

6.

7.

8.

9.

10.

PROBLEM 23.2A or 23.2B (continued)

PART II

_____

_____

_____

_____

_____

_____

_____

_____

_____

_____

_____

_____

_____

_____

_____

_____

_____

_____

_____

_____

_____

_____

_____

_____

_____

Analyze: _____

_____

_____

PROBLEM 23.3A or 23.3B

1. a.

b.

c.

d.

e.

f.

g.

h.

PROBLEM 23.3A or 23.3B (continued)

2. _____

_____

_____

3. _____

_____

_____

4. _____

_____

_____

_____

_____

_____

_____

_____

_____

_____

_____

_____

_____

_____

_____

_____

_____

_____

Analyze: _____

_____

_____

_____

_____

_____

_____

_____

_____

_____

CRITICAL THINKING PROBLEM 23.1

CRITICAL THINKING PROBLEM 23.1

_____

_____

_____

Analyze: _____

_____

CRITICAL THINKING PROBLEM 23.2

EXTRA FORM

Chapter 23 Practice Test Answer Key

Part A True-False		Part B Matching
1. F	9. F	1. b, d
2. T	10. F	2. b, d, h
3. F	11. T	3. i, j
4. T	12. F	4. b, d, h
5. F	13. T	5. i
6. F	14. T	6. a, c
7. T	15. F	
8. F		

CHAPTER 24

The Statement of Cash Flows

STUDY GUIDE

Understanding the Chapter

Objectives

1. Distinguish between operating, investing, and financing activities.
2. Compute cash flows from operating activities. 3. Compute cash flows from investing activities. 4. Compute cash flows from financing activities.
5. Prepare a statement of cash flows. 6. Define the accounting terms new to this chapter.

Reading Assignment

Read Chapter 24 in the textbook. Complete the textbook Section Self Reviews as you finish reading each section of the chapter, and the Comprehensive Self Review at the end of the chapter. Refer to the Chapter 24 Glossary or to the Glossary at the end of the book to find definitions for terms that are not familiar to you.

Activities

❏ **Thinking Critically**

Answer the *Thinking Critically* questions for Apple and Managerial Implications.

❏ **Discussion Questions**

Answer each assigned discussion question in Chapter 24.

❏ **Exercises**

Complete each assigned exercise in Chapter 24. Use the forms provided in this SGWP. The objectives covered by an exercise are given after the exercise number. If you need help with an exercise, review the portion of the chapter related to the objective(s) covered.

❏ **Problems A/B**

Complete each assigned problem in Chapter 24. Use the forms provided in this SGWP. The objectives covered by a problem are given after the problem number. If you need help with a problem, review the portion of the chapter related to the objective(s) covered.

❏ **Challenge Problem**

Complete the challenge problem as assigned. Use the forms provided in this SGWP.

❏ **Critical Thinking Problems**

Complete the critical thinking problems as assigned. Use the forms provided in this SGWP.

❏ **Business Connections**

Complete the Business Connections activities as assigned to gain a deeper understanding of Chapter 24 concepts.

Practice Tests

Complete the Practice Tests, which cover the main points in your reading assignment. Compare your answers with those in the Practice Test Answer Key for Chapter 24 at the end of this chapter. If you have answered any questions incorrectly, review the related section of the text.

Part A True-False
For each of the following statements, circle T if the statement is true or F if the statement is false.

T   F   **1.** The statement of cash flows is designed to provide information about a corporation's cash position.

T   F   **2.** The statement of cash flows provides an important link between the balance sheet and the income statement.

T   F   **3.** A three month CD is an example of a cash equivalent.

T   F   **4.** Interest expense is a cash outflow from a financing activity.

T   F   **5.** The indirect method of preparing the statement of cash flows is the preferred method of businesses when preparing this statement.

T   F   **6.** The FASB has expressed a preference for the direct method of preparing the statement of cash flows.

T   F   **7.** Repayment of a long-term note payable represents an investing activity.

T   F   **8.** The purchase of merchandise inventory for resale is an operating activity.

T   F   **9.** The issue of a mortgage payable for a building is a financing activity.

T   F   **10.** Depreciation expense is added to the net income figure in arriving at cash flow from operating activities.

T   F   **11.** Short-term borrowing is classified as a financing activity for purposes of preparing the statement of cash flows.

T   F   **12.** A corporation issued $500,000 of bonds payable, receiving in exchange a building with that value. The transaction would be included in the footnotes of the statement of cash flows.

T   F   **13.** The sale of bonds is a financing activity.

T   F   **14.** The cash received from the sale of equipment represents a cash flow from operating activities.

T   F   **15.** The amortization of premium on bonds payable is added to net income in arriving at the cash flows from operations.

T   F   **16.** The statement of cash flows reconciles the beginning and ending balances of cash and cash equivalents.

T   F   **17.** The issue of $50,000 of common stock for land with a fair market value of $50,000 represents an investing activity.

Part B Matching
For each numbered item, choose the matching term from the box and write the identifying letter in the answer column.

_____   **1.** Paid a cash dividend.

_____   **2.** Borrowed $59,000 by issuing a 90-day note payable.

_____   **3.** Purchased office furniture for cash.

_____   **4.** Paid cash on accounts payable.

_____   **5.** Paid interest on a five-year note payable.

_____   **6.** Declared but did not pay a cash dividend.

_____   **7.** Purchased land by issuing common stock.

_____   **8.** Sold land held as a long-term investment.

_____   **9.** Paid cash dividend on preferred stock.

_____   **10.** Reacquired common stock as treasury stock.

a.	Operating
b.	Investing
c.	Financing
d.	Not on statement of cash flows

Demonstration Problem

Sandwiches, Inc. was formed and began business on January 1, 2013, when Kim Lang transferred merchandise inventory with a value of $20,000, cash of $30,000, accounts receivable of $10,000, and accounts payable of $10,000 to the corporation in exchange for common stock with a recorded par value of $10 a share.

Information from the company's statement of cash flows for 2013 follows.

Instructions

Based on the data given, prepare the December 31, 2013, balance sheet for the corporation.

Cash Flows from Operating Activities		
Net Income		$ 75,000
Adjustments:		
Depreciation of building	$ 8,000	
Depreciation of equipment	5,000	
Increase in accounts receivable	(29,000)	
Increase in inventory	(10,000)	
Increase in prepaid insurance	(1,200)	
Increase in accounts payable	8,000	
Increase in income tax payable	4,000	
Total Adjustments		(15,200)
Net cash provided by operating activities		$ 59,800
Cash Flows from Investing Activities		
Purchase of land	$(20,000)	
Purchase of building*	(10,000)	
Purchase of equipment	(25,000)	
Net cash used in investing activities		(55,000)
Cash Flows from Financing Activities		
Issuance of common stock at $10	$ 80,000	
Borrowing at bank by issuance of note payable	25,000	
Net cash provided by financing activities		$ 105,000
Net Increase in Cash and Cash Equivalents		$ 109,800
Cash balance, January 1, 2013		30,000
Cash balance, December 31, 2013		$ 139,800

*A building was acquired at a cost of $80,000. Cash of $10,000 was paid, and a mortgage payable of $70,000 was given for the balance.

SOLUTION

Sandwiches, Inc.

Balance Sheet

December 31, 2013

Assets				
Current Assets				
Cash			139 8 0 0 00	
Accounts Receivable			39 0 0 0 00	
Merchandise Inventory			30 0 0 0 00	
Prepaid Insurance			1 2 0 0 00	
Total Current Assets				210 0 0 0 00
Property, Plant, and Equipment				
Land			20 0 0 0 00	
Building	80 0 0 0 00			
Less Accumulated Depreciation—Building	8 0 0 0 00		72 0 0 0 00	
Equipment	25 0 0 0 00			
Less Accumulated Depreciation—Equipment	5 0 0 0 00		20 0 0 0 00	
Total Property, Plant, and Equipment				112 0 0 0 00
Total Assets				322 0 0 0 00
Liabilities and Stockholders' Equity				
Current Liabilities				
Accounts Payable			18 0 0 0 00	
Notes Payable			25 0 0 0 00	
Income Tax Payable			4 0 0 0 00	
Total Current Liabilities			47 0 0 0 00	
Long-Term Liabilities				
Mortgage Payable			70 0 0 0 00	
Total Liabilities				117 0 0 0 00
Stockholders' Equity				
Common Stock ($10 par, 25,000 shares authorized)			130 0 0 0 00	
Retained Earnings			75 0 0 0 00	
Total Stockholders' Equity				205 0 0 0 00
Total Liabilities and Stockholders' Equity				322 0 0 0 00

WORKING PAPERS

Name _____

EXERCISE 24.1

1. _____
   _____

2. _____
   _____

EXERCISE 24.2

EXERCISE 24.3

EXERCISE 24.4

EXERCISE 24.5

EXERCISE 24.6

EXERCISE 24.7

EXERCISE 24.8

EXERCISE 24.9

PROBLEM 24.1A or 24.1B

Analyze:

PROBLEM 24.2A or 24.2B

Analyze: _____

PROBLEM 24.3A or 24.3B

_____

_____

Analyze: _____

PROBLEM 24.4A or 24.4B

Analyze: _____

CRITICAL THINKING PROBLEM 24.1

Analyze: _____

CRITICAL THINKING PROBLEM 24.2

EXTRA FORM

CRITICAL THINKING PROBLEM 24-2

Chapter 24 Practice Test Answer Key

Part A True-False

1. T	7. F	13. T
2. T	8. T	14. F
3. T	*9. F	15. F
4. F	10. T	16. T
5. T	11. T	*17. F
6. T	12. T	

Part B Matching

1. c	6. d
2. c	7. d
3. b	8. b
4. a	9. c
5. a	10. c

*Financing & Investing Activity
Not Affecting Cash Flow

MINI-PRACTICE SET 4

Financial Analysis and Decision Making
HHI Merchandise, Inc.

Introduction

HHI Merchandise, Inc. sells a variety of consumer products. Its comparative income statement and balance sheet for the years 2013 and 2012 are presented on the following pages.

Instructions

1. Prepare a horizontal and a vertical analysis of the statements. Round all dollar calculations to the nearest whole dollar. Percentage calculations should be rounded to one decimal place (e.g., 11.2%). Remember that some vertical addition of percentages may not equal 100 percent due to rounding.

2. Calculate the following ratios for each year.

   a. The rate of return on net sales.

   b. The rate of return on common stockholders' equity. Preferred dividends are $5,000 for both years. (Remember that dividend requirements on preferred stock must be deducted from net income after taxes to obtain income available to common stockholders.)

   c. The earnings per share of common stock, assuming that the preferred stock is nonparticipating, noncumulative, and has no liquidation value. The number of outstanding shares of common stock remained constant at 100,000 throughout all of 2012 and 2013.

   d. The price-earnings ratio on common stock. The market values were $3.00 in 2013 and $4.00 in 2012.

   e. The rate of return on total assets.

   f. The ratio of stockholders' equity to total liabilities.

   g. The current ratio.

   h. The acid-test ratio.

   i. The merchandise inventory turnover. Inventory was $75,000 at January 1, 2012.

   j. The accounts receivable turnover. Credit sales were $1,400,000 for 2013 and $1,300,000 for 2012. The beginning accounts receivable balance for 2012 was $123,500.

HHI Merchandise, Inc.
Comparative Income Statement
Years Ended December 31, 2013 and 2012

	2013	2012
Revenue		
Sales	1,898,000	1,642,000
Less: Sales Returns and Allowances	(29,500)	(22,000)
Net Sales	1,868,500	1,620,000
Cost of Goods Sold		
Merchandise Inventory, January 1	76,000	75,000
Purchases	945,650	800,000
Freight In	9,500	7,500
Less: Purchases Discounts	(10,000)	(8,250)
Purchases Returns and Allowances	(8,250)	(5,000)
Total Merchandise Available for Sale	1,012,900	869,250
Less Merchandise Inventory, December 31	(78,000)	(76,000)
Cost of Goods Sold	934,900	793,250
Gross Profit on Sales	933,600	826,750
Operating Expenses		
Selling Expenses		
Advertising	25,000	21,000
Sales Salaries	200,000	175,000
Payroll Taxes Sales	20,000	17,500
Supplies Expense	11,825	9,650
Miscellaneous Selling Expenses	9,575	7,950
Insurance Expense	7,700	7,500
Total Selling Expenses	274,100	238,600
Administrative Expenses		
Officers' Salaries	350,000	300,000
Office Employees	137,500	125,000
Payroll Taxes Office Employees	48,750	42,500
Office Supplies	12,250	10,000
Insurance Expense—Administrative	8,000	7,500
Uncollectible Accounts Expense	9,000	8,000
Legal and Accounting	18,000	15,000
Depreciation Expense—Building	15,000	15,000
Depreciation Expense—Furniture	12,000	10,000
Utilities Expense	18,400	16,750
Total Administrative Expenses	628,900	549,750
Total Operating Expenses	903,000	788,350
Net Income from Operations	30,600	38,400
Other Income		
Interest and Dividends	4,675	4,500
Total Other Income	4,675	4,500
Other Expenses		
Bond Interest Expense	6,930	6,930
Interest Expense	6,320	6,070
Total Other Expenses	13,250	13,000
Net Other Expenses	8,575	8,500
Net Income Before Taxes	22,025	29,900
Income Tax Expense	7,709	10,465
Net Income After Taxes	14,316	19,435

Name

HHI Merchandise, Inc.
Comparative Balance Sheet
December 31, 2013 and 2012

	2013	2012
Assets		
Current Assets		
Cash	38,157	61,942
Accounts Receivable	90,000	121,500
Merchandise Inventory	78,000	76,000
Prepaid Insurance	600	600
Supplies	975	1,000
Total Current Assets	207,732	261,042
Property, Plant, and Equipment		
Land	105,000	105,000
Building	300,000	300,000
Less: Accumulated Depreciation—Building	(45,000)	(30,000)
Furniture	60,000	50,000
Less: Accumulated Depreciation—Furniture	(22,000)	(10,000)
Total Property, Plant, and Equipment	398,000	415,000
Other Assets		
Marketable Securities (Long-Term)	40,000	40,000
Total Assets	645,732	716,042
Liabilities and Stockholders' Equity		
Current Liabilities		
Accounts Payable	119,500	125,000
Notes Payable	45,000	60,000
Bond Interest Payable	500	500
Income Taxes Payable	7,709	10,465
Sales Salaries Payable	10,000	14,000
Other Payables	5,200	7,500
Total Current Liabilities	187,909	217,465
Long-Term Liabilities		
10% Bonds Payable, due January 1, 2022	70,000	70,000
Premium on Bonds Payable	630	700
Total Long-Term Liabilities	70,630	70,700
Total Liabilities	258,539	288,165
Stockholders' Equity		
5% Preferred Stock, $100 par, 1,000 shares authorized/outstanding	100,000	100,000
Common Stock, $1 par, 500,000 shares authorized,		
100,000 shares outstanding	100,000	100,000
Paid-in Capital in Excess of Par—Common Stock	50,000	50,000
Total Paid-in Capital	250,000	250,000
Retained Earnings		
Retained Earnings—Unappropriated	112,193	152,877
Retained Earnings—Appropriated	25,000	25,000
Total Retained Earnings	137,193	177,877
Total Stockholders' Equity	387,193	427,877
Total Liabilities and Stockholders' Equity	645,732	716,042

Comparative Balance Sheet

	INCREASE OR (DECREASE)		PERCENT OF TOTAL ASSETS		AMOUNTS	
	AMOUNT	PERCENT	2012	2013	2012	2013

Comparative Balance Sheet (continued)

	AMOUNTS		PERCENT OF TOTAL ASSETS		INCREASE OR (DECREASE)	
	2013	2012	2013	2012	AMOUNT	PERCENT

Comparative Balance Sheet (continued)

	AMOUNTS		PERCENT OF TOTAL ASSETS		INCREASE OR (DECREASE)	
	2013	2012	2013	2012	AMOUNT	PERCENT

Comparative Statement of Retained Earnings–Unappropriated

	AMOUNTS		PERCENT OF TOTAL ASSETS		INCREASE OR (DECREASE)	
	2013	2012	2013	2012	AMOUNT	PERCENT

Comparative Income Statement

		AMOUNTS		PERCENT OF NET SALES		INCREASE OR (DECREASE)	
		2013	2012	2013	2012	AMOUNT	PERCENT

Name

Comparative Income Statement (continued)

	AMOUNTS		PERCENT OF NET SALES		INCREASE OR (DECREASE)	
	2013	2012	2013	2012	AMOUNT	PERCENT

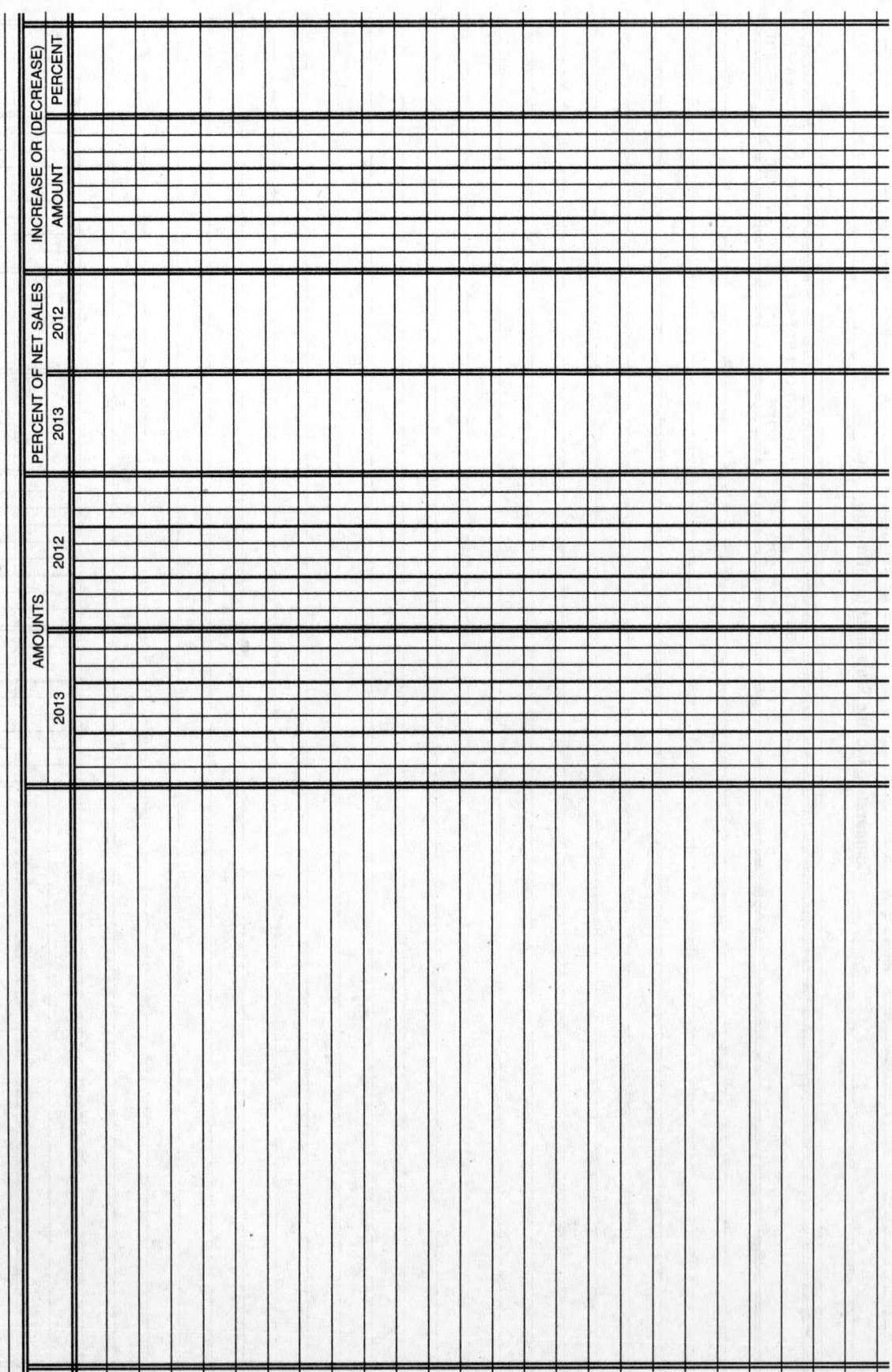

Name _____

2012

2013

RATIO

a.　b.　c.　d.　e.　f.　g.　h.　i.　j.

Name _____

COMPUTATIONS

_____

_____

_____

_____

_____

_____

_____

_____

_____

_____

_____

_____

_____

_____

_____

_____

_____

_____

_____

_____

_____

_____

_____

_____

_____

_____

_____

_____

_____

Analyze: _____

_____

CHAPTER 25

Departmentalized Profit and Cost Centers

STUDY GUIDE

Understanding the Chapter

Objectives

1. Explain profit centers and cost centers. 2. Prepare the Gross Profit section of a departmental income statement. 3. Explain and identify direct and indirect departmental expenses. 4. Choose the basis for allocation of indirect expenses and compute the amounts to be allocated to each department. 5. Prepare a departmental income statement showing the contribution margin and operating income for each department. 6. Use a departmental income statement in making decisions such as whether a department should be closed. 7. Define the accounting terms new to this chapter.

Reading Assignment

Read Chapter 25 in the textbook. Complete the textbook Section Self Reviews as you finish reading each section of the chapter, and the Comprehensive Self Review at the end of the chapter. Refer to the Chapter 25 Glossary or to the Glossary at the end of the book to find definitions for terms that are not familiar to you.

Activities

❏ **Thinking Critically**   Answer the *Thinking Critically* questions for Mattel, Inc. and Managerial Implications.

❏ **Discussion Questions**   Answer each assigned discussion question in Chapter 25.

❏ **Exercises**   Complete each assigned exercise in Chapter 25. Use the forms provided in this SGWP. The objectives covered by an exercise are given after the exercise number. If you need help with an exercise, review the portion of the chapter related to the objective(s) covered.

❏ **Problems A/B**   Complete each assigned problem in Chapter 25. Use the forms provided in this SGWP. The objectives covered by a problem are given after the problem number. If you need help with a problem, review the portion of the chapter related to the objective(s) covered.

❏ **Critical Thinking Problems**   Complete the critical thinking problems as assigned. Use the forms provided in this SGWP.

❏ **Business Connections**   Complete the Business Connections activities as assigned to gain a deeper understanding of Chapter 25 concepts.

Practice Tests

Complete the Practice Tests, which cover the main points in your reading assignment. Compare your answers with those in the Practice Test Answer Key for Chapter 25 at the end of this chapter. If you have answered any questions incorrectly, review the related section of the text.

Part A True-False *For each of the following statements, circle T in the answer column if the statement is true, or F if the statement is false.*

T   F   **1.** Responsibility accounting is designed to help management evaluate the performance of each segment of business.

T   F   **2.** A separate column should be provided in the voucher register for purchases of each sales department.

T   F   **3.** Sales discounts need not be departmentalized if they are treated as other expense.

T   F   **4.** Direct expenses are costs shared by all departments.

T   F   **5.** Cost centers are also called profit centers.

T   F   **6.** Purchases returns and allowances are not normally departmentalized in the accounts.

T   F   **7.** Semi-direct expenses cannot be allocated to a sales department on any logical basis.

T   F   **8.** If a business is profitable, it is not important to know how much each department contributed to the overall profit.

T   F   **9.** Profit centers are usually business segments that sell to customers outside the business.

T   F   **10.** Gross profit and contribution margin have the same meaning.

T   F   **11.** Payroll taxes applicable to sales salaries may be treated as an indirect expense, or as a direct expense if they are recorded by department.

T   F   **12.** Eliminating a department should eliminate all indirect expenses of that department.

T   F   **13.** Utilities expense should be allocated to departments on the basis of gross sales in each department.

T   F   **14.** Beginning and ending inventories are allocated to the departments on the basis of net sales in each.

T   F   **15.** The net income of a department should receive more attention than its contribution margin in reaching managerial decisions.

T   F   **16.** Indirect expenses are allocated to the departments at the time the expense transactions are journalized.

T   F   **17.** Nonoperating income, such as interest income, should be allocated to departments on the basis of net sales.

T   F   **18.** The contribution margin is the difference between gross profit and nonoperating expenses.

T   F   **19.** In a departmental accounting system, sales returns and allowances should be debited to the departmental sales account.

T   F   **20.** If a department has a negative contribution margin, the business would probably be more profitable if the department were eliminated.

Part B Matching

For each numbered item, choose the matching term from the box and write the identifying letter in the answer column.

_____ 1. Expenses incurred for the benefit of several departments that cannot be assigned directly to any one particular department.

_____ 2. Expenses that can be assigned to a specific department.

_____ 3. The procedure for dividing indirect expenses among several departments.

_____ 4. Expenses that are closely related to the activities in each department but cannot be allocated to any specific department.

_____ 5. The difference between gross profit and direct expense.

> a. Contribution margin
>
> b. Direct expenses
>
> c. Indirect expenses
>
> d. Semi-direct expenses
>
> e. Allocation

Demonstration Problem

FunTime, LLC is a retail store selling books, music, and videos. The store has three departments: books, music, and videos. Condensed information about the store's revenues and expenses for each department for the year ended December 31, 2013, follows. Indirect expenses have been allocated on bases similar to those discussed in the textbook chapter. The store had interest income of $300 for the year.

Instructions

1. Prepare a departmental income statement showing the contribution margin and the net profit for each department.

2. Based solely on accounting information, would you recommend closing any of the departments? Why or why not?

	Books	Music	DVDs
Allocated indirect expenses	$ 15,000	$10,000	$10,000
Beginning merchandise inventory	20,000	19,000	13,000
Direct expenses	20,000	10,000	17,000
Ending merchandise inventory	20,000	12,000	9,000
Purchases	86,000	60,000	21,500
Purchases returns and allowances	500	200	500
Sales	190,600	99,600	42,500
Sales returns and allowances	2,600	600	1,500

FunTime, LLC

Income Statement

Year Ended December 31, 2013

	BOOKS	MUSIC	DVDs	TOTAL
Sales	190600	99600	42500	332700
Less Sales Returns and Allowances	2600	600	1500	4700
Net Sales	188000	99000	41000	328000
Cost of Goods Sold				
Merchandise Inventory, January 1	20000	19000	13000	52000
Purchases	86000	60000	21500	167500
Less Purchases Returns and Allowances	500	200	500	1200
Net Purchases	85500	59800	21000	166300
Cost of Goods Available for Sale	105500	78800	34000	218300
Less Merchandise Inventory, December 31	20000	12000	9000	41000
Cost of Goods Sold	85500	66800	25000	177300
Gross Profit	102500	32200	16000	150700
Direct Expenses	20000	10000	17000	47000
Contribution Margin	82500	22200	(1000)	103700
Indirect Expenses	15000	10000	10000	35000
Net Income (Loss) from Operations	67500	12200	(11000)	68700
Other Income				
Interest Income				300
Net Income for Year				69000

Based solely on the accounting information, the DVDs Department should be closed. The contribution margin is a loss of $1,000 and the department net loss is $11,000. The department is not generating enough revenue to pay all of its direct expenses. Generally, when this situation presents itself, the management of the firm would suggest closing that department.

WORKING PAPERS

Name _____

EXERCISE 25.1

DEPARTMENT	BASIS: BOOK VALUE OF INVENTORY AND EQUIPMENT	PERCENT	TOTAL INSURANCE EXPENSE	ALLOCATION
_____	_____	_____	_____	_____
_____	_____	_____	_____	_____
_____	_____	_____	_____	_____
_____	_____	_____	_____	_____

EXERCISE 25.2

DEPARTMENT	BASIS: TOTAL SALES	PERCENT	TOTAL OFFICE EXPENSE	ALLOCATION
_____	_____	_____	_____	_____
_____	_____	_____	_____	_____
_____	_____	_____	_____	_____
_____	_____	_____	_____	_____

EXERCISE 25.3

DEPARTMENT	CREDIT SALES	CREDIT SALES RETURNS AND ALLOWANCES	BASIS: NET CREDIT SALES	PERCENT	ALLOCATION
_____	_____	_____	_____	_____	_____
_____	_____	_____	_____	_____	_____
_____	_____	_____	_____	_____	_____
_____	_____	_____	_____	_____	_____

EXERCISE 25.4

EXTRA FORM

EXERCISE 25.5

_____

EXERCISE 25.6

_____

EXERCISE 25.7

_____

PROBLEM 25.1A or 25.1B

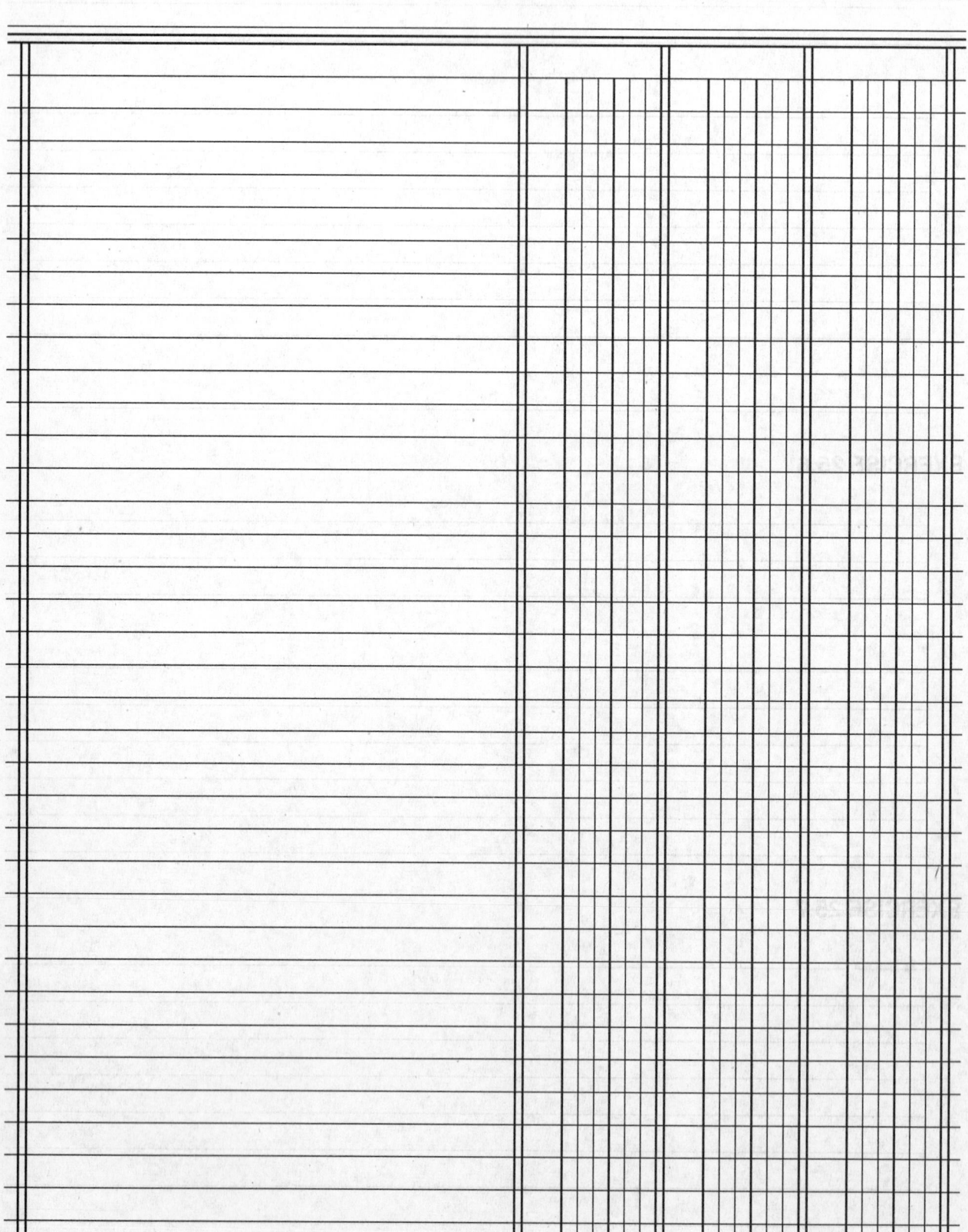

PROBLEM 25.1A or 25.1B (continued)

ALLOCATION OF INDIRECT EXPENSES

Insurance Expense

1. _____

_____

_____

Rent Expense

2. _____

_____

_____

Utilities Expense

_____

_____

_____

PROBLEM 25.1A or 25.1B (continued)

ALLOCATION OF INDIRECT EXPENSES (continued)

Office Salaries Expense

3. _____

_____

_____

Other Office Expenses

_____

_____

_____

Depreciation Expense—Office Equipment

_____

_____

_____

Uncollectible Accounts Expense

4. _____

_____

_____

Depreciation Expense—Furniture and Fixtures

5. _____

_____

_____

Analyze: _____

_____

PROBLEM 25.2A or 25.2B

1.

Income Statement

PROBLEM 25.2A or 25.2B (continued)

2. _____

_____

_____

_____

_____

_____

_____

_____

3. _____

_____

_____

_____

_____

_____

_____

_____

_____

_____

Analyze: _____

_____

CRITICAL THINKING PROBLEM 25.1

_____

_____

_____

_____

_____

_____

_____

_____

_____

_____

_____

_____

_____

_____

_____

_____

_____

_____

_____

_____

_____

_____

_____

_____

_____

_____

_____

Analyze: _____

_____

CRITICAL THINKING PROBLEM 25.2

_____

_____

_____

_____

_____

_____

_____

_____

_____

_____

_____

_____

_____

_____

_____

_____

_____

_____

_____

_____

_____

_____

_____

_____

_____

_____

_____

_____

_____

_____

_____

_____

_____

_____

_____

Chapter 25 Practice Test Answer Key

Part A True-False

1. T	6. F	11. T	16. F
2. T	7. F	12. F	17. F
3. T	8. F	13. F	18. F
4. F	9. T	14. F	19. F
5. F	10. F	15. F	20. T

Part B Matching

1. c
2. b
3. e
4. d
5. a

CHAPTER 26 Accounting for Manufacturing Activities

STUDY GUIDE

Understanding the Chapter

Objectives

1. Prepare a statement of cost of goods manufactured. 2. Explain the basic components of manufacturing cost. 3. Prepare an income statement for a manufacturing business. 4. Prepare a balance sheet for a manufacturing business. 5. Prepare a worksheet for a manufacturing business. 6. Record the end-of-period adjusting entries for a manufacturing business. 7. Record closing entries for a manufacturing business. 8. Record reversing entries for a manufacturing business. 9. Define the accounting terms new to this chapter.

Reading Assignment

Read Chapter 26 in the textbook. Complete the textbook Section Self Reviews as you finish reading each section of the chapter, and the Comprehensive Self Review at the end of the chapter. Refer to the Chapter 26 Glossary or to the Glossary at the end of the book to find definitions for terms that are not familiar to you.

Activities

❏ **Thinking Critically** Answer the *Thinking Critically* questions for Ford and Managerial Implications.

❏ **Discussion Questions** Answer each assigned discussion question in Chapter 26.

❏ **Exercises** Complete each assigned exercise in Chapter 26. Use the forms provided in this SGWP. The objectives covered by an exercise are given after the exercise number. If you need help with an exercise, review the portion of the chapter related to the objective(s) covered.

❏ **Problems A/B** Complete each assigned problem in Chapter 26. Use the forms provided in this SGWP. The objectives covered by a problem are given after the problem number. If you need help with a problem, review the portion of the chapter related to the objective(s) covered.

❏ **Critical Thinking Problems** Complete the critical thinking problems as assigned. Use the forms provided in this SGWP.

❏ **Business Connections** Complete the Business Connections activities as assigned to gain a deeper understanding of Chapter 26 concepts.

Practice Tests

Complete the Practice Tests, which cover the main points in your reading assignment. Compare your answers with those in the Practice Test Answer Key for Chapter 26 at the end of this chapter. If you have answered any questions incorrectly, review the related section of the text.

Part A True-False

For each of the following statements, circle T in the answer column if the answer is true or F if the answer is false.

T   F   **1.** In a manufacturing company, it is not necessary to take a physical inventory of the finished goods.

T   F   **2.** The entry to set up the ending work in process inventory is part of the adjustments process.

T   F   **3.** The cost of goods manufactured is the total of the direct materials, direct labor, and overhead costs involved in the manufacturing process during the period.

T   F   **4.** Small items, such as glue and nails, that become part of the finished product may be treated either as direct materials or as indirect materials, depending on company policy and cumulative cost of items.

T   F   **5.** The cost of indirect materials used is shown in the Cost of Goods Sold section of the Income Statement.

T   F   **6.** The wages of a worker who saws and forms legs for tables in a furniture factory would be classified as direct labor.

T   F   **7.** In the Cost of Goods Manufactured section of the worksheet, the excess of the total of the Debit column over the total of the Credit column represents the cost of goods manufactured.

T   F   **8.** Payroll taxes on factory wages should be classified as an administrative expense in the income statement.

T   F   **9.** On the worksheet of a manufacturing business, the amount of the ending work in process inventory is entered in the Debit column of the Balance Sheet section.

T   F   **10.** The ending inventory of finished goods is entered in the Credit column of the Cost of Goods Manufactured section of the worksheet.

Part B Completion

In the answer column, supply the missing word or words needed to complete each of the following statements.

_____   **1.** All raw materials used, direct labor costs incurred, and manufacturing costs incurred during the period make up the total _____.

_____   **2.** The cost of indirect materials used appears in the _____ section of the statement of cost of goods manufactured.

_____   **3.** All materials that become part of the manufactured product are known as _____.

_____   **4.** The adjusted balances of the manufacturing cost accounts are extended from the Adjusted Trial Balance section to the _____ section of a manufacturing company's worksheet.

_____   **5.** The partially completed product at year-end is called _____.

_____   **6.** The statement on which the beginning and ending inventories of work in process appear is the _____.

_____   **7.** In the worksheet, the cost of goods manufactured is entered in the _____ column of the Cost of Goods Manufactured section and in the _____ column of the Income Statement section.

_____   **8.** The postclosing trial balance contains the balances of the _____, _____, and _____ accounts.

Demonstration Problem

The Tee Company makes soccer equipment. Information about the company's operations follows.

Instructions

1. Prepare a statement of cost of goods manufactured for the year ended December 31, 2013.

	January 1, 2013	December 31, 2013
Finished Goods Inventory	$250,000	$ 300,000
Raw Materials Inventory	200,000	155,000
Work in Process Inventory	100,000	92,500
Direct Labor		900,000
Freight In		25,500
Indirect Labor		150,000
Indirect Materials and Supplies		20,000
Insurance—Factory		18,500
Depreciation—Factory Building and Equipment		50,000
Materials Purchases		1,900,000
Payroll Taxes—Factory		105,000
Utilities—Factory		75,000
Property Taxes—Factory		22,000
Materials Purchases Returns and Allowances		6,500
Repairs and Maintenance—Factory		39,500
Patent Amortization		1,500
Waste Removal—Factory		20,000

SOLUTION

The Tee Company

Statement of Cost of Goods Manufactured

Year Ended December 31, 2013

Raw Materials					
Raw Materials Inventory, January 1, 2013			200 0 0 0 00		
Materials Purchases	1,900 0 0 0 00				
Freight In	25 5 0 0 00				
Delivered Cost of Material Purchases	1,925 5 0 0 00				
Less Materials Purchases Returns and Allowances	6 5 0 0 00				
Net Material Purchases			1,919 0 0 0 00		
Total Materials Available for Use			2,119 0 0 0 00		
Less Raw Materials Inventory, December 31, 2013			155 0 0 0 00		
Raw Materials Used				1,964 0 0 0 00	
Direct Labor				900 0 0 0 00	
Manufacturing Overhead					
Indirect Materials and Supplies			20 0 0 0 00		
Indirect Labor			150 0 0 0 00		
Payroll Taxes—Factory			105 0 0 0 00		
Utilities—Factory			75 0 0 0 00		
Repairs and Maintenance—Factory			39 5 0 0 00		
Depreciation—Factory Building and Equipment			50 0 0 0 00		
Insurance—Factory			18 5 0 0 00		
Property Taxes—Factory			22 0 0 0 00		
Patent Amortization			1 5 0 0 00		
Waste Removal—Factory			20 0 0 0 00		
Total Manufacturing Overhead				501 5 0 0 00	
Total Manufacturing Costs				3,365 5 0 0 00	
Add Work in Process Inventory, January 1, 2013				100 0 0 0 00	
				3,465 5 0 0 00	
Less Work in Process Inventory, December 31, 2013				92 5 0 0 00	
Cost of Goods Manufactured				3,373 0 0 0 00	

WORKING PAPERS

Name _____

EXERCISE 26.1

EXERCISE 26.2

GENERAL JOURNAL

PAGE _____

	DATE	DESCRIPTION	POST. REF.	DEBIT	CREDIT	
1						1
2						2
3						3
4						4
5						5
6						6
7						7
8						8
9						9
10						10
11						11
12						12
13						13
14						14
15						15
16						16
17						17
18						18
19						19
20						20

EXERCISE 26.3

_____
_____
_____
_____
_____
_____
_____

EXERCISE 26.4

_____
_____
_____
_____
_____
_____
_____
_____

EXERCISE 26.5

_____
_____
_____
_____
_____
_____
_____

EXERCISE 26.6

_____
_____
_____
_____
_____
_____
_____

EXERCISE 26.7

_____

_____

_____

_____

_____

_____

_____

EXERCISE 26.8

_____

_____

_____

_____

_____

_____

_____

_____

EXERCISE 26.9

_____

_____

_____

_____

_____

_____

_____

EXERCISE 26.10

GENERAL JOURNAL

	DATE	DESCRIPTION	POST. REF.	DEBIT	CREDIT	
1						1
2						2
3						3
4						4
5						5
6						6
7						7
8						8
9						9
10						10
11						11
12						12
13						13
14						14
15						15
16						16
17						17
18						18
19						19
20						20
21						21
22						22
23						23
24						24
25						25
26						26
27						27
28						28
29						29
30						30
31						31
32						32
33						33
34						34
35						35
36						36
37						37

EXERCISE 26.10 (continued)

GENERAL JOURNAL

PAGE _____

	DATE		DESCRIPTION	POST. REF.	DEBIT	CREDIT	
1							1
2							2
3							3
4							4
5							5
6							6
7							7
8							8
9							9
10							10
11							11
12							12
13							13
14							14
15							15
16							16
17							17
18							18
19							19
20							20
21							21
22							22
23							23
24							24
25							25
26							26
27							27
28							28
29							29
30							30
31							31
32							32
33							33
34							34
35							35
36							36
37							37

PROBLEM 26.1A or 26.1B

Statement of Cost of Goods Manufactured

PROBLEM 26.1A or 26.1B (continued)

Income Statement

Analyze: _____

PROBLEM 26.2A or 26.2B

	ACCOUNT NAME	TRIAL BALANCE		ADJUSTMENTS	
		DEBIT	CREDIT	DEBIT	CREDIT
1					
2					
3					
4					
5					
6					
7					
8					
9					
10					
11					
12					
13					
14					
15					
16					
17					
18					
19					
20					
21					
22					
23					
24					
25					
26					
27					
28					
29					
30					
31					
32					
33					
34					

PROBLEM 26.2A or 26.2B (continued)

ADJUSTED TRIAL BALANCE		COST OF GOODS MANUFACTURED		INCOME STATEMENT		BALANCE SHEET		
DEBIT	CREDIT	DEBIT	CREDIT	DEBIT	CREDIT	DEBIT	CREDIT	
								1
								2
								3
								4
								5
								6
								7
								8
								9
								10
								11
								12
								13
								14
								15
								16
								17
								18
								19
								20
								21
								22
								23
								24
								25
								26
								27
								28
								29
								30
								31
								32
								33
								34

PROBLEM 26.2A or 26.2B (continued)

	ACCOUNT NAME	TRIAL BALANCE		ADJUSTMENTS	
		DEBIT	CREDIT	DEBIT	CREDIT
1					
2					
3					
4					
5					
6					
7					
8					
9					
10					
11					
12					
13					
14					
15					
16					
17					
18					
19					
20					
21					
22					
23					
24					
25					
26					
27					
28					
29					
30					
31					
32					

PROBLEM 26.2A or 26.2B (continued)

ADJUSTED TRIAL BALANCE		COST OF GOODS MANUFACTURED		INCOME STATEMENT		BALANCE SHEET		
DEBIT	CREDIT	DEBIT	CREDIT	DEBIT	CREDIT	DEBIT	CREDIT	
								1
								2
								3
								4
								5
								6
								7
								8
								9
								10
								11
								12
								13
								14
								15
								16
								17
								18
								19
								20
								21
								22
								23
								24
								25
								26
								27
								28
								29
								30
								31
								32

PROBLEM 26.2A or 26.2B (continued)

Statement of Cost of Goods Manufactured

PROBLEM 26.2A or 26.2B (continued)

Income Statement

PROBLEM 26.2A or 26.2B (continued)

Statement of Retained Earnings

EXTRA FORM

PROBLEM 26.2A or 26.2B (continued)

Balance Sheet

PROBLEM 26.2A or 26.2B (continued)

GENERAL JOURNAL   PAGE _____

	DATE		DESCRIPTION	POST. REF.	DEBIT	CREDIT	
1							1
2							2
3							3
4							4
5							5
6							6
7							7
8							8
9							9
10							10
11							11
12							12
13							13
14							14
15							15
16							16
17							17
18							18
19							19
20							20
21							21
22							22
23							23
24							24
25							25
26							26
27							27
28							28
29							29
30							30
31							31
32							32
33							33
34							34
35							35
36							36
37							37

PROBLEM 26.2A or 26.2B (continued)

GENERAL JOURNAL   PAGE _____

	DATE		DESCRIPTION	POST. REF.	DEBIT	CREDIT	
1							1
2							2
3							3
4							4
5							5
6							6
7							7
8							8
9							9
10							10
11							11
12							12
13							13
14							14
15							15
16							16
17							17
18							18
19							19
20							20
21							21
22							22
23							23
24							24
25							25
26							26
27							27
28							28
29							29
30							30
31							31
32							32
33							33
34							34
35							35
36							36
37							37

PROBLEM 26.2A or 26.2B (continued)

GENERAL JOURNAL   PAGE _____

	DATE		DESCRIPTION	POST. REF.	DEBIT	CREDIT	
1							1
2							2
3							3
4							4
5							5
6							6
7							7
8							8
9							9
10							10
11							11
12							12
13							13
14							14
15							15
16							16
17							17
18							18
19							19
20							20
21							21
22							22
23							23
24							24
25							25
26							26
27							27
28							28
29							29
30							30
31							31
32							32
33							33
34							34
35							35
36							36
37							37

PROBLEM 26.2A or 26.2B (continued)

GENERAL JOURNAL   PAGE _____

	DATE	DESCRIPTION	POST. REF.	DEBIT	CREDIT	
1						1
2						2
3						3
4						4
5						5
6						6
7						7
8						8
9						9
10						10
11						11
12						12
13						13
14						14
15						15
16						16
17						17
18						18
19						19
20						20
21						21
22						22
23						23
24						24
25						25
26						26
27						27
28						28
29						29
30						30
31						31
32						32
33						33
34						34

Analyze: _____

_____

CRITICAL THINKING PROBLEM 26.1

Statement of Cost of Goods Manufactured

Income Statement

CRITICAL THINKING PROBLEM 26.1 (continued)

NOTES

_____
_____
_____
_____
_____
_____
_____
_____
_____
_____
_____
_____
_____
_____
_____
_____
_____
_____
_____
_____
_____
_____
_____
_____
_____
_____
_____
_____
_____
_____
_____
_____
_____

Analyze: _____
_____

CRITICAL THINKING PROBLEM 26.2

Chapter 26 Practice Test Answer Key

Part A True-False

1.	F	6.	T
2.	T	7.	T
3.	F	8.	F
4.	T	9.	T
5.	F	10.	F

Part B Completion

1. manufacturing costs
2. manufacturing overhead
3. direct materials
4. cost of goods manufactured

5. work in process
6. statement of cost of goods manufactured
7. credit; debit
8. asset; liability; stockholders' equity

STUDY GUIDE

Understanding the Chapter

Objectives

1. Explain how a job order cost accounting system operates. 2. Journalize the purchase and issuance of direct and indirect materials. 3. Maintain perpetual inventory records. 4. Record labor costs incurred and charge labor into production. 5. Compute overhead rates and apply overhead to jobs. 6. Compute overapplied or underapplied overhead and report it in the financial statements. 7. Maintain job order cost sheets. 8. Record the cost of jobs completed and the cost of goods sold under a perpetual inventory system. 9. Define the accounting terms new to this chapter.

Reading Assignment

Read Chapter 27 in the textbook. Complete the textbook Section Self Reviews as you finish reading each section of the chapter, and the Comprehensive Self Review at the end of the chapter. Refer to the Chapter 27 Glossary or to the Glossary at the end of the book to find definitions for terms that are not familiar to you.

Activities

❑ **Thinking Critically**

Answer the *Thinking Critically* questions for The Spring Air Company and Managerial Implications.

❑ **Discussion Questions**

Answer each assigned discussion question in Chapter 27.

❑ **Exercises**

Complete each assigned exercise in Chapter 27. Use the forms provided in this SGWP. The objectives covered by an exercise are given after the exercise number. If you need help with an exercise, review the portion of the chapter related to the objective(s) covered.

❑ **Problems A/B**

Complete each assigned problem in Chapter 27. Use the forms provided in this SGWP. The objectives covered by a problem are given after the problem number. If you need help with a problem, review the portion of the chapter related to the objective(s) covered.

❑ **Critical Thinking Problems**

Complete the critical thinking problems as assigned. Use the forms provided in this SGWP.

❑ **Business Connections**

Complete the Business Connections activities as assigned to gain a deeper understanding of Chapter 27 concepts.

Practice Tests

Complete the Practice Tests, which cover the main points in your reading assignment. Compare your answers with those in the Practice Test Answer Key for Chapter 27 at the end of this chapter. If you have answered any questions incorrectly, review the related section of the text.

Part A True-False *For each of the following statements, circle T in the answer column if the statement is true or F if the statement is false.*

T   F   **1.** Perpetual inventory accounts for raw materials, work in process, and finished goods are commonly used in a job order system.

T   F   **2.** Applied overhead is usually posted each day to the job order cost sheets.

T   F   **3.** The job order cost system is often used by businesses that produce many units of the same product.

T   F   **4.** Purchases of raw materials are debited to the **Work in Process Inventory** account.

T   F   **5.** Underapplied or overapplied overhead may be closed into the **Cost of Goods Sold** account at the end of the year.

T   F   **6.** Idle time is generally treated as manufacturing overhead.

T   F   **7.** In a job order cost system, the individual job order cost sheets form a subsidiary ledger for the **Work in Process Inventory** account.

T   F   **8.** A widely used method of applying manufacturing overhead to individual jobs is based on a percentage of direct labor costs.

T   F   **9.** Under the job order system, unit costs of production are determined for all orders simultaneously.

T   F   **10.** Under a job order cost system, the selling price of goods sold will be entered on the finished goods ledger sheet for the products sold.

T   F   **11.** Charging manufacturing overhead to jobs on the basis of a predetermined rate usually results in overapplied or underapplied overhead.

T   F   **12.** The posting of labor costs to the individual job order cost sheets is made from the payroll register at the end of the week.

T   F   **13.** The materials requisition provides the information needed to enter receipt of raw materials on the raw materials ledger cards.

T   F   **14.** A just-in-time ordering system reduces the need for inventory storage space.

Part B Completion

In the answer column, supply the missing word or words needed to complete each of the following statements.

_____ 1. Materials are issued by the storeroom clerk only on presentation of a(n) _____ signed by an authorized person.

_____ 2. The receipt of materials from a supplier is reported by preparing a(n) _____.

_____ 3. The _____ shows the costs incurred for materials, labor, and overhead on a job.

_____ 4. When more overhead costs are incurred than are applied to individual jobs, overhead is said to be _____.

_____ 5. The three major inventories of a manufacturing business are generally maintained on a(n) _____ basis.

_____ 6. Depreciation of factory equipment, indirect labor, and indirect materials are examples of _____.

_____ 7. If idle time is caused by a breakdown of factory equipment, the related cost will probably be charged to _____.

_____ 8. Under the _____ method of inventory pricing, the quantities issued are priced from the oldest inventory items available in the order they were received.

Demonstration Problem

The cost data that follows is for Amor Leather Products, Inc., a maker of shoes and boots. This data covers the month of December 2013.

a. Materials purchases, $90,000.

b. Materials issued to production, $70,000; direct materials, $69,000; indirect materials, $1,000.

c. Payroll: direct labor, $20,000; indirect labor, $2,000; social security tax deducted, $1,364; medicare tax deducted, $319; income tax deducted, $3,000.

d. Manufacturing overhead of $8,000 was incurred in addition to indirect materials and indirect labor. (Credit **Accounts Payable.**)

e. Manufacturing overhead is applied to production at a predetermined rate of 60 percent of direct labor costs.

f. Jobs costing $65,000 were completed and transferred to finished goods.

g. Finished goods costing $60,000 were sold and billed to customers at $130,000.

Instructions

1. Prepare general journal entries to record each item of cost data given (the general journal is on page 679). Use the account names given in the textbook chapter. Omit explanations.

2. Compute the amount of overapplied or underapplied overhead for the month.

3. Prepare a partial income statement for the month of December, adjusted for any overapplied or underapplied overhead.

SOLUTION

OVERHEAD COMPUTATIONS

Manufacturing Overhead (Debit Balance)		
Indirect Materials	$ 1,000	
Indirect Labor	2,000	
Other Overhead Costs	8,000	
Total Charged to Manufacturing Overhead		$11,000
Manufacturing Overhead Applied (Credit Balance)		12,000
Overapplied Overhead in December (Net Credit Balance)		$ 1,000

Amor Leather Products, Inc.
Partial Income Statement
Month Ended December 31, 2013

Sales		130 0 0 0 00
Cost of Goods Sold (per ledger account)	60 0 0 0 00	
Less Overapplied Manufacturing Overhead	1 0 0 0 00	
Cost of Goods Sold (adjusted to actual)		59 0 0 0 00
Gross Profit on Sales		71 0 0 0 00

SOLUTION (continued)

GENERAL JOURNAL   PAGE _____

	DATE		DESCRIPTION	POST. REF.	DEBIT	CREDIT	
1	2013						1
2	Dec.	31	Raw Materials Inventory		90 000 00		2
3			Accounts Payable			90 000 00	3
4							4
5		31	Work in Process Inventory (Direct Materials)		69 000 00		5
6			Manufacturing Overhead (Indirect Materials)		1 000 00		6
7			Raw Materials Inventory			70 000 00	7
8							8
9		31	Work in Process Inventory (Direct Labor)		20 000 00		9
10			Manufacturing Overhead (Indirect Labor)		2 000 00		10
11			Social Security Tax Payable			1 364 00	11
12			Medicare Tax Payable			319 00	12
13			Employee Income Tax Payable			3 000 00	13
14			Salaries and Wages Payable			17 317 00	14
15							15
16		31	Manufacturing Overhead		8 000 00		16
17			Accounts Payable			8 000 00	17
18							18
19		31	Work in Process Inventory		12 000 00		19
20			Manufacturing Overhead Applied			12 000 00	20
21							21
22		31	Finished Goods Inventory		65 000 00		22
23			Work in Process Inventory			65 000 00	23
24							24
25		31	Cost of Goods Sold		60 000 00		25
26			Finished Goods Inventory			60 000 00	26
27							27
28		31	Accounts Receivable		130 000 00		28
29			Sales			130 000 00	29
30							30
31							31
32							32
33							33
34							34
35							35
36							36
37							37

WORKING PAPERS

Name _____

EXERCISE 27.1

GENERAL JOURNAL

PAGE _____

	DATE	DESCRIPTION	POST. REF.	DEBIT	CREDIT	
1						1
2						2
3						3
4						4
5						5

EXERCISE 27.2

GENERAL JOURNAL

PAGE _____

	DATE	DESCRIPTION	POST. REF.	DEBIT	CREDIT	
1						1
2						2
3						3
4						4
5						5

EXERCISE 27.3

GENERAL JOURNAL

PAGE _____

	DATE	DESCRIPTION	POST. REF.	DEBIT	CREDIT	
1						1
2						2
3						3
4						4
5						5

EXERCISE 27.4

GENERAL JOURNAL

PAGE _____

	DATE	DESCRIPTION	POST. REF.	DEBIT	CREDIT	
1						1
2						2
3						3
4						4
5						5

EXERCISE 27.5

GENERAL JOURNAL   PAGE _____

	DATE	DESCRIPTION	POST. REF.	DEBIT	CREDIT	
1						1
2						2
3						3
4						4
5						5
6						6
7						7
8						8
9						9

EXERCISE 27.6

_____

_____

_____

_____

_____

EXERCISE 27.7

_____

_____

_____

_____

_____

GENERAL JOURNAL   PAGE _____

	DATE	DESCRIPTION	POST. REF.	DEBIT	CREDIT	
1						1
2						2
3						3
4						4
5						5

EXERCISE 27.8

_____
_____
_____
_____
_____
_____
_____
_____

EXERCISE 27.9

_____
_____
_____
_____
_____
_____

EXERCISE 27.10

GENERAL JOURNAL

PAGE _____

	DATE	DESCRIPTION	POST. REF.	DEBIT	CREDIT	
1						1
2						2
3						3
4						4
5						5
6						6
7						7
8						8
9						9
10						10
11						11
12						12
13						13
14						14
15						15
16						16
17						17
18						18

PROBLEM 27.1A or 27.1B

GENERAL JOURNAL

PAGE _____

	DATE		DESCRIPTION	POST. REF.	DEBIT	CREDIT	
1							1
2							2
3							3
4							4
5							5
6							6
7							7
8							8
9							9
10							10
11							11
12							12
13							13
14							14
15							15
16							16
17							17
18							18
19							19
20							20
21							21
22							22
23							23
24							24
25							25
26							26
27							27
28							28
29							29
30							30
31							31
32							32
33							33
34							34
35							35
36							36
37							37
38							38

PROBLEM 27.1A or 27.1B (continued)

Manufacturing Overhead Computations

Partial Income Statement

Analyze: _____

PROBLEM 27.2A or 27.2B

JOB ORDER COST SHEET

For Stock _____

Customer's Name _____

Address _____

Item _____

Job No. _____ Date _____

Started _____

Completed _____

Quantity _____
          (ordered)   (completed)

MATERIAL			LABOR			OVERHEAD APPLIED				SUMMARY	
Date	Amount		Date	Amount		Date	Rate	Amount		Item	Amount
										Materials	
										Labor	
										Overhead	
										Total	
										Unit Cost	
Totals										Comments:	

JOB ORDER COST SHEET

For Stock _____

Customer's Name _____

Address _____

Item _____

Job No. _____ Date _____

Started _____

Completed _____

Quantity _____
          (ordered)   (completed)

MATERIAL			LABOR			OVERHEAD APPLIED				SUMMARY	
Date	Amount		Date	Amount		Date	Rate	Amount		Item	Amount
										Materials	
										Labor	
										Overhead	
										Total	
										Unit Cost	
Totals										Comments:	

JOB ORDER COST SHEET

For Stock _____

Customer's Name _____

Address _____

Item _____

Job No. _____ Date _____

Started _____

Completed _____

Quantity _____
          (ordered)   (completed)

MATERIAL			LABOR			OVERHEAD APPLIED				SUMMARY	
Date	Amount		Date	Amount		Date	Rate	Amount		Item	Amount
										Materials	
										Labor	
										Overhead	
										Total	
										Unit Cost	
Totals										Comments:	

PROBLEM 27.2A or 27.2B (continued)

GENERAL JOURNAL

	DATE		DESCRIPTION	POST. REF.	DEBIT	CREDIT	
1							1
2							2
3							3
4							4
5							5
6							6
7							7
8							8
9							9
10							10

OVERHEAD COMPUTATIONS

Analyze: _____

CRITICAL THINKING PROBLEM 27.1

	Job DE31	Job JA01	Job JA02
Materials			
Labor			
Overhead (1)			
Total Costs			

Cost of Goods Sold

_____

_____

_____

_____

_____

_____

_____

Notes:

_____

_____

_____

_____

_____

_____

_____

_____

_____

_____

_____

_____

_____

_____

_____

_____

_____

Analyze: _____

_____

CRITICAL THINKING PROBLEM 27.2

a. _____

_____

_____

b. _____

_____

_____

c. _____

_____

d. _____

_____

_____

e. _____

_____

f. _____

_____

_____

_____

_____

Chapter 27 Practice Test Answer Key

Part A True-False		Part B Completion
1. T	8. T	1. materials requisition
2. F	9. F	2. receiving report
3. F	10. F	3. job order cost sheet
4. F	11. T	4. underapplied
5. T	12. F	5. perpetual
6. T	13. F	6. manufacturing overhead
7. T	14. T	7. manufacturing overhead
		8. FIFO

Condensed Income Statement

CHAPTER 28 Process Cost Accounting

STUDY GUIDE

Understanding the Chapter

Objectives

1. Compute equivalent units of production with no beginning work in process inventory. **2.** Prepare a cost of production report with no beginning work in process inventory. **3.** Compute the unit cost of manufacturing under the process cost accounting system. **4.** Record costs incurred and the flow of costs as products move through the manufacturing process and are sold. **5.** Compute equivalent production and prepare a cost of production report with a beginning work in process inventory. **6.** Define the accounting terms new to this chapter.

Reading Assignment

Read Chapter 28 in the textbook. Complete the textbook Section Self Reviews as you finish reading each section of the chapter, and the Comprehensive Self Review at the end of the chapter. Refer to the Chapter 28 Glossary or to the Glossary at the end of the book to find definitions for terms that are not familiar to you.

Activities

❑ **Thinking Critically**

Answer the *Thinking Critically* questions for ConocoPhillips and Managerial Implications.

❑ **Discussion Questions**

Answer each assigned discussion question in Chapter 28.

❑ **Exercises**

Complete each assigned exercise in Chapter 28. Use the forms provided in this SGWP. The objectives covered by an exercise are given after the exercise number. If you need help with an exercise, review the portion of the chapter related to the objective(s) covered.

❑ **Problems A/B**

Complete each assigned problem in Chapter 28. Use the forms provided in this SGWP. The objectives covered by a problem are given after the problem number. If you need help with a problem, review the portion of the chapter related to the objective(s) covered.

❑ **Critical Thinking Problems**

Complete the critical thinking problems as assigned. Use the forms provided in this SGWP.

❑ **Business Connections**

Complete these Business Connections activities as assigned to gain a deeper understanding of Chapter 28 concepts.

Practice Tests

Complete the Practice Tests, which cover the main points in your reading assignment. Compare your answers with those in the Practice Test Answer Key for Chapter 28 at the end of this chapter. If you have answered any questions incorrectly, review the related section of the text.

Part A True-False

For each of the following statements, circle T in the answer column if the statement is true or F if the statement is false.

T F **1.** Raw materials are always added at the start of production.

T F **2.** The equivalent units for materials in a department are always the same as the equivalent units for labor in that department.

T F **3.** Separate cost records are kept for the various producing and service departments.

T F **4.** The balance of the **Raw Materials Inventory** account at the end of any accounting period should reflect the cost of raw materials, supplies on hand, and work in process at that time.

T F **5.** A physical inventory should be taken at least once a year to check the accuracy of the perpetual inventory figures.

T F **6.** A process cost system may be viewed as an average cost system.

T F **7.** A single **Raw Materials Inventory** account can be used for both direct materials and manufacturing supplies in a process cost system.

T F **8.** In a process cost system, the cost of service departments are allocated to the producing departments and charged to the work in process inventory accounts.

T F **9.** In a process cost system, production costs are not recorded on job order cost sheets.

T F **10.** The Quantity Schedule section of a cost of production report shows the total quantities to be accounted for and explains what happened to them.

T F **11.** A department had no beginning work in process. During the month, 500 units were started into production and 400 were completed. On the other 100 units, 50 percent of the labor had been performed. The equivalent unit production for labor is 450 units for the month.

T F **12.** If the figures from a physical inventory do not agree with the figures in the perpetual inventory records, then the records must be adjusted.

T F **13.** The entry to record the sale of finished goods is a debit to **Accounts Receivable** and a credit to **Work in Process Inventory** for the selling price.

T F **14.** The ending work in process inventory of one department becomes the beginning work in process inventory of the next department in the manufacturing process.

T F **15.** The beginning work in process inventory of one accounting period is the same as the ending work in process of the prior period.

Part B Completion   *In the answer column, supply the missing word or words needed to complete each of the following statements.*

_____ 1. A(n) _____ system is normally used in situations where different products are manufactured and are started in batches or by jobs.

_____ 2. _____ is the estimated number of units that could have been started and completed with the same effort and costs incurred during the month.

_____ 3. The maintenance department is an example of a(n) _____ department that assists in production but does not perform work on the actual product.

_____ 4. _____ is a control account with a supporting subsidiary ledger showing the detail of overhead items.

_____ 5. In a(n) _____ department, work is performed directly on the product.

_____ 6. The number of units to be accounted for and the number actually accounted for are shown in the _____ section of the cost of production report.

_____ 7. In a(n) _____ system, the total cost of a unit of production is found by adding the unit costs in each department through which the product passes as it is being manufactured.

_____ 8. The _____ report shows the costs incurred in a department, the unit cost of each element of manufacturing costs, and the cost accounted for in the department.

Part C Exercises   *Compute the following units.*

_____ 1. The beginning inventory in a department was 1,000 units, which were 25 percent complete as to overhead. During May, 5,000 units were placed in process, 5,000 units were transferred to the next department, and 1,000 units were in the ending work in process inventory. The ending inventory was 40 percent complete as to overhead. Compute the equivalent units of overhead for May.

_____ 2. A producing department had no beginning inventory. During the month, 5,000 units of product were begun in the department, of which 4,500 units were transferred to the next department and 500 units were in process at the end of the month. The 500 units were 50 percent complete as to labor. Compute the equivalent units for labor for the month.

_____ 3. The assembly department of a manufacturing business had no beginning inventory. During June, 1,000 units of product were started. All materials are added at the beginning of the manufacturing process. During the month, 900 units were transferred to the next department and 100 units were still in work in process. Compute the equivalent units of materials for June.

Demonstration Problem

Ball Products, Inc. began business in July 2013. The company manufactures soccer balls. The product is started in the cutting and assembly department and is completed in the stitching and printing department. Data for the month of July follows.

Instructions

1. Prepare equivalent production computations for the cutting and assembly department.

2. Prepare a cost of production report for the cutting and assembly department.

	Cutting and Assembly Department
Costs	
Materials	$48,750
Labor	36,890
Manufacturing Overhead	11,900
Total Costs	$97,540
Quantities	
Started in production	25,000 units
Transferred out to next department	22,000
Work in Process—ending	3,000
Stage of Completion—Ending Work in Process	
Materials	100%
Labor	60%
Manufacturing Overhead	60%

SOLUTION

1.

Ball Products, Inc.

Equivalent Unit Production Computations

Month Ended July 31, 2013

Cutting and Assembly Department					
Materials: Units Transferred Out					
To next department: 100% × 22,000 units	22	0	0	0	00
Work in Process: 100% × 3,000 units	3	0	0	0	00
Equivalent units of Production for Materials	25	0	0	0	00
Labor and Manufacturing Overhead					
Units Transferred Out					
To next department: 100% × 22,000 units	22	0	0	0	00
Work in Process: 60% × 3,000 units	1	8	0	0	00
Equivalent units of Production for Labor and Overhead	23	8	0	0	00

SOLUTION (continued)

2.

Ball Products, Inc.

Equivalent Unit Production Computations Month Ended July 31, 2013

Cutting and Assembly Department

QUANTITY SCHEDULE		UNITS	
(a) Quantity to Be Accounted For:			
Work in Process–Beginning		0 00	
Started in Production		25 0 0 0 00	
Total to Be Accounted For		25 0 0 0 00	
(b) Quantity accounted for:			
Transferred out to next department		22 0 0 0 00	
Work In Process—Ending		3 0 0 0 00	
Total Accounted For		25 0 0 0 00	

COST SCHEDULE	TOTAL COST	E.P. UNITS*	UNIT COST
(c) Costs to Be Accounted For:			
Costs in Current Department			
Materials	48 7 5 0 00	÷ 25 0 0 0 =	1 95
Labor	36 8 9 0 00	÷ 23 8 0 0 =	1 55
Manufacturing Overhead	11 9 0 0 00	÷ 23 8 0 0 =	0 50
Cummulative Cost Total	97 5 4 0 00		4 00
(d) Costs Accounted For:			
Transferred out to next department	88 0 0 0 00	= 22 0 0 0 ×	4 00
Work in Process—Ending			
Materials	5 8 5 0 00	= 3 0 0 0 ×	1 95
Labor	2 7 9 0 00	= 1 8 0 0 ×	1 55
Manufacturing Overhead	9 0 0 00	= 1 8 0 0 ×	0 50
Total Work in Process—Ending	9 5 4 0 00		
Total Cost Accounted For	97 5 4 0 00		

*Equivalent Production Units or
Equivalent Units of Production

WORKING PAPERS

Name _____

EXERCISE 28.1

_____
_____
_____
_____
_____
_____
_____

EXERCISE 28.2

_____
_____
_____
_____
_____
_____
_____

EXERCISE 28.3

_____
_____
_____
_____
_____
_____
_____

EXERCISE 28.4

_____
_____
_____
_____
_____
_____
_____
_____

EXERCISE 28.5

EXERCISE 28.6

EXERCISE 28.7

GENERAL JOURNAL   PAGE _____

	DATE	DESCRIPTION	POST. REF.	DEBIT	CREDIT	
1						1
2						2
3						3
4						4
5						5
6						6
7						7
8						8
9						9
10						10
11						11
12						12
13						13
14						14
15						15
16						16

EXERCISE 28.8

GENERAL JOURNAL   PAGE _____

	DATE	DESCRIPTION	POST. REF.	DEBIT	CREDIT	
1						1
2						2
3						3
4						4
5						5
6						6
7						7

EXERCISE 28.9

GENERAL JOURNAL   PAGE _____

	DATE	DESCRIPTION	POST. REF.	DEBIT	CREDIT	
1						1
2						2
3						3
4						4
5						5
6						6
7						7

PROBLEM 28.1A or 28.1B

Equivalent Production Computations

Analyze:

PROBLEM 28.2A or 28.2B

GENERAL JOURNAL

	DATE		DESCRIPTION	POST. REF.	DEBIT	CREDIT	
1							1
2							2
3							3
4							4
5							5
6							6
7							7
8							8
9							9
10							10
11							11
12							12
13							13
14							14
15							15
16							16
17							17
18							18
19							19
20							20
21							21
22							22
23							23
24							24
25							25
26							26
27							27
28							28
29							29
30							30
31							31
32							32
33							33
34							34
35							35
36							36
37							37

PROBLEM 28.2A or 28.2B (continued)

Computation of Equivalent Unit Production

PROBLEM 28.2A or 28.2B (continued)

Cost of Production Report—Fabricating Department

QUANTITY SCHEDULE		UNITS	

COST SCHEDULE	TOTAL COST	E.P. UNITS*	UNIT COST

PROBLEM 28.2A or 28.2B (continued)

Cost of Production Report—Assembly Department

QUANTITY SCHEDULE		UNITS	

COST SCHEDULE	TOTAL COST	E.P. UNITS*	UNIT COST

Analyze: _____

PROBLEM 28.3A or 28.3B

_____

Equivalent Unit Production Computations

PROBLEM 28.3A or 28.3B (continued)

Cost of Production Report

QUANTITY SCHEDULE		UNITS	

COST SCHEDULE	TOTAL COST	E.P. UNITS*	UNIT COST

Analyze: _____

CRITICAL THINKING PROBLEM 28.1

Equivalent Unit Production Computations

CRITICAL THINKING PROBLEM 28.1 (continued)

Cost of Production Report

QUANTITY SCHEDULE			Mixing Department		
			UNITS		

COST SCHEDULE	TOTAL COST	E.P. UNITS*	UNIT COST

CRITICAL THINKING PROBLEM 28.1 (continued)

Equivalent Unit Production Computations

Analyze: _____

CRITICAL THINKING PROBLEM 28.2

Raw Materials Inventory	Work in Process Mixing Department	Work in Process Cooking Department	Work in Process Cooling and Packaging Department

Labor Costs

Manufacturing Overhead	Finished Goods Inventory	Cost of Goods Sold

Chapter 28 Practice Test Answer Key

Part A True-False

1. F
2. F
3. T
4. F
5. T
6. T
7. T
8. T
9. T
10. T
11. T
12. T
13. F
14. F
15. T

Part B Completion

1. job order cost
2. Equivalent production
3. service
4. Manufacturing Overhead (Control)
5. producing (or production)
6. quantity schedule
7. process cost
8. cost of production

Part C Exercises

1. Transferred to next department
   (5,000 × 100%)   =   5,000
   Ending inventory of work in process
   (1,000 × 40%)   =   400
   Total equivalent units—overhead   =   5,400

2. Transferred to next department
   (4,500 × 100%)   =   4,500
   Ending inventory of work in process
   (500 × 50%)   =   250
   Total equivalent units—labor   =   4,750

3. Transferred to next department
   (900 × 100%)   =   900
   Ending inventory of work in process
   (100 × 100%)   =   100
   Total equivalent units—materials   =   1,000

EXTRA FORM

_____

_____

QUANTITY SCHEDULE		UNITS		

COST SCHEDULE	TOTAL COST	E.P. UNITS	UNIT COST

EXTRA FORM

QUANTITY SCHEDULE								UNITS								

COST SCHEDULE				TOTAL COST			E.P. UNITS			UNIT COST		

CHAPTER 29

Controlling Manufacturing Costs: Standard Costs

STUDY GUIDE

Understanding the Chapter

Objectives

1. Explain how fixed, variable, and semivariable costs change as the level of manufacturing activity changes. **2.** Use the high-low point method to determine the fixed and variable components of a semivariable cost. **3.** Prepare a fixed budget for manufacturing costs. **4.** Develop a flexible budget for manufacturing costs. **5.** Develop standard costs per unit of product. **6.** Compute the standard costs of products manufactured during the period and determine cost variances between actual costs and standard costs. **7.** Compute the amounts and analyze the nature of variances from standard for raw materials, labor, and manufacturing overhead. **8.** Define the accounting terms new to this chapter.

Reading Assignment

Read Chapter 29 in the textbook. Complete the textbook Section Self Reviews as you finish reading each section of the chapter, and the Comprehensive Self Review at the end of the chapter. Refer to the Chapter 29 Glossary or to the Glossary at the end of the book to find definitions for terms that are not familiar to you.

Activities

❑ **Thinking Critically**

Answer the *Thinking Critically* questions for Harley-Davidson and Managerial Implications.

❑ **Discussion Questions**

Answer each assigned discussion question in Chapter 29.

❑ **Exercises**

Complete each assigned exercise in Chapter 29. Use the forms provided in this SGWP. The objectives covered by an exercise are given after the exercise number. If you need help with an exercise, review the portion of the chapter related to the objective(s) covered.

❑ **Problems A/B**

Complete each assigned problem in Chapter 29. Use the forms provided in this SGWP. The objectives covered by a problem are given after the problem number. If you need help with a problem, review the portion of the chapter related to the objective(s) covered.

❑ **Critical Thinking Problems**

Complete the critical thinking problems as assigned. Use the forms provided in this SGWP.

❑ **Business Connections**

Complete the Business Connections activities as assigned to gain a deeper understanding of chapter concepts.

Practice Tests

Complete the Practice Tests, which cover the main points in your reading assignment. Compare your answers with those in the Practice Test Answer Key for Chapter 29 at the end of this chapter. If you have answered any questions incorrectly, review the related section of the text.

Part A True-False   *For each of the following statements, circle T in the answer column if the statement is true or F if the statement is false.*

T   F   **1.** A fixed budget for manufacturing costs is ideal for controlling such costs.

T   F   **2.** Direct materials is a good example of a cost that generally is classified as a variable cost.

T   F   **3.** The high-low point method may be inappropriate in determining fixed and variable costs in some circumstances.

T   F   **4.** To properly budget manufacturing costs, those costs must be separated into their fixed and variable components.

T   F   **5.** The variable costs per unit change in direct proportion to changes in the volume of activity.

T   F   **6.** Power and utility costs are likely to be semivariable costs.

T   F   **7.** In a factory, if fixed costs per unit are $50 when 500 units are produced, the fixed costs per unit should be $20 per unit if 250 units are produced.

T   F   **8.** A flexible budget shows expected costs at several levels of production activity.

T   F   **9.** It is standard practice for a company to prepare monthly budgets of manufacturing costs.

T   F   **10.** Standard costs are "ideal" costs that should generally be unattainable.

T   F   **11.** The labor rate variance is determined by multiplying the standard quantity of labor by the difference between the actual rate per hour and the standard rate per hour.

T   F   **12.** Standard costs may actually be entered into the accounts.

T   F   **13.** The human resources department should generally be held responsible for labor quantity variances.

T   F   **14.** It is possible to compute the materials quantity variance for an individual job under the job order cost accounting system if standard costs have been established.

T   F   **15.** A materials quantity variance is computed by multiplying the difference between the standard quantity of materials and the actual quantity consumed by the actual costs per unit.

T   F   **16.** Indirect labor costs in a factory consist of $25,000 per month of fixed costs and $10 per direct labor hour for variable costs. If 3,000 direct labor hours are used, the budget for indirect labor will be $55,000.

T   F   **17.** A fixed manufacturing budget is given that name because it is a budget of fixed costs.

Part B Completion

Answer each question below based on the information given for ABA Industries. ABA has set manufacturing overhead standard costs at $3.50 per unit, based on an expected volume of 100,000 units requiring 100,000 hours of direct labor, fixed costs of $100,000 per year, and variable costs of $2.50 per hour. During the year, actual production was 90,000 units requiring 96,000 hours, actual fixed costs were $110,000 and variable costs were $2.10 per hour.

_____ **1.** What are the total actual costs for the year?

_____ **2.** What are the budgeted costs for the standard hours allowed for the work?

_____ **3.** What are the standard manufacturing overhead costs of the units produced during the year?

_____ **4.** What is the amount of variable costs budgeted for the actual hours worked?

_____ **5.** What is the amount of variable costs budgeted for the standard hours for the work performed?

_____ **6.** What is the amount of fixed costs budgeted for the actual hours worked?

_____ **7.** What is the total manufacturing overhead variance for the year?

Demonstration Problem

The Baylor Company manufactures one product. Standard costs for each unit of the product are:

Direct materials, 10 gallons @ $0.50	$ 5.00
Direct labor, 2 hours @ $16	32.00
Manufacturing Overhead, 1 hour @ $8	8.00
Total Standard Cost per unit	$45.00

Actual production costs for the month are given below for the 2,000 units:

Direct materials, 20,500 gallons @ $0.52	$10,660.00
Direct labor, 3,900 hours @ $16.05	62,595.00
Manufacturing Overhead	15,600.00
Total Actual Costs	$88,855.00

Instructions

Compute the following variances:

1. Direct material price variance.
2. Direct material quantity variance.
3. Direct labor rate variance.
4. Direct labor efficiency variance.
5. Total manufacturing overhead variance.

SOLUTION

1. **Direct material price variance:** ($0.52 − $0.50) × 20,500 gallons = $410 unfavorable

2. **Direct material quantity variance:** (20,500 − 20,000) × $0.50 = $250 unfavorable

3. **Direct labor rate variance:** ($16.05 − $16.00) × 3,900 hours = $195 unfavorable

4. **Direct labor efficiency variance:** (4,000 − 3,900) × $16.00 = $1,600 favorable

5. **Total manufacturing overhead variance:** $16,000 − $15,600 = $400 favorable

WORKING PAPERS

Name _____

EXERCISE 29.1

Quarter	Direct Labor Hours	Utilities Cost
_____	_____	_____
_____	_____	_____
_____	_____	_____
_____	_____	_____
_____	_____	_____
_____	_____	_____
_____	_____	_____
_____	_____	_____

EXERCISE 29.2

Percent of Budgeted Hours

_____ _____ _____

_____	_____	_____
_____	_____	_____
_____	_____	_____
_____	_____	_____
_____	_____	_____

EXERCISE 29.3

_____

_____

_____

_____

_____

_____

EXERCISE 29.4

Cost Element	Standard Cost	Actual Cost

EXERCISE 29.5

EXERCISE 29.6

EXERCISE 29.7

EXERCISE 29.8

_____
_____
_____
_____
_____

EXERCISE 29.9

_____
_____
_____
_____
_____

EXERCISE 29.10

_____
_____
_____
_____
_____

EXERCISE 29.11

_____
_____
_____
_____
_____

PROBLEM 29.1A or 29.1B

Analyze:

PROBLEM 29.2A or 29.2B

1. _____

Flexible Budget for Manufacturing Overhead

2. _____

Manufacturing Overhead Budget Performance Report

Analyze: _____

PROBLEM 29.3A or 29.3B

1. _____

Analysis of Materials Variance

_____
_____
_____

2. _____
_____
_____
_____
_____
_____
_____

Analyze: _____
_____

PROBLEM 29.4A or 29.4B

1. _____

Analysis of Materials Variances

2. _____

Analysis of Labor Variances

Analyze: _____

_____

CRITICAL THINKING PROBLEM 29.1

Analyze:

CRITICAL THINKING PROBLEM 29.2

_____

_____

_____

_____

_____

_____

_____

_____

_____

_____

_____

_____

_____

_____

_____

_____

_____

_____

_____

_____

_____

_____

_____

_____

_____

_____

_____

Chapter 29 Practice Test Answer Key

Part A True-False		Part B Completion
1. F	10. F	1. $311,600
2. T	11. F	2. $325,000
3. T	12. T	3. $325,000
4. T	13. F	4. $240,000
5. F	14. T	5. $225,000
6. T	15. F	6. $100,000
7. F	16. T	7. $13,400 F
8. T	17. F	
9. T		

STUDY GUIDE

Understanding the Chapter

Objectives	**1.** Explain the basic steps in the decision-making process. **2.** Prepare income statements using the absorption costing and direct costing methods. **3.** Using the contribution approach, analyze the profits of segments of a business. **4.** Determine relevant cost and revenue data for decision-making purposes. **5.** Apply an appropriate decision process in three situations: **(a)** Pricing products in special cases, **(b)** Deciding whether to purchase new equipment, and **(c)** Deciding whether to make or to buy a part. **6.** Define the accounting terms new to this chapter.
Reading Assignment	Read Chapter 30 in the textbook. Complete the textbook Section Self Reviews as you finish reading each section of the chapter, and the Comprehensive Self Review at the end of the chapter. Refer to the Chapter 30 Glossary or to the Glossary at the end of the book to find definitions for terms that are not familiar to you.

Activities

❏ **Thinking Critically**	Answer the *Thinking Critically* questions for Avon and Managerial Implications.
❏ **Discussion Questions**	Answer each assigned discussion question in Chapter 30.
❏ **Exercises**	Complete each assigned exercise in Chapter 30. Use the forms provided in this SGWP. The objectives covered by an exercise are given after the exercise number. If you need help with an exercise, review the portion of the chapter related to the objective(s) covered.
❏ **Problems A/B**	Complete each assigned problem in Chapter 30. Use the forms provided in this SGWP. The objectives covered by a problem are given after the problem number. If you need help with a problem, review the portion of the chapter related to the objective(s) covered.
❏ **Critical Thinking Problems**	Complete the critical thinking problems as assigned. Use the forms provided in this SGWP.
❏ **Business Connections**	Complete the Business Connections activities as assigned to gain a deeper understanding of Chapter 30 concepts.

Practice Tests

Complete the Practice Tests, which cover the main points in your reading assignment. Compare your answers with those in the Practice Test Answer Key for Chapter 30 at the end of this chapter. If you have answered any questions incorrectly, review the related section of the text.

Part A True-False

For each of the following statements, circle T in the answer column if the statement is true or F if the statement is false.

T   F   **1.** Direct costing does not follow GAAP financial reporting.

T   F   **2.** Under direct costing, all variable costs are treated as part of the cost of goods manufactured in the period when the costs are incurred.

T   F   **3.** If the variable cost per unit remains constant, but total fixed cost increases, the contribution margin will decrease.

T   F   **4.** Fixed costs are rarely controllable.

T   F   **5.** All manufacturing costs, both fixed and variable, are assigned to the cost of goods manufactured under direct costing.

T   F   **6.** Assuming no beginning inventory, if the units produced and the units sold are equal, both direct costing and absorption costing will yield the same net income.

T   F   **7.** When a business decision is being made, only those costs that will change as a result of the decision are relevant.

T   F   **8.** Contribution margin is the difference between sales and fixed costs.

T   F   **9.** Absorption costing concentrates attention on the contribution margin.

T   F   **10.** In general, managerial decisions such as whether or not to purchase new equipment or to drop a product line can be made using only accounting and other quantitative data.

T   F   **11.** Income taxes can be ignored in making decisions such as to replace equipment, discontinue a product line, etc.

T   F   **12.** In the decision-making process, the first step is to define the problem.

T   F   **13.** It may be profitable for a company to accept an offer to sell some of its product at an amount less than the total cost per unit computed under absorption costing.

T   F   **14.** In managerial decisions, sunk costs can be ignored.

T   F   **15.** In considering whether to replace equipment, the book value of the existing equipment must be considered.

T   F   **16.** When one is deciding whether to drop a product, the contribution margin of the product is probably the most important factor to consider.

T   F   **17.** Historical costs are usually sunk costs.

T   F   **18.** If a segment of a business is not producing a positive contribution margin, management should consider eliminating that segment.

Part B Matching

For each numbered item, choose the matching definition from the box and write the identifying letter in the answer column.

_____	**1.** sunk
_____	**2.** controllable
_____	**3.** relevant
_____	**4.** manufacturing margin
_____	**5.** common or indirect
_____	**6.** incremental
_____	**7.** differential

a. The difference in cost between one alternative and another

b. Future or expected costs that will change only as a result of a decision

c. Costs that have been incurred in the past

d. Also known as differential costs

e. Costs that depend largely on the actions of the segment manager

f. Costs not traceable to any one segment of the business

g. Excess of sales over variable cost of goods sold

Demonstration Problem

Fast Tool, Inc. distributes small tools to retail hardware stores. Early in 2013, management of the business decided to develop and market a private brand line of tools. They contracted with a manufacturer to make the products and began distribution. After several months, the board of directors is rethinking the decision and has asked you to analyze the following information for the June 2013 sales.

	Fixed Costs per Month	Percent of Selling Price per Unit
Average cost of products		45%
Average cost of packaging		1%
Average freight in		2%
Average delivery costs		1%
Sales commissions		7.5%
Advertising		
Variable		4%
Fixed	$2,000	
Warehousing		
Variable		2%
Fixed	$ 800	
Other		
Variable		1%
Fixed	$ 600	

June sales were $16,000. Several of the directors think the private product line should be discontinued.

Instructions

1. Based on the information provided, what is the amount of income or loss on July sales of these products?
2. Based on the accounting analysis, should the private brand be eliminated?
3. Are there other considerations that bear on this decision to eliminate or keep the product line?

SOLUTION

1. Income for June 2013 is calculated:

	AMOUNTS	
Sales		16 0 0 0 00
Cost and Expenses		
Variable Costs		
Product cost (45% of sales)	7 2 0 0 00	
Packaging (1% of sales)	1 6 0 00	
Freight-In (2% of sales)	3 2 0 00	
Delivery Costs (1% of sales)	1 6 0 00	
Sales Commission (7.5% of sales)	1 2 0 0 00	
Advertising (4% of sales)	6 4 0 00	
Warehousing (2% of sales)	3 2 0 00	
Other Variable (1% of sales)	1 6 0 00	
Total Variable		10 1 6 0 00
Contribution Margin		5 8 4 0 00
Advertising	2 0 0 0 00	
Warehousing	8 0 0 00	
Other fixed costs	6 0 0 00	
Total fixed Costs		3 4 0 0 00
Net Income		2 4 4 0 00

2.   Based only on the calculations shown, it would be appropriate to continue the product because it contributes $5,840 toward paying the fixed costs and $2,440 additional profit.

3.   Some of the questions to be asked include: Can sales be increased? Do buyers purchase other products as a result of our carrying this item? Are our advertising techniques effective for this product? How does this product fit into our total product offering?

WORKING PAPERS

Name _____

EXERCISE 30.1

1. _____
   _____
   _____
   _____

2. _____
   _____
   _____
   _____

3. _____
   _____
   _____
   _____

4. _____
   _____
   _____
   _____
   _____
   _____
   _____
   _____
   _____
   _____
   _____
   _____
   _____
   _____
   _____
   _____
   _____
   _____
   _____

EXERCISE 30.2

1. _____

_____

_____

_____

2. _____

_____

_____

_____

_____

_____

3. _____

_____

_____

_____

_____

_____

_____

_____

_____

_____

EXERCISE 30.3

_____

_____

_____

_____

_____

_____

_____

_____

EXERCISE 30.4

_____
_____
_____
_____
_____
_____
_____
_____
_____
_____
_____
_____

EXERCISE 30.5

1. _____
_____
_____
_____
_____
_____
_____
_____
_____

2. _____
_____
_____
_____
_____

EXERCISE 30.6

_____

_____

_____

_____

_____

_____

EXERCISE 30.7

_____

_____

_____

_____

_____

_____

_____

_____

_____

EXERCISE 30.8

_____

_____

_____

_____

_____

_____

_____

_____

_____

_____

_____

_____

_____

PROBLEM 30.1A or 30.1B

1.

Income Statement (Absorption Costing)

2.

Income Statement (Direct Costing)

PROBLEM 30.1A or 30.1B (continued)

3. _____

_____
_____
_____
_____
_____
_____
_____
_____
_____
_____
_____
_____
_____
_____
_____
_____
_____
_____
_____
_____
_____
_____
_____
_____
_____
_____
_____
_____
_____
_____

Analyze: _____

_____

PROBLEM 30.2A or 30.2B

1. _____

Income Statement (Direct Costing)

2. _____

Computations

Analyze: _____

PROBLEM 30.3A or 30.3B

1.   ANALYSIS OF EFFECTS OF PURCHASING MACHINE

2.

Analyze:

PROBLEM 30.4A or 30.4B

1. _____

Analysis of Effects of Making or Buying a Part

2. _____

_____

_____

_____

_____

_____

_____

_____

_____

_____

Analyze: _____

_____

CRITICAL THINKING PROBLEM 30.1

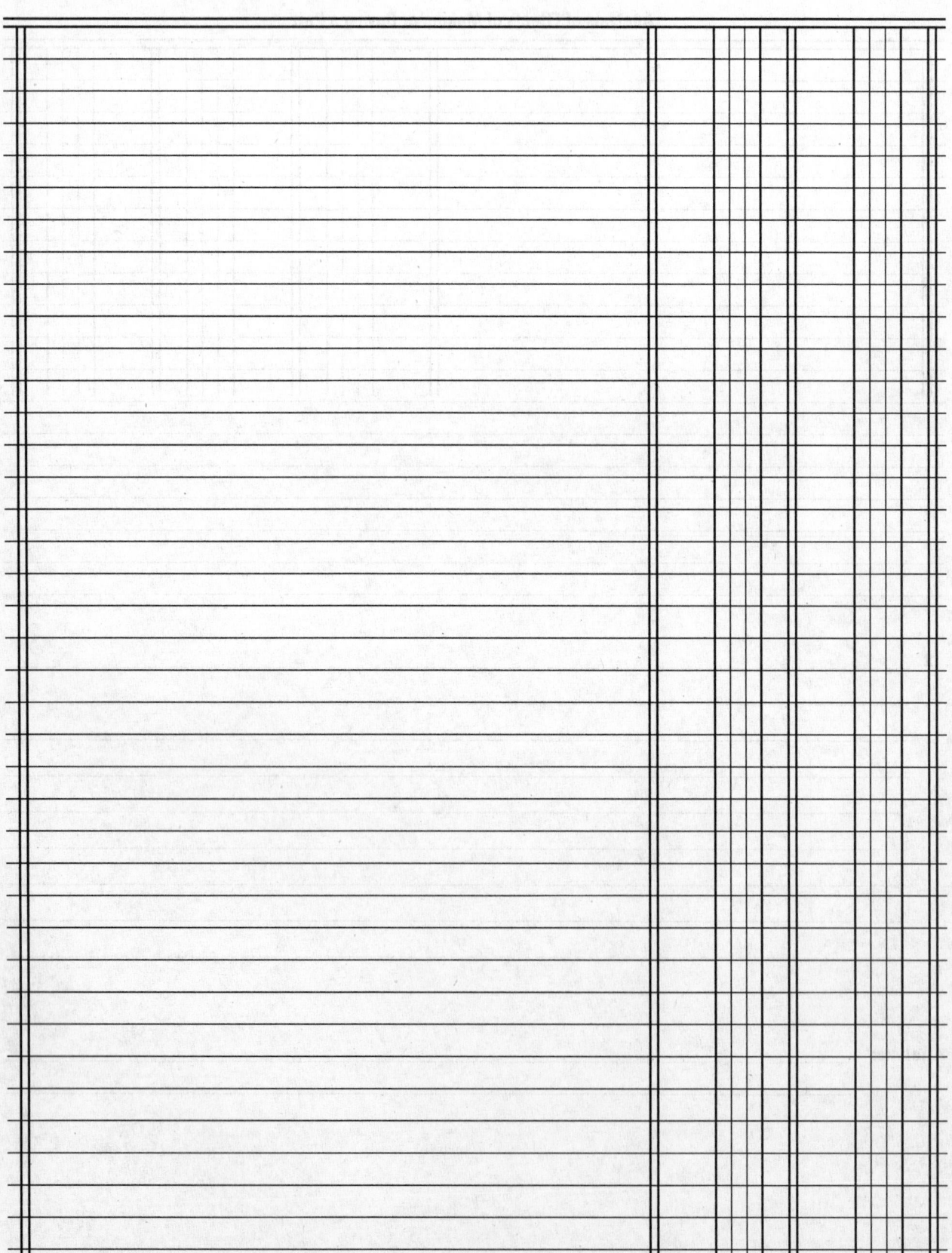

CRITICAL THINKING PROBLEM 30.1 (continued)

_____

_____

_____

_____

_____

_____

_____

_____

_____

_____

_____

_____

_____

_____

_____

_____

_____

_____

_____

_____

_____

_____

_____

_____

_____

_____

_____

_____

_____

_____

Analyze: _____

_____

CRITICAL THINKING PROBLEM 30.2

	ITEM 101	ITEM 102	ITEM 103	TOTAL